Arduino IoT Cloud for Developers

Implement best practices to design and deploy
simple-to-complex projects at reduced costs

Muhammad Afzal

BIRMINGHAM—MUMBAI

Arduino IoT Cloud for Developers

Group Product Manager: Preet Ahuja

Publishing Product Manager: Surbhi Suman

Book Project Manager: Ashwini Gowda

Senior Editor: Mohd Hammad

Technical Editor: Nithik Cheruvakodan

Copy Editor: Safis Editing

Language Support Editor: Safis Editing

Proofreader: Safis Editing

Indexer: Subalakshmi Govindhan

Production Designer: Jyoti Kadam

DevRel Marketing Coordinator: Rohan Dobhal

First published: November 2023

Production reference: 1101123

Published by Packt Publishing Ltd.
Grosvenor House
11 St Paul's Square
Birmingham
B3 1RB, UK.

ISBN 978-1-83763-717-1

www.packtpub.com

To my parents, teachers, wife, and daughter, and the memory of my grandfather Muhammad Ameer, for their sacrifices and for exemplifying the power of determination.

– Muhammad Afzal

Note from the Founding Director of EZIT

In the ever-expanding landscape of the **Internet of Things (IoT)**, where the digital and physical worlds converge, the possibilities seem boundless. This realm, once the domain of science fiction, is now a thriving reality. Behind the myriad of connected devices, intelligent systems, and seamless automation that define our modern age lies a remarkable and accessible platform – Arduino.

In *Arduino IoT Cloud for Developers*, we will embark on a journey that takes us to the heart of this transformative technology. As our world becomes more interconnected, the need for skilled developers who can harness the power of IoT becomes increasingly critical. This book is your key to unlocking that potential.

Author Muhammad Afzal is not just an expert in the field; he is a passionate advocate for democratizing technology. He understands that the true beauty of IoT is its universality, and its capacity to empower developers of all backgrounds and skill levels. This book embodies that spirit.

Whether you're a seasoned developer or a curious newcomer, this guide offers something for everyone. It walks you through the fundamentals of Arduino and IoT, empowering you to create your own innovative projects. You'll learn how to connect sensors, capture data, and make real-world decisions using Arduino's powerful and intuitive platform.

However, this book goes beyond the basics. It delves into best practices to design and deploy IoT applications, offering insights and techniques that will enable you to build not just simple projects but complex, scalable, and reliable systems. From managing data streams to securing your devices, from optimizing power consumption to designing user-friendly interfaces, this book equips you with the knowledge and skills to tackle real-world IoT challenges.

What sets this book apart is its commitment to practicality. The author understands that theory alone won't make you an IoT expert. You need hands-on experience. You need to troubleshoot, experiment, and iterate. With his guidance, you'll do just that. You'll tackle real projects, solve real problems, and gain the confidence to explore the IoT world on your terms.

In the pages that follow, you'll find a wealth of knowledge, insights, and inspiration. *Arduino IoT Cloud for Developers* is more than a book; it's a gateway to a world of endless possibilities. So, whether you're building the IoT systems of tomorrow or simply exploring the wonders of connected technology, this book is your trusted companion on the journey ahead.

Embrace the future. Dive in, learn, experiment, and create. The IoT revolution begins here.

Ehsan Elahi

Contributors

About the author

Muhammad Afzal is a senior software engineer, with more than 14 years of experience working on web-based and IoT systems in multinational organizations. He always enjoys working and solving real-world business problems with technology. He provides freelance services to IoT-based product companies to write technical reviews and projects, and he also provides consultancy to organizations.

In his free time, Muhammad creates videos and courses for YouTube and Udemy. He also runs a maker movement in his region for young students to boost their interest in adopting the latest technologies.

I want to thank the people who have been close to me and supported me, especially my wife, daughter, brothers, sister, and parents.

About the reviewer

Khadija Akter is an IoT system designer and problem solver. She has a passion for embedded electronics and IoT. She studies at the National University, at the Faculty of Electronics and Communication Engineering.

She loves to work in an arena that is very much related to the technological sector. She is currently working as an IoT developer for KaziSpin TecHub. She has been active in the field of IoT and embedded systems since 2017. She also works as a trainer and speaker at various international conferences (the 3rd Young Scientist Congress in Bangladesh, the **International Conference on Electrical Engineering and Information and Communication Technology** (**ICEEICT**), Empathy Nation, and many more).

I would like to convey my heartfelt gratitude to my family and friends who help to support and assist my busy schedule and stand by my side. I would also like to thank Mr. Redwan Hasan for his support and guidance in completing the review. It was a great learning experience. The completion of the review would not have been possible without their help and insights.

Table of Contents

2

First Look at the Arduino IoT Cloud   29

3

Insights into the Arduino IoT Cloud Platform and Web Editor   63

Part 2: Getting Hands-On with Different Communication Technologies

4

5

6

Project #3 – a Remote Asset Tracking Application with LoRaWAN   135

Part 3: Exchanging Data between Nodes and Cloud Applications

7

Enabling Communication between Different Devices   169

8

Working with the Arduino IoT Cloud SDK and JavaScript   189

9

Project 4 – Collecting Data from the Soil and Environment
for Smart Farming   227

10

Project #6 – Making Your Home Smarter with a Voice Assistant   253

Part 4: Learning Advanced Features of the Arduino IoT Cloud and Looking Ahead

11

Implementing the Arduino IoT Cloud Scheduler and Over-the-Air Features   279

12

Project #6 – Tracking and Notifying about Your Heart Rate   303

13

Scripting the Arduino IoT Cloud with Cloud CLI   325

14

Moving Ahead in the Arduino IoT Cloud   351

Index   367

Other Books You May Enjoy   378

Preface

Welcome to *Arduino IoT Cloud for Developers*. In a world increasingly interconnected through the **Internet of Things** (**IoT**), this book serves as your comprehensive guide to mastering IoT development using the versatile Arduino platform. Whether you are a newcomer to IoT or an experienced developer looking to expand your skills, this book offers a hands-on, step-by-step approach to building meaningful IoT projects with the Arduino IoT Cloud.

The IoT has revolutionized the way we interact with the world around us. Everyday objects, from home appliances to industrial machinery, are now capable of connecting to the internet and exchanging data. This transformation presents endless opportunities for innovation and efficiency.

Arduino, renowned for its simplicity and flexibility, has become a go-to platform for IoT enthusiasts and professionals alike. The Arduino IoT Cloud, an integral part of the Arduino ecosystem, offers a powerful and user-friendly platform to build and manage IoT projects. This book is your gateway to unlocking the full potential of the Arduino IoT Cloud.

Through a combination of theory and practical examples, you'll embark on a journey that starts with IoT fundamentals and culminates in advanced IoT applications. We'll explore the core features of the Arduino IoT Cloud, delve into various communication technologies, and create real-world IoT solutions.

This book is designed to be accessible to all, whether you're taking your first steps into IoT or seeking to deepen your knowledge. Each chapter provides clear explanations, code snippets, and hands-on projects to reinforce your learning.

By the end of this journey, you'll not only have a firm grasp of IoT concepts but also the ability to design, implement, and customize IoT solutions using the Arduino IoT Cloud. Let's embark on this exciting adventure into the world of IoT development together.

Who this book is for

Arduino IoT Cloud for Developers caters to a diverse audience, including IoT and Arduino enthusiasts venturing into IoT with Arduino, as well as those with prior Arduino experience eager to delve into IoT applications. It's also valuable for students and academicians pursuing electronics, computer science, or engineering degrees, seeking practical IoT knowledge and project inspiration. Additionally, makers, hobbyists, and DIY enthusiasts keen on crafting real-world IoT projects for personal experimentation will find this book beneficial. For professionals such as IoT experts, engineers, and developers aiming to elevate their IoT development comprehension, this book offers a pathway to create high-quality, commercial-grade solutions.

This book accommodates both beginners and experienced readers, providing a step-by-step learning path from IoT fundamentals to advanced IoT development with the Arduino IoT Cloud. Regardless of your background, this book equips you with the skills to design and implement innovative IoT solutions.

What this book covers

Chapter 1, Introduction to IoT and Arduino, covers IoT architecture along with security and Arduino.

Chapter 2, First Look at the Arduino IoT Cloud, explores the practical demonstration of the Arduino IoT Cloud with MKR Wi-Fi 1010 and Node-RED to connect old friends (older/non-compatible devices) with the Arduino IoT Cloud.

Chapter 3, Insights into the Arduino IoT Cloud Platform and the Cloud Editor, provides an overview of the Arduino IoT Cloud features, including things, devices, and dashboard widgets, and finally, we will take a deeper look at the Cloud Editor.

Chapter 4, Project #1 – A Smarter Setup for Sensing the Environment, offers a project that will practically demonstrate how to deploy a smart sensing node using WeMos D1 Mini, DHT22, and MQ-135 to send environment data to the Arduino IoT Cloud, visualizing it with stunning widgets.

Chapter 5, Project #2 – Creating a Portable Thing Tracker Using MKR GSM 1400, examines asset tracking and demonstrates how to track assets using MKR GSM 1400 and GPS module, visualizing the data using a map widget in the Arduino IoT Cloud.

Chapter 6, Project #3 – A Remote Asset Tracking Application with LoRaWAN, explores long-range communication using LoRaWAN technology. We will set up the LoRaWAN node, including the LoRaWAN Gateway, to track assets using MKR WAN 1300 and a GPS module.

Chapter 7, Enabling Communication between Different Devices, provides a practical demonstration of how to set up cloud variable sync across multiple things, enabling Thing to Thing communication by simply using a graphical user interface without any coding.

Chapter 8, Working with the Arduino IoT Cloud SDK and JavaScript, explores how developers can interact with the Arduino IoT Cloud using the JavaScript SDK, which includes API key setup and performing operations on Things, devices, cloud variables, and dashboards using JavaScript.

Chapter 9, Project #4 – Collecting Data from the Soil and Environment for Smart Farming, focuses on smart agriculture. We will explore how to sense soil moisture, soil temperature, and so on to make our agriculture smarter and more robust.

Chapter 10, Project #5 – Making Your Home Smarter by Voice Assistant, delves into smart homes. We will create a smart lamp using the WS2812 RGB ring and XIAO ESP32C3 and link the device to the Arduino IoT Cloud, as well as integrate the Arduino IoT Cloud with Amazon Alexa for a voice assistant experience.

Chapter 11, Implementing the Arduino IoT Cloud Scheduler and Over-the-Air Features, provides a practical demonstration of how to use the Cloud Scheduler in Arduino IoT Cloud to automate operations that are time-dependent. In the second part of the chapter, we will explore **Over-the-Air** (**OTA**) update features, which help us to send updates over the air without any physical connectivity to devices.

Chapter 12, Project #6 – Tracking and Notifying about Your Heart Rate, offers a practical demonstration of a smart health project, where we will use XIAO ESP32C3 with a heart rate monitoring sensor to build a wearable product, which will send data to the Arduino IoT Cloud. Then, we will use Webhooks to send our **beats per minute** (**BPM**) to Zapier for notification alerts.

Chapter 13, Scripting the Arduino IoT Cloud with Cloud CLI, teaches you how to perform operations on the Arduino IoT Cloud using the command-line tool, which includes operations on devices, Things, and dashboards, as well as OTA. This chapter will help you learn the commands and prepare you to create your own batch scripting for automated operations.

Chapter 14, Moving Ahead in the Arduino IoT Cloud, provides details about the different Arduino IoT Cloud pricing plans, including the features of each plan. It also looks at Arduino PRO Hardware and Software for Industrial IoT and provides a complete list of resources for further explorations.

To get the most out of this book

Before you start this book, you should have the following software and development boards, including a complete list of sensors, to get the most out of this book:

Software/hardware covered in the book	Operating system requirements
Arduino IDE desktop version	Windows, macOS, or Linux
Fritzing schematic design software	Windows, macOS, or Linux
An Arduino IoT Cloud account or a Zapier account	N/A
Amazon Alexa voice assistant	N/A

Development boards:

- MKR Wi-Fi 1010

- MKR GSM 1400

- MKR WAN 1300

- WeMos D1 Mini ESP8266

- XIAO ESP32C3

- ESP32 Dev Kit V1

- The Things Indoor Gateway for LoRaWAN

Sensors:

- DHT22/DHT11
- MQT-135
- The NEO 6-M u-blox GPS module
- Capacitive soil moisture sensors
- DS18B20 waterproof probes with long wires
- The WS2812 RGB ring
- A pulse sensor

If you are using the digital version of this book, we advise you to type the code yourself or access the code from the book's GitHub repository (a link is available in the next section). Doing so will help you avoid any potential errors related to the copying and pasting of code.

Download the example code files

You can download the example code files for this book from GitHub at `https://github.com/ PacktPublishing/Arduino-IoT-Cloud-for-Developers`. If there's an update to the code, it will be updated in the GitHub repository.

We also have other code bundles from our rich catalog of books and videos available at `https:// github.com/PacktPublishing/`. Check them out!

Conventions used

There are a number of text conventions used throughout this book.

`Code in text`: Indicates code words in text, database table names, folder names, filenames, file extensions, pathnames, dummy URLs, user input, and Twitter handles. Here is an example: "This cloud variable declaration is available in the `thingProperties.h` file."

A block of code is set as follows:

```
TinyGPSPlus gps;
unsigned long previousMillis = 0;
const long interval = 30000; //milliseconds
```

Any command-line input or output is written as follows:

```
npm install @arduino/arduino-iot-client
npm i request-promise
```

Bold: Indicates a new term, an important word, or words that you see on screen. For instance, words in menus or dialog boxes appear in **bold**. Here is an example: "After setting up the configuration, click the **Get new Access Token** button."

> **Tips or important notes**
> Appear like this.

Get in touch

Feedback from our readers is always welcome.

General feedback: If you have questions about any aspect of this book, email us at `customercare@packtpub.com` and mention the book title in the subject of your message.

Errata: Although we have taken every care to ensure the accuracy of our content, mistakes do happen. If you have found a mistake in this book, we would be grateful if you would report this to us. Please visit `www.packtpub.com/support/errata` and fill in the form.

Piracy: If you come across any illegal copies of our works in any form on the internet, we would be grateful if you would provide us with the location address or website name. Please contact us at `copyright@packtpub.com` with a link to the material.

If you are interested in becoming an author: If there is a topic that you have expertise in and you are interested in either writing or contributing to a book, please visit `authors.packtpub.com`.

Share Your Thoughts

Once you've read *Arduino IoT Cloud for Developers*, we'd love to hear your thoughts! Scan the QR code below to go straight to the Amazon review page for this book and share your feedback.

`https://packt.link/r/1837637172`

Your review is important to us and the tech community and will help us make sure we're delivering excellent quality content.

Download a free PDF copy of this book

Thanks for purchasing this book!

Do you like to read on the go but are unable to carry your print books everywhere?

Is your eBook purchase not compatible with the device of your choice?

Don't worry, now with every Packt book you get a DRM-free PDF version of that book at no cost.

Read anywhere, any place, on any device. Search, copy, and paste code from your favorite technical books directly into your application.

The perks don't stop there, you can get exclusive access to discounts, newsletters, and great free content in your inbox daily

Follow these simple steps to get the benefits:

1. Scan the QR code or visit the link below

https://packt.link/free-ebook/9781837637171

2. Submit your proof of purchase
3. That's it! We'll send your free PDF and other benefits to your email directly

Part 1:
Introduction to IoT and Communication Technologies and the Arduino IoT Cloud

This first part describes the principles of the **Internet of Things** (**IoT**), gives an overview of the Arduino IoT Cloud platform, and shows how to use it for the first time. It then provides a detailed description of its functionalities.

This part has the following chapters:

- *Chapter 1, Introduction to IoT and Arduino*
- *Chapter 2, First Look at the Arduino IoT Cloud*
- *Chapter 3, Insights into the Arduino IoT Cloud Platform and Cloud Editor*

1

Introduction to the IoT and Arduino

Connecting any device or machinery to the most advanced communication network in the world, the internet, opens endless possibilities for the progress of human beings.

The realization of an interconnected world involves many different technologies and technical aspects, regulations, and even ethical principles.

In this chapter, you will learn about the whole architecture of an end-to-end **Internet of Things (IoT)** application, including the different software layers and the communication channels required between its various components. We'll also analyze similarities and differences between the IoT and its industrial version, the **Industrial Internet of Things (IIoT)**, and we'll look at the **Industry 4.0** concept and what digital transformation for industry implies.

This information is fundamental for understanding the IoT, IIoT, and I4, as well as for evaluating its impact on our daily lives.

Finally, we will cover the principles and benefits behind the open source licensing model adopted by Arduino and some approaches to protecting your intellectual property in the source code of your projects.

By the end of this chapter, you will be able to specify the technical requirements of a commercial IoT application that implements new digital business model patterns enabled by the IoT and is built on the **Arduino IoT Cloud** platform with respect to the Arduino trademarks.

In this chapter, we're going to cover the following main topics:

- What is the Internet of Things?
- Benefits for users
- The enablement of different business models
- The architecture of an end-to-end IoT application

- Communication technologies and protocols
- Security aspects and device provisioning
- Open source

What is the Internet of Things?

There is not a single official definition of the IoT, but the following sentence covers the concept in its entirety:

The Internet of Things or, briefly, IoT is the concept of connecting physical objects to a network and other devices to let them interact with each other and with human beings to share information and take action through the Internet.

These physical objects are electronic devices using different telecommunication technologies to connect to a network. It's not surprising that the choice of network falls to the internet, not only because of the name of this technology but the characteristics of the internet itself:

- A digital network
- Worldwide coverage
- Standardized specifications
- Widely used for personal and professional communications

IoT devices are often called **IoT Nodes** because they are part of this network.

They feature sensors to detect or measure a physical property, such as the temperature of the environment or the speed of a vehicle. In other cases, they are connected to external machinery, devices, or appliances, always with the same purpose: collecting the values of physical properties, often called **Telemetry Elements**, and transmitting them to the internet. Once the values have reached the internet, they can arrive almost everywhere in the world in a few hundredths of a second.

You may think about interfacing an IoT node to an industrial machine to remotely transmit the information about its running conditions, and eventually alert a maintenance operator, in case of a fault. Or, connecting the node to your coffee machine to measure the level of the coffee grounds with the possibility to check it remotely while you are at the supermarket so that you can buy another pack only if required.

As a matter of fact, the IoT opens up the possibility to virtually infinite applications because connecting a device to the internet implies the possibility to both monitor the environment and send commands to the node remotely.

In fact, the telecommunication technologies used in the IoT are bidirectional and information can flow from the IoT node to the internet and vice versa. The interaction among IoT nodes is mainly related to the exchange of digital information by using the internet as the communication media.

Intelligence at the edge versus on the cloud

It's important to underline that IoT nodes also have processing capabilities to different extents; they can be programmed to receive information from the internet and implement some logic accordingly.

Another example might help. You can interface IoT *Node #1* to a weather station, collect information about the forecast, and transmit it to IoT *Node #2* connected to your automatic irrigation unit. You may program *Node #2* to prevent a waste of water in case rain is expected in the next few hours. Another node, *Node #3*, can embed a sensor and share the soil moisture value with *Node #2* through the internet so that irrigation is activated, if necessary, when the forecast is good and the soil requires water.

This may not be relevant to my small garden, but you might consider the benefits in the case of extensive fields, where different areas may be irrigated depending on the crop's requirements.

When the control logic is programmed directly on a node, we say that it is *at the edge*, referring to the edge between the physical and the digital world.

The logic can also be programmed *on the cloud*. In this case, there is an application running on a computer connected to the internet. In fact, the cloud empowers a huge number of computers connected together and to the internet with the aim of sharing computational and storage power, as well as balancing the computational load across multiple systems. With the *on-the-cloud* approach, the application on the cloud receives telemetry elements from one or more IoT nodes, aggregates the information, and defines the commands to send back to the same or other IoT nodes.

I talk about commands because IoT nodes can also be interfaced with actuators, such as motors, pumps, electro valves, electrical relays, and any other device responsible for moving and controlling a mechanism. This means that an IoT node can interact with the physical world by performing physical, programmed actions as a reaction to certain measures.

Considering the example of irrigation, the IoT node is electrically connected to a hydraulic servo valve and drives it to control the flow of water to the nozzles.

IoT nodes always implement embedded control logic to some extent, even when the intelligence of the application resides *on the cloud*. This is required to receive, interpret, and react to the commands from the application server on the cloud.

The distinction between *on the edge* and *on the cloud* is mainly related to the real intelligence of the application, such as the capability to understand when it's necessary to irrigate on the basis of the forecast and the moisture of the soil.

So, intelligence *on the edge* is completely programmed on the node by writing software code in a structured language such as C++ or MicroPython, or adopting artificial intelligence models based on neural networks. With the *on-the-cloud* approach, it is the responsibility of application software running on a cloud server to decide to automatically trigger a valve.

The choice between on-the-edge and on-the-cloud implementations is mainly driven by the application and the required response time. Implementations on the cloud allow more freedom in terms of programmable features. This is because the cloud is composed of multiple servers working together and it has virtually no constraints of memory and computational power. On the other hand, deployments on the edge remove some bottlenecks related to the latency of communication networks, reducing the response time of an IoT node and allowing it to interact with the physical world in real time.

It's worth noting that an implementation on the edge doesn't preclude the benefit of implementing manual remote control of the nodes in addition to automatic control. For example, an operator could interact with the devices in the field through a graphical user interface visualized on a web page (called a *dashboard*). They would see the actual values of environmental conditions and could trigger the valve as they liked.

The programmer of the application is responsible for defining and configuring the dashboards, which can be as complex as required, with widgets to visualize and insert data such as graphs and textboxes, and trigger commands such as switches, sliders, pushbuttons, and many others.

The market sees an increasing number of on-the-edge applications for various use cases where microcontroller devices can be successfully adopted as control units of IoT nodes. This trend has led to the continuous, fast improvements in hardware components, with augmented computational capabilities and a consequent decrease in their cost, as well as the mass availability of wireless telecommunication technologies characterized by very low power consumption and long-distance transmission range.

When we consider the installation of IoT nodes in remote and not easily accessible areas, energy autonomy is a very important aspect: we want to reduce the need for battery recharging as much as possible to decrease the costs of human intervention. Ideally, a good IoT application is supposed to be fully autonomous!

When you adopt one of the **Low-Power Wide Area Network** (**LPWAN**) technologies, you need to consider that a decreased power consumption comes at the expense of a reduced quantity of data that can be transmitted with a single message and a higher interval between messages. It's like considering data as a form of energy and applying the energy conservation law: if you decrease the power, you decrease the amount of data, not only the transmission range.

A decreased amount of data per message and a longer interval between two transmissions mean that you need to reduce the information exchanged with the cloud so that the cloud needs less time to collect all the values to process.

When this duration, which we may call **Cloud Latency Time**, is too long, then it's worth implementing intelligence on the edge.

The Arduino ecosystem

It's not possible to connect a single device to every type of sensor, actuator, external machinery, and device in the same way, because each element implements different electrical interfaces and ways to communicate.

Manufacturers produce IoT nodes, or components suitable for building IoT nodes, focusing on defined use cases and technologies, and adopting some of the various standards available on the market. Every person developing an IoT project has the responsibility to select the nodes with the best characteristics for their application. When a complete product with the required features is not readily available in the market, you may use electronic modules to build your IoT nodes as you like. This is where Arduino comes in handy.

We assume you know what Arduino is since you're reading this book. Anyway, I think it's worth mentioning that Arduino is not only a technology but an ecosystem maintained by the commercial business of the same name. The modular ecosystem is composed of electronic microcontroller based development boards, firmware, software libraries and tools to program boards and the cloud platform described in this book.

The Arduino team engineers every single component with particular attention to its usability and the user experience, according to the mission of the company, which is to *"enable anyone to innovate by making complex technologies open and simple to use."* (M. Banzi, cofounder of Arduino).

It's not surprising that the Arduino Cloud also follows the same approach, and you'll see how easy it is to develop an IoT cloud application with the Arduino Cloud, without programming but configuring it. The ease of use of the Arduino Cloud is related to the native on-the-edge model: Arduino follows the technology trend of implementing the intelligence on the nodes, leaving the data storage and visualization tasks to the cloud.

You may still deploy an IoT solution on the cloud with the Arduino Cloud when you interface the Arduino Cloud with third-party services where the application logic and the intelligence are implemented.

Besides officially Arduino-compatible development boards, you can also use popular development boards such as the ESP32 & ESP8266 series development boards with the Arduino IoT Cloud. This feature helps the developer to use existing hardware solutions to migrate their products to the Arduino IoT Cloud without changing existing hardware technologies.

The other important aspect of the Arduino ecosystem is related to making technologies open. Most of the hardware and software produced by Arduino is publicly released under open source licenses, and by the end of this chapter, you will know the benefits and the obligations related to open source licenses and how to protect your intellectual property. Arduino also provides professional hardware devices for industry use, such as the **Portenta series**, which is specially designed for IoT and AI solutions. **Arduino Opta Programmable Logic Controllers** (**PLCs**) are the new product line in the PRO series, which is designed for industry deployment. For more details regarding the PRO series, please visit `https://store-usa.arduino.cc/collections/pro-family`.

The IoT, big data, artificial intelligence, and machine learning

We have seen that an IoT application involves the connection between the physical and digital worlds to create some sort of digital automation of physical processes. The outcome is the result of the following:

- Connecting devices to the internet
- Allowing devices to share information to interact and collaborate
- Implementing smart applications that can take intelligent actions

When we talk about digitalization, other buzzwords are often used together with the IoT: **big data**, **artificial intelligence**, and **machine learning**. These are complementary sciences that can be used to realize complex digital projects. We'll describe what they are and how they are used in conjunction with the IoT next.

Big data refers to extremely large and complex datasets and to the science that studies how to process them. Traditional data processing software is unable to handle big data in a reasonable amount of time due to the size of the datasets and their unstructured and disaggregated nature, so dedicated technologies are necessary to extract valuable insights and knowledge used to support decision-making and strategic planning.

When we consider hundreds or thousands of IoT nodes sharing different values in real time, collected from the physical world, you may understand that the size and variety of the data require much more than a traditional database.

Big data involves an implementation of logic on the cloud. Even when an on-the-edge model is used for a fast response time in the physical world, data can be sent to the cloud for long-term processing without time constraints. Here, big data can be supportive.

For example, with reference to our example of smart irrigation, a node can use values from soil moisture sensors to control a hydraulic valve on the edge and also share information with a cloud application that uses data from multiple nodes to adapt a model for weather forecast considering, and also additional information from national weather stations.

You may consider big data as the cloud application processing raw data to extract and store valuable information.

Artificial intelligence and machine learning are often referred to as being the same science, but they are not. **Artificial Intelligence (AI)**, is a broad field that encompasses many different subdisciplines, including **Machine Learning (ML)**.

AI is the broader concept of machines being able to carry out tasks in a way that would normally require human intelligence, such as visual perception, speech recognition, decision-making, language translation, and others.

ML is a specific subfield of AI that focuses on enabling computers to learn from data and make predictions or decisions without being explicitly programmed to do so. Usually, ML involves training a model on a dataset and using the trained model to make predictions or decisions on new data.

In summary, AI is the broader concept of the mimicking of human intelligence by machines, while ML is a specific method/technique to achieve AI, which allows the machine to learn from data, instead of being explicitly programmed.

AI and ML models can be trained by using the data collected by big data tools and used to interpret other new data from the same or another big data platform.

Once trained, the models can be deployed on the cloud and on the edge as well, depending on their size and the technical features of the nodes.

While big data tools processes the data directly with analytical models, AI/ML works on patterns in data in order to recognize situations and trends.

For example, you can use big data to extract the trends of soil moisture in a wide region where thousands of sensors collect values every hour and big data can support you in distinguishing between daily, monthly, and seasonal changes over a period of years.

ML works differently; it ingests values of different types, such as weather forecast parameters, and identifies patterns that affect your observations. You may create an ML model by training a neural network with temperature, atmospheric pressure, humidity, wind speed, and soil moisture values across a period. Then you provide another set of data from a different period, without the soil moisture values, and the model is able to suggest indications about irrigation needs.

With reference to the following diagram, you may see the complete dataflow of a complex application, where the IoT senses the physical world, reacts immediately on the edge when required, and forwards the values to big data for offline or batch processing (not in real time):

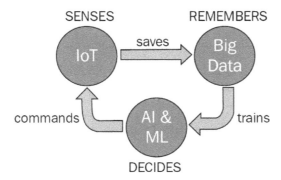

Figure 1.1 – Data integration with other technologies

Big data stores and aggregates the values that are used to train and run AI/ML models. These models make decisions and send commands back to IoT nodes that interact with the physical world.

The IoT, IIoT, and I4.0

The IoT concept has been widely applied in different aspects of our lives and some applications are already part of our daily routines.

For example, you may buy a smart doorbell online for tens of dollars. This device integrates a microphone and a loudspeaker and connects to your Wi-Fi. This IoT node remotely alerts you on your mobile when someone rings, and it allows you to have a conversation with the visitor in front of your door, even if you are miles away from your house. With some models, you may even unlock the door.

Have you ever switched on a light in your house by asking Alexa®, Google Assistant™, or Apple's Siri to do so? All those IoT nodes are examples of applications in the smart building and home vertical.

Advanced solutions manage air conditioning, windows, and curtains depending on the environmental situation, measured by presence detection, temperature, and sunlight sensors.

We've already introduced an application in the agriculture market, with others related to tracking live animals and their conditions by localizing them with GPS technologies and measuring their vital parameters. For example, a rapid heartbeat can be a symptom of stress due to overheating or the presence of a predator.

We all like to receive frequently updated tracking information about the shipping of our last online purchase. The online tracking of deliveries is also useful to freight forwarding companies to reduce the risks of complaints and the associated operative costs. All this is possible thanks to the usage of handheld devices connected to the internet and small IoT nodes attached to valuable goods, capable of sending their location wirelessly to a cloud application. Logistics is definitely one of the sectors where the IoT is successfully adopted, but the healthcare, retail, smart infrastructure, security, and surveillance markets also offer many examples of IoT applications.

The deployment of an IoT application in the industrial environment is commonly referred to as the IIoT.

IIoT applications mainly focus on collecting data from the physical world to better understand how to improve industrial processes, make better use of plants, and optimize the consumption of energy, water, human work, and other resources involved in activities.

The main target is an increase in performance and a reduction of costs in all departments.

> **Important note**
> This is not the place to cover the implications in terms of the workforce, but I would like to say that the IIoT doesn't directly imply the reduction of operators, but their training and technical growth can be managed from a cost-reduction perspective when good, fair employment policies are adopted.

The adoption of the IoT principles in the industrial environment requires particular attention in the implementation and deployment of nodes because the environment can be harsher in terms of temperatures, vibrations, and electromagnetic pollution.

The overheating caused by higher temperatures in certain industrial environments causes failures in the electronic components of nodes and reduces their lifespan.

Vibration fatigue is another main cause of failures of electronic devices. The vibrations transfer to the electronic board when a node is installed in contact with a machine, and they apply stress to the components, resulting in early failure.

Industrial environments are quite dense with industrial motors in machinery, power cables, the cellular devices of operators, and other sources of electromagnetic fields.

The preceding aspects affect IIoT nodes only, while the application of the IoT to the industrial environment has other implications on the cloud side:

- **Scalability**: Cloud infrastructures for the IIoT typically require it to easily handle and store large amounts of data from a vast number of IoT devices

- **Data security**: The industrial market requires improved cloud security measures to protect against cyber threats to cloud applications and IIoT devices

- **Data localization**: One of the frequent requests from the industrial market is that all data remains confidential and confined to the local country

Several reasons justify a request for cloud data to remain in the local country. Data privacy and security concerns are evident when you consider that keeping data within a country ensures that it is subject to the jurisdiction and protection of local laws.

Furthermore, some countries have strict regulations regarding the storage and handling of sensitive data, and keeping it within the country helps organizations comply with these regulations.

Last but not least are considerations related to performance and cost-effectiveness: accessing data and applications stored in a remote location can result in slower performance and higher latency. Likewise, transferring data across international borders can be expensive and complex, making it more cost-effective to store data within a country.

Industry 4.0, known as the **Fourth Industrial Revolution**, is a broader concept than the IIoT and refers to the application of the IIoT specifically in smart factories for the production of consumer goods.

In this way, production processes are controlled and monitored in real time and digitalization empowers machines and devices to make decisions, freeing up human workers for higher-level tasks. This is a decentralized decision-making approach, where production is driven by data collected and analyzed by machines and devices in order to speed up a continuous improvement of the production processes.

Flexible manufacturing processes allow the mass production of customized products in batches of one pace having features defined by every single customer at the time of online shopping.

Industry 4.0 means connecting a fully automated factory to the internet to improve the customer experience and optimize the overall business performance.

Customers can go to their preferred online store to buy a pair of running shoes, select the model, choose the materials, configure the colors of the different parts, and place an order. After payment by credit card, the order digitally arrives at the factory, where robots and machinery are configured in real time to get material from the warehouse, produce your custom shoes, including printing your name on them and the box, and then return the box to the warehouse ready for shipment.

Not a single piece of paper has been printed throughout the whole process. The facility managers can consult metrics online regarding the performance of the factory and the customer receives their personalized shoes delivered at home.

This is not a dream, and it's already possible with the manufacturer Nike®, famous worldwide.

Industry 4.0 requires a wider software architecture than the IIoT cloud.

You may consider that the IIoT cloud is already interfaced with the machinery and devices of a production plant in an IIoT application. Industry 4.0 additionally connects digital systems from the different departments of the business, including the following:

- **Enterprise Resource Planning (ERP)**: To automate and manage core business processes for optimal performance

- **Computerized Maintenance Management System (CMMS)**: To manage assets, schedule maintenance, and track work orders

- **Warehouse Management Systems (WMSs)**: To support inventory and manage supply chain fulfillment operations

Here, we have discussed the IoT in detail, as well as cloud versus edge processing and AI implementations. We have covered some details about the Arduino ecosystem, including their PRO line of products. Later, we discussed the IoT, big data, artificial intelligence, and machine learning, including the IIoT, as they all are very important pillars in high-level projects. In the next section, we will discuss what benefits there are for users by implementing the IoT in daily life as well as in industry.

Benefits for users

Applications based on these smart technologies offer huge benefits to end users such as automating tasks and making Things remotely controllable and monitorable.

The IoT and IIoT improve our efficiency by letting IoT applications optimize the usage of resources and allowing us to reduce costs. They also enhance our safety and security, because IoT devices can provide real-time monitoring and alerts.

Data collection and analysis by IoT nodes can be used to personalize our experiences and the augmented connectivity provided by IoT solutions creates new possibilities for communication and collaboration.

Finally, the IoT and IIoT enable new and modern business models, as we'll see in the next section.

You may ask why all this is happening now and if it comes without a cost.

The history of the IoT can be traced back to the 1980s when the term was first used by British technology pioneer Kevin Ashton in a presentation about the potential for interconnected devices.

In the early 2000s, the development of wireless networking standards such as Bluetooth and Wi-Fi made it easier to connect devices to the internet and cellular connectivity became a consumer market.

Ten years later, major technology companies, such as Microsoft, Google, and Amazon, began to invest in IoT cloud platforms.

Today, after 40 years, the progress of software technology has made big data, data analytics tools, and cloud platforms accessible and affordable for most people. The internet is a predominant medium of communication and the decreased cost of electronics, together with ecosystems such as Arduino, has made the technology easy to use.

The IoT indirectly brings costs to businesses of every size because they need to seize the moment, adopt these technologies, and keep up with progress to remain competitive in the market.

The social impact of the IoT is related to the introduction of different behaviors and the risk of human beings losing some manual and practical capabilities. For example, people who used to travel by car before navigation applications were available on mobile phones had a certain sense of orientation; nowadays, this skill has almost disappeared.

The IIoT introduces the risk of misleading managers to think that these technologies support cost savings by reducing the workforce because everything is automated. Actually, the personnel need training to maintain, troubleshoot, and improve the new systems, and it's important that business managers understand this.

In the end, it is the responsibility of everyone involved in an IoT project to consider the application and manage the social effects properly. It means that it's also your responsibility, dear reader.

The enablement of different business models

Joseph Turow, the Robert Lewis Shayon Professor of Communication at the Annenberg School for Communication at the University of Pennsylvania, said *"Despite hacks and privacy issues, people will feel a need to keep connected, partly because companies will reward them for doing so (or make life difficult if they don't)"*.

This improved connectivity among Things and people has an immediate consequence on the evolution of the patterns of digital business models.

The following figure, from the whitepaper *Business Models and the Internet of Things* by the Bosch IoT Lab, shows the evolution of web technologies and what business models were enabled in the different phases:

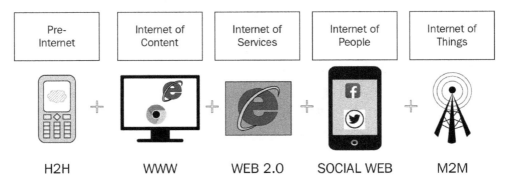

Figure 1.2 – Evolution of web technologies

We are now fully in the Web 3.0 phase where the IoT requires a drastic shift of mindset in the creation and the capture of commercial value. The Business School of Harvard University spotted this change and highlighted a series of implications.

First of all, customers require their needs to be addressed in real time. The IoT even allows businesses to address emergent needs in a predictive manner.

The possibilities offered by the IoT change the product management processes during their life cycle. The obsolescence reduces and it happens over a longer time because new versions of a product are evaluated by considering aggregated information about usage, collected automatically from products themselves, and analyzed to identify the effective requirements. Furthermore, the proposed user experience is based expressly on the *collaboration* of the products with others, eventually manufactured by third parties.

This moves the value of the products in such a way that customers perceive more benefits in the personalization of the products and their features than in commodity advantages such as lower cost, higher quality, and immediate availability. Or, in the case of professional and industrial products, brand and ownership of the intellectual property.

The appreciation for the collaboration capabilities of IoT products also suggests manufacturers should invest resources in understanding how other ecosystems work and make money, with the aim of developing a certain level of compatibility, more so than making a big effort to leverage internal core competencies and existing resources and processes.

Once the features of the new version are identified and implemented, manufacturers can often update many products at the same time, and remotely over the air. This is one of the appealing services that can be offered as the intrinsic value of a product or a paid service for subscribers.

The increased possibility to offer additional services moves the path to profit in the business strategy. The new approach is the search for the optimal balance between immediate and recurrent revenues. Immediate revenues, related to the traditional core business, often require a lot of effort and large investments to scale the number of sold products. On the other hand, the activities required to establish and maintain a good service offering, based on IoT capabilities, guarantee recurrent revenues in time.

Business models enabled by the IoT

When you buy a mobile phone from one of the two or three main manufacturers, typically, you don't pay the real value of the device itself, but the perceived value of the product. Many people are keen on spending more on a mobile that represents a status symbol, rather than on an anonymous model, even with the same features. The status symbol is a benefit perceived as product value.

In a similar way, we may calculate the price of an IoT solution on the benefits it provides, instead of its costs. For example, we may consider a smart building project for energy efficiency: the IoT system tracks and analyzes energy usage, automatically controls illumination in common areas, and allows the owner of a building to identify areas for improvement and reduce their energy costs.

According to this model, called **outcome-based**, a solution provider may propose the system for a percentage of the savings on the energy bills of the customer, plus the installation and removal costs. They maintain the property using their IoT hardware without selling it but, when they close the contract, they have created a source of recurrent revenue for a certain amount of time. At the end of the contract period, they remove and reuse the IoT products for another installation. In this way, the cost of the IoT hardware is an investment of the solution provider and, considering the product life cycle mentioned previously and the low level of wear of these devices, it can generate a good return.

Paying for the benefits provided doesn't implicitly mean paying more than the value of the product, but it can still be convenient for both parties involved. This is the case with the **pay-per-usage** model. Going back to the smart irrigation example, farmers can then use the IoT application provided by the water company to water their crops, with charges based on the amount of water used. The goal is not to make money on the IoT device itself but to use the data produced by the nodes to track usage.

The **asset-sharing** model is a pay-per-usage model characterized by the fact that the asset monitored by the IoT nodes is shared among multiple customers. For example, in the last few years, many businesses have bought and rented electric scooters in many different cities in the world. The user enrolls on the provider's platform and uses their mobile, connected to the internet, to start and stop the rental and enable the scooter accordingly. This is a very good example of an IoT application in the smart cities vertical: both the user's mobile and the scooter are connected to, and interact through, the internet. In this case, the user pays for the benefit of riding in certain areas less than they would pay to buy their own scooter because they share the IoT product, the scooter, with the local community. The asset-sharing model is based on the concept of selling extra capacity to the market and solves the big concern that everyone has when buying expensive equipment: will I be able to utilize it to its maximum capacity?

When we talk about business models related to the sale of services, the **subscription** model is the most well known: the user doesn't pay to own the solution, but they pay an amount regularly to use it. This model is usually adopted by companies offering smart home devices such as connected thermostats, security cameras, and smart locks. Customers pay a monthly or annual fee for access to the devices, as well as the ability to control and monitor them through a mobile app.

One type of IoT subscription business model with a growing trend in its adoption is **asset tracking**. The reduction in power consumption and dimensions, as well as the decreased dimensions and costs of IoT nodes, enable a progressive adoption to localize different assets they are attached to. In this case, the subscriber doesn't pay for the IoT nodes but for regular access to the localization data and the movements of the assets.

The IoT supports the proposal of other kinds of services; for example, a predictive maintenance IoT solution enables the sales of a convenient maintenance service, where the contract is appealing to both the contractor and the customer. The contractor can keep their tariffs lower because they don't need to schedule periodical visits to their customer: the system will inform them in advance to plan the intervention before it becomes urgent. At the same time, they can enlarge their customer base to justify the cost of the installed solutions.

A consultancy company can install an IoT solution to measure the performance of machinery in a production plant without stopping any machine because all data is collected by autonomous IoT nodes that don't need interfaces to the existing plant. Data is used to measure the **Overall Equipment Effectiveness** (**OEE**) and suggest how to optimize the usage of the plant. In this case, the core business of the company is not the sale of IoT solutions, but the services deriving from the data collected by the IoT application.

The **razor-blade** business model in the IoT is similar to traditional models but with the added convenience and customization of IoT technology. The goal is to get the product in the customer's hands, at cost or even less, to start selling your other products. The name comes from the company Gillette®, the inventor and first adopter: its main revenues come from the sale of the blades while razors are just the main source to bring about the sales of blades as one razor sold will generate multiple purchases of blades. In a similar way, HP® sells inkjet printers at a very low price with the aim of gaining revenues from the sale of the cartridges. The IoT can monitor the customer's habits and suggest the optimal model for the consumable. It can also increase the probability of reordering because an order can be placed automatically by a device.

There are cases where businesses provide IoT applications with their hardware for free because its purpose is to monetize by collecting and reselling users' data. This pertains to the situation involving driving habit monitoring devices. While these devices offer valuable insights to users, insurance companies derive significant benefits by analyzing driving patterns across a large number of individuals. Introducing this model can be seen as an expansion of your primary business, where you initially focus on addressing the needs of your end users and subsequently explore opportunities to generate revenue from their data. These two approaches can coexist harmoniously as long as you prioritize transparency with your customers regarding data usage and take necessary measures to safeguard their privacy.

In the preceding section, we have discussed what innovations and improvements end users benefit from due to smart products. The IoT has not only improved end users' lifestyles but has also helped new business models to emerge, as well as helping industries to shift toward Industry 4.0, which helps industries run their production lines securely, quickly, and cost-effectively.

The architecture of an end-to-end IoT application

Now that we know more about the IoT, we have seen its principles and some examples of different applications, the time is good to dig more into the technical aspects with the analysis of the architecture of an IoT application.

We have already introduced IoT nodes, cloud platforms, and applications. A picture is better than a thousand words to explain how they work together and the following diagram shows the architecture of an IoT solution in its entirety:

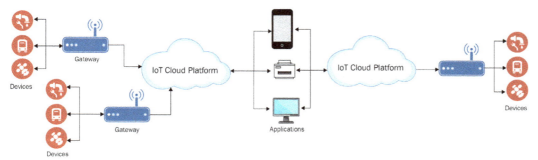

Figure 1.3 – High-level architecture of an IoT system

There is an important difference between cloud platforms and cloud applications. **Cloud platforms** implement communication, user and device management, data storage and security, and other basic services; **cloud applications** implement the logic of the application, the dashboards, and all the specific aspects of the application.

In this sense, the Arduino IoT Cloud can be considered a cloud application running on the AWS cloud platform.

Thanks to the connectivity offered by the internet, you may set up even a complex IoT solution that features many different functionalities, just by exploiting multiple cloud applications, frameworks, and services already implemented by third parties and interconnected via the internet. This means that you don't need to develop or configure everything from scratch and you may save time and headaches; it also explains the reason why multiple cloud platforms and cloud applications are visualized in the preceding figure.

Examples of these functionalities can be **Single Sign-On (SSO)**, a user authentication service that allows a user to use one set of login credentials (e.g., name and password) to access multiple applications – such as social media platforms, and tons of others. You just need to decide what you need, search on the internet for the preferred provider, and easily integrate those features in your application without the need to program them. This is also valid for the Arduino Cloud platform, which offers a couple of different ways to interface with third-party applications, as we'll see in *Chapter 12*.

The gateway is the last type of module we need to talk about. **Gateways** support the connection between nodes and cloud platforms. Or, more precisely, they are the bridge connecting nodes to the internet and allowing the exchange of data between nodes and cloud applications. There are many different types of gateways, characterized by the communication technologies they implement.

Your Wi-Fi router is a perfect example of a gateway: it's connected to the internet and it accepts connections from other devices via Wi-Fi. It converts the Wi-Fi device into the data transportation technology of your internet provider (landline, Ethernet, or fiber-optic cable).

Gateways may also implement additional functionalities, such as data filtering, protocol conversion, and security. Every IoT application includes gateways in the architecture, even when they are not directly managed by you or the programmer of the solution.

Let's consider an application with nodes using cellular connectivity. It may look like the nodes are directly connected to the internet, but it's not the case. In fact, the nodes connect to the cellular network as well as dedicated gateways managed by the network provider. It's important to clearly understand the presence of all the components in the architecture because each part can be a point of weakness in the case of an issue and can make the troubleshooting longer and more complex.

Communication technologies and protocols

Data flows through a number of different devices during the back-and-forth between IoT nodes and cloud applications. These devices implement various communication technologies and protocols and the following diagram shows the most common choices:

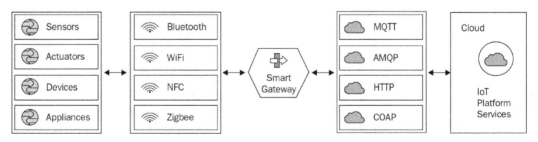

Figure 1.4 – Communication technologies and protocols

In relation to the four main communication paths in the whole chain, the main distinction is related to the wireless or wired nature of the communication.

As per the preceding figure, the *field-to-device* path is usually wired: sensors, actuators, and devices connect to an IoT node thanks to wires. They pack and exchange data according to one of the standards for wired interfaces shown in the figure.

The *device-to-gateway* path can be wired or wireless depending on the technical requirement of the node for each specific application. Wireless IoT nodes offer the following benefits compared to wired IoT nodes:

- **Mobility**: Wireless IoT nodes are not restricted by physical connections and can be easily moved or relocated, providing more flexibility and freedom

- **Ease of installation**: Wireless nodes do not require cabling and can be installed much faster and more easily, reducing installation costs and time

- **Scalability**: Adding new nodes or devices to a wireless IoT network is easier and less expensive than adding wired nodes

- **No infrastructure requirements**: Wireless IoT nodes do not require a pre-existing wired infrastructure, making them ideal for remote or hard-to-reach locations

- **Improved reliability**: Wireless nodes are less susceptible to failure caused by physical damage to cables, making them more reliable for many IoT applications

However, it's worth mentioning that wireless IoT nodes may suffer from interference from other wireless devices, limited range, and potential security issues, so it's important to consider these limitations when choosing between wired and wireless IoT nodes.

For example, the IoT nodes for the load, vibrations, and structural monitoring of a bridge over a river, which respectively provide useful information about the maintenance, traffic balance, and improvement requirements, don't need to be wireless. Many smart agriculture applications, on the other hand, benefit from long-range wireless technologies because of the difficulties and the installation costs of a wired network covering huge areas.

Considering the Kids park has a lot of IoT nodes, we can roughly divide the applications in the different market verticals into four main groups:

- **Consumer devices with a very short transmission range**: Wearables, safety devices, remote controls, and toys that typically use a Bluetooth or a **Bluetooth Low Energy** (**BLE**) connection to a mobile phone that shares the connectivity to the internet. This approach demonstrates the possibility of daisy-chaining multiple gateways with different technologies to reach the required connectivity.

- **Consumer devices with a short transmission range**: This is the case for home automation devices, such as the thermostat of your house or appliances, entertainment devices, personal instruments, and healthcare devices connected to the internet through a cabled Wi-Fi access point.

- **Wireless professional devices**: Automotive, smart agriculture, mining, and some logistics and outdoor industrial applications require very long-distance transmission ranges provided by the latest cellular technologies, which includes 3G/4G/5G or LPWAN.

- **Wired professional devices**: Some infrastructural projects, such as the monitoring of bridges and dams or indoor industrial projects, require wired nodes to increase reliability, increase the data throughput of the transmission, reduce the maintenance required for battery replacement, and increase data security.

The *gateway-to-cloud* link is wired in most IoT applications and, eventually, the gateway provides a backhaul wireless connectivity to the internet. This is the case of professional Wi-Fi and LoRa gateways that implement an Ethernet interface and also a cellular modem: the gateway automatically swaps to cellular if the Ethernet connection fails.

Defining the nature of the *cloud-to-cloud* communication path is a little bit trickier because we need to consider that cloud apps run on cloud platforms, and these are composed of servers interconnected to each other. The physical connection among the servers is definitely wired, but we may consider the logical connection between cloud applications wireless because, when compared to applications installed on a single server on the internet, wireless and wired IoT nodes offer the same benefits.

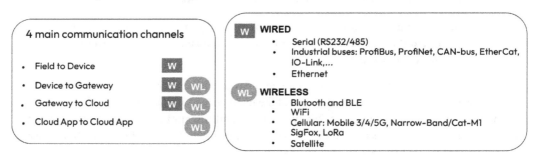

Figure 1.5 – Wired/wireless communication technologies

In this section, we discussed the high-level architecture of an end-to-end IoT application with multiple nodes, gateways, and the cloud. In the second part of the section, we discussed communication technologies and protocols, where we divided different communication technologies into wireless and wired mediums for better understanding. In the next section, we will discuss the security of IoT solutions, as well as device provisioning services, in detail.

Security aspects and device provisioning

In many applications, IoT devices collect and transmit sensitive data, such as personal information or financial data, which can be at risk of theft or unauthorized access if the data is not properly secured. Security must be a top priority in the design and implementation of any IoT application to ensure the safety and privacy of the data transmitted through the system.

The weakest link in the chain of IoT architecture in terms of security is the IoT node and the interface between the IoT device and the cloud.

I know that we said that there is always a gateway between the IoT node and the cloud. The fact is that the gateway implements all the communication layers for a reliable end-to-end communication channel between devices and the cloud. The node and the cloud are at the ends of this channel and, mainly at this layer, the data can be vulnerable to hacking, tampering, or unauthorized access, potentially compromising its security and privacy.

Hardware security

Attackers can exploit security vulnerabilities due to outdated or unpatched software, and this is even more probable when nodes are based on microcomputers running common operating systems. The probability decreases significantly when the node features a microcontroller that runs on bare metal as firmware, like in the case of the Arduino ecosystem. This is because the software running on the device is reduced to the minimum strictly necessary to run the device.

The adoption of strong data encryption algorithms on nodes protects the data transmitted over the network, making it less vulnerable to eavesdropping or tampering. In this case, too, the Arduino ecosystem demonstrates that it is a good choice for the implementation of an IoT application: Arduino devices for IoT embed secure elements, called **crypto-chips**, able to generate and manage security keys at the hardware level, without the need to include a password in the source code of the node application. We'll see what this means and how it works toward the end of this section, but it's now necessary to talk about another security risk related to IoT nodes.

That is **inadequate access controls**: some IoT devices with inadequate access controls may allow unauthorized individuals to access or control the device, potentially compromising the security of the system as a whole.

The access can be remote or even direct to the device to extract the original firmware from the device and overwrite it with a different version programmed by hackers. The extraction of the firmware could also be used just for replicating the functionalities of an original device on compatible but cloned hardware, threatening the results of an IoT business.

Arduino has engineered a safe version of their traditional bootloader to prevent these risks. A **bootloader** is the first software that is executed on the device and is responsible for loading the firmware and initializing the device's hardware.

The **Arduino Safe Bootloader** adds a secure environment to the traditional bootloader by implementing mechanisms for firmware fail-safe authentication and secure updates. These prevent unauthorized access to the device's firmware and ensure that only authorized firmware can be executed on the device.

An authenticity check of the firmware is based on digital signatures and guarantees security: the bootloader checks the digital signature of the firmware before loading it into the device's memory and doesn't proceed in the case of unauthorized or wrongly signed firmware, preventing the device from booting. In the same way, the safe bootloader protects against tampering, data corruption, and reverse engineering: it validates a new version of the firmware before overwriting the old one and can be configured to prevent the reading of the actual firmware from the device.

The programmer of the IoT node generates and manages their digital signatures, maintaining full control of the device, but excluding others at the same time.

I recommend the adoption of the secure bootloader in any IoT project because the minimal effort required to implement it is repaid immediately in terms of the security and integrity of the device and data.

Microcontroller-based nodes, with strong hardware encryption capabilities and secure boot mechanisms, address most of the security concerns on the node. Regular security audits ensure that the data exchanged between IoT devices and the backend systems is protected, while the providers of cloud platforms and cloud applications are responsible for securing the backend systems on the cloud that process and store the data by implementing secure data storage practices and regular backups, as well as regularly monitoring the systems to detect and respond promptly to potential security incidents.

Encryption for secure communication

Arduino considers the security of its IoT cloud and Arduino-based IoT nodes a top priority. The Arduino IoT Cloud requires connections with SSL/TLS encryption, and devices not implementing it cannot be provisioned to the cloud. The Arduino IoT Cloud regularly updates its security measures to address new threats and vulnerabilities and runs on the Amazon AWS platform, which has data centers and a network architecture built to meet the requirements of the most security-sensitive organizations.

The provisioning of IoT nodes refers to the process of configuring and setting up a device for operation and connecting it to a network or platform so that it can exchange data with it and interact with other devices. During this process, the device shall be configured with the information to establish a secure connection to the cloud and the cloud shall be configured to accept connections from the registered, well-known device and to manage the data exchanged with it.

Once the device is provisioned, it can connect to the cloud when required and exchange data in a secure way.

The SSL/TLS security protocols are the most adopted for secure communications on the Internet and use a combination of both symmetric and asymmetric encryption:

- **Asymmetric encryption**: Public-key cryptography, also referred to as asymmetric encryption, employs a set of public and private keys to perform encryption and decryption processes on data. In this method, the public key is utilized for encrypting the data, whereas the private key is employed for decrypting the data.

- **Symmetric encryption**, on the other hand, uses a single shared secret key to encrypt and decrypt data. It is faster and more efficient than asymmetric encryption but requires a secure method of exchanging the secret key between the client and the server.

In SSL/TLS, the initial handshake between the client and the server is performed using asymmetric encryption. The client and the server agree on a shared secret key, which is then used for symmetric encryption of the data transmitted between them. This approach provides both security and performance, making it a suitable encryption protocol for securing communications in IoT environments.

In the end, the device needs to know the public key for the SSL/TLS handshake and the cloud needs to know a unique device key or device identity to recognize the connection from a legitimate device. This data shall be configured during the provisioning phase for each IoT device that we want to deploy for our application.

The provisioning for a limited number of devices is usually manual or semi-automatic and is performed during the programming of each single device. In this phase, the programmer defines the unique identifier of their device and registers it on the cloud, then generates the security key on the cloud, and copies it to the device. It's not a difficult process, but it may become complicated because different clouds have different architectures and ways to do this.

Bulk device provisioning

IoT solutions that require a medium or mass deployment of nodes usually adopt a fully automatic process that starts from the production of the electronics. The owner of the IoT solution provides a list of unique device identifiers and a security certificate to the manufacturer of the devices. The manufacturer assigns a device identifier from the list to each device, stores the certificate, and eventually flashes the application firmware on it, making each node ready to run out of the factory.

The Arduino IoT Cloud mainly provides semi-automatic provisioning, as we'll see in detail in the next chapter. The user connects the device to a USB port of the programming PC and a web wizard is responsible for the rest of the job. The wizard recognizes the Arduino board model and flashes firmware on it responsible for the generation and storage of the security key on the crypto-chip. Finally, it completes the registration of the device on the Arduino IoT Cloud.

Even though the wizard does everything, I still consider this process semi-automatic; in fact, if you have multiple devices, you need to connect them to the USB one at a time. Actually, you may implement more automatic provisioning of Arduino boards on the Arduino IoT Cloud by programming a good script for Arduino CLI and using a smart USB hub that flexibly switches host connectivity between ports, but the topic is beyond this book.

Arduino PRO for commercial use cases

Arduino PRO can support businesses in their mass deployment by pre-provisioning devices during their production when several hundreds or thousands of devices are involved. You may contact the Arduino PRO team on the Arduino website and discuss your project with them.

We have already mentioned the crypto-chip a few times, so we'll end this section by talking about this component. The crypto-chip, also known as a **Secure Element** or **Trusted Platform Module** (**TPM**), is a hardware component used to securely store and manage cryptographic keys and perform cryptographic operations. Having its own secure processor and memory, it provides a root of trust, meaning it acts as a foundation for secure operations on the device.

Storing the device's unique identity, or a security certificate, in a secure element, as well as any other cryptographic keys used to encrypt and decrypt data, is much safer than writing them in the firmware or software code of the device. This is because the crypto-chip performs the cryptographic operations at the hardware level and the keys would not store on the hardware. Even reverse engineering activity wouldn't be able to reveal sensitive information contained on the device.

In this section, we have talked about security aspects and device provisioning in detail. To address security issues, Arduino devices for the IoT embed secure elements, called crypto-chips. It is recommended to adopt a secure bootloader in any IoT project for better security. Use SSL/TLS for device-to-cloud communication, which will provide safe passage for your devices' data for in/out operations. Next, we'll discuss open source as we proceed with this chapter.

Open source

The concept of open source software and open source licenses was first introduced in the late 1960s and early 1970s by computer scientists and programmers who believed that the sharing and collaboration of software code would lead to better, more reliable, and more innovative software.

Arduino is considered to be one of the first companies in the world to adopt open source licenses for hardware engineering too. The company released the first version of the Arduino board in 2005, along with schematics for the board and the source code of the core firmware under an open source license.

This allowed anyone to use, modify, and redistribute the design freely, which greatly contributed to the success and popularity of the Arduino platform. The open source approach also enabled a community of developers and makers to collaborate and improve the platform, creating a wide range of libraries, tutorials, and projects that are still used today.

Benefits and obligations of different open source licenses

Open source licenses are legal agreements that define the terms and conditions under which licensed software or hardware can be used, modified, and distributed. There are several different types of open source licenses, each with its own set of terms and conditions, but the main concepts are generally the same.

Open source licenses generally retain the copyright of the software or hardware, but they allow users to use, modify, and distribute the code or design freely under certain conditions. Users are allowed to create derivative works (modifications) based on the original software or hardware, but these derivative works must also be made available under the same open source license, and a copy of the license must be distributed with the product.

Most licenses require credit to be given to the original authors when using or distributing the software or hardware and the acceptance of a disclaimer of liability that excludes any responsibility of authors and distributors for any damage or problems that may arise from using the licensed software or hardware.

Some of the main open source licenses that you may find in IoT projects are the following:

- **MIT License**: This is one of the most permissive open source licenses and allows users to use, modify, and distribute software or hardware for any purpose, including commercial purposes, without the need for attribution.

- **GNU General Public License (GPL)**: This was the first widely recognized open source software license, released in 1989 by the **Free Software Free Software Foundation**.

- **GNU Lesser General Public License (LGPL)**: The LGPL is primarily used for software libraries, although it is also used by some standalone applications. The LGPL was developed as a compromise between the strong copyleft of the GNU GPL and more permissive licenses such as the BSD licenses and the MIT License.

- **Free Software Foundation (FSF)**: It is designed to ensure that software or hardware remains open source and free.

- **Apache License**: This is a permissive open source license that allows users to use, modify, and distribute the software or hardware for any purpose, including commercial purposes. However, users must provide attribution and must not use the original authors' names or trademarks to promote their products.

- **BSD Licenses, including the New BSD License and the Simplified BSD License**: These are permissive open source licenses that allow users to use, modify, and distribute software or hardware for any purpose, including commercial purposes, without the need for attribution.

- **Mozilla Public License (MPL)**: The MPL is a copyleft license that requires users to make any modifications to the software or hardware available under the same license, but allows them to add proprietary extensions to the software or hardware.

There are several benefits provided by an open source licensing model.

Open source licenses encourage collaboration and sharing, which can lead to faster innovation and better-quality software or hardware. Open source software or hardware engineering is often free, which can result in significant cost savings for users: they can modify the engineering and the products to meet their specific needs, without having to worry about proprietary restrictions. Open source brings an improved level of transparency and security because licensed products are reviewed and audited by many people, rather than just a few proprietary developers.

Arduino releases software and hardware under a combination of open source licenses. The Arduino **Integrated Development Environment (IDE)** software is released under the GPL v2 license; the hardware designs, including schematics and board layouts, are released under the **Creative Commons Attribution Share-Alike license**; while the software libraries are released under GPL v2, LGPL v2.1, and the MIT License, among others.

The protection of your intellectual property

The community of Arduino users appreciates the open source licensing model, for the benefits already mentioned earlier, while professionals still look with some reluctance at the adoption of open source for business purposes.

They may have concerns related to a lower or different level of support and maintenance that they can get compared to other proprietary products, but in many cases, they procure open source products because they compensate for that feeling with the cost savings of open source. A different thing is the consideration of intellectual property when releasing their own products: it is a critical barrier and, most of the time, professionals prefer to adopt proprietary licenses.

In my opinion, better knowledge of both the terms and conditions of the licenses and the available technologies would allow all professionals to opt in to open source, getting the benefits it provides without losing certain protection against unauthorized use or infringement of their proprietary solutions.

For example, not only may you protect the duplication of your open source IoT node just by adopting a secure bootloader, as we have seen, but you may also exploit open source software libraries without releasing the source code of your project and remaining compliant with the open source license.

In order to do this, you need to make a slight mind shift and consider your software as composed of two parts: the main software, which recalls the functionalities provided by third-party libraries, and your own proprietary library, with your know-how and proprietary technology.

If you structure your project by moving the intelligence of your device from the main application to the proprietary library, and the open source libraries provide their functionalities to the main application and not directly to your proprietary library, the game is done. In fact, your proprietary library can remain a binary library, without the need to publish its source code, and you need to publish the main application under open source and the binary code of your library only. Your main application doesn't contain any strategic or valuable knowledge but is just a wrapping for calls and back-calls to your proprietary and third-party libraries.

Now, this approach requires some programming skills but you may get paid support from Arduino and its network of System Integrator Partners. These are industrial system integrators who joined a partnership program and are officially recognized by Arduino. This network also solves concerns about the after-sales support of Arduino-based IoT nodes and applications.

Respect for the Arduino trademarks in commercial applications

We have seen that the Arduino ecosystem fulfills all the requirements of an IoT application in terms of technical and licensing requirements. It's now time to understand whether you can use it even for a commercial application without infringing any trademarks, incurring legal troubles.

Arduino technology is open source and you can copy an Arduino open source hardware design to further develop into your own product, but you must use your own brand name and logo for it.

You may use the Arduino software tools, such as the IDE, for free and as they are, to program the hardware even for commercial purposes.

If you would like to modify and further develop them, you may then redistribute them according to the included open source software license. So, the sale of derivative tools or their inclusion in commercial software products is not prohibited, but it may require modifications in order to be open sourced under the same license.

The usage of Arduino trademarks to identify hardware or software products not produced and maintained by Arduino is always forbidden. You may call them *Arduino-compatible* if you like and brand them with your own logo.

You may find many different success stories on the internet and the Arduino website of businesses that have successfully adopted the ecosystem for commercial IoT solutions in different verticals, respecting the principles mentioned here.

Some companies with large-volume projects have also successfully approached Arduino for co-branding or custom production licensing.

In the preceding section, we discussed the open source concept and discussed the details regarding different open source licenses and responsibilities while using these tools and related code in your projects. We also talked about intellectual property, which is very much related to commercial usage and preventing your product from being a copy or clone. This is the first chapter of the book and we have discussed in depth what the IoT is, its benefits, communication protocols and technologies, and a lot of other topics, giving you a broad overview of IoT architecture before starting the remainder of the book.

Summary

We have seen that two electronic devices can use the internet to interact with each other and exchange information, without the need for a direct physical connection between them. Nodes can be interfaced with other objects and cloud applications and this architecture allows the implementation of smart solutions in different markets and with huge benefits for users.

We've seen the architecture of an IoT solution, the different telecommunication technologies, and the security aspects involved.

We have talked about methods to protect your intellectual property against the duplication of your product and how to adopt open source libraries without the need to release your source code.

Finally, please respect the Arduino trademarks when implementing a commercial solution based on the Arduino ecosystem.

All this information is necessary to understand how things behind an IoT application work and for you to consider the right approach for your next IoT solution.

Before stepping into the next chapter, with the first example of an IoT project based on the Arduino IoT Cloud, it's worth recapping the main steps to engineer a good IoT solution:

1. Identify the application and define the business model.
2. Determine the requirements and goals of the IoT application.
3. Identify on the edge versus on the cloud and structured code versus AI/ML model requirements.
4. Select the most appropriate telecommunication technologies.
5. Choose the appropriate hardware for the IoT node.
6. Select the provisioning mode according to the size of the project.
7. Develop the software for the node and configure the cloud, as we'll see in the following chapters.
8. Deploy the application and periodically monitor performance and security.

2

First Look at
the Arduino IoT Cloud

Every developer/programmer/cloud engineer, when they start their coding/cloud journey, is very curious to get started with the platform immediately. Well, guys, your wait is over, and we welcome you to this chapter with a *Hello World* greeting. This chapter not only provides you with a *Hello World* example but also comes with many important core concepts of how the **Arduino IoT Cloud** works. This is the most important chapter for all readers, as this chapter will give you an overview of how to get started with the Arduino IoT Cloud, as the Arduino IoT Cloud platform has significant differences compared to other platforms. This chapter is divided into two parts; in the first part, you will learn how to use the **Arduino MKR Wi-Fi 1010** board to interact with the Arduino IoT Cloud platform, and in the second part, you will learn how to use an **API** with **Node-RED** for communication with the cloud platform.

Along with these examples, you will learn the difference between a **Thing** and a **device**, what a **variable** is, and different properties of Thing. You will also get a taste of the **Arduino Web Editor**, which is an awesome feature with interesting stuff. After that, we will move on to the dashboard, which helps a user control a Thing and visualize sensor data. So, guys, buckle up for this interesting journey.

The following topics will be covered in this chapter:

- Understanding how the Arduino IoT Cloud works
- The Arduino IoT Cloud and an MKR1010 Hello World example
- An introduction to Node-RED
- The Arduino IoT Cloud and a Node-RED Hello World example

Technical requirements

Before we start, we first need to set up an Arduino IoT Cloud-compatible board. I recommend the Arduino MKR Wi-Fi 1010, but there is a complete list of compatible boards at `https://docs.arduino.cc/arduino-cloud/getting-started/technical-reference#compatible-hardware`, which you can choose according to your requirements.

Second, you should have an Arduino IoT Cloud account. If you don't, then sign up at `https://cloud.arduino.cc/` and select a plan according to your requirements.

Third, we need to download and install the **Arduino Create Agent**. Arduino has created a beautiful web-based guide for installation at `https://create.arduino.cc/getting-started/plugin/welcome`.

The second part of the chapter is related to Node-RED, which will be used for devices that are not officially supported by the Arduino IoT Cloud such as Raspberry Pi and older versions of Arduino development boards. Download and install Node-RED according to your operating system from `https://nodered.org/docs/getting-started/local`.

> **Important note**
>
> All the Arduino IoT Cloud plans are available on the Arduino IoT Cloud website. You can visit the following link for updated plans, pricing, and features: `https://cloud.arduino.cc/plans/`. If you are from an educational institute, then there are plenty of good plans for students and faculties. Arduino also offers customized plans to business organizations according to their requirements.

Understanding how the Arduino IoT Cloud works

So, before we start our Arduino IoT Cloud journey, we need to understand how it operates because it's a little bit different from traditional IoT cloud platforms. As a result, the Arduino IoT Cloud is a more flexible, secure, and industry-deployment-ready IoT solution. Firstly, we will understand the design of the Arduino IoT Cloud with the following diagram, which will help you to understand the key pillars of the Arduino IoT Cloud:

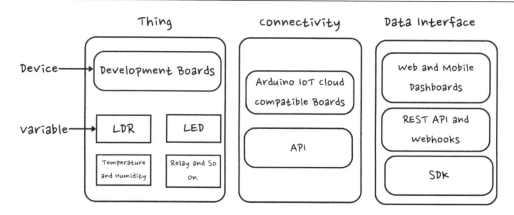

Figure 2.1 – The Arduino IoT Cloud architecture

Most cloud platforms work with the concept of devices and sensors, but in the Arduino IoT Cloud, we have the concept of the Thing, which includes devices and variables known as **sensors/actuators**. You may be thinking that a *Thing* and a *Device* are both the same; actually, they're not. It's important to make this distinction because if we do not understand it, then it will create more complications going forward.

To understand the difference between a Thing and a device, I am going to take an example from real life. Let's say we have an empty box. If we put some stuff in that box, it will be a filled box. However, what if we put the shipping label on that box? Will it still be a box? No, now it's a parcel. So, we can understand that a parcel is just a logical container that consists of the box, the stuff in the box, and the shipping label.

Like the preceding example, a Thing is a logical container that consists of a development board, variables that act as a bridge between the cloud and sensors/actuators for read/write operations, and network connectivity that makes the Thing live in an ecosystem (which is like the shipping label in the box analogy).

Next, we need to understand how device configuration works in relation to the Arduino IoT Cloud. Here, we are not talking about **network connectivity** but **device configuration**. Some cloud platforms provide **Arduino IDE** libraries or **Software Development Kits** (**SDKs**) for device configuration, but Arduino has a different, more restrictive system. Firstly, the Arduino IoT Cloud has two ways for device configuration; the first one uses compatible boards via the Arduino Create Agent (in the upcoming section, you will dive deep into the Arduino Create Agent) and the second way is through an API, which is used for non-compatible devices.

So, why does Arduino have this restriction for device connectivity? Arduino cares about security for IoT devices, and security is as vital in an IoT infrastructure as water is for living beings. Also, not all the official Arduino development boards are compatible with the Arduino IoT Cloud. You can find the complete list of Arduino IoT Cloud-compatible devices at `https://docs.arduino.cc/arduino-cloud/getting-started/technical-reference#compatible-hardware`.

The Arduino IoT Cloud directly supports some famous boards besides the Arduino official compatible boards, which include **ESP8266 Series**, **ESP32 Series**, and **LoRaWAN Nodes**. An API is available for other development boards, which can be used via any programming language. Later on in this chapter, we will explain how to use APIs with Node-RED to communicate with the Arduino IoT Cloud.

Finally, which options are available for **data visualization** and **data extraction**? The Arduino IoT Cloud platform provides a variety of options. For data visualization, the platform provides a flexible dashboard option for both web and mobile, with huge widget features as well as sharing features. For third-party application integrations, a **Representational State Transfer (REST) API** and **webhooks** are available. For custom application development or custom integrations, Arduino provides **JavaScript** and **Python SDKs**, which enrich the platform's extensibility. An organization can create custom dashboard visualization and control panels by using these SDKs.

We have discussed the Arduino IoT Cloud's main pillars; now it's time to explore the Arduino IoT Cloud by implementing basic examples, which will get you started with the Arduino MKR Wi-Fi 1010 development board and the Arduino IoT Cloud.

The Arduino IoT Cloud and the MKR1010 Hello World example

A **Hello World program** is the first program that every programmer uses when they start learning any programming technology to get a taste for a platform. However, when it comes to the IoT side, things are different; you will be working with hardware and software, which means the *Hello World* example will be different from its traditional onscreen appearance. In this section, we will demonstrate how to turn on/off a built-in LED of an Arduino MKR Wi-Fi 1010 development board using the Arduino IoT Cloud dashboard, which is a *Hello World* example for the Arduino IoT Cloud.

In a series of steps, you will learn how to work with Arduino IoT Cloud-compatible boards. This part is very important to understand how a Thing works on the Arduino IoT Cloud platform. First, you need to get the required hardware, software, and accounts, as mentioned in the *Technical requirements* section.

So, in this section, we are going to start the *Hello World* project for the Arduino IoT Cloud using MKR Wi-Fi 1010. In the next sub-section, we will cover the Arduino Create Agent. Next, we will create a Thing and cloud variables, associate the MKR Wi-Fi 1010 device with the Thing, and provide the network configuration for the Thing. Later, we will discuss the sketch/coding for the development board.

What is the Arduino Create Agent?

The Arduino IoT Cloud provides a different way to connect a device to its cloud. Arduino does not publicly reveal its cloud connectivity technique for security reasons. That's why we only have two options to connect devices with the Arduino IoT Cloud – using the Arduino Cloud IDE or the API. Also, for the Arduino Cloud IDE, it's mandatory to have the Arduino Create Agent on your machine. *Figure 2.2* shows the complete process of how the Create Agent helps devices to interact with the Arduino Web Editor.

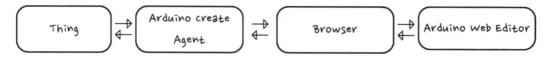

Figure 2.2 – The Arduino Create Agent process flow

As the Arduino Web Editor is a web-based tool, there is no way to talk to development boards via a browser. That's why the Arduino team developed software for all major operating systems, including Windows, Linux, and macOS, called the Arduino Create Agent. The Create Agent acts like a bridge between a device and the Arduino Web Editor. The preceding diagram explains the process in detail.

To get the Create Agent on your machine, visit `https://create.arduino.cc/getting-started/plugin/welcome` and follow the steps. After installation, start the Create Agent, as just installing it is not enough for connectivity. The Create Agent will run as a background process to provide continuous integration between a device and a browser. The following is a figure that describes all the options of the Arduino Create Agent:

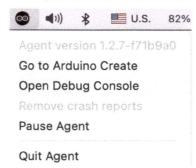

Figure 2.3 – The Arduino Create Agent menu

When we click on the Create Agent icon, it shows the Create Agent version, a **Go to Arduino Create** option, and an **Open Debug Console** option, which is like a serial monitor, where you can execute different commands to get the status and information about the current process, devices, and ports. Also from this menu, you can pause/resume the Create Agent, or if you want to close it down properly, then click on **Quit Agent**.

Setting up the Thing, device, and variable

In this section, we will create a Thing and name it. We will also learn how to add a device, along with network configuration and cloud variables.

Creating a Thing

When you first open the dashboard in the Arduino IoT Cloud (*Figure 2.4*), you will see menu links such as **Things**, **Dashboards**, **Devices**, **Integrations**, and **Templates**, and the **Create your first Thing** message. Just click on the **CREATE THING** button and your journey will start.

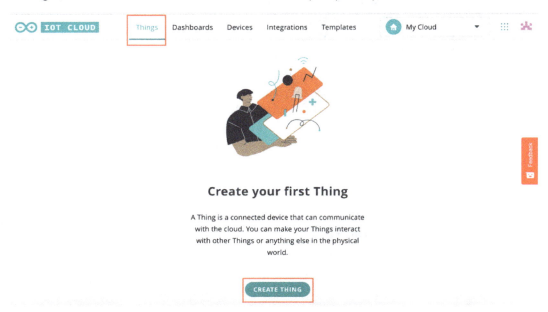

Figure 2.4 – The Thing dashboard

Adding a Thing is totally different compared to other IoT cloud platforms, as the Thing is a combination of multiple ingredients. The following figure describes all the ingredients of the Thing, such as the name, cloud variables, device, network settings, code, and Thing metadata:

Figure 2.5 – Thing creation

All the aspects indicated in the preceding screenshot are explained, step by step, as follows:

1. Assign a name to the Thing; the name should relate to the location and functionality of the device, which will help you to find the Thing easily in the following wizards.

2. Clicking on **Select Device** will show you a popup, where you can select the old device or set up a new device, as discussed in detail in a moment.

3. After attaching the device, we need to make the device network-ready by providing a Wi-Fi SSID and a password. Just click on the **Configure** button and you will see the popup for network settings.

4. Finally, we need to add a variable for the sensors/actuators to perform read/write operations. The Arduino IoT Cloud provides different types of variables, like the Arduino IDE; the only difference is that in the Arduino IDE, we declare the variables, whereas here, we need to create variables via the interface.

In this section, we have created the Thing and named it. Three further steps are required adding a device, network configuration, and adding cloud variables. We are going to cover the remaining steps in the following subsections.

Adding a device

After assigning a name to the Thing, we need to attach a device to it. When you click on the **Select Device** button, you will see a popup that shows you an available device and the option to add a new device. If there is no device, then you will see the following figure to set up a new device:

Figure 2.6 – Associating a device

In our case, we don't have any device in the portal, so we will just click on **SET UP NEW DEVICE** to configure a new device in the account.

Next, you will see the two options in the popup. The first option is **Arduino board**, and the second option is **Third party device**. Here, you will see an icon in front of both names, which means you need to use compatible devices with the Arduino IoT Cloud. Next, you will see two options: one for the Arduino official development boards and a second option for the third-party development boards.

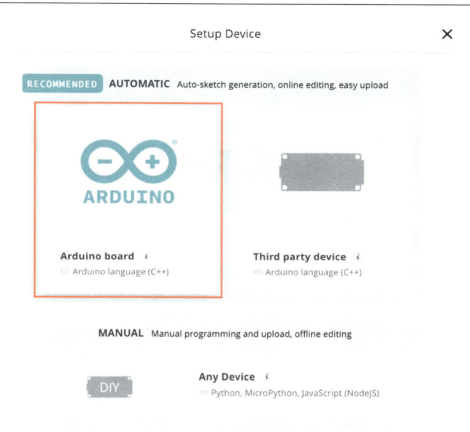

Figure 2.7 – Choosing a development device

Select one option from the popup according to the available device. For this chapter, we will click on **Arduino board**, as in this chapter, we will use the MKR Wi-Fi 1010 board. Before adding the device, make sure that the Arduino Create Agent is running on your machine.

> **Important note**
>
> You can find the Arduino IoT Cloud-compatible boards at `https://store-usa.arduino.cc/pages/cloud-compatible-boards`, and for third-party devices, we have three options, which are **ESP8266**, **ESP32**, and **LoRaWAN** devices. For some devices, we have API access, which will be discussed in the second part of this chapter.

Next, you will see the **Setup Device** popup, which will start searching for your device. So, make sure the device is properly connected to your machine. When the Arduino Create Agent detects the compatible development board device, the following popup will be shown:

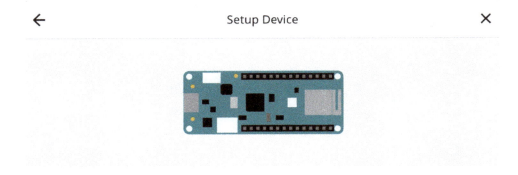

Arduino MKR WiFi 1010 found

An Arduino MKR WiFi 1010 has been detected on port
/dev/cu.usbmodem14101 and ready to be configured.

If the detected type of the device you want to configure is not
correct, try to reset your board and then refresh

Figure 2.8 – Setup Device

The wizard will find and list all the connected boards with their name and port details. Click on the **CONFIGURE** button to move forward. If the wizard doesn't show the device after searching, try to plug in a different port and click on the **refresh** link, located at the bottom. After development board configuration has been taken care of by the Arduino IoT Cloud, you will see a popup where you need to provide the name of your device:

In the next configuration wizard, provide the device's name (note that spaces and special characters are not allowed in the device name) and then click on the **NEXT** button.

Give your device a name

Name your device so you will be able to recognize it.

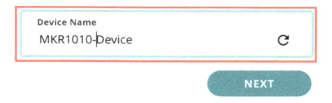

Figure 2.9 – The device configuration name

After that, the wizard will start the device configuration process, which will take up to five minutes. But in most cases, it only takes one minute to configure the device.

Eventually, you will see a popup with a **Congratulations! You are all set** message. Click on the **Done** button, and the device will be attached to your Thing.

On the Thing page, you will see the device details, which are marked in the red box in the following figure:

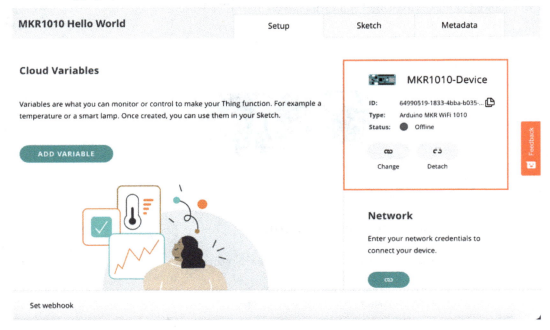

Figure 2.10 – The device attached to the Thing

The page shows the device name, the device ID, its type, its status (which is either **Online** or **Offline**), and two buttons, **Change** and **Detach**:

- **Change** is used to switch between devices – for example, if you have chosen the wrong device, then you can select a different one via this option.

- **Detach** means removing the device from the Thing. Why might we need to detach? For example, you may have created a Thing and associated the device with it, but you are now not using that Thing. If you want to set up a new Thing with that device, the platform will not allow you to do so if it's already associated with the old Thing.

> **Important note**
> The device and the Thing have a one-to-one relationship. If you want to use a device with a new Thing, then make sure it's not associated with another one.

As we have added the device, let us move toward network configuration.

Configuring the network

After attaching the device to the Thing, we can see that the device is offline. To bring it online, we need to provide Wi-Fi details. The following figure represents the network configuration popup, which only consists of two fields:

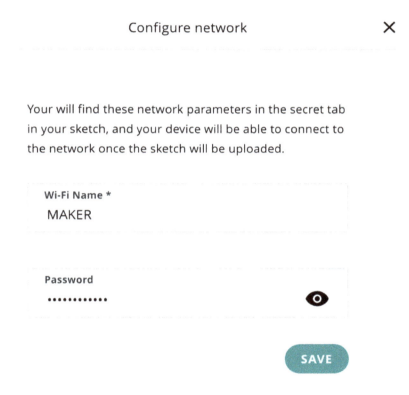

Figure 2.11 – Network configuration

On the Thing page shown in *Figure 2.5*, under the **Network** tab, click on the **CONFIGURE** button, which will take you to the **Configure network** popup with two fields, **Wi-Fi Name** and **Password**. Type the Wi-Fi SSID and password, and then click on the **SAVE** button.

In this section, we have configured the network for our device, which is MKR Wi-Fi 1010, and in the next sub section, we will create the cloud variable.

Adding a cloud variable

The final part is adding a cloud variable. Before adding a variable, you have to have an idea of what type of variables you need for your project, including the **variable type**, the **variable permission**, and the **variable update policy**.

For the current example, we need one variable to control the built-in LED, so the variable type will be **Boolean** (either on/off):

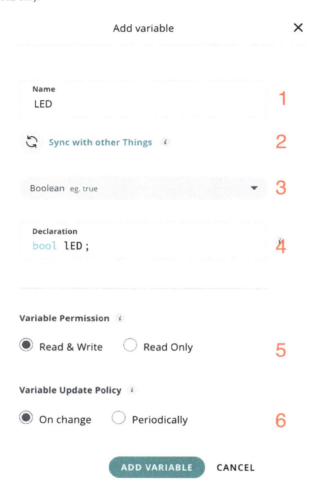

Figure 2.12 – Adding a variable

This way, we will control the LED via the dashboard:

1. Assign a meaningful name to the variable, related to the sensor/actuator type. Remember that spaces and special characters are not allowed in the name.

2. If you want to sync the variable with other Things' variables, then click on the **Sync with other Things option**. The sync option is very beneficial if you want to share data across other Things. Sync will be explained in later chapters alongside a practical demonstration.

3. Select the variable type from the dropdown; the platform provides dozens of variable types. For this example, we need a **Boolean** variable type for LED control.

4. After selecting the variable type, you will see the variable **declaration** that will be used during coding. You can see here that our variable name is LED, but the system has converted the first letter to lowercase and the rest of the characters are left as is, making the name **lED**. This declaration part is very important; you can change the declaration according to your requirements, but keep the declaration in mind, as it will be used in coding.

5. The variable permission provides two options, **Read & Write** and **Read Only**. The permission provides an extra layer of security for the Thing's control. If a sensor only senses data such as temperature/humidity, then choose the **Read Only** option. If you want to control actuators such as the relay and the LED, then choose the **Read & Write** option. For our example, we need to write data to the variable to control the LED, so we will simply choose **Read & Write**.

6. Finally, we need to choose an update policy according to our requirements. One option is event-driven (shown onscreen as **On change**), which only works when there is a change. It works when prompted by commands such as turning on/off a relay or LED. The second option is **Periodically**, which means taking data from a variable, such as temperature, humidity, air pressure, or a **Light Dependent Resistor** (**LDR**) value after a specific time. When you change the option to **Periodically**, it will ask you for a time measured in seconds, whereas for **On change**, there is a threshold option.

After adding the variable, our Thing now has all the mandatory ingredients. The following figure describes all the settings and configurations when we are done with the cloud variable, device, and network settings. Next, we need to jump to the **Sketch** tab for coding:

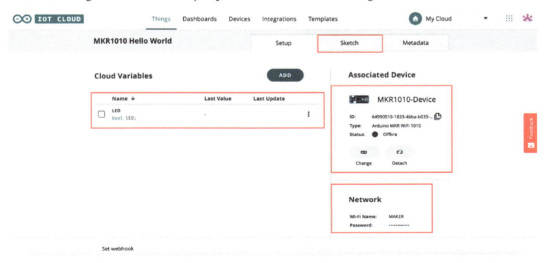

Figure 2.13 – The Thing after configuration

The preceding screenshot illustrates the device association, network configuration, and variable settings, which are essential components of the Thing. Next, click the **Sketch** tab, where you will open the Arduino Web Editor for coding. Here, we will add the code that will be associated with the LED variable. In this section, we have completed all the tasks via drag and drop, but now it's time to do some work by putting some coding into our development board. In the next section, we will explore sketches.

Writing a sketch

Most Things are set up in the cloud via a **graphical user interface** (**GUI**), but we still need to do some coding. The following figure describes all the options of the mini web editor, such as verifying and uploading the code, selecting the development board on specific ports, and the code area for writing and editing.

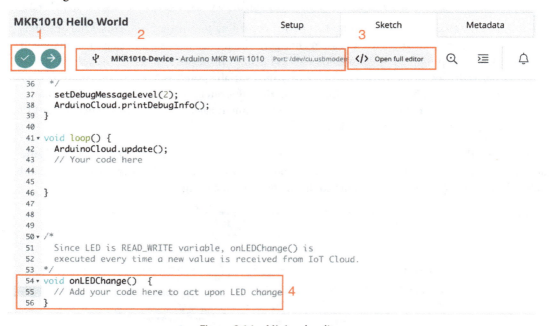

Figure 2.14 – Mini web editor

The code will associate a variable with physical sensors/actuators to make it work properly. Please see the following steps:

1. Here, you will see two buttons, like with the Arduino IDE. The tick button is used to verify code, while the arrow icon button is used to upload the code to the development board.

2. This part shows whether your device is connected to your machine or not. If the development board is connected, then it will show the device name with the port.

3. The Arduino Cloud Editor has two variants – one is basic and the other is full. In the **Thing** tab shown in *Figure 2.14*, we can see the mini version of the editor, but if you want to move to the full editor for the installation of libraries or other stuff, then click on the </> button.

4. Scroll down the editor, and at the bottom, you will see the OnLEDChange() function, which is associated with the **LED** variable. In this function, we need to write the code that will provide connectivity to the sensor/physical pins of the development board.

According to our current example project, we just want a turned-on/turned-off, built-in LED for the development board. The following is the code that will be used in the function:

```
if(lED==1)
  {
    digitalWrite(LED_BUILTIN,1);
  }else{
    digitalWrite(LED_BUILTIN,0);
  }
```

First, let's recall the declaration used during variable creation, which is shown in *Figure 2.12*. What the code does is turn the built-in LED on if the lED variable contains a true value; otherwise, it turns the built-in LED off.

To write Boolean values on development board pins, we have a method called digitalWrite, which takes two parameters. The first parameter is a pin number and in the second parameter we will place true/false or 1/0, while we are using LED_BUILTIN, which is a constant and contains *PIN #13*. The second parameter is a value, which is either 1 or 0. This parameter changes according to the lED variable state. Here we are done with our coding exercise. Now it's time to create a graphical user interface from where we turn on/off the LED. In the following section, we will set up the dashboard to control the LED.

Creating a dashboard for web and mobile with an interactive widget

After setting up a complete Thing, we are done with device setup, network settings, the variable, and coding the variable. The next question is, how can we turn the LED on/off? For that, we need to create a dashboard. *Figure 2.15* illustrates a dashboard. Click on the **Dashboards** link in the top menu. After loading the dashboard page for the first time, you will see an empty page with one green button at the bottom of the page – **Build Dashboard**.

Figure 2.15 – The Things dashboard

Click on the button, and you will be taken to the dashboard builder page to create a new stunning dashboard for your device control, as follows:

1. The dashboard has two modes, view and editing. By default, it's on editing mode, which is denoted by an edit icon, and we can switch to view mode by clicking on the eye icon. In view mode, we can't modify the widget's settings and alignment.

2. To add controls on the dashboard, click on the green **ADD** button, and a drop-down menu will appear with a variety of widgets. Here, you can select a widget by scrolling or searching.

3. This button is used to arrange the widgets. During editing, you are not able to navigate, resize, or move the widget controls.

4. As mobile icon is representing it's working from its icon, this means by click on this icon you can adjust your dashboard for mobile devices. Arduino provides both views of the dashboard for desktop and mobile. You can switch between them by clicking on the mobile/desktop icon.

5. In the textbox, type the dashboard name.

Now that we have created the dashboard, it's time to put a widget on it. Widgets will help us to control/view the sensors/actuators. When you click on the **Add** button, you will see the list of widgets. Here you can select a widget by scrolling through the list or by searching the widgets via the search bar, as shown in the following figure:

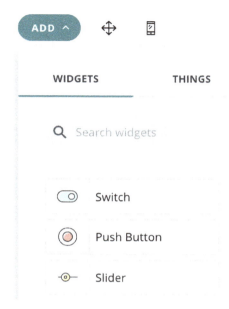

Figure 2.16 – The widgets list

Select the **Switch** widget control for the current example project. After selecting the widget control, a popup will appear, where we need to link the Thing variable with the widget control to read/write the data to the device sensors. This is because the variable is the bridge between the dashboard widget controls and the Thing sensors to read and write data.

In the widget popup, we have different settings, as shown in the following figure:

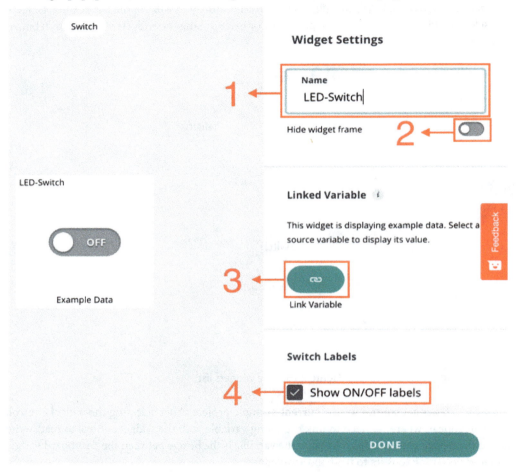

Figure 2.17 – Widget settings

The widget settings are detailed as follows:

1. Firstly, we need to assign a name to our widget. Make sure to give it a proper name that represents the sensor's name. Here, I used the name **LED-Switch**.

2. Hide or show the widget frame content, which is at the top and bottom of the widget.

3. Click on **Link Variable** to attach the Thing variable to the widget control, which will be explained in the next figure.

4. Hide/show the widget label to hide the text that overlays the widget control. In the preceding figure, it switches the **ON/OFF** button text.

It's time to attach the widget control to the variables. Note that we can add multiple controls on the same dashboard that are linked to different Things' variables, which shows the versatility of Arduino IoT Cloud dashboards, as shown in the following figure:

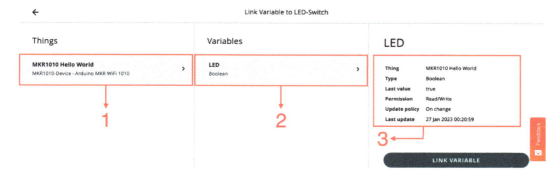

Figure 2.18 – Linking a Thing variable with a widget control

As shown in *Figure 2.18*, we have the following steps to assign the cloud variable to the widget control:

1. Select a Thing from the **Things** list. After selecting the Thing, it will show you the variables that are associated with that Thing.

2. Select a variable from the **Variables** list.

3. Here, you will see all the details of the variables, such as the Thing name, **Type**, **Last value**, **Permission**, **Update policy**, and **Last update**. The purpose of this detailed summary is to make sure to verify that you have attached the right variable to the widget control.

After selecting the variable from the specific Thing, click on the **LINK VARIABLE** button, and you will see the variable details in the widget control popup. From there, you can change or detach the variable. Finally, click on the **DONE** button; now, our dashboard is ready, with a widget control to send commands to the Thing. Just click on the eye icon on the dashboard to make it operational. After that, start testing the dashboard controls.

Here we are done with our first example project with Arduino MKR1010 and the Arduino IoT Cloud. Next, you need to solve *Assignment 1* of this section. After that, you will jump into the second section of this chapter, where you will learn how to use the Arduino IoT Cloud with non-compatible devices, such as Arduino Uno, Raspberry Pi, and so on via Node-RED.

Assignment 1

Congratulations! You have completed the first part of this chapter successfully, and I hope you enjoyed that journey. Now, it's time to verify what you have learned so far by giving you a small assignment:

1.   Attach three differently colored LEDs of any color (preferably, red, yellow, and green) to the Arduino MKR1010 development board on pin numbers 1, 2, and 3, respectively.

2.   Set up a new Thing with the name `IoT-Based Traffic Lights Control`.

3.   Associate the device, configure its network settings, and create variables according to the number of LEDs. Variable names should be based on LED colors such as `LED_Red`.

4.   Write the code that will turn the LED on/off according to the variable value. After writing the code for each LED, verify and upload the code to the development board.

5.   Finally, set up the dashboard with the name `Traffic Light Control Dashboard`.

6.   Add the **Switch** buttons according to the number of LEDs, and link them with their associated variables.

7.   Test the LEDs by switching them on/off via a dashboard.

> **Important note**
>
> Try the **Push Button** widget control along with the **Switch** button widget control. Verify whether one variable allows you to connect with more than one widget. Also, verify the behavior of the **Push Button** widget control by turning the **Switch** button on/off.

Our world is full of different types of technologies. Whenever a new innovation comes on the market, it always provides compatibility with older devices. In the Arduino IoT Cloud, we have a list of devices that are currently supported, but there are millions of devices that are not compatible with the Arduino IoT Cloud. So, while in the previous section of the chapter, we practiced an example with Arduino IoT Cloud-compatible development boards, next, we are going to look at how we can connect/use non-compatible devices with the Arduino IoT Cloud, such as Arduino UNO, Raspberry Pi, BeagleBone, and so on.

Introducing Node-RED

Node-RED is a free, open source visual programming tool for IoT and other applications. It was developed by IBM Emerging Technology and was first released in 2013. Node-RED provides a web-based interface to wire together hardware devices, APIs, and online services in new and interesting ways. The tool uses a **graphical flow-based programming language**, making it easy for users with little or no programming experience to build complex IoT systems. Node-RED has become popular in the IoT and smart home communities for its ease of use and ability to integrate with a wide range of devices and services.

Node-RED is a flow-based development tool for IoT and other applications. It provides a visual, drag-and-drop interface to connect different devices, APIs, and online services. With Node-RED, users can wire together inputs, outputs, and functions to create sophisticated IoT solutions. As well as being open source and free to use, Node-RED has a large user community and a library of pre-built components.

With all Node-RED's aforementioned benefits, the following question arises: why do we need to use the Arduino IoT Cloud? At the start of the chapter, I mentioned that the Arduino IoT Cloud only supports a few development boards natively. Even Arduino doesn't support all of their development boards, especially Arduino UNO, Arduino Mega, and Raspberry Pi from the Raspberry Pi Foundation, which are very famous among makers and hobbyists and used by industry. The solution to this is Node-RED, which is compatible with most development boards and has an Arduino IoT Cloud module, making it easier for developers to integrate non-compatible devices with the Arduino IoT Cloud.

Node-RED can be used with the Arduino IoT Cloud with several benefits:

- **Ease of development**: Node-RED's visual, drag-and-drop interface makes it easy for users to connect Arduino boards to the cloud and build IoT applications quickly

- **Integration with the Arduino IoT Cloud**: Node-RED has built-in support for the Arduino IoT Cloud, allowing users to easily connect their Arduino boards, as well as other development boards, and send data to the cloud

- **Flexibility**: The flow-based programming model of Node-RED makes it easy to build and modify complex systems

- **Flow-based programming**: Node-RED's flow-based programming model is well suited to building IoT applications, as it allows users to quickly connect inputs, outputs, and functions to create sophisticated systems

- **Open source**: Node-RED is open source, allowing users to access the source code and make modifications if necessary

- **Large user community**: Node-RED has a large and active user community, providing access to a wealth of information and pre-built components

These benefits make Node-RED a good choice for developing Arduino-based IoT applications and connecting them to the cloud. By using Node-RED, users can leverage the power of the cloud to store, analyze, and visualize data from their IoT systems. In this section, we have discussed the features and benefits of Node-RED. Now it's time to take a practical look by implementing the example project. The following sections will take you through the implementation of the project step by step.

The Arduino IoT Cloud and a Node-RED Hello World example

In this section, we will build on our project by adding some extra functionality to our system via Node-RED. This will help you to understand how you can use Node-RED to integrate non-compatible devices with the Arduino IoT Cloud.

Node-RED will monitor the LED status based on a value that is either **true** or **false**. On the basis of this status, Node-RED will send the command to another Thing variable called `LEDStatus`, which will be linked to the **Status** widget, which shows the LED as being either on or off. Using this example, you will learn how to read data from a Thing property/variable and how to write data to a Thing property/variable.

Node-RED has a module that was officially developed by Arduino for connectivity with the Arduino IoT Cloud. It provides five nodes to carry out different types of operations. For further details, visit `https://flows.nodered.org/node/@arduino/node-red-contrib-arduino-iot-cloud`.

A tour of the Node-RED editor

Before moving on, I want to first remind you that you need to set up Node-RED on your machine. If you already have, that's great; otherwise, you need to set up on a local machine by going to `https://nodered.org/docs/getting-started/local`. If you are looking for more cloud/development board options, then go to `https://nodered.org/docs/getting-started/`.

After installation, start Node-RED and type `127.0.0.1:1880` or `localhost:1880` in your browser URL bar. After that, you will see an interface, with a white space area and several different colored boxes on the left sidebar; here I have marked the following figure with different numbered boxes, which are explained in detail after the figure:

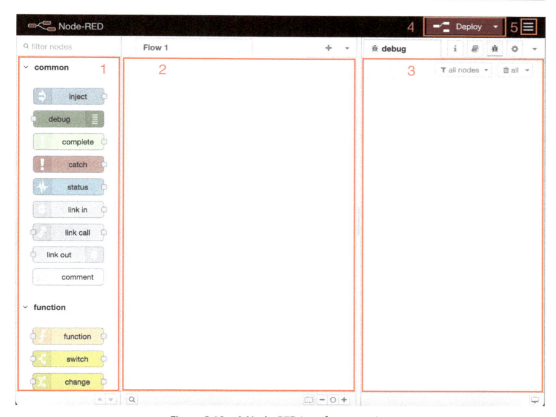

Figure 2.19 – A Node-RED interface overview

The various parts of the preceding figure are explained as follows:

1. These colorful boxes are called **nodes**. Node-RED divides different types of nodes into different groups, such as **common** and **function**.

2. This is the working area, or canvas area, where you will drag and place the nodes.

3. The **debug** area is used to debug the output and input of different operations to verify that everything is working fine.

4. Just like in other development environments, we can execute/run a program using the **Deploy** option. **Deploy** has different options; if you click on the small downward arrow icon, you will get a list of options, such as **Full**, **Modified Flows**, **Modified Nodes**, and **Restart Flows**.

5. The hamburger icon at the top right is the main navigation button, where you can find all the options to control the Node-RED configuration, especially for the installation of modules. In our case, we will install the Arduino IoT Cloud module.

Here we have discussed the interface of Node-RED with all the main options. In the following section, we will look at how to install the Arduino IoT Cloud module for Node-RED, and in the subsequent sections, we will see its implementation.

Installing the Arduino IoT Cloud module for Node-RED

For Node-RED to communicate with the Arduino IoT Cloud, we need to install the Arduino IoT Cloud module, which was officially developed by the Arduino team.

Click on the navigation icon in the top-right corner of the app and then click on **Manage palette**. After that, you will see a popup like the one in the following figure:

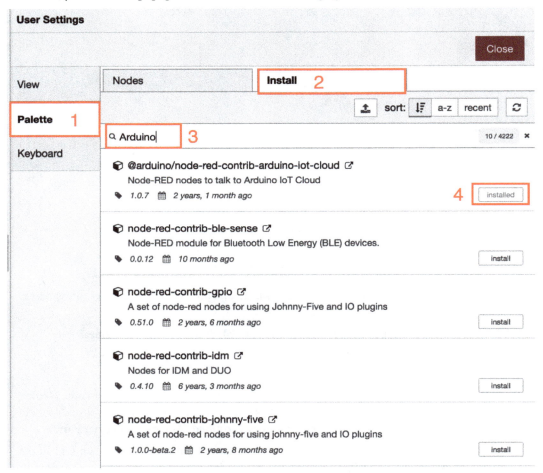

Figure 2.20 – Arduino IoT Cloud module installation

From that popup, we will install a module:

1. To install a module, click on **Palette**.

2. Next, select the **Install** tab.

3. Initially, you will see a blank area. Type `Arduino` in the search bar, which will display different modules.

4. Find the **@arduino/node-red-contrib-arduinio-iot-cloud** module and click on **install**. In the previous figure, you can see that I already have that module.

Now that we have installed the module, it's time to have a look at what type of nodes are available in the Arduino IoT Cloud module. Close the installation palette, scroll down through the nodes to the bottom, and you will arrive at the **Arduino IoT Cloud** section, as shown in the following figure:

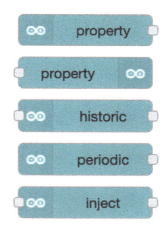

Figure 2.21 – Arduino IoT Cloud nodes

Here is a breakdown of the nodes shown in *Figure 2.21*:

1. The first one is an *IN* node (in Node-RED, we have nodes; that's why I used the word node instead of property to get the value from the Thing property/variable).

2. The second is an *OUT* node, used to write the value to the Thing property/variable.

3. The third is the **historic** node, which is used to get data from a specific property until a specific time. This node is useful when you want to get the set of values for a specific sensor, such as temperature/humidity.

4. The fourth is **periodic** and is useful when you want to get the value of a specific property after a specific period of time, such as getting the value of soil moisture after a specific time interval.

5.   The fifth, which is our last node, is **inject**. This is used to add value to the flow of the Arduino IoT Cloud variables after receiving some sort of input. *OUT* is different, as it only sends out data, but this node will inject the value into the Arduino IoT Cloud variable.

In this section, we have discussed the nodes to work with the Arduino IoT Cloud, that are available to developers from the Arduino IoT Cloud module. Next, we will set up the API, cloud variables, and dashboard to proceed further.

Setting up an API, variable, and dashboard widget

After installing the Arduino IoT Cloud module, it's time to set up an API in the Arduino IoT Cloud. In the Arduino IoT Cloud's older interface, there were API options under the **Integrations** tab, but now, the Arduino team has moved the API option to the Arduino IoT Cloud, which is available at `https://cloud.arduino.cc/home/`.

Click on **API Keys**. After that, you will be taken to the API page; click on **CREATE API KEY**. A popup will appear; type the name for API and click on the **CONTINUE** button. The following wizard will take some seconds to generate the keys, and then a new popup will appear displaying them:

Figure 2.22 – The API keys

Copy the client ID and client secret by clicking on the copy icons; never try to copy the secret name by selecting it, as it is too long. Save both the client ID and client secret to secure the location, and after that, click on the checkbox beside **I saved my Client ID and Secret** to confirm that you have saved your keys. Finally, click on the **DONE** button, and you will see your API key in the panel, ready for use.

> Important note
>
> One API key has access to all the Things and their variables. So, it's good to use one API key to gain access to all Things instead of creating separate API keys for each one. On the other hand, take care of your keys, as losing them can be a big security risk.

After API key generation, we need to set up an extra variable that will receive the value from Node-RED, and a **Status** widget that will act according to the variable value.

For variable creation, go back to the IoT Cloud dashboard shown in *Figure 2.12*, select the desired Thing, create a new variable named LEDStatus, and choose the Boolean type that we previously created for the LED. Then, navigate back to the dashboard and select the dashboard that we developed for the previous exercise. Click on the **Add** button and search for the **Status** widget from the dropdown. Link the LEDStatus variable with the **Status** widget.

Here we have created the API keys in the Arduino IoT Cloud for Node-RED, as well as a new Thing with cloud variables and a dashboard. Next, we are going to configure the API keys in Node-RED for proper communication with the Arduino IoT Cloud.

Creating a first project with Node-RED

We have done all the mandatory stuff that is required in our journey so far. Return to the Node-RED dashboard shown in *Figure 2.19*, scroll down the left side, and move your node to the Arduino IoT Cloud.

Click on the first node, which is *IN*, and drag it to the flow area. Double-click on the node, and you will see the following popup for node configuration:

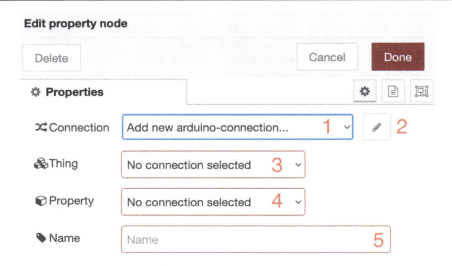

Figure 2.23 – Arduino IN node configuration

To edit the property node, follow these steps:

1. Select the Arduino connection from the dropdown (the dropdown is only there if you have multiple Arduino IoT Cloud connections).

2. If you don't have a connection, click on the pencil icon, and it will take you to a new popup where you will need to provide the name of the connection, along with the client ID and client secret that were generated in the previous section in *Figure 2.22*. When you save the connection, it will appear under the **Connection** dropdown.

3. After successfully creating and selecting a connection, a list of Things that are associated with that connection will appear. From the **Thing** dropdown, select the target Thing that you will use in your flow. If you do not see anything in the dropdown, it means there is an issue with the connection.

4. After the selection of Thing, the **Property** dropdown will list all the variables that are associated with the selected Thing. Select one variable that you want to sense; in our exercise, I chose the **LED** variable to get its status.

5. Assign a name to the node, click on the **Done** button, and then you are done with the configuration.

The following is a complete flow of nodes. It shows the entire workflow, from getting variable values to the final node, which sends a value to the cloud based on input:

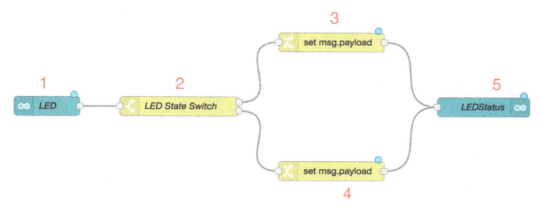

Figure 2.24 – A complete flow of the Node-RED project

The node workflow is broken down as follows:

1. The first node is the *IN* node. Select the variable that you want to read; I selected the **LED** variable.

2. Add the *switch* node (node **2**) to the flow; it can be found in the **Functions** tab on the left sidebar of the page. This node is responsible for taking the value from node **1** and selecting the specific node from **3** or **4**, according to the value. Link the Arduino *IN* node to the *switch* node. After linking, double-click on the *switch* node, where we need to specify the switch cases.

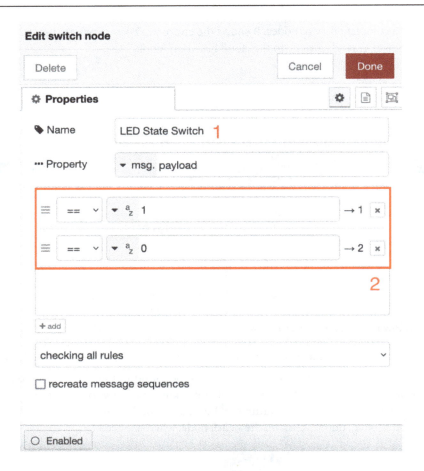

Figure 2.25 – Switch node options

To edit the *switch* node, follow these steps:

1. Firstly, assign a name to the node and then add the switch cases.

2. In our current exercise, we have two switch statements: the LED is either *true* or *false*, which means on or off. By default, there is only one option – click on the small **+add** button to insert a new case. Input the values 1 and 0, and we will then have two flows.

The *change* nodes (**3** and **4**) are responsible for sending content to the next node, which is **5**. Drag **3** and link it with the *switch* node, as shown in *Figure 2.24*. Node **3** represents the True/1/On value. Double-click on this node. Now, click on the drop-down icon, which is marked by a red box in the following figure, select the **Boolean** type, and then select **true**.

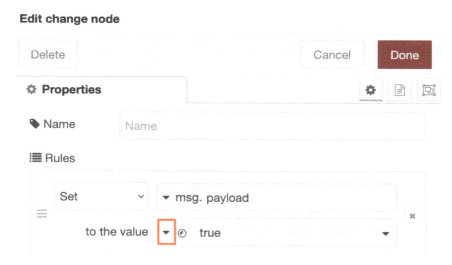

Figure 2.26 – Changing the node configuration

To edit the change node, follow these steps:

1. Again, insert the *change* node and link it with the *switch* node (node **4**) shown in *Figure 2.24*. This will represent the `False/0/Off` value. Double-click the *change* node, select the Boolean data type, and select the **false** value.

2. Everything is ready now. We just need to add a node that will send data to a specific Arduino IoT Cloud Thing variable. To send the data, we need the Arduino *OUT* node, which is the second node under the Arduino IoT Cloud tab shown in *Figure 2.21*. Drag this node, and connect both *change* nodes (**3** and **4**) to the Arduino *OUT* node (**5**) as shown in *Figure 2.24*. This node has the same configuration as the *IN* node. Select the connection, then the Thing, and finally, select the variable where you want to send the data. For the current exercise, we will select the `LEDStatus` variable.

Finally, we are done with all the node configurations and linkage. Click on the **Deploy** button shown in *Figure 2.19* and move back to the device dashboard in the Arduino IoT Cloud. Remember to keep MKR1010 on and connected to the internet. Now, click on the **switch** button to turn the LED on/off, and wait for a few seconds to get an updated value from Node-RED. In the background, Node-RED will send the value to the `LEDStatus` Arduino IoT Cloud variable according to the Node-RED **LED** variable, and the status widget will be changed accordingly.

In the second part of the chapter, we have explored how to connect non-compatible IoT development boards with the Arduino IoT Cloud using Node-RED. Next up is *Assignment 2*, which is specially designed for you to practice with different experiments.

Assignment 2

Continue the previous assignment, where you connected three LEDs to MKR Wi-Fi 1010 and the Arduino IoT Cloud setup:

1. Create three status variables in the Thing, according to the LED name such as Red, Yellow and Green, to the previously-set-up Thing.

2. Add three status widgets to the previously-set-up dashboard and attach newly created status variables to them.

3. Set up three different flows for each LED and deploy the flows.

4. Verify the status widgets by turning the LEDs on/off with the **Switch** button widget.

Summary

This chapter is the first chapter where we explored how to connect devices with the Arduino IoT Cloud using a basic LED on/off example. In the first part, we used an Arduino IoT Cloud-compatible development board, which was the MKR Wi-Fi 1010 board, where we learned how to create Things and cloud variables, how to associate devices, how to configure networks, and how to create sketches. At the end of that section, there was an assignment for you to practice on.

In the second part of this chapter, we explored how to connect non-compatible development boards, such as Arduino UNO, Arduino Mega, and Raspberry Pi, with the Arduino IoT Cloud, using Node-RED and the Arduino API interface. Here we have explored Node-RED, the Node-RED module for the Arduino IoT Cloud, and generating API keys in the cloud. This part of the chapter helped teach you how to use non-compatible existing technologies with the Arduino IoT Cloud.

Arduino has a lot of options in the Arduino IoT Cloud, such as Things, devices, dashboards, and a lot of widgets for dashboards and the Arduino Web Editor. So, in the next chapter, we will explore all those options in detail before moving on. *Chapter 3* is very important for you to better understand all of the Arduino IoT Cloud options.

3

Insights into the Arduino IoT Cloud Platform and Web Editor

Before getting started with any development or cloud platform, it's important to get a broad idea about the platform's functionality, including its functions, controls, widgets, and so on. These platforms are like a kitchen full of spices, vegetables, meat, and other ingredients. To cook a good meal in a new kitchen, you need to get an idea about what's in the kitchen – what types of tools, ingredients, spices, and other stuff are available. Product development is just like cooking a meal – if you have a good idea about what the platform provides, then you will be able to develop an awesome project. Another benefit of getting an overview of a platform is that it will save your time in the long run and give you confidence in your product design, because you already have a good understanding of the platform and can combine different things logically to develop something new according to your requirements.

So, in this chapter, we will first cover the main ingredients of the **Arduino IoT Cloud** in detail, namely **Things**, **devices**, **dashboards**, **integrations**, and **templates**. In the next part, we will take a look at all the **dashboard input/output widgets** and will see in detail what their purposes are, where to use them, and what type of variables they support. We will also have a brief comparison between some different control widgets that resemble each other.

In the last part, we will cover the complete **Arduino Web Editor** functionality, learning how to import new libraries, what the Web Editor storage and memory limits are, how to share your code with others, and how to debug code with the **cloud-based Serial Monitor**.

In this chapter, we will cover the following topics:

- Introducing the Arduino IoT Cloud interface
- Input controls
- Output controls

- The Arduino Web Editor
- An assignment

Technical requirements

For this chapter only, Arduino IoT Cloud access is required to explore the different functionalities and dashboard control widgets we'll cover in this chapter.

Introducing the Arduino IoT Cloud interface

The Arduino IoT Cloud's main interface is composed of five primary components – Things, devices, dashboards, integrations, and templates, as shown in *Figure 3.1*. Each component has its own properties, which will be discussed in detail in this section.

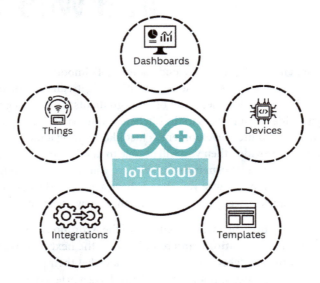

Figure 3.1 – Arduino IoT Cloud components

Things, devices, and dashboards are highly coupled with each other in every project. For example, for even a small project, we require a Thing and a device to get onboard the cloud platform. Is it enough to just configure a Thing and a device? No – a dashboard is also mandatory, from which the user can give input to the Thing and over which the system can show Thing data for user visualization.

However, integrations are a more optional component, with use cases varying from project to project and only being used by developers when they want to connect any non-compatible device to the Arduino IoT Cloud, build a custom interface to fetch data from the Arduino IoT Cloud, or integrate with third-party services such as **Zapier** and **AWS services**.

Templates are good for beginners as well as geeks, providing ready-made generic projects, including documentation, code, cloud templates, and a list of the hardware used in a given project. By using these templates, you can expose yourself to new things, which is good for learning purposes.

Here, we have discussed the Arduino IoT Cloud's key interface components. In the following section, we will discuss all the components in detail step by step. This chapter is very important with respect to all Arduino IoT Cloud features.

Devices and things

In *Chapter 2*, we explored a *hello world* example, where we used devices, Things, and other stuff to complete the example. In this section, we will discuss in more detail about devices and Things.

A device is a **Wi-Fi/LoRa-enabled microcontroller** that acts as a bridge between the Arduino IoT Cloud and sensors. The Arduino IoT Cloud has a very specific list of compatible development boards. Follow `https://support.arduino.cc/hc/en-us/articles/360016077320-What-devices-can-be-used-with-Arduino-IoT-Cloud` to see the complete list of compatible boards. Besides these official boards, the **ESP8266** and **ESP32** boards are also compatible with the IoT Cloud and are very low-cost and widely used development boards. There is good news for **LoRaWAN** geeks – any brand of LoRaWAN node is compatible with the Arduino IoT Cloud.

Now, it's time to look at the device page. Click on the **Device** menu in the dashboard. On this page, we have three main things. The first is the search bar, where we can search for devices by name as well as using the four device filters available – **Device Type**, **Serial Number**, **Device Status**, or **Thing**. The search filters offer awesome functionality for those scenarios where we have dozens of devices connected to the platform. The second notable thing on this page is the **ADD** button, with which we will attach new devices to the Arduino IoT Cloud. The third is the device list table, which shows a complete list of the devices connected to the Arduino IoT Cloud along with their statuses, either online or offline.

From the device list table, we can see the relationship between a given device and a Thing. The device is either attached to a Thing or is still available to join with another Thing. One device is only able to connect with one Thing at a time. Besides all of this, the device list shows other important properties that can be shown/hidden via the **Table Settings** icon, according to your requirements. When set to be shown, you can see a lot of new properties under the table settings, such as the ID, type, **Fully Qualified Board Name** (**FQBN**), serial number, connectivity module firmware, last activity, and device addition date.

You can also get all the device properties by clicking on the device. Of all the aforementioned device properties, **Last Activity** is one of the most important, as it helps to measure device downtime. You can delete devices one by one, or you can use the checkbox option to bulk-delete devices. There is another **Update** icon below the **Table Settings** icon, which is used to refresh the device table list.

> **Important note**
>
> A device is only attachable to one Thing in a one-to-one relationship. If you want to use a device associated with any other Thing, then it's mandatory to detach the device from the previously associated Thing before associating it with a new Thing.

The concept of a Thing is a bit like a dish containing pieces of steak, veggies, mashed potato, and so on. A Thing holds cloud variables, network connectivity, and the device, and is it responsible for managing code and metadata, such as the device time zone and the **meta tags** for the Thing.

Now, it's time to explore Things more closely in the Arduino IoT Cloud. The following diagram summarizes the whole Thing interface:

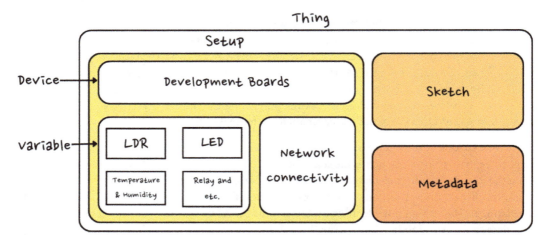

Figure 3.2 – The Thing interface

Let's start by exploring the Thing main page (shown in *Figure 2.4* in *Chapter 2*) by clicking on **Thing** menu, which is very similar to the menu for devices but with a few differences in the **Search** and **Thing** table list. We can see a **CREATE** button for Thing creation, instead of **ADD** as there is for devices. The search functionality for Things has totally different filters compared to those for devices, allowing us to filter Things by **Device**, **Device Type**, and **Time Zone**.

As the relationship between devices and Things is a one-to-one relationship, it will show you only one Thing, but **Device Type** is a good feature to show a whole bunch of Things with a particular device type. For example, let's say we have deployed two different projects, and each project contains 25 nodes. One project was developed by **MKR Wi-Fi 1010**, while the other was developed by **ESP32**. The **Device Type** filter provides you with the option to filter down the Things to just those using the ESP32 board type. The third filter is **Time Zone**, which is very beneficial if you have projects deployed in different regions across the world. To return the devices in specific regions, you can simply use this **Time Zone** filter.

By default, the Thing list table provides us with a list of Things with their **Device**, **Variables**, and **Last Modified** properties. We can rearrange the list by any property in ascending or descending order by clicking on the property column. The Thing **option** menu provides us options to delete the Thing. In the device property, it shows either the associated device or gives you the option to associate a device. The **Last modified** property is good for auditing purposes and indicates the last time your Thing was modified.

Besides all of these properties, we have some hidden properties, **Creation Date** and **Time Zone**, that can be enabled via the **Table Settings** icon, located on the right side of the page. If we add meta tags to the Thing, then this will also appear under **Table Settings**. Meta tags will be covered in more detail in the following few paragraphs.

It's time to explore the internal options for Things (*Figure 2.5* from *Chapter 2*). Click on the **CREATE** button or click on any Thing from the table. On the page that appears, you will see three different tabs, **Setup**, **Sketch**, and **Metadata**, along with the Thing name in bold font. You can also modify the Thing name by clicking on it.

The **Setup** tab is used for cloud variable creation and associating devices with Things (if not already linked). The **Change/Detach Device** option is available for devices associated with the Thing. Finally, there is the option to configure the Wi-Fi network settings for the development board.

The second tab is **Sketch**, which provides a mini version of the Arduino Web Editor, from where we can write/modify code as well as verify and upload it to the associated device. I like the **Sketch** option for Things, as it helps us to maintain the code for each device within a separate Thing container, with no need for local backups or code management. The mini cloud editor also provides the option to open the full editor. Beside that is the search icon, which opens the web-based Serial Monitor to verify whether your device is working.

The third tab is for Thing metadata. Normally, people don't concern themselves with these settings, but they are used to classify and provide ease of management when you have dozens of Things. Here, we can add tags to classify our Things. **Tags** also appear in the Thing table list, as well as in the search bar as a filter option. So, let's see how tags work. A tag consists of two parts – one is the key and the other is a value. The key is used in search filters. For example, if you have dozens of devices for different organizations and each organization contains multiple devices, then how you can filter the specific organization devices? The answer is by tag; you create a tag, where the key will be the organization name and the value will be the type of device. When you type the organization name in the search bar, you will see all the devices that are associated with these meta tags. The next option is the time zone, which is the perfect option to get Thing data according to the time zone of its native region. By default, it shows the time zone according to your location, but you can manually override the time zone. Resetting it will show some details regarding the Thing, such as **Thing ID**, **Last Modified**, **Last Sync**, and **Created At**.

At this point, the following question arises: *What is the difference between Last Modified and Last Sync?*

I recommend that you have a think and find a solution to it before you proceed.

> **Important note**
>
> Let's imagine you have written the code for a Thing and it is associated with an MKR Wi-Fi 1010 device, but you have changed the association of the device to **Arduino Nano RP2040** or any other development board. In this scenario, you will get the prewritten code for the RP2040. You will get this code, as the code belongs to the Thing, not the device. However, it may require some minor modifications in code, as pins and libraries vary from development board to development board.

In this section, we discussed the device and Thing pages in detail, regarding search options, creations, and other options on the pages. Now, we will discuss *dashboards*, which will help us to create beautiful graphical user interfaces to control and display device data.

Dashboards

The Arduino IoT Cloud offers very versatile dashboards with lots of options, providing an awesome experience for users. **Dashboards** consist of different features, including widgets, which are categorized into input and output, responsive design options for mobile and web, and lots of other features. The following figure summarizes all the features of a dashboard, which will be discussed in detail step by step in the following sections:

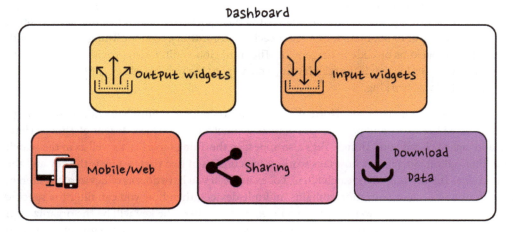

Figure 3.3 – An Arduino IoT Cloud dashboard

The dashboard interface is very similar to Thing and device interfaces, but it's simpler in terms of search and tables. Let's now examine input/output widgets in the context of the IoT Cloud but not in terms of devices (although devices are relevant, as if we provide input to the IoT cloud, it will, in turn, provide input to the Thing, and if a device sends output data to the IoT cloud, it will be displayed on the dashboard).

Arduino IoT dashboards provide a wide variety of widget controls for input/output. We will examine all of the widgets in detail later, while here, we will discuss some other major features, such as *responsive design* and *sharing and downloading data*.

Dashboards provide a responsive grid design system for both mobile/web. To enter into editing mode, firstly click on the **Edit** icon on the **Dashboard** page (*Figure 2.15* in *Chapter 2*) and then on the **Navigation** icon, which is also known as *Arrange Widgets*. You can modify the design by making widgets larger or smaller, or by dragging them to any location on the canvas. You should see the **Lock** icon on every widget control as well, which lets you fix their locations. After placing the widget at the appropriate location, click on that lock to fix the position. In the top menu near the **Add** button, there is an icon for mobile/desktop mode to align the widgets.

There will come a time when you need to share these dashboards with your stakeholders so that they can monitor their systems easily. The Arduino IoT Cloud provides a secure way to share your dashboard with others. Just click on the **Sharing** icon – from there, we can share our dashboard with other users (although note that it's mandatory that all users' emails need to be registered with the Arduino IoT Cloud to take part in sharing).

Getting sensor data from the cloud is an essential element of IoT cloud platforms, as researchers use data in a variety of applications, including training **Machine Learning/Artificial Intelligence** (**ML/AI**) models or visualizing data on different platforms, such as **Google Looker** and **Tableau**. Arduino provides a vast functionality wizard to download all data or the specific data of a given cloud variable. Click on the **Download** icon, and you will get a lot of options. From there, you can select the variables (either single, multiple, or all, according to your requirements) and provide the date range. Arduino will then process the data according to your query and share it with you in the CSV format at your registered email.

Here, we have talked about different features of dashboards, such as the alignment of widgets, responsive design for mobile and web dashboards, and how to download sensor data. In the following section, we will cover integrations and templates.

Integrations and templates

Templates page contains example projects for learning and practice purpose and are great for beginners to try different projects, from the beginner's level all the way up to advanced level. Each project is properly documented with a project description, hardware list, code, and imported cloud template. On the **Templates** page, you will initially see a very small list of projects, but more can be found at `https://projecthub.arduino.cc/`, where makers/professionals around the globe upload the projects they've created with full documentation.

Integrations provide interoperability to link the Arduino IoT Cloud with other third-party services, as well as custom-developed applications. Arduino provides three ways to interact with different platforms, **Application Programming Interface** (**APIs**), **Webhooks**, and **Software Development Kits** (**SDKs**), as shown in the following figure:

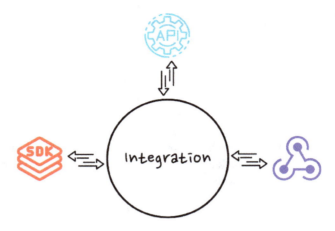

Figure 3.4 – Arduino IoT cloud integrations

First, let's talk about APIs, as this technique is widely used by developers to interact with different platforms. In the Arduino IoT Cloud, APIs are used for two purposes – the first purpose is to set up a non-compatible device with the IoT Cloud, including **Raspberry Pi** and **Beagle Bone**, while the second purpose is to fetch data from the IoT Cloud using different predefined APIs. These APIs will be discussed in detail in *Chapter 8*.

Webhooks are used as triggers when a specified event happens in a Thing, such as an update in the cloud variables. To set up a Webhook, you need to visit the specific Thing's page, click on **Set Webhook** at the bottom, and assign a URL where you want to send the Thing data. Makers and developers mostly use **IFTTT** or Zapier to receive data and route it to tons of other applications/platforms. Webhooks send the data in the JSON format with lots of details, which will be discussed further in *Chapter 12*.

It's very important to understand the concepts behind APIs and Webhooks. Third-party applications use an API's interface to request data from the cloud, but with Webhooks, the Arduino IoT Cloud sends the data to a specific platform when any predetermined event happens within the Thing. So, if you develop an alert system, then Webhooks are the preferred choice, as they send data instantly when any change is detected within the Thing. Conversely, if you develop an application where you only need data periodically, then APIs are the best solution. To put it simply, Webhooks work like **push requests** and APIs work like **pull requests**.

The Arduino IoT Cloud team has also released official SDKs for different programming languages, such as **JavaScript** (**Node.js**), **Python**, and **GoLang**. SDKs make development easy for developers by allowing them to use predefined functions to get data from the cloud, instead of playing with raw APIs. For authentication purposes, SDKs use API keys for access and authentication. The Node.js SDK will be discussed in detail in *Chapter 8*.

In this section, we discussed APIs, SDKs, and Webhooks. Now, we will explore a dashboard's widget controls. We have divided Arduino Dashboard widget controls into two categories, *input* and *output*. In the following section, we will first explore the complete range of input controls, and in the subsequent section, we will explore the complete range of output controls.

Exploring input controls

Input controls are very important in IoT product development, where users control the flow of operations according to metrics. The latest trends and technologies in the **User Interface/User Experience** (**UI/UX**) field bring lots of different input controls that vary in size, shape, and design, providing a better end user experience.

The Arduino IoT Cloud team has taken account of the latest trends in the market and provided nine different, stunning input widgets, each of which provides users the ability to give input to Things in various ways. Each widget is linked to a single cloud variable; you can link multiple widgets to a single cloud variable, but the data type must be the one specified by the widget control. In the following subsections, I have categorized the input widgets into various groups, based on their resemblance with each other.

Switch, push button, slider, and stepper

Let's start with the very basic input control widgets – **switch**, **push button**, **slider**, and **stepper**. These widgets allow users to control their Things in an effective and efficient manner. All the widgets are shown in *Figure 3.5*:

Figure 3.5 – Switch, Push Button, Slider, and Stepper

Switch and **Push Button** work on the same binary principle (`on/off`) and consume the `Boolean` type cloud variable. The only difference between these two controls is the UI/UX design. When the user clicks the switch control, it slides on/off and stays in the same state until clicked again. **Push Button** also retains its state but is *pressed* in or out to change between on/off states.

> **Important note**
>
> To understand the proper working of **Switch** and **Push Button**, just place both controls on a dashboard and link them to the same cloud variable. Afterward, click on **Push Button** and release it, and then try clicking on the switch.

The **Slider** and **Stepper** controls both work in the same manner but are totally different in UI/UX design. The slider uses a simple slide to change values, while the stepper has an input control where a user can directly insert a specific number, as well as increment and decrement buttons. The **Slider** orientation is horizontal by default but can be changed to a vertical orientation. Both controls can be linked with the `integer` or `float`-type cloud variables. These controls are useful to control stepper motor angles, the speed of motors, and light intensity, or even to set the threshold for an alert system for temperature and humidity monitoring. For example, say you want to set an alarm threshold for temperature and humidity values, and also the weather. These controls will help you to get values from the stakeholder via the dashboard and process them in the Thing, without needing to modify the Thing code.

Here, we explored four different input widget controls, **Switch**, **Push Button**, **Slider**, and **Stepper**, and their uses in detail. Now, we are going to cover input widget controls related to light control.

Color, dimmed light, and colored light

Arduino has introduced three new widgets specific to light color and intensity control, which developers can use when building real-world products for smart homes. *Figure 3.6* shows these three widgets, which help you to control your smart bulb/light solutions:

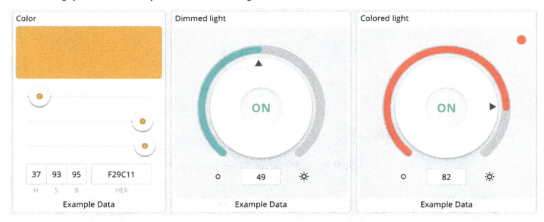

Figure 3.6 – Color and light widgets

Here, we have seen all the widget controls regarding light/bulb control; now, we will discuss all the widgets, step by step, in the upcoming subsections. First, we will start with the **Color** widget control.

Color

Our first widget here is the **Color** widget. This widget works with the `Color` type cloud variable, for which we fetch the **Red Green Blue** (**RGB**) color values with Arduino code for the final device input. The color widget provides an RGB slider to adjust the color, or the desired value can be directly entered in the RGB or hex formats. This widget is very useful to control RGB LED colors, RGB lamps, and the **WS18B20** module.

The following code snippet for the Arduino IDE or the Web Editor shows how to convert the color type cloud variable into RGB variables:

```
int red, green, blue;
RGBVariable.getValue().getRGB(red, green, blue);
```

`RGBVariable` is a cloud variable of the `Color` type. We have to use the RGB format to input our color codes into RGB LEDs, and for that reason, we will declare three integer type variables, `red`, `green`, and `blue`, and use `RGBVariable.getValue().getRGB(red, green, blue);` to convert our single cloud variable value into the RGB format.

Dimmed light

The **Dimmed light** widget, as shown in *Figure 3.6*, provides us the ability to turn a light on/off as well as control the intensity of the light. This widget is useful if you have a single-color bulb/light strip and want to control its luminous intensity. It consumes the `Dimmed Light` cloud variable, which contains the switch status and brightness values.

Before moving to the code, we first need to understand what values are required by the development board. Two values are required here – the on/off status and the light brightness level. The following code shows how we get the brightness level and on/off status from the `Dimmed Light` cloud variable:

```
//retrieve and map brightness value from cloud variable
  int brightness = map(dimmedLightVariable.getBrightness(), 0, 100, 0,
255);

  //then check if switch is on/off
  if (dimmedLightVariable.getSwitch()) {
    analogWrite(5, brightness); //write brightness value to pin 5
  }
  else{
    analogWrite(5, LOW); //turn off lamp
  }
```

To get the brightness, we need to transform the `dimmedLightVariable` brightness property value into the 0-255 range, using the `map` function. Then, we need to get the on/off status by calling the `getSwitch` property of that cloud variable. If it's on, then we will use the `analogWrite` function on *Pin #5* to adjust the brightness; if the switch is off, the LED/lamp will be turned off.

Colored light

Finally, it's time to play with colorful strips with the **Colored light** widget, as shown in *Figure 3.6*. This widget provides three functionalities, two of which resemble the **Dimmed light** widget (an on/off switch and a luminous intensity control), while the third is a color selection option via a color palette. This widget works with the `Colored Light` cloud variable type.

The following code for the Arduino IDE/Web Editor fetches values from the `Colored Light` variable type. Before diving into the code, note that we need to get three values from that cloud variable – the RGB color, brightness level, and on/off status:

```
//retrieve RGB color values from cloud variable
int red, green, blue;
ColoredLightVariable.getValue().getRGB(red, green, blue);

//retrieve and map brightness value from cloud variable
int brightness = map(ColoredLightVariable.getBrightness(), 0, 100, 0,
255);

//then check if switch is on/off
bool switch= ColoredLightVariable.getSwitch();
```

Firstly, we fetch the RGB color value in the `int` format by using the `ColoredLightVariable.getValue().getRGB` method. Second, we fetch the brightness using the `ColoredLightVariable.getBrightness()` method and transform the values with the `map` method. Finally, we fetch the on/off status with the `ColoredLightVariable.getSwitch()` method. All the values are stored in three different variables that could be used to control LED/lamp or RGB strip functionality.

Here, we discussed in detail smart light/bulb controls, which contain **Color**, **Dimmed light**, and **Colored light** widget controls, including their code to fetch and set the values from them. Now, we will discuss another important input control, time picker, which is used for configuration.

Time picker (configuration)

The **time picker** widget is a very important configuration widget control used to set/get the time on a device without modifying the code on the device. With this feature, it's easy to maintain the device time without a **Real-Time Clock (RTC)** module. Whenever a Thing is turned on, it will automatically sync the device time with the time cloud variable.

The following screenshot shows the **Time Picker** widget with the date and time, and you have the option to set the date, the time, or both. The widget also gives you the ability to change the date and time format according to your region.

Figure 3.7 – The Time Picker widget

The time picker widget is linked to the Time type cloud variable and stores all date and time data in the seconds format. The following code takes the local time from Arduino Cloud and stores it in a variable:

```
CloudTimeVariable = ArduinoCloud.getLocalTime();
```

After fetching the local time, you can use CloudTimeVariable to sync your Thing operations. Use the preceding code in the setup method.

In this section, we discussed the time picker widget, including how to set the time for this widget control by using the Time cloud variable type. Now, we will discuss another configuration widget control, the Scheduler Widget control, which helps you set the time to automate your operations on IoT devices.

Scheduler (configuration)

Scheduler is another important utility in Arduino IoT Cloud to automate a process. With this widget, we can automate lots of operations without human intervention, just like a **cron job** that executes processes/methods at a specific time.

So, where we can use this Scheduler feature in our IoT solutions? There are many use cases, including outdoor light automation, watering systems in agriculture, and animal feeders for poultry farms.

The following screenshot of the **Scheduler** widget shows the many options to schedule our processes/methods:

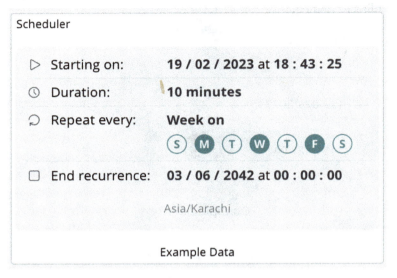

Figure 3.8 – The Scheduler Widget

The Scheduler Widget uses the `Schedule` cloud variable type. When configuring it, we specify at what time and on which day we want the process to start and end.

The following code snippet is very simple, using a `true`/`false` interface to start/stop operations, respectively, instead of going into complex stuff:

```
if (scheduleVariable.isActive()) {
    digitalWrite(LED, HIGH); // whenever the job is "active", turn on
the LED
}
else{
    digitalWrite(LED, LOW); // whenever the job is "not active", turn
off the LED
}
```

We can get the active/not active status of every `Schedule` cloud variable by accessing its `isActive()` method. Use the aforementioned code in a device loop – if the `Schedule` cloud variable is active, then execute the given processes/methods; otherwise, stop them. Why do we need to execute the preceding code snippet in a loop? Because the `loop()` method is the main method in Arduino, which always executes.

In this section, we discussed Scheduler in detail, what type of cloud variable is used by this widget, and how to access the Scheduler status to perform a specific job. This is the last control in input widgets. Now, we will look at the output control widgets. In the following section, all the output controls will be discussed in detail to give you a better understanding of how to implement these controls in your professional projects.

Delving into output controls

In the previous sections, we discussed input widget controls. Arduino IoT Cloud dashboards also feature stunning output controls. There are nine widgets here (although two are **non-device widgets** – **messenger** and **sticky note**).

Value, status, gauge, percentage, and LED

Let's start with the basic output widgets commonly used by developers in almost every solution. These output widgets are used to display a single value either in numerical or graphical format. *Figure 3.9* shows all the main and basic output control widgets:

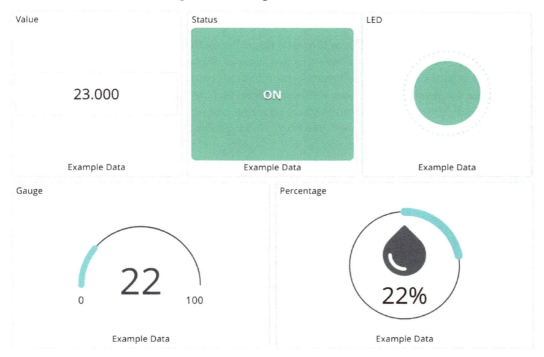

Figure 3.9 – The Value, Status, LED, Gauge, and Percentage widgets

In this section, we will discuss in detail five different output widget controls in separate sections. First, we will start with the value widget control.

Value

The **value** widget is a very basic and important widget that is widely used in projects to display **sensor/actuator** values, such as temperature or humidity, or to write some numeric values to sensors/actuators. This widget can be linked with the `integer` type variables, but I also tested it with the `time` variable, and it worked fine, as the `time` variable stores all information in seconds. You can also use the value widget control to set thresholds for sensors, automating the process flow.

The following simple code snippet takes the value from analog pin #0 and stores it in `valueCloudVariable`:

```
valueCloudVariable = analogRead(A0);
```

Here, we discussed the value widget control, which is used for both input and output purposes. Now, we will explore the status and LED control widgets.

Status and LED

Our next widgets are **status** and **LED**, as shown in *Figure 3.9*. Both widgets work very similarly but are different in UI/UX. These widgets have only two states to display either `true` or `false`. These widgets only display the state; they don't provide any option to control them, and they both work with the `bool` type cloud variable. Use cases for these widgets include indicating the Thing status (on/off) – for example, a water pump's status in smart agriculture, or whether a door is open or closed in a smart home. Just assign `true`/`false` to the `bool` cloud variable type, which is linked to the status widget after performing a specific task.

The following example code demonstrates how we can change the value of `statusCloudVariable` to change the status/LED widgets' appearance:

```
Void loop() {
digitalWrite(1,HIGH);
statusCloudVariable=true; //Assign true to Status Widget
delay(5000);
digitalWrite(1,LOW);
statusCloudVariable=false;//Assign false to Status Widget
delay(500);
}
```

The preceding code shows how, after performing the `digitalWrite` operation, we change the value of `statusCloudVariable` according to the current condition to update the status widget.

Gauge and percentage

Finally, we have the **gauge** and **percentage** widgets shown in *Figure 3.9*, which can be used to make your dashboard spicy and provide a stunning information display experience to your users. Both of these widgets can be linked to the `integer` or `float` cloud variable types. Comparing the gauge and percentage widgets, we can see a clear difference in UI/UX design – gauge uses a half-circle to display a sensor reading, while the percentage widget uses a full circle featuring icons, for which you can specify the color if a value goes below or above a given threshold. However, the working of both widgets is essentially the same. Gauge can be used to display gas-related readings, such as air quality, carbon dioxide levels, and temperature, while the percentage widget is best for displaying humidity, battery level, **Light-Dependent Resistor (LDR)** values, and so on.

Here, I haven't provided the sample code for the gauge and percentage widgets, as it's very similar to the preceding example – just assign the values of the sensors to the gauge- and percentage-linked cloud variables.

> **Important note**
>
> As a little exercise, create an integer type variable named `MultiDimmVariable`, and drop a gauge, percentage, and slider widget on the dashboard. Link these three widgets with the same `MultiDimmVariable` cloud variable you created. Now, you can have a bit of fun; just change the slider position and see how the gauge and percentage widgets react.

In this section, we discussed all the major output controls, which include value, status, gauge, percentage, and LED, step by step, and their usage and code. Now, we will look at maps and charts widgets, which are the most important widgets to display for location and time-series data.

Maps and charts

Our next two widgets are very interesting – one is used to display maps with specific coordinates, and the other is used to display the `integer/float` type sensor readings in graph format. *Figure 3.10* shows the **Map** and **Chart** widget controls. The map widget is used to display the location of a device using coordinates, and the chart widget is used to display the values in a time-series manner.

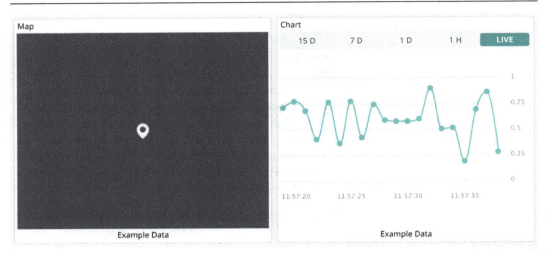

Figure 3.10 – The Map and Chart widgets

First, we will start with the map widget, where we will discuss how we can display the location, and then, we will explore the chart widget to display the historical data of a sensor.

Map

There are many use cases where we need to display the current location of an object on a map, which is much easier to understand visually than simple coordinate values. The Arduino IoT Cloud provides us with a **map** widget to display the current location of an object. The map widget works with the location cloud variable type, which consists of latitude and longitude values. The object could be anything from a child or animal to a delivery bike, a courier truck, or even food/vegetable parcels.

The following code demonstrates how you can assign the latitude and longitude values to the location cloud variable:

```
location=Location(32.045948421308715, 72.72505696868048);
```

The preceding code is used to assign a location whenever your device receives data from a **GPS module**. This map widget is only capable of showing one location at a time. If you have multiple objects for which you want to display tracking, then each object will need its own map widget.

Chart

So, we can use the gauge or percentage widgets to display the current value of a sensor, but what if we want to display the current value as well as historical data? For this, **chart** is your best option, which is used to display current readings alongside historical readings for better visualization and comparison.

The **Chart** widget shown in *Figure 3.10* uses the `integer` or `float` cloud variable types, which as discussed previously are appropriate to monitor temperature, humidity, air quality, and so on. Just link any cloud variable with the chart widget for data visualization. Other use cases include light levels, energy consumption, and levels of different gases in industry.

> **Important note**
>
> For quick testing, just drop the slider and chart widgets on a dashboard and link both of them with the same `integer` cloud variable type. After that, just change the value of the slider, and you can observe how charts work.

Here, we discussed both the map and chart widget controls in detail. Now, we will explore messenger and sticky note controls.

Messenger and sticky notes

Our last two widgets are **messenger** and **sticky notes**. Both widgets are non-essential elements but do help you to make your dashboard interactive. *Figure 3.11* shows both the widget controls:

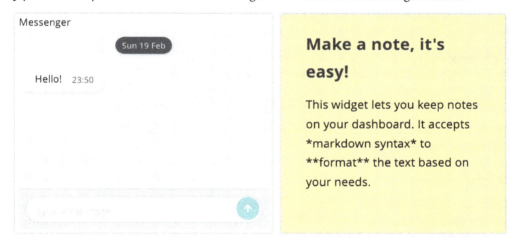

Figure 3.11 – The Messenger and sticky note widgets

In the figure, the first widget is **Messenger**, and the second widget is sticky notes. Both widgets will be discussed in the following sections.

Messenger

The **messenger** widget works like any traditional messenger app. But the question arises, why would we need this widget on a dashboard? In my opinion, it's simply not essential on any dashboard currently, but in the future, it could become an awesome widget and inspire people to develop products where you communicate textually with Things, just as we already have the **Amazon Echo Dot** and **Google Assistant** devices that users interact with verbally, where you ask questions to the device and it responds audibly.

In the future, you may see many messenger applications linked to your Things, where you ask questions such as, *where is my child?*, and the Thing connected to your child will respond to you with their exact location. Alternatively, you could ask a question about the temperature/humidity conditions in your room, and the Thing would respond with the required answer.

You could also use the messenger widget to create some sort of small search engine for your Thing that understands some keywords and responds to users' queries. Remember, the early bird catches the worm.

The messenger widget works with the `string` cloud variable type. The following simple code snippet demonstrates how you can write to the messenger widget from the device end:

```
stringMessengerVariable = "Hello Sir, My name is Arduino MKR1010 and I
will be your host. How may I help you Sir?";
```

When you assign a new value to the string variable, messenger will append the new content to the widget. The following code is used to clear the whole widget at the device end:

```
stringMessengerVariable = PropertyActions::CLEAR;
```

You can also integrate the messenger widget with third-party tools such as **Slack** and **Discord**, via either an API or Zapier integration.

Sticky notes

The sticky note widget works just like simple Windows OS Sticky Notes. It helps you to write down your project progress, or you can write anything on a sticky note to maintain your dashboards. It helps you in a situation where you have dozens of dashboards and you want to add some comments about specific dashboards.

For the latest updates and details about dashboard widget controls, please visit `https://docs.arduino.cc/arduino-cloud/getting-started/dashboard-widgets`.

In this section, we discussed both the messenger and sticky note widgets. Sticky notes make it easy to maintain projects and write down comments about project progress or maintenance, while messenger has a broader use. We also discussed how sensor data is related to AI. We have now completed all of our input and output widget controls, Now, we will dive deep into the Arduino Web Editor, where we will explore all the options step by step.

Understanding the Arduino Web Editor

Arduino has also launched a web-based editor that is independent of Arduino IoT Cloud and the desktop IDE. It works with any board compatible with the Arduino IDE without needing to install boards via the board manager. The Web Editor is compatible with a majority of web browsers, including Chrome, Firefox, Microsoft Edge, and Safari. To work with the Web Editor, your machine should have the **Arduino Create Agent**, which acts as a bridge between the device and the Web Editor. All code is stored on the cloud, so there is no risk of losing code or any need to make backups.

To visit the Arduino Web Editor, go to `https://create.arduino.cc/editor`, where you will see something like the following:

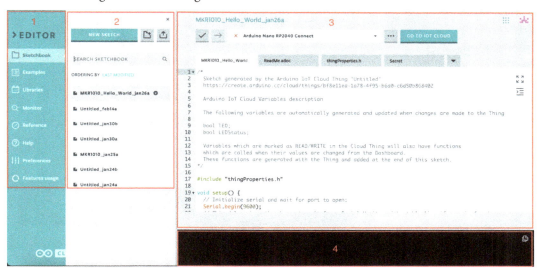

Figure 3.12 – The Arduino Web Editor

The numbers in the preceding screenshot correspond to the following elements of the Web Editor:

1. This is the main menu of the Web Editor, where you will find all the navigation links, such as **Sketchbook**, **Examples**, **Libraries**, and **Monitor**.

2. This tab is a sub-menu, displaying options/content according to the current main menu selection. In the screenshot, this tab shows content related to the sketchbook.

3. This area is the coding/sketch area, where you can find all the options to work with code, such as code verification/uploads, board selection, and the code editor.

4. This tab is the output terminal, which provides you with information regarding code upload status, any errors found in your code, and so on.

Here, we discussed the Arduino Web Editor interface. Now, we will discuss **Sketchbook**, **Examples**, **Libraries**, **Monitor**, **References**, and **Help**, as well as the **Preferences** and **Features** menus in detail. We will discuss all the options in depth so you will get a broader overview of the Arduino Web Editor, allowing you to utilize its features fully during your development.

Sketchbook

This menu option is responsible for sketch organization, creation, code download and upload, and so on.

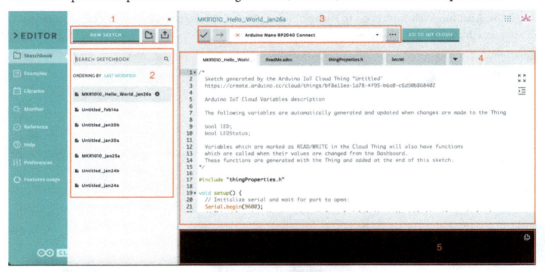

Figure 3.13 – The Arduino Web Editor sketchbook

The numbers in the preceding screenshot correspond to the following elements of the sketchbook screen:

1. The **NEW SKETCH** button is used to initialize a new set of files for a new project. To the right of this button are two icons – the first is used to create a folder for project organization, and the second is used to import any existing Arduino IDE code/libraries into the Web Editor if required.

2. Here is where you will find all of your sketches/folders, and you can also search your sketchbooks with the help of the search bar.

3. The tick icon is used to verify the code, while the arrow icon is used to upload the code to the development board. From the dropdown to the right of these icons, you can select the development board and port. Finally, the ellipses button contains a range of options regarding sketches, such as **Save**, **Save as**, **Rename Sketch**, and **Download Sketch**.

4. This area is a playground for developers to write code for their devices. Here, you will find two icons to the right of the screen, the first of which is used to make the code editor full-screen, while the second is used for code indentation.

5. This is the output terminal where you can get all the information about code compilation progress and any errors found in your code.

Examples

One of the top features of Arduino IDE is **Examples**, which is a great resource for beginners, who can benefit from examples provided by library and sensor developers. This is presented as a separate menu in the Arduino Web Editor. *Figure 3.14* shows the **Example** menu with two different tabs. The first tab shows the **BUILT IN** examples, while the second tab shows the **FROM LIBRARIES** examples.

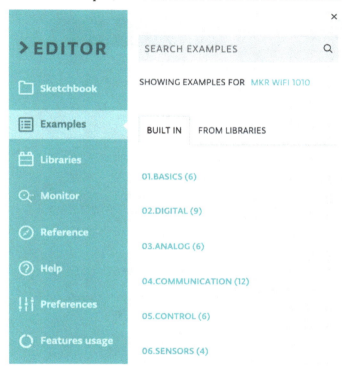

Figure 3.14 – The Arduino Web Editor examples

When you click on the **Examples** menu, the next tab will be displayed, showing options for examples either built-in or from libraries. All the examples are organized in different categories, just as in the Arduino IDE. You can also use the search bar to find examples from a specific library. By default, the Arduino Web Editor only displays development board-specific examples and libraries. The preceding screenshot only shows examples compatible with MKR Wi-Fi 1010, but you can click on the **MKR WIFI 1010** link and shift to **ALL Boards**, and vice versa.

Libraries and the Library Manager

There are thousands of libraries for the Arduino platform, developed by developers and sensor and module manufacturers around the world. Libraries provide vast integration possibilities for sensors/modules in the Arduino IDE as well as, by default, example code. Libraries are the main source of learning for beginners and professional developers. *Figure 3.15* shows the **Libraries** menu with different options, such as **LIBRARY MANAGER**, which helps us to install the libraries, and the **DEFAULT**, **FAVORITES**, and **CUSTOM** tabs are also shown, which will be discussed in detail step by step:

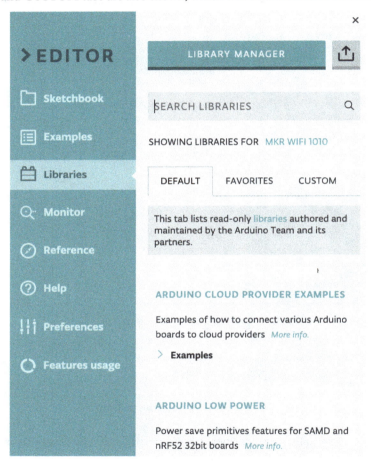

Figure 3.15 – The Arduino Web Editor libraries

In the Arduino Web Editor, we have access to a vast collection of pre-installed libraries, and we can mark libraries as favorites and include them in our code. When we open the **Libraries** menu option, we will see the aforementioned three main tabs – **DEFAULT**, **FAVORITES**, and **CUSTOM**. The **DEFAULT** tab displays all the libraries developed by the Arduino team and verified partners. The

FAVORITES tab contains the libraries that you have favorited in the Library Manager. If you can't find a library specific to your work, then you can import your own library into the Arduino Web Editor by clicking on the **CUSTOM** tab.

The Library Manager contains a complete list of libraries from all around the world. To add a library to your project that you can't find in the **DEFAULT** tab, just click on **LIBRARY MANAGER**, and a new popup will appear, where you can search for a library by its name or company name. When found, mark it as a favorite by clicking on the star icon.

Monitor AKA the Serial Monitor

The **Serial Monitor** plays a vital role in the verification of **process execution**, **sensor testing**, and **code debugging**. It works similarly to a console in a web browser, where developers print messages for process verification according to their requirements. In the Arduino Web Editor, it has been renamed **Monitor**.

Figure 3.16 – The Arduino Web Editor | Monitor

Clicking on the **Monitor** link will only activate the Monitor when there is a board connected to the system. Make sure your Arduino Create Agent is running in the background as well. At the top of the **Monitor** screen, you will see the name of the development board and the port name/number to which it's connected.

Next, set the **baud rate** on which a device is configured during a sketch, using the `Serial.begin()` method. Developers mostly use 9,600 baud rates for serial communication. The large text area in the bottom half of the Monitor shows all communication between the device and the developer. By default, **AUTOSCROLL** is enabled in this window, so new messages will automatically be shown.

Reference, help, and preferences

The **Reference** option provides helpful material related to **FUNCTIONS**, **VARIABLES**, and **STRUCTURES** across three different tabs. You can also search for a specific Thing via the search bar. For example, say we wanted to find information about the `Delay` function; just find and click on the `Delay()` method, and it will show you a description, with example syntax and code for better understanding.

The **Help** menu provides lots of new information about product updates and much more. Information is divided into three tabs, **INFO**, **TUTORIALS**, and **GLOSSARY**. The **INFO** tab provides all the latest updates regarding versions, compatibility, and bug fixes. The **TUTORIALS** tab contains links to small projects that help beginners to learn new stuff. **GLOSSARY** is just like a glossary in a book, but here, you will get a specific list related to Arduino, electronics, sensors, and so on.

Finally, we arrive at the **Preferences** menu, from where we can modify the Web Editor's theme and font size, show/hide the output panel, and set code to auto-save or be manually saved.

Arduino IoT Web Editor features

In the Arduino IDE, we don't have any restrictions regarding sketch creation, compilation, or storage, but in the Arduino Web Editor, we do encounter some restrictions. This is because, with Arduino IDE on desktop machines, we use our own resources, but everything involved with the Web Editor is hosted on the cloud. On the cloud, everything has to be paid for, including storage, processor, and memory usage for code verification and compilation.

For that reason, the Arduino Web Editor has some restrictions and limitations on storage size, sketches, and compilations. Arduino has different resource allowances for different types of subscribers, which should be compared with other plans before purchase. Visit `https://cloud.arduino.cc/plans` for complete details and a comparison of the plans.

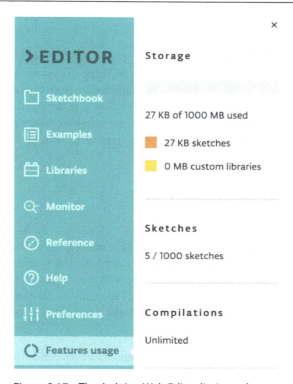

Figure 3.17 – The Arduino Web Editor limits and usage

The preceding screenshot displays stats regarding the Web Editor features. Firstly, we can see how much storage space has been used from the total made available as part of the subscription plan. I have 1,000 MB of storage in total with my Maker Pro plan. The screenshot also shows how many sketches can be created, and finally, how many compilations are allowed. In my case, I have unlimited, but the Free plan only had 100 MB of space allowed for sketch storage and limits of 25 compilations per day.

> **Important note**
>
> The Arduino Web Editor features are subject to change over time, so please visit the official page for up-to-date information: `https://cloud.arduino.cc/plans`.

Here, we successfully discussed the different options in the new Arduino Web Editor in depth, which will help you to use the Editor effectively and efficiently in your development projects, helping you to boost your productivity. The following section, *Assignments*, cover different questions for you, which will help to test out what you have learned in this chapter and through internet searches, helping you to utilize your new skills effectively.

Assignments

This chapter is longer in length than the previous ones, as we want to give you an in-depth overview of Arduino IoT Cloud and its main pillars, which include Things, devices, dashboards, integrations and templates, progressing to further chapters. In this chapter, we have discussed dashboards, input and output widget controls, as well as the Arduino Web Editor in detail. To consolidate what you have learned in this chapter, we have created three different assignments for you. These assignments will help you to understand the core concepts necessary to proceed with the book, as well as in your professional projects.

Make sure to attempt all the assignments given ahead.

Assignment 1

ASNA Group is a leading ISO-certified salt supplier organization in Pakistan. The organization processes salt according to international standards, but they are facing issues in warehouse monitoring, where they want to maintain the temperature/humidity in line with the standards, to avoid issues with the finished product. Right now, they have five warehouses to monitor. They want multiple views for data monitoring and analysis. You need to keep the following questions in mind while developing a solution for ASNA Group:

1. Firstly, identify what type of industrial-grade sensors/development boards are required for this monitoring scenario.
2. Is there any calibration required for the sensors? If so, how will you calibrate the sensors? If not, provide a reason why it's not mandatory.
3. What type of widgets are required to visualize the information on a dashboard?
4. How you could visualize readings from five warehouses on one dashboard?
5. What type of widgets will be used on the dashboard to allow users to analyze readings covering a long period of time?
6. By what means will you give the company access to the dashboard?

Assignment 2

Imzlab Technologies Private Limited is a leading smart agriculture solution provider. The company has deployed custom-designed sensors in the field, using ESP32 and the Arduino IoT Cloud, to measure soil moisture, soil temperature, and outdoor temperature/humidity. On the dashboard, they have different widgets for data visualization. They now have a new requirement from a customer to integrate a water pump control and display its status history (on/off). The customer also requires that on Monday and Thursday, the water pump will run from 5:00 p.m. to 7:00 p.m., and on Sunday, from 4:00 a.m. to 6:00 a.m., in the GMT+5 time zone. On other days, the pump status will be controlled manually. You need to keep the following questions in mind while developing a solution for Imzlab Technologies Private Limited:

1. What type of control widgets are required to display and control the water pump status?

2. How can you provide a solution for automatic pump control on specific days and at specific times?

3. Is it possible to visualize the water pump on/off status history using charts? If so, how? If it's not possible, provide an alternative solution to meet the customer's requirements.

Assignment 3

A group of researchers at Imzlab Technologies Private Limited is working on a monitoring system to monitor carbon dioxide levels. They are using MKR 1010 and the Arduino IoT Cloud, but they are trying to use a custom sensor developed by Tingstack LLC. In the Arduino Web Editor, there is no library for this sensor, but Tingstack LLC has developed an in-house library for the Arduino platform. The researchers also want to share their code with the Tingstack LLC team for review.

Identify the problems from the preceding paragraph, and write down their solutions.

Summary

This chapter was just like understanding the ingredients and kitchen tools we have before we start cooking. Firstly, we learned about how the Arduino IoT Cloud components work, including Things, devices, dashboards, integrations, and templates. Then, we studied all the input/output widget controls to get a proper idea of their potential usage, including some example code and the cloud variable types. In the following section, we examined what the Arduino Web Editor is and how its different features work, including examples, libraries, and the Serial Monitor. You should now have a good understanding of all the different ingredients of the Arduino IoT Cloud and the Web Editor and how to employ them appropriately.

This chapter was most important before starting the next chapters, as it gives you an in-depth overview of all the main pillars of the Arduino IoT Cloud and how they work in real time, which will help you to understand how the Arduino IoT Cloud works. Arduino dashboard widgets are also very important to us, as we will use different widgets in different projects throughout the book, so giving you an overview here has prepared you for upcoming chapters, helping you to understand what types of things are mandatory for professional projects and what type of controls make your project more robust and professional.

In the following chapter, we will start work on our first project, where we will build an air-quality monitoring system from scratch to deployment. You will learn why air-quality monitoring is necessary and what types of development boards/sensors are required. We will also use a **Printed Circuit Board (PCB)** for proper deployment, which will be explained in depth. After a section on the necessary hardware, we will set up Things, cloud variables, devices, and network configurations and coding for a device, as well as a dashboard for proper data visualization. So, gear up for the upcoming chapter, which will be fun for all of you.

Part 2: Getting Hands-On with Different Communication Technologies

The second part of the book describes the different communication technologies involved in IoT projects and provides four different practical projects to demonstrate their usage and how third-party components can be adopted in combination with the Arduino IoT Cloud.

This part has the following chapters:

- *Chapter 4, Project #1 – A Smarter Setup for Sensing the Environment*
- *Chapter 5, Project #2 – Creating a Portable Thing Tracker Using MKR GSM 1400*
- *Chapter 6, Project #3 – A Remote Alarming Application with LoRaWAN*

4

Project #1 – a Smarter Setup for Sensing the Environment

This chapter guides you through the reasons why a clean environment is necessary for human beings and how to implement air quality, temperature, and humidity monitoring by using low-cost **ESP-series boards**, with different open source sensors and the **Arduino IoT Cloud**. Moreover, you will learn how to visualize the relevant data and use the Arduino IoT Cloud features to expand the functionalities of your applications/projects.

In this chapter, you will gain confidence in how to build real-world solutions as we demonstrate **Printed Circuit Board** (**PCB**) design, its implementation, and its deployment in the real world. We will cover the following topics:

- Why is air quality monitoring necessary?
- Hardware components – sensors and development boards
- Project architecture
- Setting up the **Thing**, network credentials, cloud variables, and code
- Setting up a dashboard for web and mobile
- What's next?

Technical requirements

The following hardware components are required to understand this chapter:

- **WeMos D1 MINI ESP8266**
- A **DHT11/DHT22** sensor/module
- The **MQ-135** air quality module

- A PCB (a link is available in the *PCB design and assembling hardware components* section)
- Female headers
- Jumper cables

For coding, we will use the **Arduino Web Editor**, which includes a large collection of development boards and sensor libraries, and the **Arduino IoT Cloud** for Thing and dashboard setup. To develop hardware and sensor designs, we will need **Fritzing** desktop software.

The code for this chapter is available at the book's official GitHub repository, or you can directly download the code by following this link: `https://github.com/PacktPublishing/Arduino-IoT-Cloud-for-Developers/tree/main/Chapter%234%20Project%231%20Sensing%20and%20Monitoring%20the%20Air%20for%20Clean%20Environment`.

Why is air quality monitoring necessary?

Air quality monitoring is necessary for human beings because air pollution can have significant negative effects on our health and well-being. Poor air quality can cause a variety of respiratory and cardiovascular problems, such as asthma, chronic bronchitis, lung cancer, and heart disease. It can also exacerbate existing health conditions and reduce our ability to fight off infections and illnesses.

Air pollution can also impact the environment, including ecosystems, wildlife, and plants. Polluted air can lead to **acid rain**, which can damage crops, forests, and bodies of water and harm wildlife. It can also lead to the depletion of the ozone layer, which protects us from harmful UV radiation.

By monitoring air quality, we can identify areas where pollution levels are high and take steps to reduce exposure. This can include reducing emissions from factories, power plants, and transportation, as well as encouraging the use of clean energy and transportation alternatives. By improving air quality, we can help to protect our health, support the environment, and promote sustainable development.

Air quality monitoring is necessary to assess the level of pollutants present in the air we breathe. It helps to identify the sources of pollution and to track changes in air quality over time. There are several reasons why air quality monitoring is important:

- **Regulatory compliance**: Many countries have regulations in place to limit the amount of pollutants that can be released into the air. Air quality monitoring is necessary to ensure that these regulations are followed and to identify areas where additional regulations may be necessary.
- **Economic concerns**: Poor air quality can have a negative impact on economic activity, including reduced productivity, increased healthcare costs, and decreased tourism. Monitoring air quality can help to identify areas where pollution levels are high and take steps to improve air quality and support economic growth.

Overall, air quality monitoring is an essential tool to protect public health, preserve the environment, and promote sustainable economic development. Now we've had a theoretical review of air quality monitoring, it's time to explore the project practically. Firstly, we will start with the hardware, where we will explore all the required components such as development boards, sensors, design diagrams, and PCB design for implementation. Later, we will set up the Thing and cloud variables, upload code to the development board, and set up the dashboard for data visualization.

Exploring the hardware requirements

Before moving forward, we will first look at what types of development boards and sensors are required to accomplish the project. We aim to use a board that provides Wi-Fi connectivity, is small in size, and is low in cost. If we talk about Wi-Fi-enabled development boards, then there are a lot of organizations providing them, such as **Arduino**, the **ESP32 series**, and the **ESP8266** series. Arduino development boards such as **MKR Wi-Fi 1010** and **MKR Wi-Fi 1000** are expensive compared to ESP32 and ESP8266. Now, we have two options: we either go with ESP32 or ESP8266 and leave the Arduino development boards. In this project, we will be using the WeMos D1 Mini, which is part of the ESP8266 series. Although the ESP32 series offers similar features, it is equipped with **Bluetooth Low Energy** (**BLE**) connectivity, which is not currently compatible with this project. Thus, we have opted for the ESP8266 series development boards, which are not only compact in size but also more affordable.

Among the sensors, there is a diverse range of options for measuring temperature, humidity, and air quality. However, our primary goal is to provide sensors that are affordable and readily available to users worldwide. For temperature and humidity measurements, we rely on the widely available and reasonably priced DHT11/DHT22 sensors. The MQ-135 sensor provides a wide detecting scope, fast response, and high sensitivity. It is a stable and long-life, simple drive circuit application. These sensors are used in air quality control equipment and are suitable for detecting NH_3, NOx, alcohol, benzene, smoke, CO_2, and more. They are easily obtainable on the market and well-suited for small-scale projects.

The ESP8266 series has a wide collection of development boards that vary in size and pins. In this chapter, I'm using the WeMos D1 Mini development board, as it's very compact compared to other boards and, of course, cheaper in cost, and it provides 5V as well as 3.3V pins. The following figure is the complete overview of the WeMos D1 Mini board, and demonstrates all the digital/analog Arduino-based pin numbers, ground and power pins, and so on:

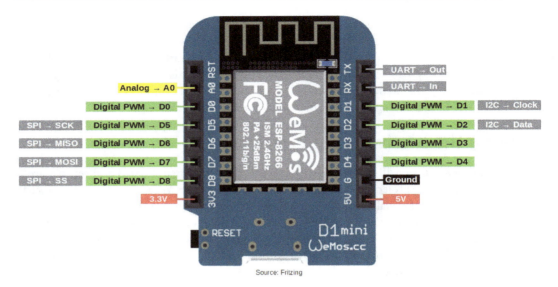

Figure 4.1 – WeMos D1 Mini ESP8266

WeMos provides multiple pins for digital input/output, but there is only one analog pin for input/output operations. If you want to use multiple analog sensors, then **analog-to-digital converters** are available. One of the most famous analog-to-digital converters is the **ADS1115/ADS1015 module**, which provides four analog pins that help cater to the requirement of using multiple sensors.

However, for the current project, we need one digital pin for the **DHT11/DHT22 sensor** and one analog pin for the **MQ-135 air quality sensor**. One of the best features of the WeMos D1 Mini development board is the 5V power pin, which is not available on most ESP8266 series development boards.

Next, we will use the DHT11 sensor to sense temperature and humidity, but you can also use the DHT22 sensor, depending on your requirements. With regard to features, the DHT22 provides a broader range of sensing compared to the DHT11, but its cost is higher. The following diagram shows the pinout layout of both sensors:

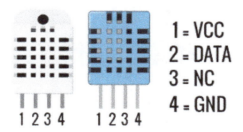

Figure 4.2 – The DHT22 and DHT11 pinout layouts

Pin #1 is the **voltage common collector** (**VCC**) and works with both 3.3V and 5V. Pin #2 is a **data** pin that connects with any digital pin of a development board, and Pin #4 is a **ground** (**GND**) pin that connects with the GND pin of a development board. There is another pin in the sensor, Pin #3, which is **Not Connected** (**NC**) – this pin is not used by us during development.

The following table explains all the specification differences between DHT22 and DHT11; the most notable things are the **sensing range** and the **sensing period**:

Model	DHT22	DHT11
Power supply	3.3–5V	
Output signal	A digital signal via a single bus	
Sensing element	Polymer capacitor	
Sensing range	Humidity: 0–100% RH Temperature: 40~80 Celsius	Humidity: 20–90% RH Temperature: 0~50 Celsius
Accuracy	Humidity: ± 2% RH (Max ±5% RH) Temperature: <±0.5 Celsius	Humidity: ±1% RH (Max ± 5% RH) Temperature: <±2 Celsius
Sensing period	Average 2s	Average 1s

Table 4.1 – DHT11 vs DHT22 comparison

Finally, we will look at the main sensor for our project. The MQ-135 sensor is used to monitor the air quality of a specific area. It is a low-cost environment-monitoring sensor, and it monitors a wide range of parameters, such as smoke, carbon dioxide, ammonia, benzene, nitrogen oxides, and alcohol. The MQ-135 senses all these parameters and provides the value of air quality in **parts per million** (**ppm**). The following figure shows the MQ-135's shape and its pin layout diagram as well as indicators for the LED and regulator:

Figure 4.3 – MQ-135 sensor and pinout

The MQ-135 sensor module consists of four pins, and each pin is marked with a code: **Analog Output (AO)**, **Digital Output** (DO), GND, and VCC. The module provides readings on both analog and digital modes, but analog mode is best to get values in PPM. The sensor operates better with 5V power, but you can still use 3.3V, although I recommend the former. The MQ-135 requires 20 seconds of preheating to provide better readings, so make sure to get readings after an interval of every 20 seconds, or at least wait 20 seconds for the first-time boot of the development board.

The module also contains a regulator to control the sensitivity of sensors, which could be adjusted according to the environment. Different indicator **Surface Mount Device (SMD)** LEDs are available to verify the module status, which includes **Logic Out LED** and **Power LED**.

Understanding the project architecture

In the preceding sections, we discussed the sensors and development board in detail. Now, it's time to cook the recipe. In hardware development, before getting to work with sensors and development boards, we need to develop design concepts to get a better understanding of how things will be connected. There is a lot of software available to design and develop design concepts regarding electronics projects, but we will opt for Fritzing.

In the next subsection, we will talk about the schematics and the design of the project, which explains how to connect the pins to the development board. In the subsection after that, we will talk about the PCB design and its implementation to make a product ready for deployment in the field.

Schematics and design

The purpose of our design is to get a clear understanding of how sensors will connect with the development board. It helps engineers develop a prototype on a **breadboard** or **Veroboard** by using our design files. The other major benefit of designing is that Fritzing builds hardware schematics and the PCB design in the background according to your design, which can be adjusted by designers according to system requirements. The following design provides a full overview of how you can connect sensors to a development board:

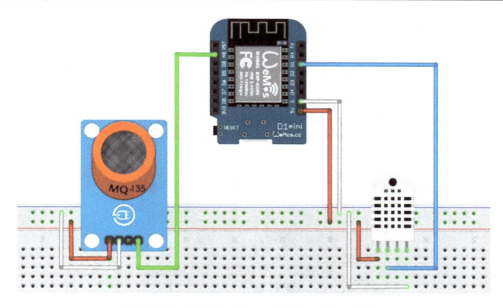

Figure 4.4 – An air quality-monitoring system design

For better understanding we have developed the schematics diagram shown in *Figure 4.4* as well *Table 4.2* for easy understanding. The pin configuration will be discussed in detail in proceeding paragraph.

We Mos D1 mini	MQ-135	DHT22
5V	VCC	VCC
GND	GND	GND
A0	A0	-
D1	-	Data

Table 4.2 – Pin configuration table for sensors

According to the design (*Figure 4.4* and *Table 4.2*), we have a common 5V output and GND from the development board to both sensors. The MQ-135 sensor is an analog sensor, so we connected its AO pin to the AO pin of the WeMos development board, while DHT11/DHT22 are digital sensors, and their Pin 2 is connected to the D1 pin of the development board.

PCB design and the assembly of hardware components

In the preceding subsection, we looked at a design that is ideal for creating a prototype using a breadboard or Veroboard, but what if we want to deploy that solution in the field? **Fritzing** is a great tool that provides the option to design the PCB, but when you develop the design, it automatically creates the PCB design in the backend, which is accessible via the **PCB Design** tab. Automatic PCB design is just a basic footprint and not suitable for direct production, so it's mandatory to review and rearrange the design according to professional practices. The following diagram demonstrates the final PCB design of the project:

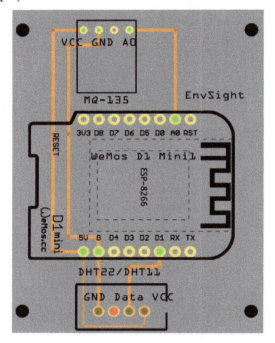

Figure 4.5 – An air quality-monitoring system PCB design

It's easy to develop the PCB; just make sure that the connection line doesn't intersect with other connection lines. There are many different tools available for PCB design, such as EasyEDA, CircuitMaker, and Altium, but it is thanks to Fritzing that I could create that design so easily.

After the PCB design, you have two options. First, you can develop the PCB by yourself using a DIY method, which is good for learning purposes but not suitable for a large-scale product. The second method is to choose a professional organization that manufactures the PCB professionally. Many organizations in China provide PCB manufacturing and fabrication services, such as **Seeed Studio**, **JLCPCB**, and **PCBWay**. I have tried PCBWay and was impressed with their manufacturing and shipment delivery time. I have uploaded the PCB design to the PCBWay project repository; from there, you can select and order it easily: `https://www.pcbway.com/project/shareproject/Low_cost_Outdoor_Air_Quality_Monitoring_System_0157f1af.html`.

After getting the PCB board, it's time to solder the female headers for the development boards and sensors. Never solder the development board and sensors directly on the PCB, as if anything stops working, then it's easy to detach and replace. So finally, here we have a product ready where the sensors and development board are soldered on the PCB for final deployment.

Figure 4.6 – An air-quality monitoring system on the PCB

After the female headers are soldered onto the PCB, WeMos and the other sensors are plugged into the headers, as shown in the preceding diagram. In this section and the previous section, we explored what types of sensors and development boards will be used in our project, and the latter part of this section discussed design, which demonstrates the wiring system for connectivity between sensors and the WeMos D1 Mini. Finally, we explored PCB design and assembled all the components of the PCB. Next, we need to set up the Thing, code, and dashboard in the Arduino IoT Cloud to get ready for the final product.

Setting up the Thing, network credentials, cloud variables, and code

After setting up the hardware, it's time to set up the Thing in the Arduino IoT Cloud. For this project, we need three cloud variables to fetch the monitoring parameters from the device, and the Wi-Fi network settings will be different as compared to Arduino development boards, due to the ESP series-based development board. The following figure provides an overview of the Thing, including **Cloud Variables**, **Associating a device**, and **Network** settings with numbers, which will be discussed next step by step:

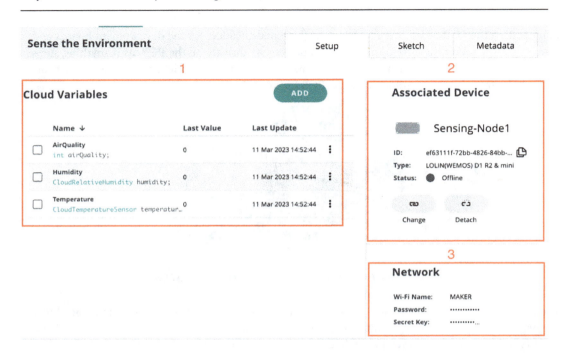

Figure 4.7 – The air quality-monitoring system Thing setup

Set up a new Thing with the name `Sense the Environment`. Follow the next steps to create variables, the associated device, the network configuration, and finally, the code:

1. Firstly, we need to set up three cloud variables regarding air quality, humidity, and temperature. The complete details regarding cloud variables are available in the next subsection.

2. After that, we need to associate the device with the Thing. In the current project, we will use the WeMos D1 Mini so the wizard will be different from the Arduino boards. The complete details are available in the *Associating a device* subsection.

3. Finally, we need to set up the network configuration for the device, but this time, we need to provide a security key for ESP series boards to make the connection secure. The Arduino-compatible boards are configured by the Arduino IoT Cloud automatically during the device setup wizard.

4. After the setup of cloud variables, device, and network settings, we will go through the code.

Here, we have given an overview of the Thing and we also discussed the required steps that will be carried out to complete the Thing setup.

Cloud variables

The following table explains all the properties of the variable that we need to use when we create the cloud variable. An integer is a very famous data type, but we will use two new variable types for humidity (`CloudRelativeHumidity`) and temperature (`CloudTemperatureSensor`), which measure data in percentage and Celsius, respectively. Next, make sure to declare the variables exactly as stated in the given table, including case-sensitive names and variable types. If the example code does not match your naming, you will need to modify it accordingly.

S#	Variable name	Variable type	Declaration	Permission	Update policy
1	AirQuality	int	airQuality	Read-only	On change
2	Humidity	CloudRelative Humidity	humidity	Read-only	On change
3	Temperature	CloudTemperature Sensor	temperature	Read-only	On change

Table 4.3 – Cloud variables details

Here, we made the **permission** read-only; although we have a read/write option, in our project, we only want to receive data from the device instead of a dashboard modification. That's why read-only mode is used to prevent issues in data consistency. **Update policy** is set to **On change**, as the device will send the data after five minutes, and this option is more appropriate compared to periodic updates.

Associating a device

After creating the variables, it's time to add a device and associate it with the Thing. Before adding the device, connect the development board to the computer and open the **Arduino Create Agent** application. The following figure shows the different types of third-party boards that are supported by the Arduino IOT Cloud, and in that step, we will select the **ESP8266** series board.

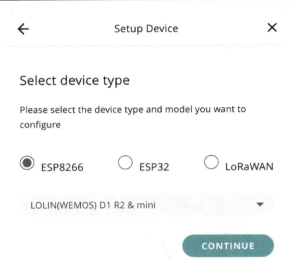

Figure 4.8 – The device selection wizard

Please follow these steps to add the device to the Arduino IoT Cloud:

1. Click on the **Select Device** button under the **Associating a device** section on the Thing page.
2. A popup will appear, where you can see all the devices that are already available. If you have already added your WeMos D1 Mini, select it. Otherwise, click on **SET UP NEW DEVICE**.
3. Next, click on the **Third party device** option.
4. Select **ESP8266** and **LOLIN(WEMOS) D1 R2 mini** from the dropdown, and click on the **CONTINUE** button.
5. Provide the device name and click on the **Next** button.
6. In the final wizard, the device ID and secret key will be displayed. Copy the secret key to a safe place, as it will be used during the network configuration.

After setting up the device and associating it with the Thing, it's time to configure the device network settings. The following sections will cover all the steps to configure your device for a Wi-Fi network.

Network

After associating the device with the Thing, it is time to configure the Wi-Fi settings for device communication. Fill in the form with **Wi-Fi Name** and **Password**:

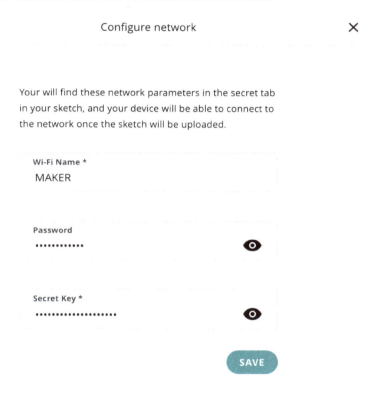

Figure 4.9 – The network configuration for the Thing

In *Figure 4.9*, you will find a new field for **Secret Key**. Paste the secret key that we received from the system during the device association process, which is explained in *step 6* in the preceding subsection.

Now, we are done with the device association to the Thing as well as with network settings. The next step is to understand and upload the code. The following section will guide you through the code.

Coding

The chapter's code is available at the book's official GitHub repository, or you can directly download the code by following this link: `https://github.com/PacktPublishing/Arduino-IoT-Cloud-for-Developers/tree/main/Chapter%234%20Project%231%20Sensing%20and%20Monitoring%20the%20Air%20for%20Clean%20Environment/Sense_the_Environment_feb24a`

You can download the code and put it into your Thing by navigating to the **Sketch** tab. We will not discuss the code any further, as you will get an idea of how it works after reading it. Instead, we will explain the main workflow, which involves initializing all the things in the setup method and using milliseconds to calculate the delay time. Remember to never try using the `delay` method, as it will block the `ArduinoCloud.update()` method and then call the `STHAM` method every five minutes. The following code is demonstrating how to fetch Temperature and Humidity values from `dht` object, and for `airQuality` we are simply using `analogRead()` method.

```
dht.temperature().getEvent(&event);
if (isnan(event.temperature)) {
  temperature=0;
}
else {
  //Send Temperature to Cloud
  temperature=event.temperature;
}

// Get humidity event and print its value.
dht.humidity().getEvent(&event);
if (isnan(event.relative_humidity)) {
  humidity=0;
}
else {
  //Send Humidity to Cloud
  humidity=event.relative_humidity;
}
//Send Air Quality to Cloud
airQuality=analogRead(A0);
```

The preceding code snippet was taken from the `STHAM` method; here, we just modified the code to show you how we send values to the Arduino IoT Cloud after taking values from the sensors.

In a previous section, we created the cloud variables. Just recall the cloud variable declaration and assign the sensor readings to those variables. This cloud variable declaration is available in the `thingProperties.h` file. So, when you assign the values to these variables, the `ArduinoCloud.update()` method in the loop will automatically send data to the cloud.

Upload the code to the device and verify the connectivity and readings. If you want to change the reading time, then just modify the `interval` variable value. Make sure you provide the time in milliseconds, where 1 second equals 1,000 milliseconds.

> **Important note**
>
> If you used different naming in the variable declaration, then update the code according to your naming scheme. However, it's better that you first follow all the steps according to the book and later change the cloud variable names and modify your code, in that order.
>
> Never try to use `delay` method, which will create a block for the `ArduinoCloud.update()` method. Always use milliseconds to calculate the waiting time. Review the `loop()` method to understand how we call the method after 5 minutes.
>
> The Arduino IoT Cloud only updates the value on the dashboard whenever a variable value is changed. For example, if the temperature is 30 and is still the same after 5 minutes, then the Arduino IoT Cloud will not record the value, so don't get confused if values don't change on a graph. This is another benefit of the Arduino IoT Cloud: you will not get duplicated data when you export the content.

We have successfully set up the Thing, which includes cloud variables, device association, network configuration, and code, and uploaded it to the development board. Now, it's time to explore the dashboard and sensor values visualization in the following section.

Setting up a dashboard for web and mobile

After uploading the code to the device, it's time to set up a dashboard for web and mobile to visualize the data with different widgets. Complete details about widgets and their usage are available in *Chapter 3*. If you have directly skipped to this chapter, I recommend going back to *Chapter 3* to get a detailed overview of widgets and their usage as this will help you to understand how widgets work and their usage for different use cases. The following figure demonstrates the visualization of readings with different widgets:

Figure 4.10 – The Thing dashboard

We have three different readings, **Temperature**, **Humidity**, and **Air Quality**. For each reading, we use different widget controls to demonstrate how they all work, but for historical data, graphs are the best widgets.

The **Temperature** reading is visualized by **Gauge**, the **Humidity** reading is connected to the **Percentage** widget, and the **Air Quality** reading is connected to the **Value** widget. These widgets are only capable of displaying current readings of sensors. However, we also want to monitor the historical data, and graphs are the best widgets to display live as well as older data. Here, we have used three graphs, and each one is connected to a specific cloud variable.

What's next?

We still have a lot of options available to explore, but now it's your turn to use different sensors and development boards to do some more experiments and learn from them. In this chapter, we have only used two sensors, which only offer three parameters, but there are a lot of sensors on the market that provide a wide variety of functionalities, such as air pressure and measurements for different gases.

Try out the following sensors to enhance your practical knowledge and compare them with other sensors in terms of features, range, and cost:

- The **BMP280** (pressure and temperature) sensor

- The **MH-Z19C/D/E series** sensors for carbon dioxide monitoring

- The **MQ series** sensors, which are designed to sense different specific gases, including MQ-2, MQ-3, MQ-4, MQ-5, MQ-7, MQ-8, and MQ-9

- **Seeed Studio SCD30** (temperature, humidity, and CO_2)

- **Gravity**: **Analog Electrochemical Carbon Dioxide Sensor** (0–10,000 PPM)

Summary

In this chapter, we explored how to develop a low-cost air quality monitoring system using DHT11, MQ-135, and the WeMos D1 Mini development board. We set up the Thing, which involved creating cloud variables, associating the device, configuring the network, and coding the development board. Later, we created a dashboard to visualize the Thing's sensor readings with different types of widgets, displaying the current readings as well as historical data with the help of graphs. Through this project, you will get the confidence to set up the Thing practically and deploy it in the field using a PCB. You have learned about new types of cloud variables for sensor readings and storage, as well as dealing with different types of dashboard widgets.

In the next chapter, we will study GSM technology for IoT. We will learn about different types of global IoT SIM cards and their usage. This project will also demonstrate a Smart Assets tracing example, where we will track the asset with a GPS module and send the data to the Arduino IoT Cloud via global IoT SIM cards. In the end, you will also learn about new widgets in the Arduino IoT Cloud to visualize the location of your assets on the basis of GPS coordinates.

5

Project #2 – Creating a Portable Thing Tracker Using MKR GSM 1400

This chapter is dedicated to **smart transportation** and **smart remote monitoring**. It shows how cellular communication-enabled devices can be integrated with the **Arduino IoT Cloud** platform, and it also offers an example of using a **global IoT SIM card** for communication.

Here, we will practically explore **Long-Term Evolution (LTE)** technologies, which are very useful in remote monitoring and control, whether they involve asset tracking or remote operation monitoring. This project uses the **Arduino MKR GSM 1400** development board, which is equipped with the latest communication bands and was specially designed for **Industrial Internet of Things (IIoT)** and **Internet of Things (IoT)** use cases. This project practically explains how you can develop a tracking solution based on cellular communications for different use cases. This chapter will help you to understand cellular communication technology, global IoT SIM cards, and the integration of Arduino IoT Cloud using cellular technology. By the end of this chapter, you will be able to develop solutions for remote areas using cellular technology.

In this chapter, we're going to cover the following main topics:

- Enhancing operations with IoT asset tracking and remote control
- Exploring the advantages of GSM/LTE/NB-IoT communication technologies
- Seamless global connectivity with IoT SIM cards
- Building blocks – sensors and development boards for IoT
- Designing the project architecture
- Activating SIM cards for IoT deployment

- Configuring the Thing, network credentials, cloud variables, and code
- Creating comprehensive web and mobile dashboards

Technical requirements

The following are the hardware components required to complete this chapter:

- MKR GSM 1400/MKR NB 1500
- A Hologram global IoT SIM card
- A NEO-6M GPS module
- A breadboard
- Jumper cables

For coding, we will use the **Arduino Web Editor**, which includes a large collection of development boards and sensor libraries, as well as Arduino IoT Cloud for Thing and dashboard setup. To develop hardware and sensor designs, we need the **Fritzing** desktop software, and we need **Arduino IDE** for GPS module testing.

In this chapter, we will use the **Arduino IoT SIM card** for communication instead of local SIM providers. Arduino provides a wide variety of data plans for global IoT sim cards that can be chosen according to requirements. The code for this chapter is available at the book's official GitHub repository at this link: `https://github.com/PacktPublishing/Arduino-IoT-Cloud-for-Developers`.

Enhancing operations with IoT asset tracking and remote control

IoT technology can be very useful for asset tracking and remote controlling and monitoring operations. By installing sensors on assets and connecting them to a central network, you can track the location and status of your assets in real time. Here are some ways in which IoT can be used for asset tracking and remote controlling and monitoring operations:

- **Asset tracking**: By installing GPS trackers or RFID tags on your assets, you can track their location and movements in real time. This can be very useful for logistics and supply chain management, as well as fleet management.
- **Condition monitoring**: By installing sensors on your assets, you can monitor their condition and performance in real time. This can help you identify potential problems before they become serious and take corrective action to prevent downtime and reduce maintenance costs.

- **Predictive maintenance**: By analyzing data from your sensors, you can use machine learning algorithms to predict when maintenance is needed on your assets. This can help you schedule maintenance at the most convenient time and avoid unplanned downtime.

- **Remote control**: By connecting your assets to a central network, you can control them remotely from a central location. This can be very useful for operations that are located in remote areas or difficult to access.

- **Remote monitoring**: By installing cameras and other sensors on your assets, you can monitor their operations remotely in real time. This can help you identify potential problems and take corrective action quickly.

Overall, IoT technology can be very useful for asset tracking and remote controlling and monitoring operations. By leveraging the power of sensors, data analytics, and machine learning, you can improve the efficiency and reliability of your operations while reducing costs and downtime. In this section, we have discussed IoT for asset tracking and remote monitoring using cellular technology. Next, we will cover different communication technologies that are available now and coming to market in the future.

Exploring the advantages of GSM/LTE/NB-IoT communication technologies

Global System for Mobile communication (**GSM**), LTE, and **NarrowBand-Internet of Things** (**NB-IoT**) are all wireless communication technologies that are widely used for mobile communications and IoT devices. Each technology has its own pros and cons, and the choice of which technology to use depends on the specific requirements and solution design.

Here are some of the reasons why GSM, LTE, or NB-IoT are often chosen over other communication technologies:

- **Wide coverage**: GSM and LTE networks have extensive coverage and are available in most parts of the world, making them ideal for global connectivity. NB-IoT, on the other hand, has been designed specifically for IoT devices and offers greater coverage in hard-to-reach areas.

- **High data rates**: LTE offers high data rates, making it suitable for applications that require fast and reliable data transfer. NB-IoT, although slower, still offers better data rates than other **Low-Power Wide-Area Network** (**LPWAN**) technologies.

- **Security**: GSM and LTE networks offer high levels of security, with features such as encryption and authentication to protect against eavesdropping and other forms of cyberattacks. NB-IoT also provides end-to-end encryption for data security.

- **Compatibility**: GSM and LTE networks are backward compatible with previous generations of technology, allowing for seamless integration with existing infrastructure. NB-IoT is also designed to be compatible with LTE networks, making it easy to add IoT capabilities to existing LTE networks.

- **Battery life**: NB-IoT and other LPWAN technologies are designed to consume minimal power, resulting in longer battery life for connected devices.

Overall, GSM, LTE, and NB-IoT are widely used communication technologies that offer reliable connectivity, high data rates, security, and compatibility with existing infrastructure. Here, we have discussed the benefits of GSM/LTE/NB-IoT communication technologies over other wireless communication technologies. In the next section, we are going to cover global IoT SIM cards, which is the main pillar of this chapter.

Seamless global connectivity with IoT SIM cards

Global IoT SIM cards are specifically designed for IoT devices that require cellular connectivity to communicate with the internet or other connected devices. These SIM cards provide access to multiple networks, allowing devices to roam across different countries and regions without the need to switch between SIM cards.

Global IoT SIM cards typically offer features such as the following:

- **Multi-network coverage**: These SIM cards can connect to multiple cellular networks, including GSM, LTE, and other emerging technologies, such as NB-IoT and **Cat-M**, to provide reliable coverage in different locations.

- **Over-the-air (OTA) updates**: Many global IoT SIM card providers offer OTA updates, enabling devices to receive firmware and software updates without the need for physical intervention, improving efficiency and reducing maintenance costs.

- **Data plans**: Global IoT SIM card providers offer flexible data plans that can be customized to suit the specific needs of a device or application. This includes data allowances, data speed, and the ability to add more data as needed.

- **Security**: Global IoT SIM cards typically come with security features such as encryption and authentication to protect data and prevent unauthorized access.

- **Management tools**: Many global IoT SIM card providers offer web-based portals or mobile apps that allow users to monitor and manage their SIM cards, including data usage, network performance, and billing information.

Global IoT SIM cards provide a cost-effective and flexible solution for companies, allowing them to deploy IoT devices worldwide. They allow seamless connectivity, ensuring that devices are always connected to the best available network, regardless of location.

There are many IoT global SIM service providers. Here is a list of some of them:

- Hologram
- Soracom
- Arduino SIM
- Twilio
- Emnify
- Aeris
- KORE Wireless
- Sierra Wireless
- Teleena
- Thales Group
- Truphone
- UROS
- 1oT

> **Important note**
>
> Before buying an IoT global SIM card from any service provider, please verify whether it works in your region or not and, if so, what type of services it offers, such as GSM, **3G/4G**, or NB-IoT, as there are many regions where, for example, NB-IoT services are still not available.
>
> Please note that this is not a complete list, and there are many other IoT SIM providers available in the market. It's important to research and compare different providers based on your specific requirements and needs before making a decision.

Here, we have discussed global IoT SIM cards in detail and listed all the top global IoT SIM card service providers. Next, we are going to cover what types of hardware and sensors are required to complete the chapter's project.

Building blocks – sensors and development boards for IoT

The Arduino series has a wide collection of development boards that vary in size, pins, and communication technologies. In this chapter, I will use an Arduino MKR GSM 1400 development board, as it's compact, battery-enabled, and provides the support of GSM/3G/4G. *Figure 5.1* shows the pinout diagram for the MKR GSM 1400.

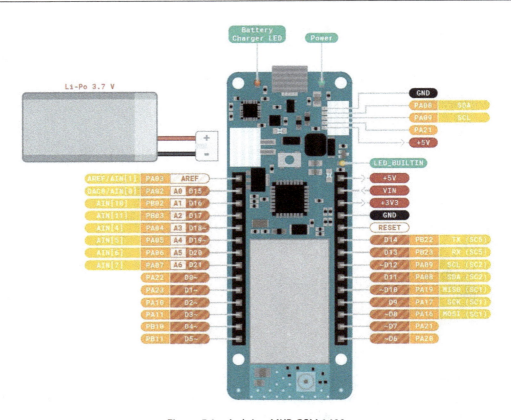

Figure 5.1 – Arduino MKR GSM 1400

Arduino MKR GSM 1400 provides 7 analog pins and 14 digital input/output pins, with built-in battery charging and a LiPo battery connector for standby power, which helps developers build prototypes and solutions for remote monitoring/operations without worrying about power backups. For further details, please visit the official website at https://store-usa.arduino.cc/products/arduino-mkr-gsm-1400.

Arduino's latest development board, MKR NB 1500, only supports NB-IoT, **LTE-M**, and **Enhanced GPRS (EGPRS)** for SMS. NB-IoT and LTE-M are specially designed for IoT devices, and their popularity is spreading very rapidly across different regions. For complete details and specifications, visit https://store-usa.arduino.cc/products/arduino-mkr-nb-1500. For a list of updated regions where NB-IoT and LTE-M are deployed, visit https://www.gsma.com/iot/deployment-map/.

In this chapter, we will track the assets based on GPS location. To get the GPS coordinates, we will use the **GY-GPS6MV2 GPS module**, which is based on the **NEO-6M u-blox** chip. The GPS module communicates on both software serial and hardware serial ports, but MKR GSM 1400 provides a built-in hardware serial, so we will use *Pins 13* and *14* to communicate with the GPS module.

The GPS module provides latitude, longitude, satellite count, altitude feet, and speed per mile data. We will display these properties on the dashboard for proper asset tracking. This module was developed in China and is available on the market at affordable prices, but there are many other organizations that develop GPS modules based on the NEO-6M u-blox chip, such as **SparkFun**, **Seeed Studio**, and **Adafruit**. *Figure 5.2* shows the NEO-6M u-blox GPS module and its pinout diagram:

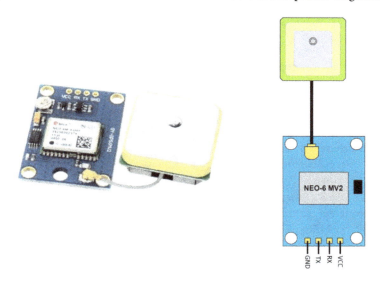

Figure 5.2 – The NEO-6M u-blox GY-GPS6MV2 GPS module and a pinout diagram

The preceding figure illustrates the pinout layout of the GPS module. *Pin #1* is a **ground** (**GND**) pin that connects with the onboard GND, while *Pin #2* and *Pin #3* are **transmit** (**TX**) and **receive** (**RX**) pins, respectively, and connect to *Pin #13* and *Pin #14* of MKR GSM 1400, respectively. *Pin #4* – the **voltage common collector** (**VCC**) – works with both onboard VCC and 5V pins. You can solder the male headers with the GPS module or directly solder the cables without any header pins.

> **Important note**
>
> The GPS module works optimally in an outdoor environment. Make sure there is no rooftop during testing and deployment to receive a proper signal from satellites.
>
> If you are using the module in a lab, then there will be a chance that the GPS module will not work properly. Remember that there is a built-in light in the GPS module that blinks when you start receiving signals from satellites.

In this section, we discussed the MKR GSM 1400 development board, which is a SIM-enabled board, and the NEO-6M u-blox GPS module, which will provide the GPS coordinates to the development board. We also discussed their pin layouts. Next, we will discuss how to connect the GPS module with the MKR GSM 1400 development board.

Designing the project architecture

In the preceding sections, we discussed the module and development board in detail. Now, it's time to cook the recipe. In hardware development, before starting to work with sensors and development boards, we need to develop the design concepts to get a better understanding of how things will connect. There is a lot of software that is available to design and develop design concepts for an electronics project, but in this case, we will use Fritzing.

In the following two subsections, we will talk about schematics and designing a project, while explaining how to connect pins with a development board and soldering. Then, we will do some tests to fetch GPS coordinates, which is very important before sending data to the cloud.

Schematic design and assembly

The purpose of your schematic design is to get a clear understanding of how sensors will connect with a development board. Schematic diagram helps you to develop a prototype on a breadboard or a **Veroboard,** which is shown in *Figure 5.3*. Another major benefit of designing is that Fritzing builds hardware schematics and PCB design in the background according to your design, which can be adjusted according to system requirements. *Figure 5.3* shows the schematic diagram of how to connect MKR GSM 1400 with the NEO-6M u-blox GPS module:

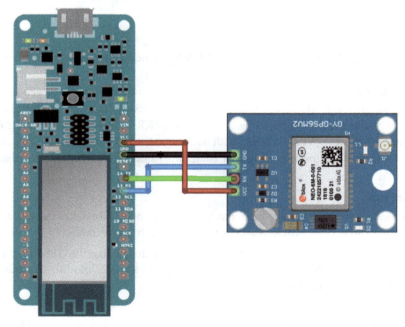

Figure 5.3 – MKR GSM 1400 and the GPS module schematic

Figure 5.3 is schematic diagram of project, but for ease I also created *Table 5.1,* which demonstrates MKR GSM 1400 to GPS Module pin numbers and names.

MKR GSM 1400 Board	GPS Module
5V	VCC
GND	GND
14 TX	RX
13 RX	TX

Table 5.1 – MKR GSM 1400 and the GPS module pin connections list

The preceding design provides a full overview of how you can connect a module to a development board. According to our design, we have 5V and GND from the development board to the GPS module. The GPS module TX is connected to the RX (*Pin #13*) and the GPS module RX pin is connected to the TX (*Pin #14*) of the development board. *Table 5.1* shows the pin information. Finally, we have built our prototype by using a breadboard, which is shown in *Figure 5.4*:

Figure 5.4 – The final prototype

After soldering the male headers to the GPS module, connect the pins according to the schematic diagram. There is only one sensor, so there is no requirement for the Veroboard. Next, we are going to test the GPS module using a serial monitor to verify that our GPS module is working properly and getting the values from GPS.

Testing GPS module data

For module testing, we need a **serial monitor** to verify whether the GPS module works properly or not. Select the Arduino MKR GSM 1400 board from **Tools** > **Board** > **Arduino SAMD** > **Arduino MKR GSM 1400** in the Arduino IDE. Select the port of the development board. Next, we need to install a library for the GPS module. Navigate to **Sketch** > **Include Library** > **Manage Libraries**. Type tinygps into the search bar.

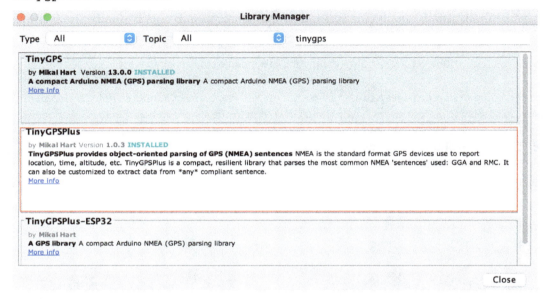

Figure 5.5 – The TinyGPSPlus library

After searching, **Library Manager** shows a lot of libraries. Select the **TinyGPSPlus** library and install its latest version. The library comes with a lot of examples, but all are based on software serial. However, **Arduino SAMD** boards provide hardware serial, so I modified the code that uses hardware serial to communicate with the GPS module.

Download the code from the book's official GitHub repository in the chapter folder, open the MKR-1400-NEO-6M-GPS-Module code, and upload it to the development board:

```
while(Serial1.available()>0)//While there are characters to come from
the GPS
  {
    gps.encode(Serial1.read());//This feeds the serial NMEA data into
the library one char at a time
  }
  if(gps.location.isUpdated())//This will pretty much be fired all
the time anyway but will at least reduce it to only after a package of
```

```
NMEA data comes in
  {
    //Get the latest info from the gps object which it derived from
the data sent by the GPS unit
    Serial.println("Satellite Count:");
    Serial.println(gps.satellites.value());
    Serial.println("Latitude:");
    Serial.println(gps.location.lat(), 6);
    Serial.println("Longitude:");
    Serial.println(gps.location.lng(), 6);
    Serial.println("Speed MPH:");
    Serial.println(gps.speed.mph());
    Serial.println("Altitude Feet:");
    Serial.println(gps.altitude.feet());
    Serial.println("");
  }
```

In the setup, we have initialized `Serial` and `Serial1`. `Serial` is used to display the content on the serial monitor, while `Serial1` is the hardware serial that is used to communicate with the GPS module. The preceding code belongs to the `loop()` method.

First, the GPS module will read the data from satellites using the `Serial1.read()` method and encode the data via the `gps.encode()` method. `Serial1` only reads one character at a time, so it will take a little bit of time to update the values. Next, we will verify whether there is any update in location by using the `gps.location.isUpdated()` method. If there is a change, then data will be printed on the serial monitor.

> **Important note**
>
> Make sure that your GPS module is placed in an open environment where you have a clear sky without any obstructions, such as a roof or anything similar, to properly receive signals from satellites.
>
> The GPS module has an onboard built-in LED that starts blinking when it receives data from GPS.
>
> The same code will work with MKR NB 1500 without any modification.

Figure 5.6 shows the serial monitor with values from the GPS, which includes latitude and longitude, along with other parameters:

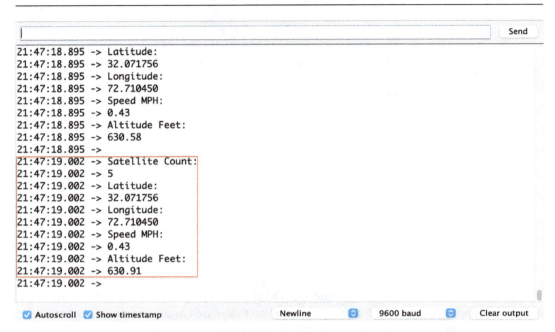

Figure 5.6 – GPS module data on the serial monitor

The preceding figure shows the data that is received by the GPS module from GPS satellites and printed on the serial monitor. The data includes the satellite count, the latitude and longitude that represent the location coordinates, the speed in **miles per hour** (**MPH**) based on current and previous GPS coordinates, and the altitude in feet.

In this section, we tested the NEO-6M u-blox GPS module in the Arduino IDE. First, we installed the TinyGPSPlus library for the module and then we used the preceding code for the development board, which shows the readings on the serial monitor. In the next section, we are going to start with the global IoT SIM card activation.

Activating SIM cards for IoT deployment

After assembling the GPS module with MKR GSM 1400 and testing it, it's time to activate the Hologram global IoT SIM card, which will act as a bridge between the device and the Arduino IoT Cloud. You can purchase the IoT SIM card from https://store.hologram.io/store/. It provides different types of SIM cards for industries, such as the **Hyper EUICC IoT SIM card**, which is an industrial-grade and simple SIM card for learning projects, and these are available in different sizes according to the SIM slots in the development boards. You can order its **pilot SIM card** for free, but you need to pay for its shipment.

After receiving the SIM card, create an account at `hologram.io`, where you will be able to activate and manage all your SIM cards. The Hologram dashboard provides full details regarding the data utilization of devices, packages, billing, and routes. By setting up routes, you can forward your device data to a different IoT cloud if you directly send it to the Hologram cloud. However, in our case, we will just use the Hologram SIM card as a carrier to transfer data from a device directly to the Arduino IoT Cloud, so there will be no requirements to set up a route. Just activate the SIM card and insert it into the MKR GSM 1400 development board.

In this section, we discussed how we can proceed with Hologram global IoT SIM card activation as well as the different types of SIM cards available at `hologram.io` for researchers as well as industry. In the next section, we are going to set up the Thing in the Arduino IoT Cloud, which will include cloud variables creation, device association, network configuration, and code.

Configuring the Thing, network credentials, cloud variables, and code

After setting up the hardware, it's time to set up the Thing in the Arduino IoT Cloud. For this project, we need four cloud variables to fetch different properties from the device. The network settings will be different as we are using a GSM series board instead of Wi-Fi. *Figure 5.7* shows the complete overview of the Thing:

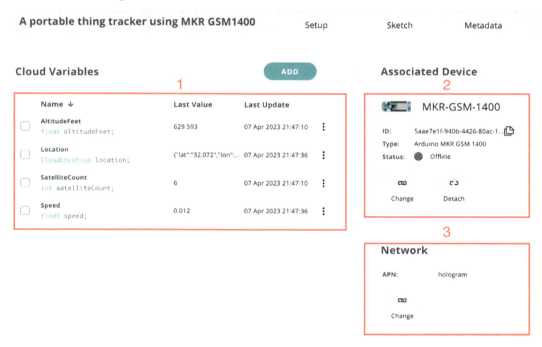

Figure 5.7 – A portable Thing tracker using the MKR GSM 1400 Thing setup

Set up a new Thing with the name A portable thing tracker using MKR GSM1400. Then, follow these steps to create cloud variables, an associate device, a network configuration, and finally, the code:

1. Firstly, we need to set up four cloud variables for location, altitude feet, satellite count, and speed. The complete details regarding these cloud variables are available in the following section.

2. Then, we need to associate the device with the Thing. In the current project, we will use the MKR GSM 1400, so the wizard will be the same one used for the Arduino boards. The complete details are available in the *Associating a device* section.

3. Finally, we need to set up a network configuration for the device, but this time, we need to provide different settings for the GSM board, which will be covered in the *Network* subsection.

Here, we have discussed what steps will be involved in the Thing creation. In the following subsections, we will create cloud variables, associate a device to the Thing, and network settings in separate subsections step by step.

Cloud variables

The following table explains all the properties that we need to use during cloud variable creation. For Location, we need two different variables to store latitude and longitude, but thanks to the Arduino IoT Cloud extended group of variables, we have a Location type variable. Next, make sure each variable matches the declaration in the table; otherwise, you need to modify the example code according to your naming.

In *Table 5.2*, during the cloud variables creation, I made the permission *read-only*. Although we have the read/write option, in this project, we only want to receive data from the device instead of modifying it on the dashboard. That's why read-only mode is used – to prevent issues with data consistency. **Update Policy** is set to **On change**, as the device will send the data when the GPS module receives new data from satellites.

#	Variable name	Variable type	Declaration	Permission	Update policy
1	AltitudeFeet	Float	altitudeFeet	Read-only	On change
2	Location	CloudLocation	location	Read-only	On change
3	SatelliteCount	Int	satelliteCount	Read-only	On change
4	Speed	Float	speed	Read-only	On change

Table 5.2 – Cloud variables list for the Thing

In this section, we have discussed what type of cloud variables are required for this project. Here, we have listed four cloud variables of different types but in read-only mode, as we only want to take the values from the device. In the next subsection, we are going to associate the MKR GSM 1400 with the Thing.

Associating a device

After creating the variables, it's time to add the device and associate it with the Thing. Before adding the device, connect the development board to the computer and open the **Arduino Create Agent** application. *Figure 5.8* shows a popup in which we have options to either select the existing device for association or set up a new device that is not available in the list:

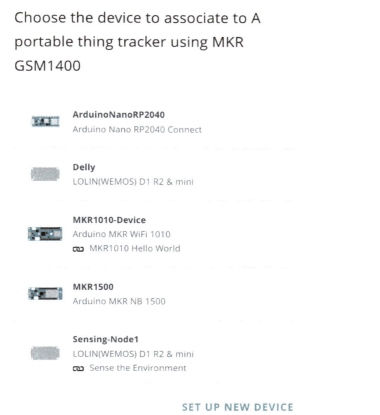

Figure 5.8 – Associate device

In our case, we already have different devices in the portal, but we want to add a new MKR GSM 1400 device, so just click on **SET UP NEW DEVICE** to configure the new device in the account.

Then, you will see two options in the popup (*Figure 5.9*). The first option is to set up an Arduino board, and the second option is to set up a third party device. Here, you will see a note under both options, **Compatible devices** (*i*), which means you can only use certain types of Arduino devices as well as third-party devices in the Arduino IoT Cloud.

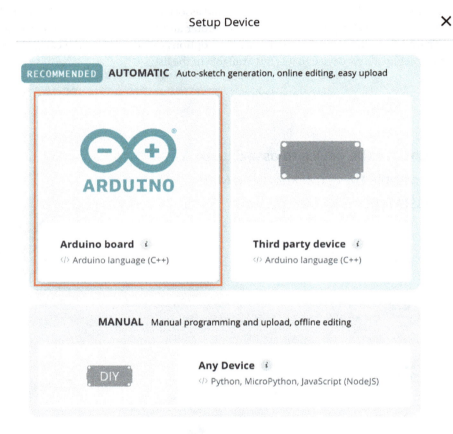

Figure 5.9 – Choosing a development device

We can select any one option from the popup, according to the available device. However, in this case, click on the option to set up an Arduino device, as, in this chapter, we will use the MKR GSM 1400 board. Before adding the device, make sure that Arduino Create Agent runs on your machine.

In this subsection, we have associated the MKR GSM 1400 development board with the Thing. Next, we will configure the network settings in the **Thing** tab.

Network

After associating the device with the Thing, it is time to configure the network settings for device communication. These network settings are different from the Wi-Fi network settings. Both the MKR GSM 1400 and MKR NB 1500 development boards use SIM technology for communication. For that reason, their network configurations are different and will vary according to the IoT SIM card service provider. The following figure (*Figure 5.10*) shows the **Configure network** popup for the MKR GSM 1400, which is totally different to the Wi-Fi configuration due to cellular communication:

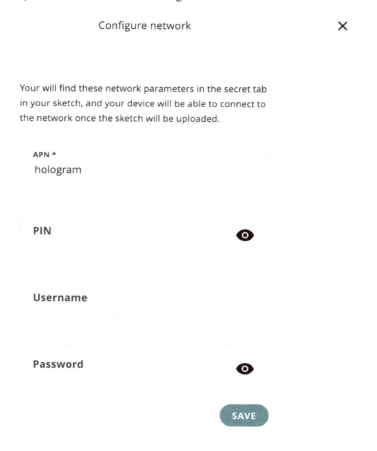

Figure 5.10 – The network configuration for the MKR GSM 1400

Currently, we are using the Hologram global IoT SIM card, and only need to mention `hologram` under **APN**; there is no requirement for the **PIN**, **Username**, and **Password** details. However, if you use the Arduino SIM, then **APN** will be `prepay.pelion`, **PIN** will be `0000`, and **Username** and **Password** will both be `arduino`. Before using any other global IoT SIM card, first, take its APN information to set up the network properly.

Here, we have discussed the network configuration for the Arduino MKR GSM 1400, which includes the APN, PIN, username, and password. In the next section, we will cover the code for the development board.

Coding

The chapter's code is available at the book's official GitHub repository. Download A_portable_ thing_tracker_using_MKR_GSM1400_apr07a.zip and import it into the Arduino Web Editor.

You can download the code and put it into your Thing by navigating to the **Sketch** tab. Here, I will explain the main workflow instead of all code, we are initializing all the objects and variables in the setup() method; remember to never try to use the delay method, as it will block the ArduinoCloud.update() method:

```
TinyGPSPlus gps;
unsigned long previousMillis = 0;
const long interval = 30000; //milliseconds
```

In the preceding code snippet, we declare the gps instance and two variables, which will be used to wait for 30,000 milliseconds (30 seconds) before taking the next readings without blocking the code.

Next, we will move toward the loop method. Here, we call the FetchGPS() method after every 30 minutes, which is carried out by comparing currentMillis and previousMillis without the use of delay:

```
unsigned long currentMillis = millis();
if (currentMillis - previousMillis >= interval) {
  //speed=currentMillis;
  FetchGPS();
  previousMillis = currentMillis;
}
```

In the following snippet, I have just picked a small part of the code from the FetchGPS() method. Here, I assign the latest values from the GPS module to the Arduino cloud variables, which will be used to send data to the cloud as well as print it on the serial monitor:

```
if (gps.location.isUpdated())
  {
    altitudeFeet = gps.altitude.feet();
    satelliteCount = gps.satellites.value();
    speed = gps.speed.mph();
    location = Location(gps.location.lat(), gps.location.lng());
    Location cordinates = location.getValue();
```

```
    .
    .
    .
}
```

Upload the code to the device and open up the Arduino Web Editor serial monitor to verify the values. After successfully uploading the data to the cloud, it's time to set up a beautiful dashboard for web and mobile for end users.

> **Important note**
>
> If you used different names in the variable declaration, then update the code according to your naming scheme. However, it's better to first follow all the steps according to the book and later change the cloud variable names, modifying your code respectively.
>
> Never try to use the `delay` method, which will create a block for the `ArduinoCloud.update()` method.
>
> The Arduino IoT Cloud only updates a value on the dashboard whenever a variable value is changed. For example, if the GPS location of the device is the same after an interval of time, then it means the device is not moving. Then, the Arduino IoT Cloud will not record the value, so don't get confused if values are not changing on the map. Another benefit of this feature is that you will not get duplicate data when you export the content.
>
> The same code will work with MKR NB 1500 without any modification. However, here, you need to associate the MKR NB 1500 device with the Thing instead of the MKR GSM 1400.

Creating comprehensive web and mobile dashboards

After uploading the code to the device, it's time to set up a dashboard for web and mobile to visualize the data with different widgets. The following figure demonstrates the visualization of readings with different widgets:

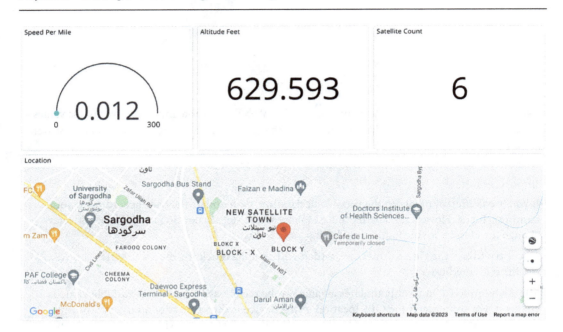

Figure 5.11 – The Thing dashboard

We have four readings from the GPS module to visualize; here, I have used three widgets, **Gauge**, **Value**, and **Map**, but **Map** is used twice as it takes two values (i.e., latitude and longitude). The **Gauge** widget shows **Speed Per Mile**, while two **Value** widgets have been used to display **Altitude Feet** and **Satellite Count**. The **Map** widget has been used to display **Location** based on the latitude and longitude coordinates, which are stored in a cloud-based `location` variable. Currently, the Map widget is only capable of displaying the location of the asset device based on coordinates; if you have multiple assets to track, then you need to set up multiple Map widgets according to the number of tracking devices.

Well, this was the last section of our chapter. Here, we have created a stunning dashboard for GPS tracking that shows the location using the Map widget on the dashboard, the speed per mile, and some other parameters.

What next?

We still have a lot of options available to explore, but now it's your time to use different sensors and development boards to do some more experiments and learn from them. In the current chapter, we only used one GPS module, which gave us only four parameters but, on the market, there are a lot of GPS modules that provide a wide variety of functionalities; they work under the roof as well as under clear sky, and have several accuracy features.

While monitoring an asset's location, there are some other parameters that are very important to monitor in different industries, such as temperature and humidity, which are very important in food and medical products. CO_2 and LPG gases are very important to monitor during fuel transportation. Try different sensors with a GPS module to set up different tracking prototypes for different industries.

Summary

In this chapter, we explored how to develop a GPS-based tracking system using a global IoT SIM card and GPS module. We set up the Thing, which included cloud variable creation, device association, GSM network configuration, and coding a development board. Later, we created a dashboard to visualize the Thing readings with different types of widgets to display current readings, with the most important widget of the chapter being the Map widget. It is a very interesting and important widget to display the location of IoT devices using GPS coordinates.

GPS tracking is a very important aspect that we covered in this chapter, and it helps us to develop a device for our asset tracking, which will help us in asset tracking and monitoring. This chapter demonstrated how we can display the location of a device on the dashboard, which gives you the confidence to build more solutions regarding asset tracking. In the next chapter, we will explore another long-range communication technology, called **LoRaWAN**. We will use this technology to build a solution for remote monitoring distant areas as well as compare this technology with GSM/4G/LTE and NB-IoT technology for proper guidance.

6

Project #3 – a Remote Asset Tracking Application with LoRaWAN

This chapter is dedicated to **smart transportation** and **smart remote monitoring** using low-power and long-range communication technology. The project in this chapter will take you through the implementation and deployment of a remote alarming application based on **Long Range Wide Area Network (LoRaWAN)**, connected to the public, global, and decentralized The Things Network. The project in this chapter provides localization features by using a GPS module. The **Arduino IoT Cloud** will be used for data visualization and remote configuration of the device. The application will be used in real use cases, showing the benefits offered by LoRaWAN technologies compared to other wireless technologies.

Here, we will practically explore LoRaWAN technologies, which are very useful in remote monitoring and control, whether it's **asset tracking** or **remote operation monitoring**. This project uses the **Arduino MKR WAN 1300** development board, which is equipped with the latest communication frequencies, 433/868/915 MHz US/EU. It is specially designed for **Internet of Things (IoT)** and **Industry 4.0** use cases. This project explains how you can practically develop a tracking solution based on LoRaWAN communication for different use cases.

In this chapter, we will cover the following main topics:

- Understanding LoRaWAN and its IoT applications
- LoRaWAN versus other communication technologies
- Components of a LoRaWAN IoT application
- Essential hardware – sensors and development boards
- Designing the project architecture

- Setting up the Thing, adding devices, cloud variables, and code
- Configuring the The Things Indoor Gateway
- Creating web and mobile dashboards

Technical requirements

The following hardware components are required to complete the exercise in this chapter:

- MKR WAN 1300 or MKR WAN 1310
- The Things Indoor Gateway
- The NEO-6M u-blox GPS module
- A breadboard
- Jumper cables

To code, we will use the **Arduino Web Editor,** which includes a large collection of development boards and sensor libraries, and the Arduino IoT Cloud for the Thing and dashboard setup. To develop hardware and sensor designs, we need the **Fritzing** desktop software, and we need the **Arduino IDE** for GPS module testing.

In this chapter, we will use the **The Things Indoor Gateway** for LoRaWAN communication. The code used in the chapter is available in the book's official GitHub repository by following this link: https:// github.com/PacktPublishing/Arduino-IoT-Cloud-for-Developers.

Understanding LoRaWAN and its IoT applications

LoRaWAN is a wireless communication protocol and network architecture specifically designed for **Low-Power Wide Area Networks (LPWANs),** enabling long-range communication between devices in the context of the IoT. LoRaWAN technology is optimized for applications that require low data rates, long battery life, and long communication ranges, making it well-suited for various IoT use cases.

Usage in IoT

LoRaWAN has been widely adopted in various IoT applications due to its unique features. Some common use cases include the following:

- **Smart agriculture**: LoRaWAN can be used for soil moisture monitoring, crop health monitoring, livestock tracking, and precision farming, allowing farmers to optimize their operations and increase yield
- **Smart cities**: LoRaWAN can enable smart street lighting, waste management, parking management, and environmental monitoring, helping cities become more efficient and sustainable

- **Industrial monitoring**: LoRaWAN can monitor equipment health, track assets, and improve supply chain management in industrial settings, leading to better maintenance practices and reduced downtime

- **Utilities**: LoRaWAN can be used for smart meters and to remotely monitor utility infrastructure, such as water and gas meters, improving billing accuracy and resource management

- **Environmental monitoring**: LoRaWAN can support applications such as air quality monitoring, water quality monitoring, and wildlife tracking, helping researchers and organizations gather valuable environmental data

- **Asset tracking**: LoRaWAN enables real-time tracking of assets, such as shipping containers, vehicles, and valuable equipment, ensuring their security and efficient utilization

Overall, LoRaWAN's combination of long communication ranges, low power consumption, and scalability makes it a powerful technology to build IoT networks that cover large areas and connect a wide range of devices for various applications.

In this section, we have discussed the different use cases of LoRaWAN in the field of IoT, and in the next section, we will discuss why to choose LoRaWAN over other communication technologies.

LoRaWAN versus other communication technologies

LoRaWAN offers several advantages over other communication technologies, making it a preferred choice for certain IoT applications. Here are some reasons why LoRaWAN might be chosen over other alternatives:

- **Long range**: LoRaWAN provides exceptional long-range communication capabilities, enabling devices to communicate over several kilometers in open areas. This is particularly useful for applications that require connectivity over large distances, such as agriculture, environmental monitoring, and asset tracking.

- **Low power consumption**: Devices using LoRaWAN can operate on very low power, extending battery life for years. This is crucial for remote or hard-to-reach locations where changing or recharging batteries is impractical or costly.

- **Deep indoor penetration**: LoRaWAN can penetrate buildings and other obstacles effectively, ensuring connectivity even in challenging environments. This makes it suitable for applications such as smart building management and indoor asset tracking.

- **Cost-effective**: Implementing and maintaining a LoRaWAN network is often more cost-effective than deploying traditional cellular networks. This makes LoRaWAN a viable option for businesses and organizations looking to deploy IoT solutions on a larger scale.

- **Scalability**: LoRaWAN networks can handle a massive number of devices within a single network. This scalability is essential for IoT applications that involve a high density of devices, such as smart city deployments.

- **Low data rate applications**: LoRaWAN is optimized for applications that transmit small amounts of data at low data rates. For IoT use cases involving sensor data, meter readings, and periodic updates, LoRaWAN provides a suitable and efficient communication solution.

- **Network flexibility**: LoRaWAN supports both public and private network deployments. Organizations can choose to set up their own private LoRaWAN network or use existing public networks, giving them flexibility in terms of ownership and control.

- **Adaptive data rate**: LoRaWAN devices can adjust their data rate based on signal strength and interference, optimizing communication for the current conditions. This adaptive feature enhances reliability and ensures the efficient use of available resources.

- **Global standard**: LoRaWAN is a global standard, and devices designed to work with it can operate seamlessly across different regions and countries. This standardization simplifies device development and deployment for international projects.

- **Diverse applications**: LoRaWAN's versatility enables its use in various application domains, from agriculture and industrial monitoring to smart cities and environmental sensing.

While LoRaWAN offers these advantages, it's important to note that no single communication technology is universally superior. The choice between LoRaWAN and other technologies (such as cellular, Wi-Fi, Bluetooth, or Zigbee) depends on the specific requirements of the IoT application, including factors such as range, power consumption, data rate, cost, and scalability. Each technology has its strengths and weaknesses, and the selection should be based on a careful analysis of a project's needs.

In this section, we have discussed the benefits of using LoRaWAN. In the next section, we will explore the important components of LoRaWAN.

Components of a LoRaWAN IoT application

LoRaWAN is a wireless communication protocol and network architecture designed to enable long-range, low-power communication between IoT devices. It's specifically tailored to connect devices that require extended battery life, reliable long-distance communication, and efficient use of the wireless spectrum. LoRaWAN is one of the key technologies in the realm of LPWANs. *Figure 6.1* illustrates the whole architecture of the LoRaWAN solution, including the end nodes, gateway, network server, and application server.

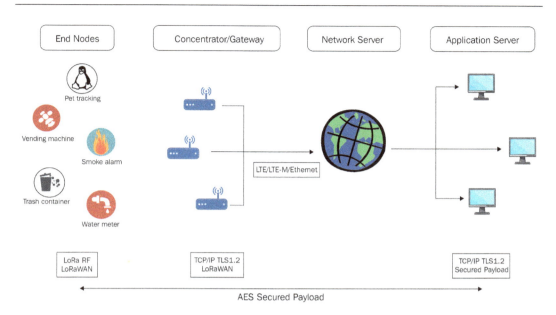

Figure 6.1 – The components of a LoRaWAN network

The LoRaWAN architecture consists of four main components:

- **End nodes/devices**: These are the IoT devices that gather data from sensors or perform specific tasks. They communicate with gateways using the LoRa modulation technique, sending data packets at low data rates.

- **Gateways**: Gateways serve as intermediate points that receive data packets from end devices and transmit them to a centralized network server. They are typically connected to the internet via wired or wireless connections.

- **Network server**: The network server manages communication between gateways and end devices. It handles functions such as authentication, encryption, and the routing of data packets to their respective application servers.

- **Application server**: The application server is responsible for processing data received from the network server and performing specific actions based on the data. It interfaces with an end user's application or backend system to present data, trigger alerts, perform analytics, or control devices. The application server can be hosted on the cloud or on-premises.

In this section, we have discussed LoRaWAN components in detail, and in the next section, we are going to explore the hardware and sensors that are required to execute the practical exercise of this chapter.

Essential hardware – sensors and development boards

The Arduino series has a wide collection of development boards that vary in size, pins, and communication technologies. In this chapter, we will use the Arduino MKR WAN 1300 development board, as it's compact, battery-enabled, and provides support for different frequencies from different regions around the world, including 433/868/915 MHz. *Figure 6.2* shows a pinout diagram of the MKR WAN 1300.

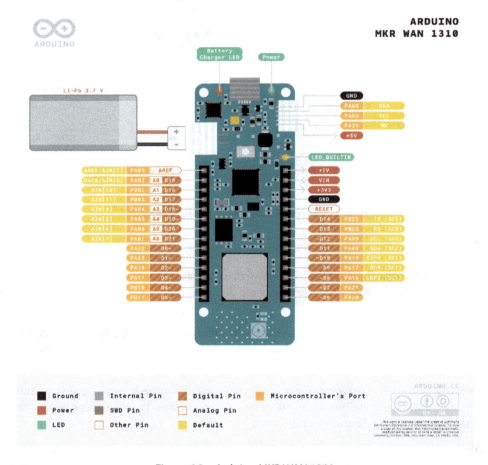

Figure 6.2 – Arduino MKR WAN 1300

The Arduino MKR WAN 1300 provides seven analog pins, which start with **A** (**A0, A1**, and so on), and eight digital input/output pins, which start with **D** (**D0, D1**, and so on), with built-in battery charging and a **lithium polymer** (**LiPo**) battery connector for standby power, which helps developers build prototypes and solutions for remote monitoring/operations without worrying about power backups. For further updates and the latest product development news, please visit the official website at https://store.arduino.cc/products/arduino-mkr-wan-1300-lora-connectivity.

Arduino's latest development board is the MKR WAN 1310, which contains the same processor and module for LoRa communication as the MKR WAN 1300. However, the MKR WAN 1310 has an updated in-battery charger, 2 MB of **Serial Peripheral Interface** (**SPI**) flash, and enhanced power consumption. This board is specially designed for IoT devices and is quickly growing in popularity in different regions. For its complete details and specifications, visit `https://store.arduino.cc/products/arduino-mkr-wan-1310`.

In this chapter, we will track the device via GPS coordinates. To get the GPS coordinates, we will use the GY-GPS6MV2 GPS module, which is based on the NEO-6M u-blox chip. The GPS module operates on both a software serial and a hardware serial, but the MKR WAN 1300 provides a built-in hardware serial, so we will use *ins 13* and *14* to communicate with the GPS module shown in *Figure 6.3*.

The GPS module provides latitude, longitude, satellite count, altitude feet, and speed-per-mile properties. These properties will be displayed on a dashboard for proper asset tracking. This module was developed in China and is available at affordable prices, but many other organizations are developing GPS modules that are also based on the NEO-6M u-blox chip, such as SparkFun, Seeed Studio, and Adafruit. *Figure 6.3* shows a NEO-6M u-blox GPS module and its pinout diagram:

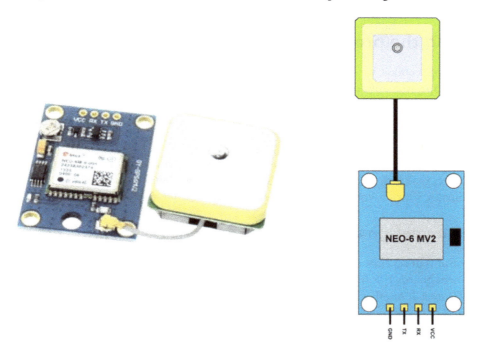

Figure 6.3 – The GY-GPS6MV2 NEO6MV2 GPS module and a pinout diagram

The preceding diagram describes the pinout layout of the GPS module. *Pin #1* is the **GND** pin that connects with the onboard GND pin of the MKR WAN 1300. *Pin #2* and *Pin #3* are **TX** and **RX**, respectively, and will connect to *Pin #13* and *Pin #14* of the MKR WAN 1300, respectively. *Pin #4*, **VCC**, works with both an onboard VCC and the 5V pins of the MKR WAN 1300. You can solder the male headers with the GPS module or directly solder the cables without any header pins.

> **Important note**
>
> The GPS module works best in an outdoor environment. Make sure there are no rooftops above during testing and deployment to properly receive a signal from satellites.
>
> If you are using the module in the lab, then there will be a chance that the GPS module will not work properly. Remember that there is a built-in light on the GPS module that starts blinking when you receive signals from satellites.

In this section, we have discussed the development board and GPS module in detail, including their pinout diagrams. In the next section, we will start exploring how to connect the GPS module with the MKR WAN 1300.

Designing the project architecture

In the preceding sections, we discussed the module and development board in detail. Now, it's time to cook the recipe. In hardware development, before getting to work with sensors and development boards, we need to develop the design concepts to get a better understanding of how things will connect. There is a lot of software that is available to design and develop design concepts for an electronics project, but in this case, we will use Fritzing.

In the following two subsections, we will talk about schematics and designing a project, while explaining how to connect pins with a development board and soldering. Then, we will do some tests to fetch GPS coordinates, which is very important before sending data to the Arduino IoT Cloud.

Schematics design and assembly

The purpose of your schematic design is to get a clear understanding of how sensors will connect with a development board. This helps engineers develop a prototype on a breadboard or Veroboard, as shown in *Figure 6.4*. Another major benefit of designing is that Fritzing builds hardware schematics and PCB design in the background according to your design, which can be adjusted according to system requirements. *Figure 6.4* shows a schematic diagram of how to connect the MKR WAN 1300 with the NEO-6M u-blox GPS module:

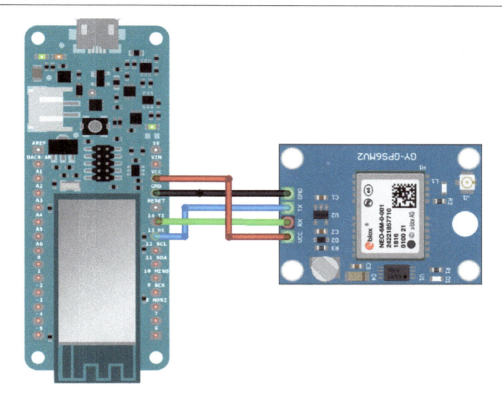

Figure 6.4 – The MKR WAN 1300 and GPS module schematic

While *Figure 6.4* illustrates the design of the MKR WAN 1300 and GPS module, we have created *Table 6.1* for easier understanding, which illustrates (in row format) how to connect pins.

MKR WAN 1300	NEO-6M u-blox GPS module
14 (TX)	RX
13 (RX)	TX
VCC	VCC
GND	GND

Table 6.1 – MKR WAN 1300 to GPS module pinout

The preceding design provides a full overview of how you can connect a module to a development board. According to our design, we have 5V and GND pins going from the development board to the GPS module. The GPS module **TX** pin is connected to the **RX** pin (*Pin #13*), and the GPS module **RX** pin is connected to the **TX** pin (*Pin #14*) of the development board. Finally, we built our prototype by using a breadboard, which is shown in *Figure 6.5*:

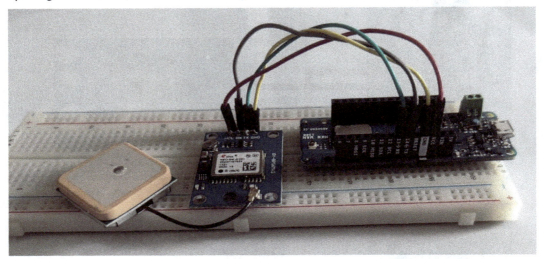

Figure 6.5 – The final prototype MKR WAN 1300 and GPS module

After soldering the male headers to the GPS module, connect the pins according to the schematic diagram. There is only one sensor, so there is no requirement for the Veroboard. Next, we will test the GPS module using Arduino's **Serial Monitor** tool to verify that our GPS module works properly and gets values from GPS satellites.

Testing GPS module data

Before moving toward the Arduino IoT Cloud, firstly, we need to verify that our GPS module is working. So, in this section, we will test the GPS module by using the Arduino IDE and its Serial Monitor tool to observe the readings from the GPS module. The following steps will guide you on how we will set up the testing environment:

1. For module testing, we need the Serial Monitor tool to verify whether the GPS module works properly or not. Click on the **Tools** menu and select **Serial Monitor**. Select the Arduino MKR WAN 1300 board from **Tools | Board | Arduino SAMD | Arduino MKR WAN 1300** in the Arduino IDE.

2. Select the port of the MKR WAN 1300.

3. Next, we need to install the library for the GPS module in the Arduino IDE. Navigate to **Sketch | Include Library | Manage Libraries**. Type tinygps into the search bar.

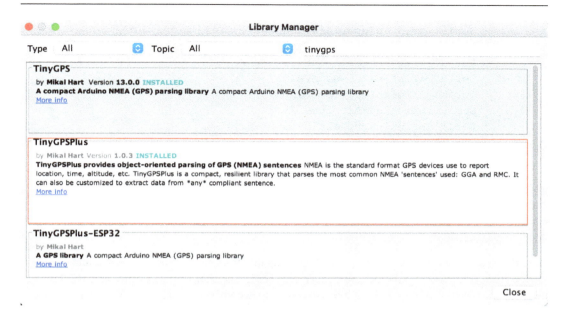

Figure 6.6 – The TinyGPSPlus library

4. After searching, the Library Manager brings up a lot of libraries. Select the **TinyGPSPlus** library and install its latest version. The library comes with a lot of examples, and all of them are based on a software serial. However, Arduino SAMD boards provide a hardware serial. Therefore, I've modified the code to use a hardware serial to communicate with the GPS module.

5. Download the code from the book's official GitHub repository, and under the `chapter#6` folder, open the `MKR-WAN-1300-NEO-6M-GPS-Module` ZIP folder, extract it, and upload the code to the development board:

```
while(Serial1.available()>0)//While there are characters to come
from the GPS
   {
     gps.encode(Serial1.read());//This feeds the serial NMEA data
into the library one char at a time
   }
   if(gps.location.isUpdated())//This will pretty much be fired
all the time anyway but will at least reduce it to only after a
package of NMEA data comes in
   {
     //Get the latest info from the gps object which it derived
from the data sent by the GPS unit
     Serial.println("Satellite Count:");
     Serial.println(gps.satellites.value());
     Serial.println("Latitude:");
```

```
        Serial.println(gps.location.lat(), 6);
        Serial.println("Longitude:");
        Serial.println(gps.location.lng(), 6);
        Serial.println("Speed MPH:");
        Serial.println(gps.speed.mph());
        Serial.println("Altitude Feet:");
        Serial.println(gps.altitude.feet());
        Serial.println("");
    }
```

In the setup, we have initialized `Serial` and `Serial1`. `Serial` is used to display the content to the Serial Monitor (the magnifier icon in the top right of the Arduino IDE) on screen, while `Serial1` is the hardware serial that is used to communicate with the GPS module. The preceding code belongs to the `loop()` method.

First, the GPS module will read data from satellites using the `Serial1.read()` method and encode it via the `gps.encode()` method. `Serial1` only reads one character at a time, so it will take a little bit of time for the updated values. Then, we will verify whether there is any update in `Latitude` and `Longitude` coordinates by using the `gps.location.isUpdated()` method. If there is a change, then the data will be printed on the Serial Monitor.

> **Important note**
>
> Make sure your GPS module is placed in an open environment where you have a clear sky, without any obstruction such as a roof or anything that stops you from receiving proper signals from satellites.
>
> The GPS module has an onboard built-in LED that starts blinking when it starts receiving data from GPS satellites.
>
> The same code will work with the MKR WAN 1310 without any modification.

Figure 6.7 shows the Serial Monitor with values from the GPS, which includes `Latitude`, `Longitude`, and other parameters:

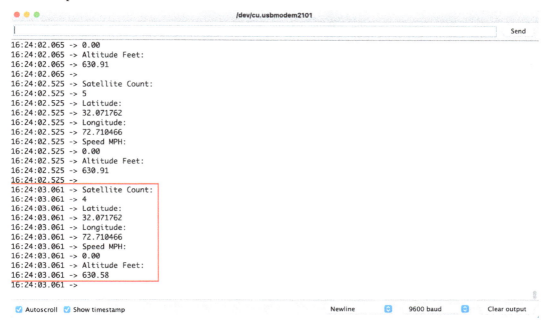

Figure 6.7 – The GPS module data on the Serial Monitor

The preceding figure shows the data that is received by the GPS module from GPS satellites and printed on the Serial Monitor. The data includes the satellite count, the latitude and longitude that represent the location coordinates, the speed in MPH based on current and previous GPS coordinates, and the altitude in feet.

In this section, we tested the NEO-6M u-blox GPS module in the Arduino IDE. First, we installed the `TinyGPSPlus` library for the module, and later, we used the aforementioned code for the development board, which shows the readings on the Serial Monitor. In the next section, we will start with the Thing setup in the Arduino IoT Cloud.

Setting up the Thing, device association, cloud variables, and code

After setting up the hardware, it's time to set up the Thing in the Arduino IoT Cloud. For this project, we need four cloud variables to fetch different properties from the device. The device association settings will be different due to the LoRa series board. Also, network configuration will happen automatically when we upload the code/sketch to the MKR WAN 1300. *Figure 6.8* shows a complete overview of the Thing:

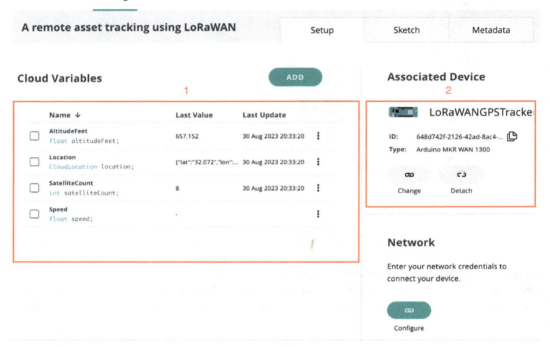

Figure 6.8 – Remote asset tracking using the LoRaWAN Thing setup

Set up a new Thing with the name **A remote asset tracking using LoRaWAN**, and then follow the next steps, which will take you to the next subsections to create variables, an associate device network configuration, and finally, code. We have marked the preceding figure with red boxes and numbers according to the following steps.

Firstly, we need to set up four cloud variables – `Location`, `AltitudeFeet`, `SatelliteCount`, and `Speed`. The complete details regarding cloud variables are available in the following subsection.

After that, we need to associate the device with the Thing. In the current project, we will use the MKR WAN 1300, so the process will be the same as the one used for Arduino boards, but here, we will see some different options due to LoRaWAN. The complete details are available in the *Associating a device* section.

Cloud variables

The following table explains all the properties of the variables that we need to create. For the location, we need two different variables to store the latitude and longitude, but thanks to the Arduino IoT Cloud extended group of variables, we have a Location-type variable. Then, make sure each variable matches the declaration in the table; otherwise, you will need to modify the example code according to your naming.

As shown in *Table 6.2*, when creating the cloud variables, we set the permission to **Read-Only**. Although we have the *Read/Write* option, in this project, we only want to receive data from the device instead of modifying the data via the dashboard. That's why **read-only** mode is used – to avoid issues in data consistency. **Update policy** is set to **On Change**, as the device will send the data when the GPS module receives new data from satellites.

S#	Variable name	Variable type	Declaration	Permission	Update policy
1	AltitudeFeet	Float	altitudeFeet	Read-Only	On Change
2	Location	CloudLocation	location	Read-Only	On Change
3	SatelliteCount	Int	satelliteCount	Read-Only	On Change
4	Speed	Float	speed	Read-Only	On Change

Table 6.2 – The cloud variables list for the Thing

In this section, we discussed what type of cloud variables are required for this project. Here, we listed four cloud variables of different types but in **read-only** mode, as we only want to extract the values from the device. In the next subsection, we will associate the MKR WAN 1300 with the Thing.

Associating a device

After creating the variables, it's time to add the device and associate it with the Thing:

1. Before adding the device, connect the development board to the computer and open the **Arduino Create Agent** application. *Figure 6.9* shows a popup in which we have options to either select the existing device for association or set up a new device that is not available on the list.

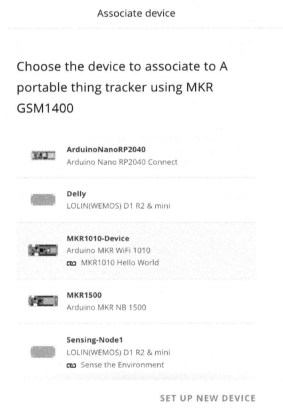

Figure 6.9 – Associate device – selecting a device

In our case, we already have different devices in the portal, but we want to add a new one, MKR WAN 1300, so just click on **SET UP NEW DEVICE** to configure the new device in the account.

2. Then, you will see three options in the popup. The first option is **Arduino board**, the second option is **Third party device**, and the third option is **Any Device**, which is for non-compatible devices. This means you can now use all types of Arduino devices as well as third-party devices with the Arduino IoT Cloud, which supports Python, MicroPython, and JavaScript.

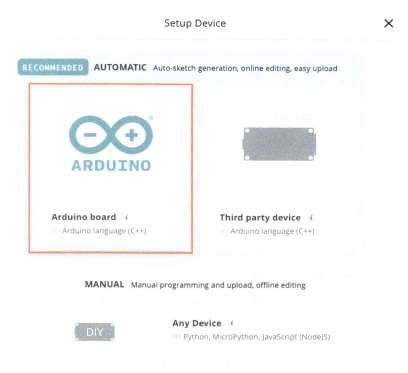

Figure 6.10 – Choosing a development device

3. Click on **Arduino board** (marked with a red box in *Figure 6.10*) and the next step will automatically detect the MKR WAN 1300 board, which we are using in this chapter. Before adding the device, make sure that **Arduino Create Agent** is running on your machine. *Figure 6.11* shows that the Arduino IoT Cloud detected the MKR WAN 1300.

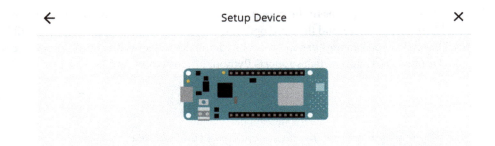

←   Setup Device   ✕

Arduino MKR WAN 1300 found

An Arduino MKR WAN 1300 has been detected on port
/dev/cu.usbmodem2101 and ready to be configured.

CONFIGURE

If the detected type of the device you want to configure is not
correct, try to reset your board and then refresh

Figure 6.11 – The device found

When the popup finds the device, click on the **CONFIGURE** button, which will take you to the next screen.

4. *Figure 6.12* shows a screen that provides some details about the **The Things Stack** portal link. You will also see a message saying that you need an active LoRaWAN gateway for the MKR WAN 1300 to communicate with the Arduino IoT Cloud.

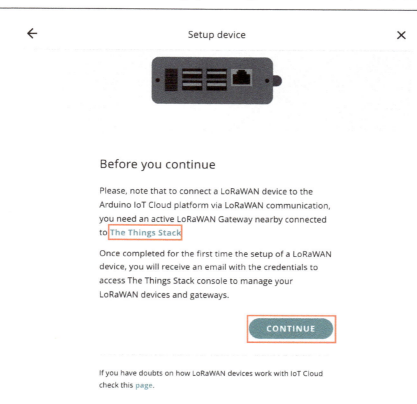

Figure 6.12 – The active LoRaWAN gateway

If you already have the gateway set up, then that's fine; otherwise, in the *Configuring the The Things Indoor Gateway* section, read up on how to set up the The Things Indoor Gateway, which will provide connectivity to your MKR WAN 1300 development board.

This message also informs you that the Arduino IoT Cloud will automatically configure your device in the The Things Stack portal.

5. After associating the device, you will receive an email with a username and password, as well as a URL for the The Things Stack portal login, which contains all the information about LoRaWAN nodes. Here, the Arduino IoT Cloud will automatically add the MKR WAN 1300 to the The Things Stack portal after the final steps. Next, *Figure 6.13* shows that we need to select a frequency for our device.

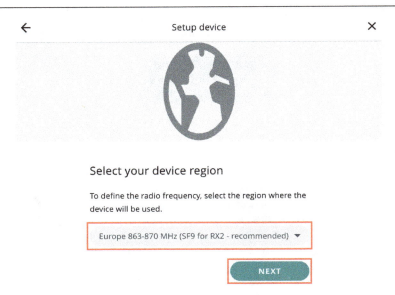

Figure 6.13 – The MKR WAN 1300 frequency selection

As we discussed earlier, LoRaWAN operates on different frequencies according to region. So, from the dropdown, select the specific frequency according to your region. I selected **Europe 863-870 MHZ (SF9 for RX2 - recommended)** according to my LoRaWAN gateway. After selecting the frequency from the dropdown, click on the **NEXT** button.

6. Now, we need to provide a name for the device, as shown in *Figure 6.14*.

Figure 6.14 – Assigning a name to the MKR WAN 1300

Here, I assigned the name `LoRaWanGPSTracker` to the device, but you can use any name related to your project structure. After assigning the name, click on the **NEXT** button.

7. Then, another popup will appear, as shown in *Figure 6.15*, which will prepare your device for the Arduino IoT Cloud.

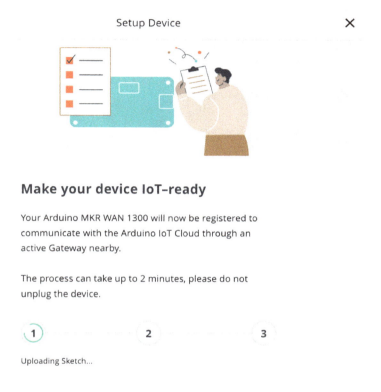

Setup Device   ✕

Make your device IoT-ready

Your Arduino MKR WAN 1300 will now be registered to communicate with the Arduino IoT Cloud through an active Gateway nearby.

The process can take up to 2 minutes, please do not unplug the device.

1   2   3

Uploading Sketch...

Figure 6.15 – MKR WAN 1300 configuration

Here, the Arduino IoT Cloud configures the MKR WAN 1300 via **Arduino Create Agent**. It will take one to two minutes to set up the development board with the necessary configuration.

8. When the device has been configured successfully, you will see the following popup. Just click on the **DONE** button and your device will be associated with your Thing.

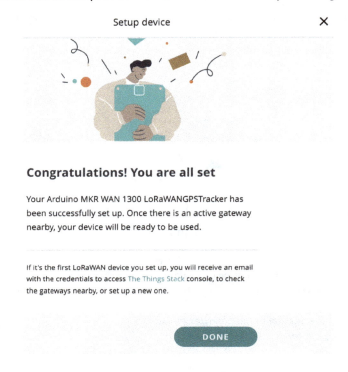

Figure 6.16 – A successful device setup

In this section, we have associated the MKR WAN 1300 with our Thing. We have also seen a lot of new options regarding LoRaWAN such as frequency, gateway, and so on. In the upcoming sections, we will discuss the network and code.

Network

In previous chapters, after associating the device with the Thing, we configured the network settings for device communication. However, this time, we don't need to configure any network settings, as the device will be configured automatically when we upload the sketch to the MKR WAN 1300 development board. At first, you will see an empty area in the **Network** configuration, as shown in *Figure 6.8*, but after the sketch uploads, you will see the LoRaWAN network configuration parameters.

Coding

The code for this chapter is available in the book's official GitHub repository. Download the A_ remote_asset_tracking_using_LoRaWAN_aug30a.zip file and import it into your Arduino Web Editor.

You can download the code and put it into your Thing by navigating to the **Sketch** tab. Here, I will explain the main workflow in which we are initializing all the variables and serial instances in the setup() method. Remember to never try to use the delay() method, as it will block the ArduinoCloud.update() method:

```
TinyGPSPlus gps;
unsigned long previousMillis = 0;
const long interval = 30000; //milliseconds
```

In the preceding code snippet, we declare the gps instance and two variables, which wait for 30000 milliseconds (30 seconds) before the next readings are taken without blocking the code.

Now, we will explore the loop() method. Here, we call the FetchGPS() method every 30 minutes, which will be carried out by comparing currentMillis and previousMillis without the use of delay():

```
  unsigned long currentMillis = millis();
  if (currentMillis - previousMillis >= interval) {
    //speed=currentMillis;
    FetchGPS();
    previousMillis = currentMillis;
  }
```

In the following snippet, I have just picked a small part of the code from the FetchGPS() method. Here, I assign the latest values from the GPS module to the Arduino cloud variables, which will be used to send data to the cloud as well as print it on the Serial Monitor:

```
if (gps.location.isUpdated())
  {
    altitudeFeet = gps.altitude.feet();
    satelliteCount = gps.satellites.value();
    speed = gps.speed.mph();
    location = Location(gps.location.lat(), gps.location.lng());
    Location cordinates = location.getValue();
    .
    .
    .
  }
```

Upload the code to the device, and open up the Arduino Web Editor Serial Monitor to verify the values. After successfully uploading the data to the cloud, it's time to set up a beautiful dashboard for web and mobile for end users.

> **Important note**
>
> If you used different *naming* when declaring the variables, update the code according to your naming scheme. However, it's recommended to first follow all the steps in the book and change the cloud variable names later, modifying your code respectively.
>
> Never try to use the `delay()` method, which will create a block for the `ArduinoCloud.update()` method.
>
> The Arduino IoT Cloud only updates values on its dashboard whenever the variable value changes. For example, if the GPS location is the same after some time, then it means an asset has not moved from its original location. Then, the Arduino IoT Cloud will not record the value, so don't get confused if values don't change on the map. Another benefit of this feature is you will not get duplicate data when you export the content.
>
> The same code will work with the MKR WAN 1310 without any modification. However, in this instance, you need to associate the MKR WAN 1310 device with the Thing instead of the MKR WAN 1300.

In this section, we have explored our code step by step to understand how it works. In the next section, we will set up the The Things Indoor Gateway. If you already have the gateway in your region/area, then you can skip this, but if you don't have any gateway near your location, then you need to set up the gateway; otherwise, your MKR WAN 1300 will not be able to communicate with the Arduino IoT Cloud.

Configuring the The Things Indoor Gateway

In this section, we will set up the The Things Indoor Gateway. It is available in different frequencies but I have a gateway with the EU868 MHz frequency. If you already have the LoRaWAN gateway in your area and want to skip this section, you're good to go, but if you don't have the gateway in your area, then this section is mandatory for MKR WAN 1300 communication. Without the gateway, your module will not communicate with the Arduino IoT Cloud. To set up the gateway, please follow these steps:

1. Open your gateway box, set it up with a power cable, and turn on the gateway. If you are using a brand-new gateway, then it will be in setup mode; otherwise, you can put the gateway into setup mode by pressing the **SETUP** button for a few seconds when the orange and green lights start blinking. This means the gateway has entered setup mode.

2. Select the Wi-Fi network of your the The Things Indoor Gateway, and connect to it. The Wi-Fi password is written on the back of the device. *Figure 6.17* shows the **Setup** page for the The Things Indoor Gateway.

Figure 6.17 – The Things Indoor Gateway setup page

After connecting to the indoor gateway, open up your browser and type http://192.168.4.1. This will open up the **MiniHub Setup** page, as shown in the preceding figure. Click on the plus icon (+) to select the Wi-Fi network that is connected to the internet, and provide its Wi-Fi password. Then, click on the **SAVE & REBOOT** button. It will take some seconds to restart, and eventually, your LoRaWAN indoor gateway will be connected to the internet via your selected Wi-Fi network.

3. Now, it's time to configure the LoRaWAN gateway in the **The Things Stack** portal, as shown in *Figure 6.18*.

Figure 6.18 – LoRaWAN gateway registration – step 1

When you associate the MKR WAN 1300 to the Thing in the Arduino IoT Cloud, you will receive an email from the The Things Stack Cloud that contains the portal URL, along with your username and password details. Log in to the portal, where you will be given a clusters list to add your gateway to a recommended cluster. In the *Associating a device* section, I chose the **Europe 863-870 MHZ (SF9 for RX2 - recommended)** frequency for the MKR WAN 1300, so here, I will choose **Europe 1** for my gateway. This way, my gateway and MKR WAN 1300 development board both sit under the same cluster.

4. After choosing the cluster, you will be redirected to the main page of the portal. From here, we will start adding the gateway, as shown in *Figure 6.19*.

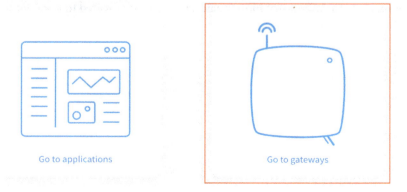

Figure 6.19 – LoRaWAN gateway registration – step 2

On the main page, we have some menus and two big icons, as shown in the preceding figure. From there, click on the **Go to gateways** icon.

5. Then, we will be on the page that shows the complete list of gateways, as well as the option to register a new gateway, as shown in *Figure 6.20*.

Figure 6.20 – LoRaWAN gateway registration – step 3

Click on the blue + **Register gateway** button.

6. This will take us to a new page where we can add a gateway to the the The Things Stack network, as shown in *Figure 6.21*.

Register gateway

Register your gateway to enable data traffic between nearby end devices and the network. Learn more in our guide on Adding Gateways ☑ .

Owner *

Gateway EUI ⓘ

To continue, please confirm the Gateway EUI so we can determine onboarding options

Figure 6.21 – LoRaWAN gateway registration – step 4

Firstly, we need to select the owner from the **Owner** dropdown. Here, you will see two names. One is your personal username, and the other is **arduino-iot-cloud-user**. Just select your personal username, as you are the main person adding the gateway. In the next field, insert the **Gateway EUI** details. The EUI will be written on the back of the gateway. After that, click on the **Confirm** button.

7. Now, we will verify our gateway and select the frequency plan, as shown in *Figure 6.22*.

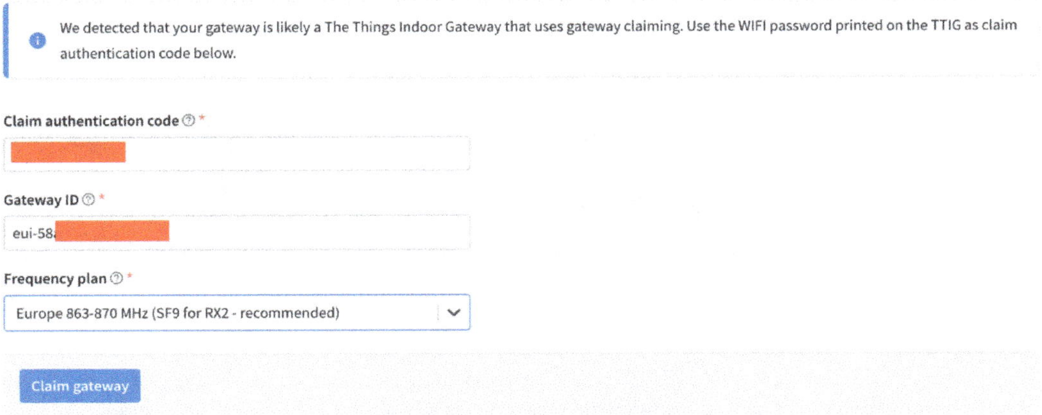

Figure 6.22 – LoRaWAN gateway registration – step 5

You will see the **Claim authentication code** field at the top. Here, we need to provide the gateway with a Wi-Fi password for authentication. You can get the gateway Wi-Fi password from the back of the gateway, from where you previously took it to connect with the device's Wi-Fi network.

Now, we need to select the frequency plan for our gateway. We already selected **Europe 863-870 MHZ (SF9 for RX2 - recommended)** during the MKR WAN 1300 association, so we will select the same frequency from the dropdown. After selecting the frequency, click on the **Claim gateway** button.

8. After successfully registering the gateway, we will see a page like the one in the following figure, which provides you with the gateway connectivity status, as well as **Live data**, **Created at**, **Last updated at**, and lots of other information.

Figure 6.23 – The LoRaWAN gateway successfully registered on The Things Network

In this section, we explored how to set up the The Things Indoor Gateway step by step. In the next section, we will create a dashboard for our Thing on mobile and web to track our assets.

Creating web and mobile dashboards

After uploading the code to the device, it's time to set up a dashboard for web and mobile to visualize data with different widgets. *Figure 6.24* demonstrates the visualization of readings with different widgets.

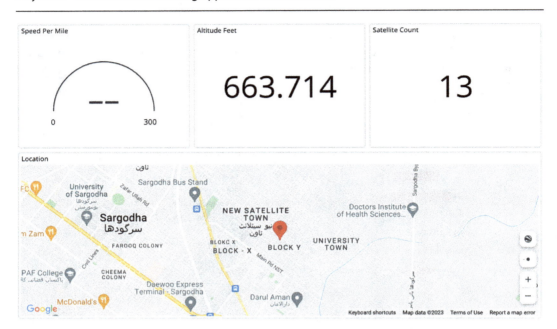

Figure 6.24 – The Thing dashboard

We have four readings from the GPS module to visualize. Here, I have used four widgets: one gauge, two values, and one map. The gauge widget shows **Speed Per Mile**, while the two value widgets have been used to display **Altitude Feet** and **Satellite Count**. The map widget was used to display **Location** based on the latitude and longitude coordinates, which are stored in a cloud-based `location` variable. Currently, the map widget is only capable of displaying the location of the asset device based on coordinates; if you have multiple assets to track, then you need to set up multiple map widgets according to the number of tracking devices.

Well, this is the last section of our chapter. Here, we created a stunning dashboard for GPS tracking that shows **Location** using a map widget on the dashboard, **Speed Per Mile**, and some other parameters.

What next?

We still have a lot of options available to explore, but now it's your turn to use different sensors and development boards to do some more experiments and learn from them. In this chapter, we only used one GPS module, which gave us only four parameters, but there are a lot of GPS modules on the market that provide a wide variety of functionalities, such as working under a roof and accuracy features.

While monitoring the location of assets, some other parameters are very important to monitor in different industries, such as temperature and humidity, which are very important in food and medical products. CO2 and **liquefied petroleum gas (LPG)** gases are very important to monitor during fuel transportation. Try using different sensors with a GPS module to set up different tracking prototypes for different industries.

Summary

In this chapter, we explored how to develop an asset-tracking system using LoRaWAN and a GPS module. We set up the Thing, which included cloud variable creation, device association, the The Things Indoor Gateway, and coding a development board. Then, we created a dashboard to visualize the Thing readings with different types of widgets to display current readings. The most important widget of the chapter is the map widget, which is very interesting and important for plotting the current location of the device.

GPS tracking is a very important topic that helps us to develop a device for our assets, assisting us in asset tracking and monitoring. We can use LoRaWAN for a specific region, as it has a longer range, but that range only operates in a specific area, unlike other wireless technologies. This chapter demonstrated how we can display the location of a device on a dashboard, giving you more confidence to build more asset-tracking solutions.

In the next chapter, *Enabling Communication between Different Devices*, we will explore how the Arduino IoT Cloud makes it easy to send data between devices. Using this method, we will sync IoT nodes with each other for seamless operations.

Part 3:
Exchanging Data
between Nodes
and Cloud Applications

This third part of the book describes how to exchange data between IoT nodes provisioned on the Arduino IoT Cloud and between the Arduino IoT Cloud and external cloud applications.

These functionalities are required in many real cases to build a distributed and reliable network, to implement some interdependent visualization and logic on the IoT application, and to expand the functionalities of the Arduino IoT Cloud with external tools.

This part has the following chapters:

- *Chapter 7, Enabling Communication between Different Devices*
- *Chapter 8, Working with the Arduino IoT Cloud SDK and JavaScript*
- *Chapter 9, Project #4 – Collecting Data from the Soil and Environment for Smart Farming*
- *Chapter 10, Project #5 – Making Your Homes Smarter with a Voice Assistant*

7

Enabling Communication between Different Devices

This chapter is dedicated to **thing-to-thing communication** (TTC), which is a very important concept and requirement in the field of the **Internet of Things** (**IoT**). You can also call it **Device-to-Device** (**D2D**) communication. D2D communication plays a vital role in complex systems where one device's operations are totally dependent on another device. For example, say you want to control your room's AC according to outdoor weather conditions; here, D2D communication plays a vital role by sending the outdoor temperature to the room's AC controller device so it knows whether it needs to cool or heat the room according to the weather outside.

Arduino IoT Cloud provides a cloud variable synchronization feature across multiple things, as well as for dashboards, which helps us to build complex systems easily. This chapter explains the usage of the synchronization feature for the implementation of cloud **graphical user interfaces** (**GUIs**) and D2D communication purposes.

In this chapter, you will learn how to sync a cloud variable across things using the GUI without writing any complex code. This chapter will help you set up communication between things with just a couple of clicks without writing any lengthy code. It will also help you to develop solutions that are totally dependent upon other device's sensor data. You will also learn how to create a single dashboard for multiple things so you can display their readings in one place, which helps the user monitor everything from one display without navigating to other dashboards.

In this chapter, we're going to cover the following main topics:

- What is D2D communication in the IoT cloud?
- The benefits of Arduino IoT Cloud thing-to-thing communication
- Hardware components – sensors and development boards
- Project architecture
- Setting up a Thing

- Implementation of GUIs using synchronized cloud variables

- Limitations of cloud variable/property synchronization

- What next?

Technical requirements

The following are required to complete this chapter's exercise:

- Complete *Chapter 4* of this book

- MKR Wi-Fi 1010

- 1x 5 mm red LED and 1x 5 mm green LED

- A breadboard

- Jumper cables

We will use the **Arduino Web Editor** for coding, which includes a large collection of development boards and sensor libraries, and **Arduino IoT Cloud** for thing and dashboard setup. The chapter code is available in the official book GitHub repository by following this link: `https://github.com/PacktPublishing/Arduino-IoT-Cloud-for-Developers`.

What is D2D communication in the IoT cloud?

D2D communication in the context of IoT and the IoT cloud refers to the ability of IoT devices to directly exchange data or information with each other without relying on a central server or cloud-based service as an intermediary. This form of communication is also known as **Peer-to-Peer** (**P2P**) communication among IoT devices.

Here are some key points to understand about D2D communication in the IoT cloud:

- **Direct communication**: In traditional IoT architectures, devices send data to a cloud platform, where it is processed and potentially shared with other devices. D2D communication allows devices to talk to each other directly, bypassing the cloud when necessary.

- **Low latency**: D2D communication can reduce latency because data doesn't have to travel to a remote server and back. This is crucial in applications where real-time or near-real-time responses are required, such as in industrial automation or connected vehicles.

- **Efficiency**: By enabling devices to communicate directly, it can reduce the load on cloud servers and bandwidth usage, making the IoT system more efficient and cost-effective.

- **Offline operation**: D2D communication can work even when devices are not connected to the internet or the cloud. This can be especially useful in scenarios where intermittent connectivity is common, such as in remote areas or emergency situations.

- **Security**: Implementing direct communication between devices requires robust security measures to protect data and ensure the authenticity of messages. Encryption and authentication mechanisms are essential to prevent unauthorized access.

- **Use cases**: D2D communication can be used in various IoT applications. For example, in a smart home, IoT devices such as thermostats and lights can communicate directly to coordinate actions without needing to send data to a central server. In agriculture, sensors on farm equipment can communicate directly to optimize tasks.

- **Protocols**: Various communication protocols can facilitate D2D communication in IoT, including **Message Queuing Telemetry Transport (MQTT)**, **Constrained Application Protocol (CoAP)**, Bluetooth, and **Zigbee**. The choice of protocol depends on factors such as range, data volume, and power consumption.

- **Challenges**: While D2D communication provides many benefits, it also presents challenges, such as ensuring interoperability between devices from different manufacturers and managing the complexities of decentralized communication.

In summary, D2D communication in IoT cloud environments allows IoT devices to communicate directly with each other, which provides benefits such as reduced latency, improved efficiency, and offline operation. However, it also requires careful planning and security measures to ensure the reliability and integrity of the communication network.

In this section, we explored the benefits and challenges of D2D communication, which is very important in IoT infrastructure and solution development. In the next section, we will explore what type of option Arduino IoT Cloud is providing for TTC.

The benefits of Arduino IoT Cloud thing-to-thing communication

Arduino IoT Cloud is a platform that's designed to simplify the development and management of IoT projects using Arduino boards and other compatible hardware. When it comes to TTC in the context of Arduino IoT Cloud, there are several benefits:

- **Ease of integration**: Arduino IoT Cloud provides a user-friendly interface for connecting and configuring IoT devices, making it easier to establish communication between devices. Users can quickly set up and manage the connections between their Arduino boards and other IoT devices.

- **Remote control**: You can use TTC to control one Arduino device from another. For example, you could use one Arduino device to control a light bulb in another room.

- **Scalability**: Arduino IoT Cloud allows you to scale your IoT projects easily. You can add new devices to your network and configure their communication parameters without extensive programming, making it suitable for both small-scale and large-scale IoT deployments.

- **Reduced latency**: Direct communication between IoT devices within the same network can significantly reduce latency compared to sending data to an external cloud server and back. This is crucial for real-time applications, where low latency is essential.

- **Energy efficiency**: Arduino IoT Cloud allows you to optimize the power consumption of your devices by controlling when and how they communicate with each other. This can extend the battery life of battery-powered IoT devices.

- **Customizable logic**: You can program custom logic for TTC to suit your specific project requirements. This flexibility enables you to implement complex behaviors and automation in your IoT system.

- **Security**: Arduino IoT Cloud provides security features to help protect the communication between your devices, including encryption and authentication mechanisms. This ensures that data exchanged between devices remains secure.

- **Cost efficiency**: By reducing the reliance on external cloud services and minimizing data transfer costs, Arduino IoT Cloud can be a cost-effective solution for IoT projects, especially when dealing with a large number of devices.

- **Compatibility**: Arduino IoT Cloud supports a wide range of Arduino boards and compatible hardware, making it accessible to a broad user base. This compatibility simplifies the process of implementing TTC for Arduino-based IoT projects.

In summary, Arduino IoT Cloud simplifies TTC in IoT projects, providing features such as ease of integration, scalability, reduced latency, energy efficiency, offline operation, customization, security, cost efficiency, and broad hardware compatibility. These features make it a valuable platform for developing and managing IoT systems that rely on direct communication between devices.

In this section, we have discussed the benefits of Arduino IoT Cloud TTC. In the next section, we will explore what hardware components we require to do this chapter's exercise.

Hardware components – sensors and development boards

In this chapter, we are going to explore how to sync cloud variables across multiple Arduino IoT Cloud things. So, here we will use the same thing, including a development board and sensors, that was used in *Chapter 4*. For this chapter's demonstration, we are going to use Arduino MKR Wi-Fi 1010 along with two 5 mm LEDs, a red one and a green one. The complete project is summarized in *Figure 7.1*.

Thing-to-Thing Cloud Variable Sync

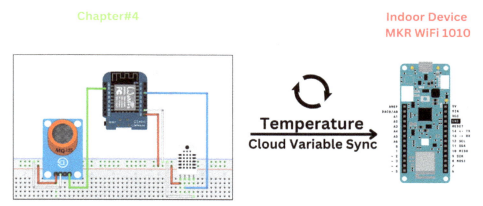

Figure 7.1 – Project architecture

As shown in *Figure 7.1*, we use one WeMos D1 mini development board, which is based on ESP8266, and the whole project is demonstrated in *Chapter 4*. The purpose of using different types of boards in this chapter is to demonstrate how easy it is to sync the cloud variables across different types of development boards. In the next section, we will talk in detail about project architecture.

Project architecture

In this section, we will discuss how cloud variable synchronization works. As shown in *Figure 7.1*, we have taken the project from *Chapter 4*. In that project, we set up a device that monitors outdoor temperature, humidity, and air quality. Now, we want to share the outdoor temperature with our indoor device, which is the MKR Wi-Fi 1010. To make things easier, we just used LEDs with MKR Wi-Fi 1010, which is shown in *Figure 7.2*. Our indoor device will turn on the red LED if the temperature exceeds the specified threshold and turn on the green LED if it comes down below a specified threshold. You can also use relays instead of LEDs to control the heating and cooling system of your room.

We already have one complete thing in Arduino IoT Cloud that is working, but now we need to create another thing for MKR Wi-Fi 1010 named **Indoor MKR Wi-Fi 1010** with a bunch of cloud variables. We will then sync the temperature cloud variable of the Indoor MKR Wi-Fi 1010 thing with the Sense the Environment thing, which was created in *Chapter 4*.

In the preceding sections, we discussed the module and development board in detail. Now, it's time to begin the exercise. In hardware development, before we start working with sensors and development boards, we need to develop design concepts to get a better understanding of how things will connect. There is a lot of software available for designing and developing design concepts for an electronics project, but in this case, we will use **Fritzing**.

In the following subsection, we will talk about the schematics of a project while explaining how to connect pins with a development board.

Schematics design and assembly

The purpose of schematic design is to get a clear understanding of how sensors/LEDs will connect with a development board. This helps engineers to develop a prototype on a breadboard or a **Veroboard**. *Figure 7.2* shows a schematic diagram of how LEDs are connected to the MKR Wi-Fi 1010 development board.

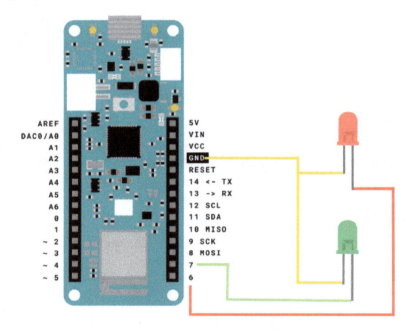

Figure 7.2 – MKR Wi-Fi 1010 and LEDs schematic diagram

In *Figure 7.2*, we have one common ground from MKR Wi-Fi 1010, which is shared with both LEDs using a yellow line. The red LED is connected to MKR Wi-Fi 1010 by using *Pin #6* and the green LED is using *Pin #7* of the MKR Wi-Fi 1010 development board.

In this section, we have discussed how cloud sync works and how we connect the LEDs with MKR Wi-Fi 1010. In the next section, we will set up the Thing for MKR Wi-Fi 1010 as well as device association and network configuration; and, most importantly, we will create the cloud variables and sync them with other things.

Setting up a Thing

After setting up the hardware, it's time to set up a thing in Arduino IoT Cloud. For this project, we need three cloud variables. Later on, we will associate MKR Wi-Fi 1010 with our thing. Next, we will perform the Wi-Fi network configuration. *Figure 7.3* shows a complete overview of the Thing:

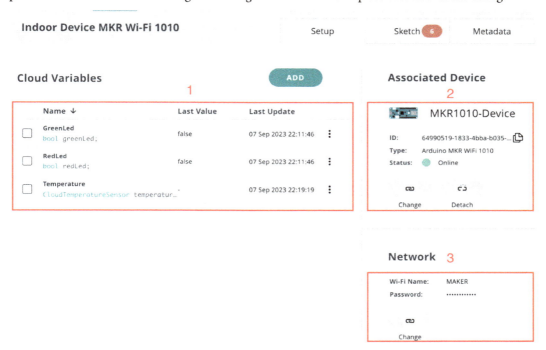

Figure 7.3 – Indoor device MKR Wi-Fi 1010 thing setup

Set up a new thing called `Indoor Device MKR Wi-Fi 1010`. In *Figure 7.3*, the following steps are marked with red boxes. Follow these steps to create variables, associate a device, configure the network, and, finally, write the code:

1. Firstly, we need to set up three cloud variables for the green LED, the red LED, and temperature (which will be synced with another thing cloud variable). A more detailed discussion of cloud variables is in the upcoming section.

2. After that, we need to associate the device with the Thing. In the current project, we are using MKR Wi-Fi 1010. More details are available in the *Associating a device* subsection of this chapter.

3. After attaching the device, we need to make the device network-ready by providing an SSID and a password for the Wi-Fi network. Just click on the **Configure** button (if the network is empty, then you will see the **Configure** button. Otherwise, you will see the **Change** button) and you will see the popup for network settings.

We have discussed the process of setting up a thing, and all these steps will be explained in detail in the proceeding subsections. We will start with the *Cloud variables* subsection, where we will create cloud variables for our thing as well as synchronize them.

Cloud variables

The following table describes all the properties of the cloud variables that we need to configure. For this project, we need three cloud variables, as listed in *Table 7.1*. Next, make sure each variable matches the **Declaration** in the table; otherwise, you need to modify the example code according to your naming.

When we created the cloud variables, we made the permission read-only for all variables except `Temperature` because we need this cloud variable to sync with the `Temperature` cloud variable of the Sense the Environment thing in *Chapter 4*. That's why this variable's permissions are set to **Read & Write**. **Update Policy** is set to **On change** for all variables.

S#	Variable Name	Variable Type	Declaration	Permission	Update Policy
1	GreenLed	Boolean	greenLed	Read Only	On change
2	RedLed	Boolean	redLed	Read Only	On change
3	Temperature	Temperature sensor	Temperature	Read & Write	On change

Table 7.1 – Cloud variables list for things

Use *Table 7.1* to create the `GreenLed` and `RedLed` cloud variables. The creation of the `Temperature` cloud variable will be discussed step by step; we are going to sync this cloud variable with the Thing cloud variable from *Chapter 4*. *Figure 7.4* shows the first step of creating the `Temperature` cloud variable.

Add variable   ✕

Name
Temperature

↻ Sync with other Things ⓘ

Select variable type   ▼

Declaration   ⓘ

Variable Permission ⓘ

⦿ Read & Write   ◯ Read Only

Variable Update Policy ⓘ

⦿ On change   ◯ Periodically

Threshold
0

ADD VARIABLE   CANCEL

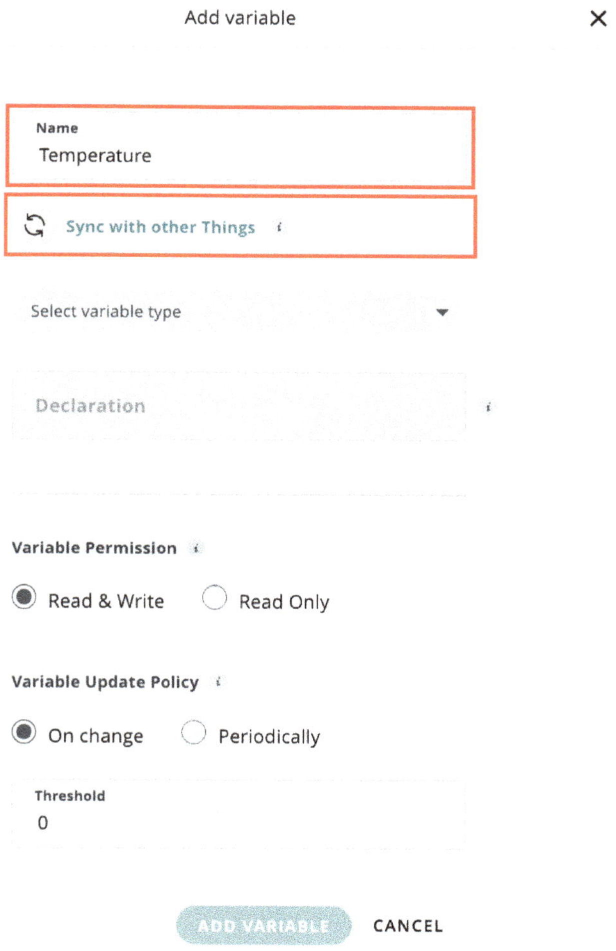

Figure 7.4 – Temperature cloud variable step 1

In this step, we will assign a name to the cloud variable, which is shown in *Figure 7.4*. Next, we will click on **Sync with other Things**. This will open a new popup, which is shown in *Figure 7.5*.

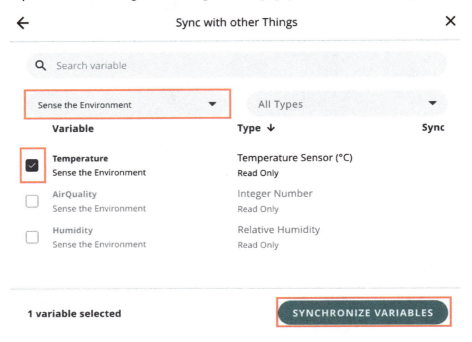

Figure 7.5 – Temperature cloud variable step 2

In this popup, you will find a complete list of cloud variables across all the things that are available in your Arduino IoT Cloud. To prevent complexity and errors, select a specific thing. We selected the **Sense the Environment** thing from the dropdown, which is marked by a red box in *Figure 7.5*. After selecting the Thing from drop down, you will only see the associated cloud variable of that thing in popup. Click on the **Temperature** cloud variable checkbox and then click on the **SYNCHRONIZE VARIABLES** button. *Figure 7.6* shows the final popup, where you will find the final status of the cloud variable sync status.

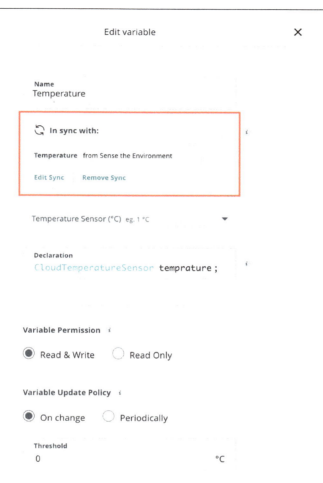

Figure 7.6 – Temperature cloud variable step 3

In *Figure 7.6*, you will see the status of the cloud variable sync status, which is marked by a red box. Remember that for sync variables, you must choose **Read & Write** permission or it will not work properly. Then save the cloud variable, and we are good to go. After going through these steps, you should have an idea of how easy it is to sync cloud variables across multiple things within seconds by just using a simple interface.

Important note

Remember that for sync variables, you must choose the **Read & Write** permission or it will not work properly.

In this section, we discussed the types of cloud variables that are required for this project. We listed three cloud variables of different types and also discussed in detail how to sync the cloud variable from one thing to another thing. Next, we are going to associate the MKR Wi-Fi 1010 with the Thing.

Associating a device

After creating the variables, it's time to add the device and associate it with the Thing:

1. Before adding the device, connect the development board to the computer and open the **Arduino Create Agent** application. *Figure 7.7* shows a popup where we have two options: either select the existing device for association or set up the new device if it is not available in the list:

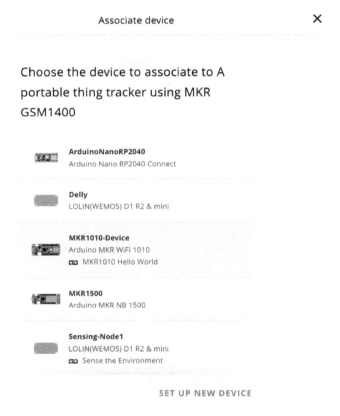

Figure 7.7 – Associate device – select device

In our case, we already have different devices in the portal, but we want to add a new MKR Wi-Fi 1010. Just click on **SET UP NEW DEVICE** to configure a new device in the account.

2. Next, you will see the three options in the popup. The first option is **Arduino board** and the second option is **Third party device**. The third option is **Any Device**, which is for non-compatible devices. It means you can use any type of Arduino device, as well as third-party devices with Arduino IoT Cloud, which supports Python, MicroPython, and JavaScript.

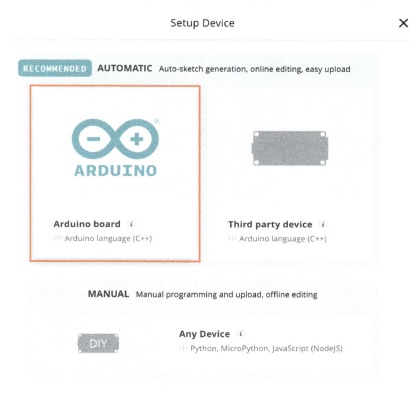

Figure 7.8 – Choosing a development device

3. Select the right option from the popup for your project. For this example, click on **Arduino board** because in this chapter, we are using an MKR Wi-Fi 1010 board. Before adding the device, make sure **Arduino Create Agent** is running on your machine. *Figure 7.9* shows that Arduino IoT Cloud detected the MKR Wi-Fi 1010 device.

Arduino MKR WiFi 1010 found

An Arduino MKR WiFi 1010 has been detected on port /dev/cu.usbmodem101 and ready to be configured.

CONFIGURE

If the detected type of the device you want to configure is not correct, try to reset your board and then refresh

Figure 7.9 – Device found

When the popup displays that it has found the device, just click on the **CONFIGURE** button, which will take you to the next configuration step, where you will provide the name of the device, and later, another popup will perform some configuration on your development board and associate the development board with Arduino IoT Cloud. Once this is done, a successful device association message will be displayed.

4.   When the device is configured successfully, you will see a popup saying congratulations. Just click on the **DONE** button and your device will be associated with your thing.

In this section, we associated the MKR Wi-Fi 1010 device with our thing, and in the upcoming sections, we will talk about the network and code.

Network

After attaching the device to the Thing, we can see that the device is offline. To bring it online, we need to provide Wi-Fi details. The following screenshot shows the network configuration popup, which only consists of two fields:

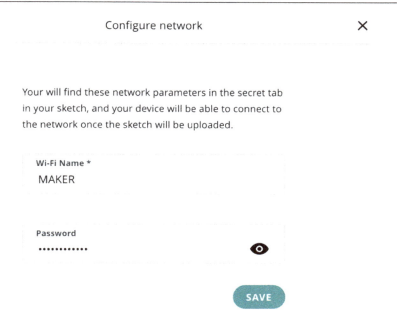

Figure 7.10 – Network configuration

On the Thing page, shown in *Figure 7.10*, on the **Network** tab, click on the **CONFIGURE** button, which will take you to the **Configure network** popup with two fields, **Wi-Fi Name** and **Password**. Type the Wi-Fi SSID and password, and then click on the **SAVE** button.

In this section, we have configured the network for our device, which is MKR Wi-Fi 1010. In the next subsection, we will create the cloud variable.

Coding

This chapter's code is available in the official GitHub repository for the book. Download `Indoor_Device_MKR_Wi-Fi_1010_sep07a.zip` and import it into your Arduino Web Editor.

You can download the code and put it into your thing by navigating to the **Sketch** tab. Here, I will explain the main workflow. First, we have defined two constants for the red and green LED pins called `RLED` and `GLED` in the following snippet and assigned them pin numbers 6 and 7, respectively:

```
#define RLED 6
#define GLED 7
```

Then, we initialize all the required pins and methods in the setup() method. Specifically, we are changing the modes of the pins to output by using the pinMode() method:

```
void setup() {
  pinMode(RLED, OUTPUT);
  pinMode(GLED, OUTPUT);

  // Initialize serial and wait for port to open:
  Serial.begin(9600);
  // This delay gives the chance to wait for a Serial Monitor without
blocking if none is found
  delay(1500);

  // Defined in thingProperties.h
  initProperties();

  // Connect to Arduino IoT Cloud
  ArduinoCloud.begin(ArduinoIoTPreferredConnection);

  setDebugMessageLevel(2);
  ArduinoCloud.printDebugInfo();
}
```

The next important method is onTemperatureChange(). Whenever the value of the Temperature cloud variable changes on the Sense the Environment thing, it will be automatically synced with the Temperature cloud variable of the Indoor Device MKR Wi-Fi 1010 thing. Then, when the value changes, this method will be called:

```
void onTemperatureChange()  {
  // Add your code here to act upon Temperature change
  if(temperature>30)
    {
      //if Temperature is more then 30 then turn on the Red LED and
turn off Green LED
      redLed=true;
      greenLed=false;

    }else{
      //If Temperature is 30 or less then turn on Green LED and turn
off Red LED
      redLed=false;
      greenLed=true;
```

```
    }

    digitalWrite(RLED,redLed);
    digitalWrite(GLED,greenLed);
}
```

In the preceding code snippet, we have defined the manual threshold for `temperature`. If the `temperature` value is greater than 30 degrees Celsius, then assign `redLed` the `true` value and `greenLed` the `false` value; otherwise, assign `redLed` with `false` and `greenLed` with `true`. At the end of the method, we are controlling the LEDs according to the `redLed` and `greenLed` values. Here, you can use relays instead of LEDs to control the heating and cooling system of your indoor environment.

Upload the code to the device and you will see that either the red or green LED will be turned on, depending on the temperature. After successfully uploading data to the cloud, it's time to set up a beautiful dashboard for web and mobile for the users. This time, we will create a dashboard that will show the values of two things' cloud variables.

> **Important note**
>
> If you used different *naming* in the variable declaration, then update the code according to your naming scheme. But it's better if you first follow all the steps according to the book and later change the cloud variable names and modify your code.

Never try to use the `delay()` method, which will create a block for the `ArduinoCloud.update()` method. Also, don't put the code in an end-of-loop method as it will create a delay in the pulse sensor readings.

In this section, we have explored the code, and we are using the `Temperature` cloud variable, which is synced with the `Temperature` cloud variable in *Chapter 4*, and we are turning on and off the LEDs according to temperature value. In the next section, we will explore how to display the cloud variables of multiple things on a single dashboard.

Implementation of GUI using synchronized cloud variables

After uploading the code to the device, it's time to set up a dashboard for web and mobile to visualize the data with different widgets. *Figure 7.11* demonstrates the visualization of readings with different widgets.

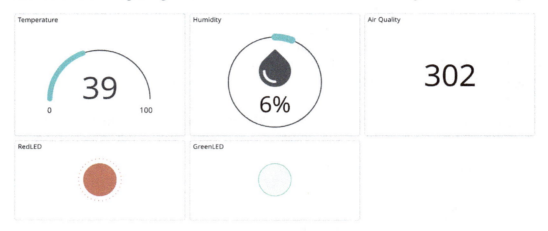

Figure 7.11 – Thing dashboard

We have three different readings, **Temperature, Humidity**, and **Air Quality**, from the Sense the Environment thing and two readings, **RedLED** and **GreenLED**, from the Indoor Device MKR Wi-Fi 1010 thing. As the temperature from the Indoor Device MKR Wi-Fi 1010 thing is synced with the Sense the Environment thing, we are only displaying one temperature value here. For every reading, we use different widget controls to demonstrate how they all work. But for the LED status, we used an LED widget control.

The main thing to note about this dashboard is that we are using values from two different things but the same dashboard to visualize the values. This example demonstrates that we can display the values from multiple things on a single dashboard. *Figure 7.12* shows how easy it is to link any cloud variable to a widget control.

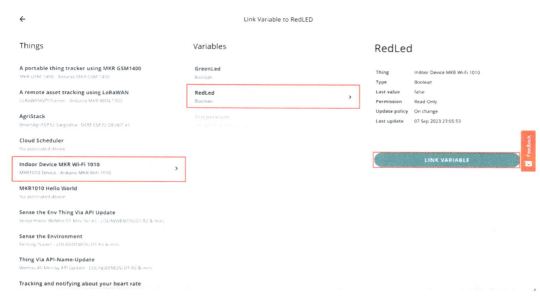

Figure 7.12 – Linking a cloud variable to a widget control

Figure 7.12 shows how to link the **RedLed** cloud variable from **Indoor Device MKR Wi-Fi 1010** to a widget. But, as you can see, you can select any cloud variable from any thing and link it with the widget control. So, we can see how the Arduino IoT Cloud dashboard allows us to create a single dashboard for multiple things easily.

In this section, we discussed how to set up a dashboard that contains widgets attached to multiple things. In the next section, we will discuss limits and cloud variable synchronization in detail.

Limitations of cloud variable/property synchronization

Arduino IoT Cloud offers a platform for IoT device management and communication, including TTC between devices. While it provides valuable features for connecting and managing IoT devices, there are some drawbacks to consider:

- **Latency**: TTC can introduce latency, which is the delay between when a change is made to a variable on one device and when it is reflected on the other device. This can be a problem for applications that require very low latency, such as controlling a robot in real time.

- **Offline device challenges**: Devices that are temporarily offline may miss important messages or updates from other devices. Ensuring that devices can catch up on missed communications when they reconnect to the network can be complex to implement.

- **Dependency on internet connectivity**: Arduino IoT Cloud relies on an internet connection for communication between devices. If the internet connection goes down, the devices may lose their ability to communicate with each other.

- **Limited functionality**: TTC is not as flexible as some other IoT communication protocols. For example, you cannot use TTC to send arbitrary data between devices.

- **Dependency on the cloud**: TTC relies on Arduino IoT Cloud to function. This means that if the cloud is unavailable, your TTC connections will not work.

When considering Arduino IoT Cloud for TTC in your IoT project, it's essential to weigh these drawbacks against the platform's benefits and assess whether it aligns with your specific project requirements and constraints. Additionally, exploring alternative IoT platforms and communication solutions may be necessary to ensure the best fit for your needs.

In this section, we have discussed in detail the limitations of Arduino IoT Cloud TTC. In the next section, we will explore how you can use TTC for different types of cloud variables.

What next?

We still have a lot of options available to explore, but now it's your turn to use different sensors and development boards to do some more experiments and learn from them. In this chapter, we have only used one `Temperature` cloud variable synced between two things, but you can try using this feature to sync multiple cloud variables with multiple things. Next, create a dashboard for multiple things to visualize all the values in one place. We configured simple LEDs to turn on and off according to the temperature, but you can also use relays to control the heating/cooling system of your indoor home/office and warehouse environment, or you can create an alarm in case of a temperature increase using this TTC feature.

Summary

In this chapter, we explored D2D communication and the benefits of Arduino IoT Cloud for thing-to-thing communication. We discussed how to develop a solution for thing-to-thing communication. We also explored how easy it is to sync the cloud variable with other things just using a GUI. We set up a dashboard, where we linked the widget controls with multiple thing cloud variables. Finally, we discussed the limits of Arduino IoT Cloud thing-to-thing communication in detail.

In the next chapter, we are going to explore how to use the Arduino IoT Cloud SDK. This chapter is for developers who are eager to learn how to use Arduino IoT Cloud programmatically and develop custom solutions using Arduino IoT Cloud or integrate Arduino IoT Cloud with third-party platforms.

8

Working with the Arduino IoT Cloud SDK and JavaScript

Every platform provides **APIs** and **SDKs** to make their product compatible with other platforms, and these endpoints are used by developers to create new functionalities to solve real-world issues. Likewise, the **Arduino IoT Cloud** comes with its own built-in features and functionalities, but there are also three different ways to extend the Arduino IoT Cloud platform's functionality or make it compatible with other tools and services: namely, **REST APIs**, **SDKs**, and **webhooks**.

In this chapter, we will talk about APIs and SDKs and how they work. Specifically, we will use the **Node.js SDK** to illustrate different coding exercises. This chapter will cover **Create, Read, Update, and Delete** (**CRUD**) operations for devices, Things, properties (aka variables), and dashboards. Beyond that, we will explore some other features such as how to set/get values of properties.

By the end of this chapter, you will understand how to interact with the Arduino IoT Cloud platform via an API or the Node.js SDK to create custom dashboards, interface with the data using other tools/apps, and use the SDK for bulk device creation and management.

In this chapter, we're going to cover the following main topics:

- Demystifying the Arduino IoT Cloud SDK – functionality and operation
- Securing access – unveiling API keys and authentication
- Step-by-step – installing the Arduino Node.js SDK client
- Initial exploration – test drive using Postman
- Diverse platform compatibility – SDKs for various environments
- Interacting with devices – hands-on with the Node.js SDK
- Engaging with Things – Node.js SDK implementation guide

- Exploring properties – Node.js SDK interaction techniques
- Crafting dashboards – unleashing potential via the Node.js SDK
- Fine-tuning with the Node.js SDK – property value management

Technical requirements

There are no specific hardware requirements for this chapter as we are focusing on the SDK and will work through different coding exercises to perform different operations on the Arduino IoT Cloud platform using the Node.js SDK. To follow along with the coding and testing exercises, the following software is required:

- Node.js
- The **Node.js Arduino IoT Cloud module** installed
- The **VSCode editor**
- **Postman**
- An Arduino IoT Cloud account

Postman will be used for **cURL testing** and authentication, which will help other developers when doing request and response testing. For SDK coding, we will use Node.js and the VSCode editor. The code for this chapter is available from the book's official GitHub repository at `https://github.com/PacktPublishing/Arduino-IoT-Cloud-for-Developers`.

Demystifying the Arduino IoT Cloud SDK – functionality and operation

The Arduino IoT Cloud offers a range of features, but there are inevitably situations where developers need to integrate their tools/systems/apps with the Arduino IoT Cloud for improved operations management and control. To cater to these requirements, the Arduino IoT Cloud provides different techniques and tools that can be used by developers and organizations to extend the product's functionality and provide solutions for real-world issues.

As shown in the following diagram, the Arduino IoT Cloud provides three main interfaces to developers to help meet their requirements. First is webhooks, which we used in the previous chapter to send the data from an Arduino IoT Cloud Thing to a custom **endpoint** or any well-known platform including **Zapier** or **IFTTT** for further integration. Following webhooks, we have the REST API and SDK, both of which are very handy features for developers to mold the system according to their requirements.

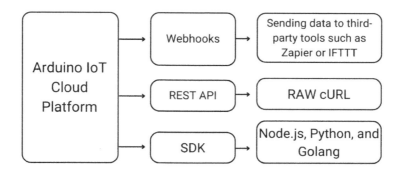

Figure 8.1 – Arduino IoT Cloud interface

In this chapter, we are going to focus specifically on the Node.js SDK. However, it's important first to give a proper overview of the Arduino IoT Cloud functionalities that can help developers make better decisions during integration with other platforms. The Arduino team has created REST API endpoints for different operations such as *create*, *delete*, *list*, *update*, and so on, and placed them into different categories according to the main terms used on the Arduino IoT Cloud platform, such as Thing, device, property, and so on. The developer can send a request to these endpoints via different methods such as PUT, DELETE, or GET with different parameters, and in return they will get their desired response from the Arduino IoT Cloud in JSON format that they can then use for further product development.

REST APIs are like raw material for developers in that they need to process them by writing code in their preferred language and sending and receiving requests and responses using the **cURL library**. On the other hand, the Arduino team offers an SDK, which is basically a programming wrapper for REST API endpoints. This allows us to save time as we get access to a lot of methods and sample code to accomplish our tasks just using library methods. At the time of writing, the Arduino team has developed SDKs for three programming platforms: Node.js, **Python**, and **GoLang**.

In this chapter, we will work with the Node.js SDK specifically to create different scripts to perform CRUD operations on Things, devices, properties, and dashboards. We will also develop scripts that allow you to *fetch/set* the latest values of Thing properties and much more. Overall, this chapter will be fun for developers, as we are going to explore different techniques and methods that will help us extend IoT operations from small scale to enterprise level.

In this section, we have discussed what type of features the Arduino IoT Cloud API/SDKs provide to developers. In the next section, we will talk about API keys for authentication.

Securing access – unveiling API keys and authentication

Before heading into the meat of the chapter, we first need to talk about the authentication mechanism of the platform. The Arduino IoT Cloud uses a **token authentication mechanism** to validate API requests. This involves the SDK/tool sending the **Client ID** and **Client Secret** to `https://api2.arduino.cc/iot/v1/clients/token` to get a token that is used later to authenticate for `requests/responses`.

Before we get started with the SDK installation and testing with Postman, we need to set up the API in the Arduino Cloud that will provide us the Client ID and Secret. In older versions of the interface, the API options are under the **Integrations** tab, but have now moved to the Arduino Cloud, which is available at `https://cloud.arduino.cc/home/`.

After visiting the Integration page click on **API Keys** and you will be taken to the API page. Click on **CREATE API KEY**. A popup will appear; provide a name for the API and click on the **CONTINUE** button. The wizard that appears will take a few seconds to generate the keys and then a new popup will appear displaying the keys:

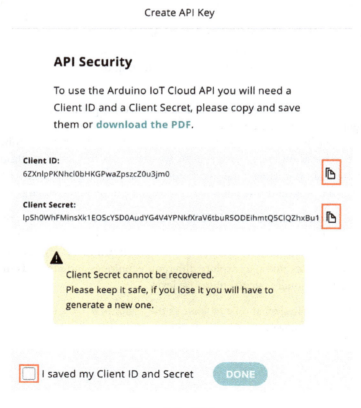

Figure 8.2 – API keys

Copy the **Client ID** and **Client Secret** values by clicking on the copy icons – never try to copy by manual selection as the **Client Secret** is very long, so clicking the copy icon is the best option. Save the both Client ID and Client Secret in a secure location and then click the checkbox confirming that you have saved your keys. Lastly, click on **DONE** and you will see your API key in the panel – it's now ready for use.

> **Important note**
>
> A single API key is used to give access to all the Things and their variables. Having access to all infrastructure with just one API key is handy, instead of having to create separate API keys for each Thing, but you must take care of your key! This is a big security risk, as if you were to lose the key, a hacker could gain access to your whole account.

In this section, we have set up and created API authentication keys consisting of a Client ID and Client Secret. This section is most important, as without these keys we can't use any APIs. In the next section, we are going to try our first API call using the Postman tool.

Initial exploration – test drive using Postman

Before diving into the SDK, we will try the **naked REST APIs** endpoints using Postman, a tool that helps developers to debug *requests/responses* for other programming-language platforms not available as SDKs. Postman is a well-known tool among backend developers and is used to expose API requests/responses without any coding. Postman also helps developers to analyze responses via a **graphical user interface** (**GUI**).

Download Postman from `https://www.postman.com/`, choosing the correct version for your operating system. Before getting to work with Postman, firstly create a new workspace for the Arduino IoT Cloud to put all the requests in a separate group. To do this, click on **Workspaces** and then **Create Workspace**:

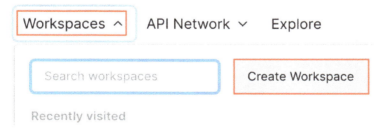

Figure 8.3 – Postman workspace

A new window will be opened: provide a workspace name and description and set the visibility policy according to your requirements. After creating the new workspace, navigate to **File > New…** and select **HTTP Request**. Before sending any request to the Arduino IoT Cloud, an authentication token is mandatory. Refer to the following screenshot: click on the **Authorization** tab and select **OAuth 2.0** from the **Type** dropdown. Scroll down the **Authorization** page to find the **Configure New Token** section and click on the **Configuration Options** tab under this section.

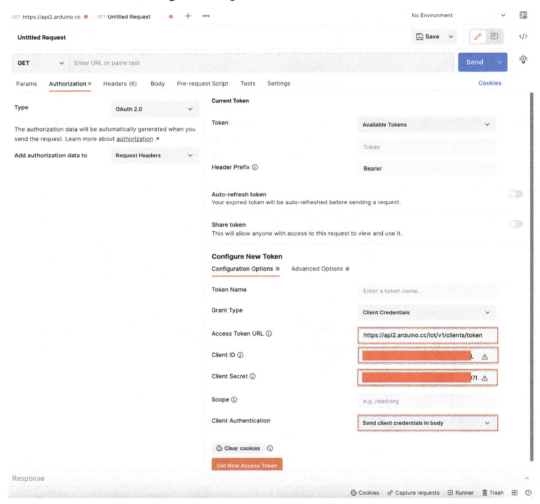

Figure 8.4 – Authorization Configuration Options

We need to provide three things under **Configuration Options**. Firstly, add the `https://api2.arduino.cc/iot/v1/clients/token` URL to the **Access Token URL** field, then insert the values that we generated previously in the Arduino IoT Cloud API into the **Client ID** and **Client Secret** fields. Lastly, select **Send client credentials in body** from the **Client Authentication** dropdown. Now click on the **Advanced Options** tab, where we will set the API audience who will receive the requests.

Figure 8.5 shows the **Advanced Options** where we need to provide the Arduino IoT Cloud authentication URL with which we can authenticate and authorize requests.

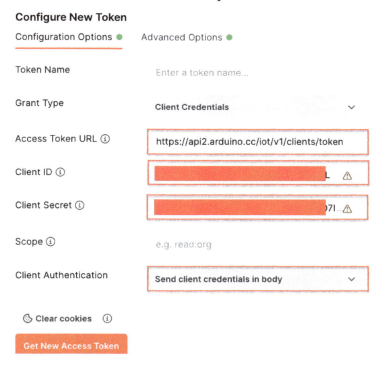

Figure 8.5 – Authorization Advanced Options

Add the `https://api2.arduino.cc/iot` URL into the **Audience** field. After setting up the configuration, click the **Get new Access Token** button. It will return either an error or a success message. If there is any error, then please repeat all the steps one by one, ensuring the configuration is as described previously. If you are successful, then click on **Proceed** and you will get your token for authentication.

After getting the authentication token, it's time to do some experiments. The Arduino team has documented all the endpoints with cURL and the Node.js SDK samples in different categories, available at `https://www.arduino.cc/reference/en/iot/api/`. So here, we want to see the list of cloud variables/properties for specific Thing. Open up the preceding API documentation URL, find the **API Methods – PropertiesV2** category, and click on **propertiesV2List**. Here you will see cURL and the Node.js SDK. Copy the URL from the cURL sample, which is `https://api2.arduino.cc/iot/v2/things/{id}/properties?show_deleted=`. Here we need to replace `{id}` in the URL with the specific Thing ID (*Figure 8.6*). The Thing ID is available under the Thing's **Metadata** tab in the Arduino IoT Cloud. Add `true` to the end of the URL just after `show_deleted`. After adding all the required data to the URL, it will look something like `https://api2.arduino.cc/iot/v2/things/8aee742e-4492-423d-9f19-79fec856b917/properties?show_deleted=true`.

Click on **Send** and you will receive a response from the Arduino IoT Cloud in JSON format containing all the cloud variables properties of the Thing, including the property ID, name, type, last value of the cloud variable, and so on:

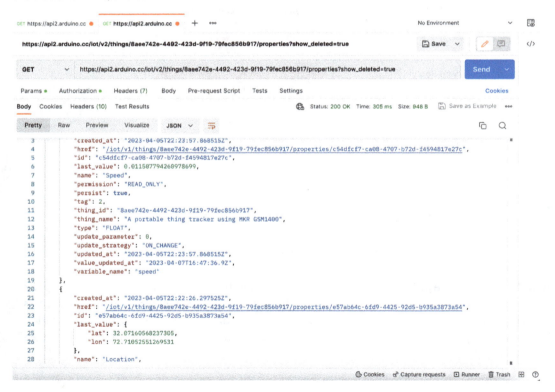

Figure 8.6 – Postman request response

The preceding screenshot shows the response in Postman. You can convert the response into plain text as well as other formats including **XHTML**, **HTML**, and so on, but Postman has excellent visualization functionality for **JSON** data responses. This way, developers can easily understand and tweak the nature of the response and prepare the scripts according to their data structure. It also helps developers to choose specific content from the response more quickly, reducing the time and effort required.

In this section, we used Postman to generate our first request to the Arduino IoT Cloud. We began by configuring the API authentication keys in Postman and then requested the list of cloud variables/properties of Thing. The Arduino IoT Cloud successfully returned the response with all the required data in JSON format. In the following section, we will examine the SDKs available for different platforms.

Diverse platform compatibility – SDKs for various environments

After testing *request/response* with Postman, it's time to explore the SDKs available for the Arduino IoT Cloud. Earlier I mentioned the Arduino Team has developed official SDKs for three programming platforms, Node.js, Python, and GoLang.

Node.js is a very well-known language among backend developers and is used by both web and mobile developers. So, if you are planning to create a mobile or web app for Arduino IoT Cloud automation with custom visualizations, then Node.js is the best language, providing a wide variety of libraries for HTTP services.

On the other hand, Python is also a very well-known and rapidly growing language among web, IoT, and **AI/ML** developers. Python seems to be trending toward AI/ML, and IoT is very close as a field to AI/ML. If you are planning to develop a solution focused on AI/ML, such as **predictive maintenance**, **time series analysis**, or predictions then the Python SDK is the best choice to interact with the Arduino IoT Cloud.

GoLang is the last platform for which an SDK was developed by the Arduino team. GoLang was developed by Google and follows the **C-type syntax**. The GoLang platform is good for operating system and network/API service development. If you are planning to maintain a high-performance system with the Arduino IoT Cloud or planning to run concurrent operations, then GoLang is the better choice.

We discussed here the three different platforms and their specialized domains of application. Node.js is best for **Web APIs**, Python is good for machine learning, and GoLang is an awesome choice for high-performance systems. You can either choose one SDK platform for your development or consume all the SDKs depending on your project requirements.

In the next section, we will start our journey with the Node.js SDK, beginning by installing the official Arduino IoT Cloud Node.js SDK on our machines.

Step-by-step – installing the Arduino Node.js SDK client

From this point, we are going to use the Node.js SDK for our exercises and experiments. Before moving to the practical exercises, we need to first install the Arduino IoT Cloud package for Node.js. Download and install Node.js from `https://nodejs.org/`. After the installation of Node.js is complete, open up the Windows/Mac/Linux **Terminal** and navigate to the directory where you will set up your coding workspaces using **VSCode**:

```
npm install @arduino/arduino-iot-client
npm i request-promise
```

Type the two preceding commands in the **Terminal** and wait for the installation to complete. After a successful installation, open up VSCode and add the folder (where you have installed the Node.js Arduino IoT Cloud SDK) to the workspace where you installed the Arduino IoT Cloud and request-promise modules.

Navigate to the book's official GitHub repository and download all the code from this chapter's folder. Copy the files into the VSCode `Workspace` folder and extract the downloaded `.zip` file. Navigate to the `start` folder and open up the `main.js` file in VSCode.

Here we have two methods, `getToken()` and `ThingProperty()`. The `getToken()` method will be same across the coding exercises and will be used to fetch the authentication token from the Arduino IoT Cloud on the basis of the Client ID and Client Secret:

```
client_id: '-----Paste ClientID Here-----',          client_secret:
'-----Paste Client Secret Here-----',
```

The preceding code snippet is from the `getToken()` method. Insert your Client ID in the `client_id` variable and your Client Secret in the `client_secret` variable. Likewise, insert your `Thing ID` and `Property ID` in the following code snippet under the `ThingProperty()` method. You can get your Thing ID by navigating to Thing and then the **Metadata** tab in the Arduino IoT Cloud. The property ID can be found by clicking on the cloud variable on the Thing page in the Arduino IoT Cloud:

```
var id = "Paste -----Thing ID-----"; // {String} The id of the thing
var pid = "-----Property ID-----"; // {String} The id of the property
```

Open the **integrated terminal** in VSCode and type the following command; Node will execute the `main.js` code and provide a response in the console:

```
node main.js
```

You will receive the following response in the console if everything works fine:

```
API called successfully. Last Value of Property=259
```

If you receive a `401 error`, it means your Client ID and/or Client Secret are not correct. If a `404 error` is returned, it means you are not using the proper method to fetch property data. If you get a `500 error`, it means the server is down or there is a network blockage for the Arduino IoT Cloud from your ISP.

In the *First try with Postman* section, we discussed how to use Arduino IoT Cloud endpoints with Postman for request/response tasks as well as installing the Node.js module for the cloud and testing it with an example where we fetched the last value of the Thing cloud variable/property.

Building on this foundation, we are going to start a new journey where we will play around with the Arduino IoT Cloud. Firstly, we will start with devices. In the next section, we will create, update, delete, list, and view a specific device. Later in the chapter, we will do the same for Things, properties (also known as cloud variables), and dashboards.

Interacting with devices – hands-on with the Node.js SDK

In this section, we are going to get hands-on and practical with devices. We will perform CRUD operations on a device as well as listing all the devices and showing all the parameters of specific devices. Open up VSCode and navigate to this chapter's example code. Then click on the `device` folder: here you can find all the code related to device operations.

Creating a device

Firstly, we will start with device creation. The documentation on device creation can be found at `https://www.arduino.cc/reference/en/iot/api/#api-DevicesV2-devicesV2Create`. Open `create-device.js` under the `device` folder in VSCode.

There are two methods in the code: one is `getToken()`, which is the same method as in all our coding exercises and helps us to fetch the authentication token for requests. The second method is `CreateDevice()`, which is responsible for device creation. Consulting the documentation, we can see we need to initiate the `api` variable with the `AiotApi.DevicesV2Api()` object, which is related to devices:

```
var DeviceProperties = {
        'name':'Sense Home XIAO Series',
        'connection_type':'wifi',
        'fqbn':'esp32:esp32:XIAO_ESP32C3',
        'type':'login_and_secretkey_wifi'
    };
    var options = {
    };
    api.devicesV2Create(DeviceProperties, options).then(function(data)
{
        console.log('Device Created successfully. Returned data: ' +
util.inspect(data));
```

```
}, function(error) {
  console.error(error);
});
```

`api.devicesV2Create` is the method responsible for device creation and takes two parameters as input. `DeviceProperties` covers things such as the device name, type, and **Fully Qualified Board Name (FQBN)**. Let's start with name first – this could be anything you fancy, but avoid using special characters. Next, we need to provide a choice for `connection_type`, such as Wi-Fi, GSM, LoRa WAN, and so on. All available types are provided by the documentation. For `fqbn`, we need to provide the details of the development board. Taking the **XIAO ESP32C3** board as an example, it belongs to the **ESP32** family, so its FQBN would be `esp32:esp32:XIAO_ESP32C3`.

`options` are optional, so I left it blank, but you can provide the `X-Organization` value according to your requirements. Both arrays are passed to the `api.devicesV2Create` method, which will return the response. The `util.inspect` method is used to display the JSON response on the console with proper formatting. Type the following command to execute the `create-device.js` program:

```
node create-device.js
```

After successful execution of the script, it will print a response like the following:

```
Device Created successfully. Returned data: ArduinoDevicev2 {
  href: '/iot/v2/devices/e88b84a7-7ad7-4c2b-b79c-ab426e47dc67',
  id: 'e88b84a7-7ad7-4c2b-b79c-ab426e47dc67',
  label: 'Login and secret key for wifi device',
  name: 'Sense Home XIAO Series',
  serial: '',
  type: 'login_and_secretkey_wifi',
  user_id: 'f067c1e9-3ff8-4b9f-a9b4-f8c5c1d0ceb4',
  fqbn: 'esp32:esp32:XIAO_ESP32C3'
}
```

In the response, you will get your device ID, which will be used later in the chapter for Thing creation when we associate the device with the Thing. The remaining properties are the same as already covered in the code.

> **Important note**
>
> If you are unable to get the correct FQBN, then add the device manually from the dashboard, finding and clicking on the device from the dropdown. This will give you the `fqbn`, `type`, and `connection_type` details. You can use these details later in your Node.js script for automated creation of devices.

Updating a device

In this section, we are going to explore how we can update a device using the device ID. Let's suppose we mistakenly added a device with the wrong FQBN and name. We will update both properties using the device ID. The documentation on updating devices is available at `https://www.arduino.cc/reference/en/iot/api/#api-DevicesV2-devicesV2Update`. Open the `update-device.js` file under the `device` folder in VSCode:

```
var api = new AiotApi.DevicesV2Api();
var DeviceID="e88b84a7-7ad7-4c2b-b79c-ab426e47dc67";
var DeviceProperties = {
        'name':'Sense Home WeMos D1 Mini Series',
        'connection_type':'wifi',
        'fqbn':'esp8266:esp8266:d1_mini',
        'type':'login_and_secretkey_wifi'
};
var options = {
};
api.devicesV2Update(DeviceID,DeviceProperties, options).
then(function(data) {
        console.log('Device Created successfully. Returned data: ' +
util.inspect(data));
    }, function(error) {
        console.error(error);
});
```

The preceding code is almost the same as the `create-device` code. Here we have one extra variable, `DeviceID`, with which we will update the specific device. The rest of the code has the same device properties and options as previously. Now, fill in the correct `fqbn` and `name` values in the `DeviceProperties` variable. Lastly, we call the `api.devicesV2Update()` method. Execute the following command in the Terminal:

node update-device.js

After successful execution of the script, it will print a response like the following:

```
Device Updated successfully. Returned data: ArduinoDevicev2 {
  href: '/iot/v2/devices/e88b84a7-7ad7-4c2b-b79c-ab426e47dc67',
  id: 'e88b84a7-7ad7-4c2b-b79c-ab426e47dc67',
  label: 'Login and secret key for wifi device',
  name: 'Sense Home WeMos D1 Mini Series',
  serial: '',
  type: 'login_and_secretkey_wifi',
  user_id: 'f067c1e9-3ff8-4b9f-a9b4-f8c5c1d0ceb4',
```

```
created_at: 2023-04-17T00:47:40.700Z,
fqbn: 'esp8266:esp8266:d1_mini'
}
```

As we can see, after our update, the response sends back the new content. We provided a change of name and FQBN and it is reflected successfully in the response.

Deleting a device

In this section, we are going to explore how we can delete a device using the device ID. The documentation for deleting devices is available at https://www.arduino.cc/reference/en/iot/api/#api-DevicesV2-devicesV2Delete.

Open the delete-device.js file under the device folder in VSCode:

```
var api = new AiotApi.DevicesV2Api();
var DeviceID='e88b84a7-7ad7-4c2b-b79c-ab426e47dc67';
var options = {
};
api.devicesV2Delete(DeviceID, options).then(function(data) {
   console.log('Device Deleted successfully. Returned data: ' +
data);
}, function(error) {
   console.error(error);
});
```

The preceding code snippet is taken from the DeleteDevice() method. In this method, we need to supply DeviceID and options variables as parameters. DeviceID is mandatory for the deletion process while the options variable is not. Execute the following command in the Terminal:

```
node delete-device.js
```

After successful execution of the script, it will print a response to the console reporting that the device has been deleted successfully.

Listing devices

In this section, we will list all the devices. Note that there is a difference between listing devices and showing devices: *listing* devices means displaying all the devices with their properties, while *showing* a device only returns a specific device's properties based on the device ID.

The documentation on listing devices is available at `https://www.arduino.cc/reference/en/iot/api/#api-DevicesV2-devicesV2List`. Open the `list-device.js` file under the `device` folder in VSCode. The following code snippet is taken from the `ListDevice()` method from the `list-device.js` file:

```
var api = new AiotApi.DevicesV2Api()
var opts = {
    'acrossUserIds': true // {Boolean} If true, returns all the
devices
  };
  api.devicesV2List(opts).then(function(data) {
    for(var i=0;i<data.length;i++){
        console.log("Device ID:"+data[i].id+" Device
Name:"+data[i].name);
    }
}, function(error) {
  console.error(error);
});
```

Here we need to provide the criteria that will be used to filter out the devices and return the desired response. In the current code, we only mention one parameter, `'acrossUserIds'`, which is `true` to fetch all types of devices. But if required, you can filter the devices listed on the basis of `tags`, `serial`, and `X-Organization`. Execute the following command in the Terminal:

`node list-device.js`

After successful execution of the script, it will print a response in JSON format with the device properties, which will clog up the **Terminal** console with extensive output. I modified the code to only display the device ID and device name on the console:

```
Device ID:04d8025a-4270-4d7e-aa04-45db87a594f5
Device Name:SmartAgriESP32-Sargodha
Device ID:5aae7e1f-940b-4426-80ac-1c953839cdb2
Device Name:MKR-GSM-1400
Device ID:fae0951d-3169-4d6a-a8e5-739c347eafc1
Device Name:MKR1500
Device ID:ca711f68-6de9-497a-ac45-780219ad2bb8
Device Name:Wemos d1 Mini by API Update
Device ID:64990519-1833-4bba-b035-978fcaa33466
Device Name:MKR1010-Device
Device ID:62e8600b-2733-4f24-9654-1fac549af27f
Device Name:XIAO-ESP32C3-Pulse-Sensor
Device ID:e88b84a7-7ad7-4c2b-b79c-ab426e47dc67
Device Name:Sense Home WeMos D1 Mini Series
Device ID:b9f3ff20-ebf1-4260-ad16-f434466458ac
```

```
Device Name:ArduinoNanoRP2040
Device ID:047d8316-dcdb-4bf5-af30-4319bb5a5eb0
Device Name:Delly
```

In the preceding code, we are displaying two parameters on the console, but you can choose whichever and however many you want by specifying their names in the for loop. Using this, we can send the output in JSON format to a web/mobile client, which will display the information either in a list box or in menus.

Showing a device

This is the second-to-last subsection of the *Interacting with devices – hands-on with the Node.js SDK* section. Here we will fetch all the properties of a specific device by providing the device ID. The documentation on showing devices is available at https://www.arduino.cc/reference/en/iot/api/#api-DevicesV2-devicesV2Show.

Open the show-device.js file under the device folder in VSCode. The following code snippet is taken from the ShowDevice() method from the show-device.js file:

```
var api = new AiotApi.DevicesV2Api()
    var id = '62e8600b-2733-4f24-9654-1fac549af27f'; // {String} The
id of the device
    var opts = {
    };
    api.devicesV2Show(id, opts).then(function(data) {
       console.log('Device Created successfully. Returned data: ' +
util.inspect(data));
    }, function(error) {
      console.error(error);
    });
```

The devicesV2Show() method only takes two parameters: the first one is the DeviceID and the second is options, which includes X-Organization. DeviceID is mandatory to fetch a proper response while the opts variable is optional, hence we pass this variable as empty. Execute the following command in the Terminal:

```
node show-device.js
```

After successful execution of the script, it will print the response in JSON format with the device properties as well as the details of any cloud variables if any associated variable is present:

```
ArduinoDevicev2 {
   id: '62e8600b-2733-4f24-9654-1fac549af27f',
   label: 'Login and secret key for wifi device',
   name: 'XIAO-ESP32C3-Pulse-Sensor',
```

```
.................................. . .
thing: ArduinoThing {
  id: '6b6cd076-5859-4a6d-9b4e-18879893c6cb',
  name: 'Tracking and notifying Your Heart Rate',
.................................. . .
  webhook_active: true,
  webhook_uri: 'https://hooks.zapier.com/hooks/
catch/14930971/324me7k/'
  }
}
```

The preceding code is the edited response of the script regarding device properties, which includes all the details of the given device such as last activity, the cloud variables count, the Thing ID associated with the device, webhook details (if active), sketch ID, and so on.

In this sub-section, we have explored how to get all the devices list from the Arduino IoT Cloud using the Node.js SDK. Next, let's explore how to get the list of cloud variables/properties associated with the device.

Device properties/variables

Here, we will fetch all the cloud variable details for a specific device by providing the device ID. The documentation on showing devices is available at https://www.arduino.cc/reference/en/iot/api/#api-DevicesV2-devicesV2GetProperties.

To begin, open the properties-device.js file under the device folder in VSCode. The following code snippet is taken from the ListPropDevice() method in the properties-device.js file:

```
var api = new AiotApi.DevicesV2Api()
var id = '62e8600b-2733-4f24-9654-1fac549af27f'; // {String} The
id of the device
var opts = {
};
api.devicesV2GetProperties(id, opts).then(function(data) {
  console.log('Device Properties.' + util.inspect(data));
}, function(error) {
  console.error(error);
});
```

The devicesV2GetProperties() method only takes two parameters: the first one is device ID and the second is options, which includes showDeleted and X-Organization. DeviceID is mandatory to fetch a proper response, while the opts variable is optional, so we leave this variable empty when we pass it. Execute the following command in the Terminal:

```
node properties-device.js
```

After successful execution of the script, it will print a response in JSON format containing the cloud variable details associated with that particular device ID:

```
Properties: [
  ArduinoProperty {
    href: '/iot/v1/things/6b6cd076-5859-4a6d-9b4e-18879893c6cb/
properties/b357a513-ad2b-4e1f-a76b-6dac078e36d5',
    id: 'b357a513-ad2b-4e1f-a76b-6dac078e36d5',
    name: 'BPM',
    permission: 'READ_ONLY',
    thing_id: '6b6cd076-5859-4a6d-9b4e-18879893c6cb',
    type: 'HEART_BEATS',
    update_strategy: 'ON_CHANGE',
    created_at: 2023-03-31T16:41:33.103Z,
    persist: true,
    tag: 1,
    thing_name: 'Tracking and notifying Your Heart Rate',
    update_parameter: 0,
    updated_at: 2023-03-31T17:05:19.564Z,
    variable_name: 'bPM'
  }
]
```

The preceding response is the edited response of the script regarding the device cloud variables, including variable_name, type, permission, thing_id, update_strategy, and so on. We have now seen how to get the cloud variable details, and in the next section we'll move on to cover Things.

Engaging with Things – Node.js SDK implementation guide

The Thing is one of the most important elements in the Arduino IoT Cloud, and acts as defined container holding all of its ingredients such as cloud variables, the device, a sketch for the device, and the device's network configuration. In this section, we will try a range of different coding exercises to get a feel for Thing CRUD operations.

Creating a Thing

Firstly, we will start with Thing creation. The relevant documentation can be found at `https://www.arduino.cc/reference/en/iot/api/#api-ThingsV2-thingsV2Createe`. Open the `create-thing.js` file under the `thing` folder in VSCode.

There are two methods in this code: one is `getToken()`, which is the same method as in all our coding exercises and helps us to fetch an authentication token for our requests. The second method is `CreateThing()`, which is responsible for Thing creation. Referring to the documentation, we can see that we need to initiate the `api` variable with the `AiotApi.ThingsV2Api()` object, which relates to the Arduino IoT Cloud Thing. This object is responsible for performing operations on the Thing:

```
var api = new AiotApi.ThingsV2Api()
var thingCreate = {'name':' Sense the Env Thing Via API'}; //
{ThingCreate}
var opts = {
  'force': true // {Boolean} If true, detach device from the other
thing, and attach to this thing
};
api.thingsV2Create(thingCreate, opts).then(function(data) {
  console.log('Thing Created successfully. Returned data: ' +
util.inspect(data));
}, function(error) {
  console.error(error);
});
```

`api.thingsV2Create` is the method responsible for Thing creation and takes two parameters as input: `name` and `opts`. Firstly, we start with `name`, which can be anything you like, but make sure to avoid special characters. For now, we provide just the Thing name in the variable, but in the upcoming update section, we will additionally pass the time zone and device ID parameters.

`opts` here is optional, hence I left it blank, but you can provide the `X-Organization` value if required. Both variables are passed to the `api.thingsV2Create` method, which will return the response. The `util.inspect` method is used to display the JSON response on the console with proper formatting. Type the following command to execute the `create-device.js` script:

```
node create-thing.js
```

After successful execution of the script, it will print a response as follows:

```
Thing Created successfully. Returned data: ArduinoThing {
  href: '/iot/v1/things/d99e244d-f245-4e27-9ead-717e52ac5a96',
  id: 'd99e244d-f245-4e27-9ead-717e52ac5a96',
  name: 'Sense the Env Thing Via API',
  timezone: 'America/New_York',
  user_id: 'f067c1e9-3ff8-4b9f-a9b4-f8c5c1d0ceb4',
```

```
created_at: 2023-04-18T16:46:35.767Z,
properties_count: 0,
updated_at: 2023-04-18T16:46:35.767Z,
webhook_active: false
}
```

In the response, you will get your Thing ID, which will be used shortly in the following Thing update/delete operations – so make sure to paste this Thing ID into a Notepad file or something similar. Also returned are the time zone, properties count, and webhook status.

Updating a Thing

In this section, we are going to explore how to update a Thing using the Thing ID. Let's suppose we mistakenly added the Thing without setting the proper time zone and without device association. In this scenario, we have the option to update the Thing with new properties. The documentation covering updating devices is available at https://www.arduino.cc/reference/en/iot/api/#api-ThingsV2-thingsV2Update. Open the update-thing.js file under the device folder in VSCode:

```
var api = new AiotApi.ThingsV2Api()
var id = 'd99e244d-f245-4e27-9ead-717e52ac5a96'; // {String} The
id of the thing
var thingUpdate = {
    'name':'Sense the Env Thing Via API Update',
    'timezone':'Asia/Karachi',
    'device_id':'e88b84a7-7ad7-4c2b-b79c-ab426e47dc67'
};
var opts = {
    'force': true // {Boolean} If true, detach device from the other
thing, and attach to this thing
};
api.thingsV2Update(id,thingUpdate, opts).then(function(data) {
    console.log('Thing Updated successfully. Returned data: ' +
util.inspect(data));
}, function(error) {
    console.error(error);
});
```

The preceding code is similar to the create-thing code. Here we have one extra variable, id, which will help us to update the specific Thing. We also have the timezone, device_id, and name in the thingupdate variable. Lastly, we call the api.thingsV2Update() method. Execute the following command in the Terminal:

```
node update-thing.js
```

After successful execution of the script, it will print a response like the following:

```
Thing Updated successfully. Returned data: ArduinoThing {
  href: '/iot/v1/things/d99e244d-f245-4e27-9ead-717e52ac5a96',
  id: 'd99e244d-f245-4e27-9ead-717e52ac5a96',
  name: 'Sense the Env Thing Via API Update',
  timezone: 'Asia/Karachi',
  user_id: 'f067c1e9-3ff8-4b9f-a9b4-f8c5c1d0ceb4',
  created_at: 2023-04-18T16:46:35.767Z,
  device_id: 'e88b84a7-7ad7-4c2b-b79c-ab426e47dc67',
  properties_count: 0,
  updated_at: 2023-04-18T16:46:35.767Z,
  webhook_active: false
}
```

After our update, the response will return the new content. We provided new values for name and device_id, along with the correct time zone. Everything is updated successfully and reflected in the response.

Creating a Thing sketch

With Thing creation out of the way, we now need to create a sketch for the Thing. The relevant documentation can be found at https://www.arduino.cc/reference/en/iot/api/#api-ThingsV2-thingsV2CreateSketch. Open the create-sketch-thing.js file under the thing folder in VSCode.

There are two methods in the code: one is getToken(), which is the same method as used in all our coding exercises and fetches the authentication token for our requests. The second method is CreateSketch(), which handles creating the sketch for our specific Thing:

```
    var api = new AiotApi.ThingsV2Api()
    var id = 'd99e244d-f245-4e27-9ead-717e52ac5a96'; // {String} The
id of the thing
    var thingSketch = {'sketch_version':'v1'}; // {ThingSketch}
    var opts = {
    };
    api.thingsV2CreateSketch(id, thingSketch, opts).
then(function(data) {
        console.log('Thing Sketch Created successfully. Returned data: '
+ util.inspect(data));
    }, function(error) {
        console.error(error);
    });
```

`api.thingsV2CreateSketch` is the method responsible for Thing sketch creation and takes three parameters as input. The Thing ID is the first parameter; the second is the sketch version. `opts` is optional, so I left it blank, but you can provide the `X-Organization` value according to your requirements. All variables are passed to the `api.thingsV2CreateSketch` method, which will return the response. The `util.inspect` method is used to display the JSON response on the console with proper formatting. Type the following command to execute the `create-device.js` script:

```
node create-sketch-thing.js
```

After successful execution of the script, it will print the following response:

```
Thing Sketch Created successfully. Returned data: ArduinoThing {
   href: '/iot/v1/things/d99e244d-f245-4e27-9ead-717e52ac5a96',
   id: 'd99e244d-f245-4e27-9ead-717e52ac5a96',
   name: 'Sense the Env Thing Via API Update',
   timezone: 'Asia/Karachi',
   user_id: 'f067c1e9-3ff8-4b9f-a9b4-f8c5c1d0ceb4',
   created_at: 2023-04-18T16:46:35.767Z,
   device_id: 'e88b84a7-7ad7-4c2b-b79c-ab426e47dc67',
   properties_count: 0,
   sketch_id: '93297fc6-835d-46b3-89bc-1c6738a8ec7b',
   updated_at: 2023-04-18T17:10:34.779Z,
   webhook_active: false
}
```

In the response, you will see your Thing ID along with some other properties indicating that the sketch for the given Thing has been created successfully. You can also verify the sketch by navigating to the given Thing on the Arduino IoT Cloud.

> **Important note**
> Before sketch creation, it's important to associate a device with the Thing.

In this section, we created the Sketch for our Thing as the Arduino IoT Cloud will not do this by default. As a result, it's mandatory to create a Sketch after creating a Thing in the Arduino IoT Cloud. Next we are going to explore how we can delete a Thing using the Arduino IoT Cloud API.

Deleting a Thing

In this section, we are going to explore how we can delete a Thing using the Thing ID. The documentation covering Thing deletion is available at `https://www.arduino.cc/reference/en/iot/api/#api-ThingsV2-thingsV2Delete`. Open the `delete-thing.js` file under the `thing` folder in VSCode:

```
var api = new AiotApi.ThingsV2Api()
var id = 'ac9fc5fd-a946-406e-983d-715dcc2571b6'; // {String} The
id of the thing
var opts = {
  'force': true // {Boolean} If true, detach device from the other
thing, and attach to this thing
};
api.thingsV2Delete(id, opts).then(function(data) {
  console.log('Thing Deleted successfully. Returned data: ' +
data);
}, function(error) {
  console.error(error);
});
```

The preceding code snippet is taken from the `DeleteThing()` method. In the `DeleteThing()` method, we need to supply the `id` (Thing ID) and `opts` variables as parameters. `id` (Thing ID) is mandatory for the deletion process, while the `opts` variable is not. Execute the following command in the Terminal:

```
node delete-thing.js
```

After successful execution of the script, it will print a response on the console indicating that the device was deleted successfully.

Listing Things

In this section, we will list all the Things. Note that there is a difference between *listing* Things and *showing* a Thing: listing Things will display all the Things with their properties, while showing a Thing only shows the specific Thing properties related to a given Thing ID.

The relevant documentation on listing Things is available at `https://www.arduino.cc/reference/en/iot/api/#api-ThingsV2-thingsV2List`. Open the `list-thing.js` file under the `thing` folder in VSCode. The following code snippet is taken from the `ListThing()` method:

```
var api = new AiotApi.ThingsV2Api()
var opts = {
    'acrossUserIds': false
};
```

```
api.thingsV2List(opts).then(function(data) {
    for(var i=0;i<data.length;i++){
        console.log("Thing ID:"+data[i].id+" Thing Name:"+data[i].
name);
    }
}, function(error) {
    console.error(error);
});
```

Here we need to provide criteria that will be used to filter out the Things and return the response. In the current code, we have provided only one parameter, 'acrossUserIds', which is true and so will fetch all types of Things. But you can also filter Things on the basis of tags, IDs, X-Organization, and so on. Execute the following command in the Terminal:

node list-thing.js

After successful execution of the script, it will print the response in JSON format with the Thing properties, which will fill the console with an extensive output. I modified the code to only display the Thing ID and Thing name on the console:

```
Thing ID:6b6cd076-5859-4a6d-9b4e-18879893c6cb Thing Name:Tracking and
notifying Your Heart Rate
Thing ID:6e3d308c-dfb2-49ad-aa61-998227f214ab Thing Name:Thing Via
API-Name-Update
Thing ID:85b04a9c-e335-4842-bf4b-c13f726e0522 Thing Name:AgriStack
Thing ID:8aee742e-4492-423d-9f19-79fec856b917 Thing Name:A portable
thing tracker using MKR GSM1400
Thing ID:bf8e11ea-1a78-4f95-b6a0-c6d50b868402 Thing Name:MKR1010 Hello
World
Thing ID:d99e244d-f245-4e27-9ead-717e52ac5a96 Thing Name:Sense the Env
Thing Via API Update
```

As can be seen in the preceding output, I am only displaying two parameters on the console but you can choose whichever parameters you would like to be displayed by specifying their names in the for loop. This way we can send the output in JSON format to a web/mobile client where the information will be displayed in either a list box or in menus.

Showing a Thing

This is the last subsection of the *Engaging with things – Node.js SDK implementation guide* section. Here we will fetch all the properties regarding a specific Thing by providing the Thing ID. The documentation covering showing Things is available at `https://www.arduino.cc/reference/en/iot/api/#api-ThingsV2-thingsV2Show`. Open the `show-thing.js` file under the `thing` folder in VSCode. The following code snippet is taken from the `ShowThing()` method:

```
var api = new AiotApi.ThingsV2Api()
var thingid='6b6cd076-5859-4a6d-9b4e-18879893c6cb';
var opts = {
};
api.thingsV2Show(thingid, opts).then(function(data) {
    console.log('API called successfully. Returned data: ' +util.
inspect(data));
    }, function(error) {
        console.error(error);
    });
```

The `thingsV2Show()` method only takes two parameters: the first one is the `thingid` and the second is `opts`, which include `X-Organization`. `thingid` is mandatory to fetch a proper response, while the `opts` variable is not compulsory, hence I passed this variable empty. Execute the following command in the Terminal:

```
node show-thing.js
```

After successful execution of the script, it will print the response in JSON format containing the device properties as well as the details of cloud variables, if any associated variable is present:

```
API called successfully. Returned data: ArduinoThing {
  name: 'Tracking and notifying Your Heart Rate',
  timezone: 'Asia/Karachi',

  .................................. . .
  device_fqbn: 'esp32:esp32:XIAO_ESP32C3',
  device_id: '62e8600b-2733-4f24-9654-1fac549af27f',
  device_name: 'XIAO-ESP32C3-Pulse-Sensor',
  device_type: 'login_and_secretkey_wifi',
  properties: [
    ArduinoProperty {
      id: 'b357a513-ad2b-4e1f-a76b-6dac078e36d5',
      name: 'BPM',
      permission: 'READ_ONLY',
      thing_id: '6b6cd076-5859-4a6d-9b4e-18879893c6cb',
      type: 'HEART_BEATS',
      update_strategy: 'ON_CHANGE',
```

```
        created_at: 2023-03-31T16:41:33.103Z,
        last_value: 50,
        ....................................... . .
        variable_name: 'bPM'
      }
    ],
    properties_count: 1,
    sketch_id: 'f490fec5-b62a-41f9-9ff7-2b5c3f2ed7d1',
    updated_at: 2023-04-01T16:42:47.152Z,
    webhook_active: true,
    webhook_uri: 'https://hooks.zapier.com/hooks/
catch/14930971/324me7k/'
  }
```

The preceding code snippet shows an edited section from the output response regarding the Thing properties, which includes all the details of the Thing, the device properties, cloud variables such as last value, webhook details (if active), the sketch ID, and so on.

In this section, we explored how we can get the complete details of a specific Arduino IoT Cloud Thing using the Thing ID in JSON format. Next, we will start playing with cloud variables/properties.

Exploring properties – Node.js SDK interaction techniques

Properties, also called **cloud variables**, are one of the most important ingredients for Things in the Arduino IoT Cloud, responsible for storage of sensor data from the device to the cloud or vice versa. In this section, we will explore how to create, update, delete, and list cloud variables using the Node.js SDK.

Creating a property

Firstly, we will start with property creation. The property creation documentation can be found at https://www.arduino.cc/reference/en/iot/api/#api-PropertiesV2-propertiesV2Create. Open the create-property.js file under the properties folder in VSCode.

There are two methods in the code: one is getToken(), which is the same method used in all our coding exercises to fetch the authentication token for our requests. The second method is CreateProperty(), which handles cloud variable creation. Consulting the documentation, we can see that we need to initiate the api variable with AiotApi, the PropertiesV2Api() object, which is related to properties:

```
    var api = new AiotApi.PropertiesV2Api()
    var thing_id="d99e244d-f245-4e27-9ead-717e52ac5a96";
    var property = {
        'name':'Temperature',
```

```
        'variable_name':'temperature',
        'permission':"READ_ONLY",
        'persist':true,
        'type':'TEMPERATURE_C',
        'update_strategy':'ON_CHANGE'
    };
    api.propertiesV2Create(thing_id, property).then(function(data) {
        console.log('Property Created successfully. Returned data: '
+util.inspect(data));
    }, function(error) {
        console.error(error);
    });
```

`api.propertiesV2Create` is the method responsible for property creation and takes two parameters as input. One is the Thing ID and the other variable contains mandatory details regarding the cloud variable. The Thing ID is simple and easily fetchable from the Thing metadata, but cloud variables have a variety of different parameters including `type`, `permission`, and `update_strategy`, available on the official documentation page (the URL was provided at the start of this section). Both variables are passed to the `api.devicesV2Create` method, which returns the response. The `util.inspect` method is used to display the JSON response with proper formatting on the console. Type the following command to execute the `create-device.js` script:

`node create-property.js`

After successful execution of the script, it will print the following response:

```
Property Created successfully. Returned data: ArduinoProperty {
    href: '/iot/v1/things/d99e244d-f245-4e27-9ead-717e52ac5a96/
properties/c4dc8f92-b62f-44df-9455-74cdd08041bc',
    id: 'c4dc8f92-b62f-44df-9455-74cdd08041bc',
    name: 'Temperature',
    permission: 'READ_ONLY',
    thing_id: 'd99e244d-f245-4e27-9ead-717e52ac5a96',
    type: 'TEMPERATURE_C',
    update_strategy: 'ON_CHANGE',
    created_at: 2023-04-18T23:49:46.610Z,
    persist: true,
    tag: 1,
    updated_at: 2023-04-18T23:49:46.610Z,
    variable_name: 'temperature'
}
```

In the response, you will get your cloud variable ID, creation date, and update date, along with other details already mentioned during our cloud variable creation exercise.

Updating a property

In this section, we are going to explore how we can update a cloud variable using the cloud variable ID. Suppose we mistakenly added a cloud variable with the wrong data type and some other parameters – in the event of this scenario, we have the option to update it. The documentation covering updating properties is available at `https://www.arduino.cc/reference/en/iot/api/#api-PropertiesV2-propertiesV2Update`. Open the `update-property.js` file under the `property` folder in VSCode:

```javascript
var api = new AiotApi.PropertiesV2Api()
var thing_id="d99e244d-f245-4e27-9ead-717e52ac5a96";
var property_id="c4dc8f92-b62f-44df-9455-74cdd08041bc"
var property = {
    'name':'OutdoorTemperature',
    'variable_name':'outdoorTemperature',
    'permission':"READ_ONLY",
    'persist':true,
    'type':'TEMPERATURE_F',
    'update_strategy':'ON_CHANGE'

};
api.propertiesV2Update(thing_id,property_id, property).
then(function(data) {
    console.log('Property Updated successfully. Returned data: '
+util.inspect(data));
    }, function(error) {
    console.error(error);
    });
```

The preceding code is very similar to the `create-property` code. Here we have one extra variable, `property_id`, used to update the given property. Besides that, we have the same cloud variable properties with their updated content. Lastly, we call the `api.propertiesV2Update()` method. Execute the following command in the Terminal:

```
node update-property.js
```

After successful execution of the script, it will print a response something like the following:

```
Property Updated successfully. Returned data: ArduinoProperty {
  href: '/iot/v1/things/d99e244d-f245-4e27-9ead-717e52ac5a96/
properties/c4dc8f92-b62f-44df-9455-74cdd08041bc',
  id: 'c4dc8f92-b62f-44df-9455-74cdd08041bc',
  name: 'OutdoorTemperature',
  permission: 'READ_ONLY',
  thing_id: 'd99e244d-f245-4e27-9ead-717e52ac5a96',
```

```
    type: 'TEMPERATURE_F',
    update_strategy: 'ON_CHANGE',
    created_at: 2023-04-18T23:49:46.610Z,
    persist: true,
    updated_at: 2023-04-18T23:58:07.496Z,
    variable_name: 'outdoorTemperature'
}
```

After the update, the response will return the new content. We provided updated information for the name, type, and variable name and this is reflected successfully in the response.

Deleting a property

In this section, we are going to explore how to delete a property using the Thing ID and property ID. The documentation covering deleting a property is available at https://www.arduino.cc/reference/en/iot/api/#api-PropertiesV2-propertiesV2Delete. Open the delete-property.js file under the property folder in VSCode:

```
var api = new AiotApi.PropertiesV2Api()
var thing_id="d99e244d-f245-4e27-9ead-717e52ac5a96";
var property_id="c4dc8f92-b62f-44df-9455-74cdd08041bc";
var options = {
    'force':true
};
api.propertiesV2Delete(thing_id,property_id, options).
then(function(data) {
    console.log('Property Deleted successfully. Returned data: '
+data);
}, function(error) {
    console.error(error);
});
```

The preceding code snippet is taken from the DeleteProperty() method from delete-property.js file. In the DeleteProperty() method we need to supply the thing_ID, property_id, and options variables as parameters. thing_id and property_id are both mandatory for the deletion process while the options variable is optional. Execute the following command in the Terminal:

```
node delete-property.js
```

After successful execution of the script, it will print a response on the console reading that the property has been deleted successfully.

Listing properties

In this section, we will list all the properties for a given Thing using the Thing ID. As previously outlined with devices and Things, there is a difference between *listing* properties and *showing* a property. Listing properties means displaying all the cloud variables of a Thing, while showing a property only shows the specific cloud variable properties related to the given Thing ID and property ID.

The documentation on listing properties is available at https://www.arduino.cc/reference/en/iot/api/#api-PropertiesV2-propertiesV2List. Open the list-property.js file under the property folder in VSCode. The following code snippet is taken from the ListProperty() method:

```
var api = new AiotApi.PropertiesV2Api()
var thing_id="6b6cd076-5859-4a6d-9b4e-18879893c6cb";
var options = {
    'showDeleted':true
};
api.propertiesV2List(thing_id, options).then(function(data) {
    console.log('Property Updated successfully. Returned data: '
+util.inspect(data));
    }, function(error) {
      console.error(error);
    });
```

Here we only need to provide the Thing ID and options to get a complete list of cloud variables associated with the Thing. Execute the following command in the Terminal:

```
node list-property.js
```

After successful execution of the script, it will print the response in JSON format with the cloud variable's properties. I chose a Thing that only has a single cloud variable:

```
Returned data: [
  ArduinoProperty {
    href: '/iot/v1/things/6b6cd076-5859-4a6d-9b4e-18879893c6cb/
properties/b357a513-ad2b-4e1f-a76b-6dac078e36d5',
    id: 'b357a513-ad2b-4e1f-a76b-6dac078e36d5',
    name: 'BPM',
    permission: 'READ_ONLY',
    thing_id: '6b6cd076-5859-4a6d-9b4e-18879893c6cb',
    type: 'HEART_BEATS',
    update_strategy: 'ON_CHANGE',
    created_at: 2023-03-31T16:41:33.103Z,
    last_value: 50,
    persist: true,
```

```
    tag: 1,
    thing_name: 'Tracking and notifying Your Heart Rate',
    update_parameter: 0,
    updated_at: 2023-03-31T17:05:19.564Z,
    value_updated_at: 2023-04-01T16:43:12.293Z,
    variable_name: 'bPM'
  }
]
```

The preceding response contains all the values related to the cloud variable, such as last value, updated time, and so on. If you want to fetch the last value of a cloud variable then this method could be used in your application to do so.

Next, we have another API endpoint related to showing the properties of a single cloud variable. The code is available in the `property` folder, and the execution of the code along with checking out how it works is left to you as an exercise.

In this section, we discussed in depth how to get the complete details of a cloud variable/property in JSON format using the Arduino IoT Cloud API, which provides lot of data including `last_value` and `value_update_at`. In the next section, we will start working with dashboards and learn how to perform operations on them using the Node.js SDK.

Crafting dashboards – unleashing potential via the Node.js SDK

Dashboards are the most important ingredient in the Arduino IoT Cloud pertaining to **data visualization**. In the SDK, we have dashboard-specific methods to perform CRUD operations on dashboards, as well as other operations such as sharing, requesting access, and so on, but here we will only focus on the CRUD operations.

Creating a dashboard

Let's start first with dashboard creation. The relevant documentation can be found at `https://www.arduino.cc/reference/en/iot/api/#api-DashboardsV2-dashboardsV2Create`. Open the `create-dashboard.js` file under the `dashboard` folder in VSCode.

There are two methods in this code: one is `getToken()`, which is the same method as in all our coding exercises to fetch the authentication token for our requests. The second method is `CreateDashboard()`, which is responsible for dashboard creation. Referring to the documentation, we can see we need to initiate the `api` variable with the `AiotApi.DashboardV2Api()` object, which is used to perform operations on dashboard objects:

```
var api = new AiotApi.DashboardsV2Api();
    var dashboardprop = {
```

```
        'name':'Dashboard Created via API'
    };
    var opts = { };
    api.dashboardsV2Create(dashboardprop,opts).then(function(data) {
        console.log('Dashboard Created successfully. Returned data: '
+ util.inspect(data));
        }, function(error) {
        console.error(error);
    });
```

`api.dashboardsV2Create` is the method responsible for dashboard creation and takes two parameters as input: the first is the dashboard properties and the second variable is `opts`, which is not mandatory, hence I leave it empty. Both variables are passed to the `api.dashboardsV2Create` method, which returns the response. The `util.inspect` method is used to display the JSON response on the console with proper formatting. Type the following command to execute the `create-dashboard.js` script:

```
node create-dashboard.js
```

After successful execution of the script, it will print a response like the following:

```
Dashboard Created successfully. Returned data: ArduinoDashboardv2 {
  id: '5b872702-059c-4895-a677-808981f31588',
  name: 'Dashboard Created via API',
  updated_at: 2023-04-19T17:31:39.487Z,
  created_by: ArduinoDashboardowner {
    user_id: 'f067c1e9-3ff8-4b9f-a9b4-f8c5c1d0ceb4',
    username: 'mafzalattari'
  }
}
```

In the response you will get your dashboard ID, creation date, update date, and other things we already covered during dashboard creation.

Updating a dashboard

In this section, we are going to explore how to update a dashboard using the dashboard ID. There is an option to add widgets to a dashboard via an API but it will make the code significantly more complex due to the JSON data involved. For this reason, we will just update the dashboard name instead of adding widgets. The documentation for updating properties is available at `https://www.arduino.cc/reference/en/iot/api/#api-DashboardsV2-dashboardsV2Update`. Open the `update-dashboard.js` file under the `dashboard` folder in VSCode:

```
    var api = new AiotApi.DashboardsV2Api()
        var dashboard_id="5b872702-059c-4895-a677-808981f31588";
```

```
    var dashboardprop = {
        'name':'Dashboard Created via API Update'
    };
    var opts = {
    };
    api.dashboardsV2Update(dashboard_id,dashboardprop, opts).
then(function(data) {
        console.log('Dashboard Updated successfully.'+ util.
inspect(data));
    }, function(error) {
        console.error(error);
    });
```

The preceding code is almost the same as the `create-dashboard` code. Here we have one extra variable, `dashboard_id`, used to update the specific dashboard. Besides that, we have the same dashboard properties with their updated content. Lastly, we call the `api.dashboardsV2Update()` method. Execute the following command in the Terminal:

node update-dashboard.js

After successful execution of the script, it will print a response like the following:

```
Dashboard Updated successfully.ArduinoDashboardv2 {
   id: '5b872702-059c-4895-a677-808981f31588',
   name: 'Dashboard Created via API Update',
   updated_at: 2023-04-19T17:39:28.378Z,
   created_by: ArduinoDashboardowner {
     user_id: 'f067c1e9-3ff8-4b9f-a9b4-f8c5c1d0ceb4',
     username: 'mafzalattari'
   }
}
```

After our update, the response will return the new content, reflecting the updated data for the name that we provided.

Deleting a dashboard

In this section, we are going to explore how to delete a dashboard using the dashboard ID. The relevant documentation on deleting dashboards is available at https://www.arduino.cc/reference/en/iot/api/#api-DashboardsV2-dashboardsV2Delete. Open the `delete-dashboard.js` file under the `dashboard` folder in VSCode:

```
    var api = new AiotApi.DashboardsV2Api()
    var dashboard_id="3681cdbe-ecb2-4237-a834-e3423c6bd8e3";
    var opts = {
```

```
  };
  api.dashboardsV2Delete(dashboard_id, opts).then(function(data) {
    console.log('Dashboard Deleted successfully.');
  }, function(error) {
    console.error(error);
  });
```

The preceding code snippet is taken from the DeleteDashboard() method from delete-dashboard.js file. In the DeleteDashboard() method we need to supply the dashboard_id and opts variables as parameters. dashboard_id is mandatory for the deletion process, while the opts variable is optional. Execute the following command in the Terminal:

```
node delete-dashboard.js
```

After successful execution of the script, it will print the response on the console indicating that the dashboard was deleted successfully.

Listing dashboards

In this section, we will list all the dashboards with complete details and widgets. The difference between listing dashboards and showing a dashboard is that listing dashboards will display all the dashboards available in the Arduino IoT Cloud, while showing a dashboard only shows the specific dashboard properties and widgets related to the given dashboard ID.

The documentation for listing dashboards is available at https://www.arduino.cc/reference/en/iot/api/#api-DashboardsV2-dashboardsV2List. Open list-dashboard.js under the dashboard folder in VSCode. The following code snippet is taken from the ListDashboard() method:

```
var api = new AiotApi.DashboardsV2Api()
var opts = { };
api.dashboardsV2List().then(function(data) {
  console.log(util.inspect(data));
}, function(error) {
  console.error(error);
});
```

Execute the following command in the Terminal:

```
node list-dashboard.js
```

After successful execution of the script, it will print the response in JSON format containing the dashboard properties and widgets:

```
[
  ArduinoDashboardv2 {
    id: '36287c03-5034-4a64-b40a-102740c998c6',
    name: 'SmartAgri-Sargodha',
    updated_at: 2023-03-05T11:00:18.395Z,
    created_by: ArduinoDashboardowner {
      user_id: 'f067c1e9-3ff8-4b9f-a9b4-f8c5c1d0ceb4',
      username: 'mafzalattari'
    },
    widgets: [
    ]
  },
  ArduinoDashboardv2 {
    id: '28ea7839-7a81-460e-a871-368d45d82cee',
    name: 'Tracking and notifying Your Heart Rate Dashboard',
    updated_at: 2023-04-19T16:41:36.604Z,
    created_by: ArduinoDashboardowner {
      user_id: 'f067c1e9-3ff8-4b9f-a9b4-f8c5c1d0ceb4',
      username: 'mafzalattari'
    },
    widgets: [ [ArduinoWidgetv2], [ArduinoWidgetv2] ]
  },
]
```

The preceding response contains all the properties related to dashboards such as widgets, creation date, update time, and so on. Next, we have another API endpoint related to showing a dashboard, which is used to display all the information regarding a single dashboard. The code is available in the `dashboard` folder; the execution of the code and checking out how it works is left to you as an independent exercise.

In these sub-sections, we discussed how to work programmatically with dashboards, including actions such as dashboard creation, updating, deletion, and showing the list of dashboards via the Arduino IoT Cloud Node.js SDK. In the next section, we will explore how we can use the Node.js SDK to fine-tune our cloud variables/properties.

Fine-tuning with the Node.js SDK – property value management

In this section, we will look at how we can *set*/*get* cloud variable values using the SDK. This is very useful for performing bulk operations; for example, if you have 100 lights connected to the Arduino IoT Cloud, it will be difficult to control them all manually from a dashboard. Suppose switching one device on/off takes 3 seconds from the dashboard – with 100 devices this will require 300 seconds, a total of 5 minutes, along with the chance of human error (maybe the user misses one device due to bulk processing). But with the help of the SDK, we can perform bulk operations on Things, saving time and improving confidence in our ability to reach zero-error operations.

Get a property value

Let's first see how to get the last value of the cloud variable. To do this, we need the Thing ID and cloud variable ID. More precisely, we will get the complete properties of the cloud variable in JSON format here, but will only fetch `last_value` of the cloud variable. The relevant documentation can be found at `https://www.arduino.cc/reference/en/iot/api/#api-PropertiesV2-propertiesV2Show`. Open the `get-prop.js` file under the `getset` folder in VSCode:

```
var api = new IotApi.PropertiesV2Api()
    var thingid = "8aee742e-4492-423d-9f19-79fec856b917"; // {String}
The id of the thing
    var propertyid = "182d7319-5c36-4988-a5b8-ace2df7bd08a"; //
{String} The id of the property
    var opts = {
    'showDeleted': false // {Boolean} If true, shows the soft deleted
properties
    };
    api.propertiesV2Show(thingid, propertyid, opts).
then(function(data) {
    console.log('Last Value of Property=' + data.last_value);
    }, function(error) {
    console.error(error);
    });
```

The preceding code snippet was taken from the `GetProperty()` method. We have defined `thingid` and `propertyid` and then passed these variables to the `api.propertiesV2Show` method later in the snippet. After getting the response in JSON format, we only use the `last_value` property to display its data on the console. Run the following command on the Terminal:

```
node get-prop.js
```

After successful execution, you will get the response with the value.

Set a property value

In the previous section, we discussed how to get the last value of a cloud variable, and in this section, we will explore how to set/publish the value to a cloud variable. The relevant documentation can be found at https://www.arduino.cc/reference/en/iot/api/#api-PropertiesV2-propertiesV2Publish. Open the set-prop.js file under the getset folder in VSCode:

```
var api = new IotApi.PropertiesV2Api()
    var thingid = "8aee742e-4492-423d-9f19-79fec856b917"; // {String}
The id of the thing
    var propertyid = "182d7319-5c36-4988-a5b8-ace2df7bd08a"; //
{String} The id of the property
    var propertyValue = {
        'device_id':'5aae7e1f-940b-4426-80ac-1c953839cdb2',
        'value':true
    }; // {PropertyValue}
    api.propertiesV2Publish(thingid, propertyid, propertyValue).
then(function(data) {
    console.log('Value Published to Property Successfully');
    }, function(error) {
    console.error(error);
    });
```

The preceding code snippet was taken from the SetProperty() method. Here, we provide three variables to the api.propertiesV2Publish method. The first is thingid, the second is propertyid, and the third variable contains the two further properties of device_id and value. Run the following command on the Terminal to execute the script:

```
node set-prop.js
```

After successful execution, you will get a response indicating that the value has been updated successfully.

In the section, we discussed in detail how to get/set the value of a cloud variable programmatically. This helps developers to fetch values and display them in their custom dashboards, or set the values of cloud variables to control device operations. Next, you have an assignment of an example project for practice, which will help you to refine your skills and chapter study.

Assignment

After playing with SDK, it's now time to do some more experiments so you can apply your learning in new scenarios and solidify your learning. For this assignment, you will create a script for Thing automation with the following properties:

1. Set up a method for **WeMos D1 Mini** device creation. This device belongs to the **ESP8266** category.

2. Set up a Thing named `Sense Environment` and create a sketch for a Thing. Then, associate the previously created device with the Thing.

3. Create three cloud variables/properties for temperature, humidity, and air quality and attach these variables to the previously created Thing.

Create the required script in one file containing all the methods, where we just provide the Thing name and it will automatically set up the device, Thing, and sketch, handle device association with the Thing, and take care of variable creation. Successfully completing this task will teach you to automate workflows and processes efficiently and effectively.

Summary

In this chapter, we covered API endpoints, SDKs, and the types of SDK platforms available to us on the Arduino IoT Cloud. We also learned how to test APIs with Postman. Next, we explored the Node.js SDK by performing different types of operations, particularly CRUD operations, on devices, Things, properties, and dashboards. Finally, we saw how to get and set the value of a cloud variable.

This chapter was specially designed for backend developers seeking to use the Arduino IoT Cloud as a foundation and wanting to develop a custom frontend for their solution, which is possible when you know how to interact with the Arduino IoT Cloud programmatically using the Node.js SDK. Likewise, the ability to create custom services allows us to integrate with third party cloud services and applications.

The next chapter will be more interesting as we are going to dive into smart agriculture, implementation a project where you will learn how to measure the soil moisture, soil temperature, and outdoor temperature and humidity. We will design a device that will allow us to monitor four different crops/plants. You could use this project to monitor your home plants as well as helping your friends working in the field of agriculture.

Project 4 – Collecting Data from the Soil and Environment for Smart Farming

This chapter is dedicated to **smart agriculture**. Our population is growing rapidly and food consumption is directly proportional to population. Fortunately, we have the latest tools and technologies that help us to boost our crop yields by using fewer natural resources. In smart agriculture, there are different parameters to monitor, but we will only focus on soil moisture and soil temperature as both are linked to water consumption; access to clean water is another issue with the rapid growth of industries and population.

In this chapter, we will practically explore smart agriculture by monitoring the soil moisture level, soil temperature, and outdoor temperature and humidity, which will help us to understand how our soil responds to changes in the outside environment and for how many days the soil retains moisture after watering the crop. Our smart agriculture device will send all the data to the Arduino IoT Cloud, where we will monitor it in real time and make decisions that will help us to use controlled watering for crops, which will save water and improve the soil quality.

In this chapter, we are going to use open source and cost-effective sensors to carry out experiments in labs as well as in the field. For the development board, we are using the **ESP32** and **ADS1115 analog-to-digital converter** (**ADC**) modules in combination with four capacitive soil moisture and four **DS18B20** sensors for soil temperature monitoring, as well as a **DHT22** module for outdoor temperature and humidity monitoring. This project will help you optimize your crops with precision farming, tunnel farming, and drip irrigation, as well as be useful for home gardening.

In this chapter, we will cover the following topics:

- Smart farming with IoT
- Essential hardware for your agri-tech project

- Architecting your agriculture IoT system
- Perfecting sensor calibration
- Setting up things, networks, and cloud variables
- Creating web and mobile dashboards

Technical requirements

The following hardware components are required to complete this chapter:

- ESP32 development board
- ADS1115 ADC module
- DHT22 module
- Soil moisture sensor x4
- DS18B20 x4
- PCB (link is available in the *PCB design and the assembly of hardware components* section)
- 2.54 mm three-pin connectors
- Female headers
- Jumper cables

For coding, we will use the Arduino Web Editor, which includes a large collection of development board and sensor libraries, and we will use the Arduino IoT Cloud for Thing and dashboard setup. To develop hardware and sensor designs, we need the Fritzing desktop software.

The chapter code is available in the book's official GitHub repository, or you can directly download the code at `https://github.com/PacktPublishing/Arduino-IoT-Cloud-for-Developers`.

Smart farming with IoT

Internet of Things (**IoT**) technology is used in smart agriculture to optimize farm operations, improve crop yields, reduce waste, and increase profits. Here are some examples of how IoT is used in smart agriculture:

- **Automated irrigation**: IoT sensors can be used to monitor soil moisture levels and weather conditions to determine when to irrigate crops. Automated irrigation systems can then be triggered to deliver the right amount of water to crops, which can reduce water wastage and increase crop yields.

- **Livestock management**: IoT sensors can be used to monitor the health and behavior of livestock, such as their movement, feeding habits, and sleeping patterns. This data can be used to detect early signs of illness, track breeding cycles, and ensure optimal conditions for the livestock.

- **Crop monitoring**: IoT sensors can be used to monitor crop growth, detect pests and diseases, and identify areas that need attention. This data can be used to make timely interventions and improve crop yields.

- **Precision farming**: IoT sensors can be used to gather data on individual plants or crops, enabling farmers to optimize their use of resources, such as water, fertilizers, and pesticides. This can help reduce waste, improve yields, and save money.

- **Smart harvesting**: IoT sensors can be used to monitor crop ripeness and determine the optimal time for harvesting. This can help reduce waste and improve the quality of harvested crops.

- **Weather monitoring**: IoT sensors can be used to monitor weather conditions such as temperature, humidity, and rainfall. This data can be used to make informed decisions about planting, harvesting, and other farming operations.

Overall, IoT technology is transforming the way that agriculture is practiced. By using real-time data and analytics, farmers can make better decisions and achieve better outcomes, ultimately leading to a more sustainable food supply for the world.

In this section, we have discussed smart agriculture and different terms and techniques that are common in smart agriculture. In the next section, we will discuss the hardware components that we are going to use in this chapter's project.

Essential hardware for your agri-tech project

In this project, we have chosen open source and easily available hardware components. To demonstrate how the Arduino IoT Cloud works with ESP32 series development boards, we have chosen the following hardware. In the ESP32 series, we have a wide selection of development boards that vary in size and number of pins. In this chapter, we are using **ESP32-DevKit V1** as it's very compact and smaller in size compared to other boards. It is, of course, also cheaper and provides a 5V pin, which is also known as VIN, as well as having the option of a 3.3V pin. The following figure shows the **pin layout (pinout)** diagram of ESP32 V1.

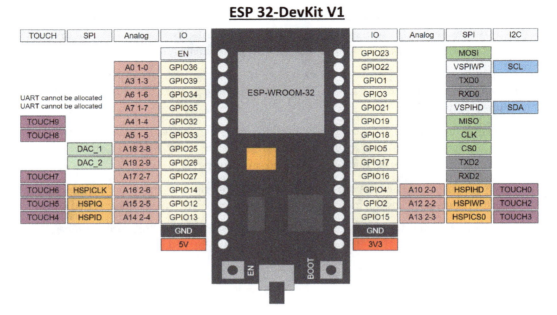

Figure 9.1: ESP32-DevKit V1

ESP32 provides multiple pins for digital and analog input/output. If you want to use multiple analog sensors, then ADCs are available. One of the most well-known ADCs is the ADS1115/ADS1015 module, which provides four analog pins and is good when you need to add additional analog pins to your project. In this project, four analog pins are required to fetch soil moisture sensor values; this board has enough analog pins but I am using ADS1115 to demonstrate how we can use the ADC module to add extra analog pins to our projects.

In the current project, we need five digital pins for the DHT22 module and DS18B20 temperature probe and four analog pins for the capacitive soil moisture sensors. One of the good features of this development board is that it provides a 5V power pin, which is not available in most ESP32 series development boards.

Next, we are using the DHT22 module to sense outdoor temperature and humidity, but you can also use the DHT11 sensor, depending on your requirements. If specifically talking about features, then the DHT22 provides a broader range of sensors compared to the DHT11, but it costs more. The following figure shows the DHT22 module, and we have labeled the pins for better understanding.

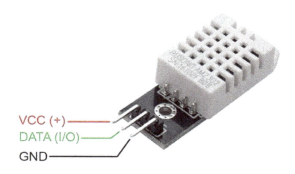

Figure 9.2: DHT22 and DHT11 module pinout

The preceding figure shows the pinout of the DHT22/DHT11 sensor module; the complete pin connection configuration can be seen in *Table 9.3*. The first pin (**VCC**) works with both 3.3V and 5V. The second pin is the **DATA** pin, which connects with any digital pin of ESP32-DevKit V1. The third pin is the **GND** pin, which connects with the GND pin of the development board.

Before moving on, the following table explains all the specification differences between the DHT22 and DHT11. The most notable things are the sensing range and sensing period:

Feature	DHT22	DHT11
Power supply	3.3 to 5V	
Output signal	Digital signal via a single bus	
Sensing element	Polymer capacitor	
Sensing range	Humidity 0-100% Relative Humidity (RH) Temperature 40-0°C	Humidity 20-90% RH Temperature 0-50°C
Accuracy	Humidity: +-2% RH (max +-5% RH) Temperature: <+-0.5°C	Humidity: 1% RH (max 5% RH) Temperature: <2°C
Sensing period	Average 2 s	Average 1 s

Table 9.1: DHT22 and DHT11 sensor specification

The main sensor of the project is a capacitive soil moisture sensor and it is used to monitor the soil moisture of a specific area. It is a low-cost soil moisture monitoring sensor and is rustproof due to its use of PCB (PCB sheets use plastic and paint, making them rustproof). It senses the soil moisture by passing a small amount of electric current into the soil moisture sensors, as shown in *Figure 9.3*, and determining the soil moisture based on the returned current. If the sensor receives a higher current, then it means the moisture is high; if it receives a low current, then there is little or no moisture content in the soil.

Figure 9.3: Capacitive soil moisture sensor pinout

The soil moisture sensor consists of three pins: **GND**, **VCC**, and **AOUT**. The sensor provides readings in analog format. These values will later be converted into percentages using the map() method under the FetchSoilMoisture() method. The complete code is available on GitHub in the folder for this chapter. The sensor operates with both 5V power as well as 3.3V, but 5V is recommended.

The other main sensor of this project is the DS18B20 waterproof temperature sensor probe, which is used to monitor the soil temperature of a specific area, along with soil moisture levels. It is a low-cost waterproof temperature monitoring sensor and is rustproof due to its steel enclosure. The following figure shows the DS18B20 waterproof temperature probe and its pinout and connection diagram with ESP32-DevKit V1.

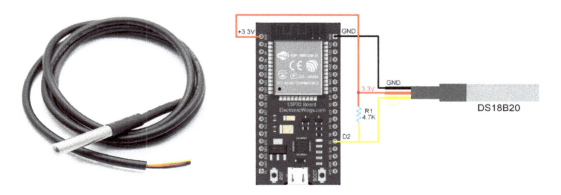

Figure 9.4: DS18B20 waterproof temperature probe

The preceding figure shows the sensor and its pinout diagram. DS18B20 contains three colored wires: the black wire is used for GND, the red wire is used to connect VCC either with 3.3V or 5V, and the yellow wire is used to connect with any digital pin but with a 4.7k pull resistor, as shown in the figure. If we're talking about sensor specifications, then its temperature sensing range is good – it is capable of measuring a temperature from -55 to 125°C. All the other details are given in the following table for further exploration:

Feature	DS18B20
Power supply	3.3 to 5V
Output signal	Digital signal/one wire
Temperature sensing range	-55~125°C
Temperature accuracy	Temperature ± 0.5°C
Sensing period	<750 ms

Table 9.2 – DS18B20 specification table

In this section, we have discussed development boards and sensors in detail, with complete specifications and pinout diagrams. In the next section, we will talk about how these sensors connect to ESP32-DevKit V1 as well as the PCB design of the project.

Architecting your agriculture IoT system

In the previous sections, we discussed the sensors and development board in detail. Now it's time to put things into practice. In hardware development, before starting to work with sensors and development boards, we need to develop the design concepts to get a better understanding of how things will be connected. There are many pieces of software available to design and develop design concepts for electronic projects, but we are going to use **Fritzing**.

In the following two subsections, we will first talk about the schematics and design of the project and explain how to connect the pins with the development board. Then, we will talk about PCB design and its implementation to make the product ready for deployment in the field.

Schematics and design

The purpose of the design is to get a clear understanding of how sensors will connect with the development board. It helps engineers develop prototypes on a breadboard or Veroboard by basing them on these design files. A major benefit of designing using Fritzing is that it builds hardware schematics and PCB design in the background according to your design, which can be adjusted by designers according to the system requirements. The following figure shows the whole project diagram, illustrating how the sensors and ADS1115 module connect to the ESP32-DevKit V1 board.

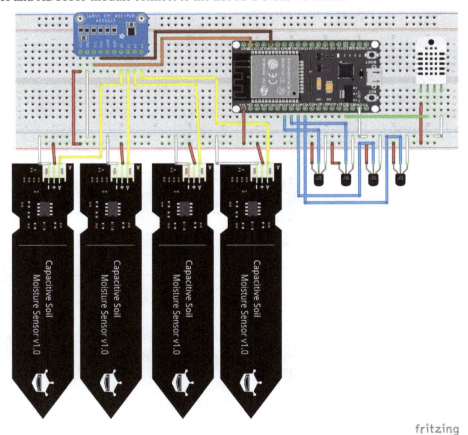

Figure 9.5: Smart agriculture system design

Figure 9.5 depicts the whole project schematic diagram, which also includes the pin numbers. But to make it easier for you, we have provided the following tables with all the pin numbers. *Table 9.3* contains the pin configuration for DHT22 with ESP32:

ESP32	**DHT22**
D13	Data (I/O)
GND	GND
3.3V	VCC

Table 9.3: ESP32 and DHT22 pinout table

Table 9.4 contains the pin configuration for DS18B20 temperature probes with ESP32. Here, we are using four DS18B20 temperature probes, and in each column of sensors, we have mentioned the ESP32 pin number that will connect with the DS18B20 data pin. GND and VCC pins of ESP32 development board will be common to all sensors:

Soil Temperature Sensor #1	**Soil Temperature Sensor #2**	**Soil Temperature Sensor #3**	**Soil Temperature Sensor #4**
Data pin with ESP32 (D32)	Data pin with ESP32 (D33)	Data pin with ESP32 (D25)	Data pin with ESP32 (D26)
ESP32 GND to GND	ESP32 GND to GND	ESP32 GND to GND	ESP32 GND to GND
ESP32 3.3V to VCC	ESP32 3.3V to VCC	ESP32 3.3V to VCC	ESP32 3.3V to VCC

Table 9.4: ESP32 and DS18B20 temperature probes pinout table

Table 9.5 illustrates ESP32 to ADS1115 pin configuration. The rest of the soil moisture sensors will connect to the system via ADS1115 analog pins, which are explained in *Table 9.6*:

ESP32	**ADS1115**
D22	SCL
D21	SDA
3.3V	VCC
GND	GND

Table 9.5: ESP32 and ADS1115 pinout table

In *Table 9.6*, you will see how we have attached soil moisture sensors to the system using ADS1115. The second row of the table states which pin of ADS1115 will be used to connect soil moisture sensors to the system:

Soil Moisture Sensor #1	Soil Moisture Sensor #2	Soil Moisture Sensor #3	Soil Moisture Sensor #4
Soil moisture analog pin to ADS1115 (A0)	Soil moisture analog pin to ADS1115 (A1)	Soil moisture analog pin to ADS1115 (A2)	Soil moisture analog pin to ADS1115 (A3)
ESP32 GND to GND	ESP32 GND to GND	ESP32 GND to GND	ESP32 GND to GND
ESP32 VCC to VCC	ESP32 VCC to VCC	ESP32 VCC to VCC	ESP32 VCC to VCC

Table 9.6: ADS1115 and soil moisture sensors pinout table

The preceding design provides a full overview showing how you can connect the sensors to the development board. According to the design, we have only one 5V and one GND from the development board, which will be used across all the sensors. Soil moisture sensors are analog sensors, so we connected all the sensors with ADS1115 module pins from the AO pin to the A4 pin, as shown in *Figure 9.5* and *Table 9.6*, while the DHT22 module and DS18B20 are digital sensors and are connected to the D12, D32, D33, D25, and D26 pins of ESP32, as shown in *Figure 9.5* and in *Table 9.3* and *Table 9.4*, respectively. The ESP32 to ADS1115 pinout is shown in *Table 9.5* as well as in *Figure 9.5*.

PCB design and the assembly of hardware components

In the preceding section, we saw a design that is good for creating prototypes using a breadboard or Veroboard, but what if we want to deploy that solution in the field? Fritzing is a great tool that provides the option to design a PCB, and when you develop the design, it automatically creates the PCB design in the backend, which is accessible in the Fritzing software via the **PCB Design** tab. Automatic PCB design is just a basic functionality and is not suitable for direct production, so it's mandatory to review and rearrange the design according to professional practices. The following figure shows the PCB design for the current project.

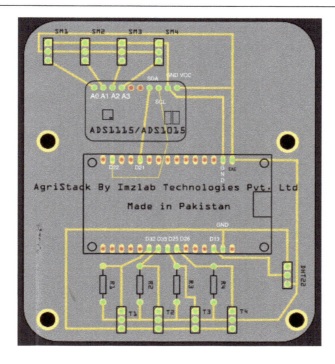

Figure 9.6: Smart agriculture system PCB design

The preceding figure shows the final PCB design of the project. (I was able to create this design easily thanks to Fritzing.) There are many different tools available for PCB design, such as **EasyEDA**, **Circuit Maker**, and **Altium**. It's easy to develop a PCB; just make sure that the connection line on the PCB doesn't intersect with other connection lines.

After the PCB design, you have two options: either develop the PCB yourself using the DIY method (which is good for learning purposes but not suitable for large-scale products) or choose a professional organization that will manufacture the PCB professionally. Many organizations in China provide PCB manufacturing and fabrication services, such as Seeed Studio, JLCPCB, and PCBWay. We tried PCBWay and were impressed with their working and delivery time. We have uploaded the PCB design to the PCBWay project repository, and from there, you can select the PCB design and order easily: `https://www.pcbway.com/project/shareproject/ESP32_Based_Smart_Agriculture_Node_11223e5a.html`.

After getting the PCBs, it's time to solder the female headers and 2.54 mm three-pin connectors for development boards and sensors. Never solder the development board and sensors directly on a PCB so that if anything stops working, then it's easy to detach and replace. The following figure shows the final face of the PCB which contains 2.5mm three-pin connectors in white color for soil moisture sensors, DS18B20 & DHT22 while black female headers are used to insert the ESP32-DevKit V1 and ADS1115 module.

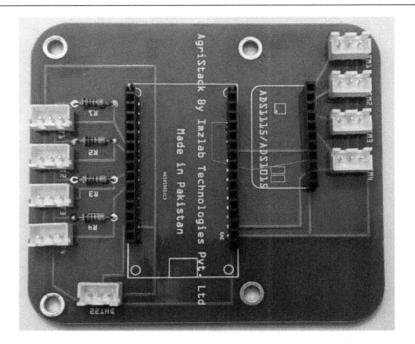

Figure 9.7: Smart agriculture system PCB

The preceding figure shows how the PCB looks after soldering the three-pin 2.54 mm connectors and female headers. Soil moisture connectors are marked with **SM** while DS18B20 connectors are marked with **T** and resistances are marked with **R**, as shown in *Figure 9.7*. Now it's time to plug all the connectors to get our smart agriculture node ready for further procedures. But wait – by default, soil moisture sensors come with a very small length of wire, which is not enough, so here you need to extend the cable lengths by putting 2.54 mm female connectors on both ends, as soil moisture sensors also use the same connectors for connectivity. DS18B20 also comes with a naked terminal but we plugged a 2.54 mm female connector for easy and clean connectivity. The following figure shows the complete setup with all the sensors and cabling arrangement.

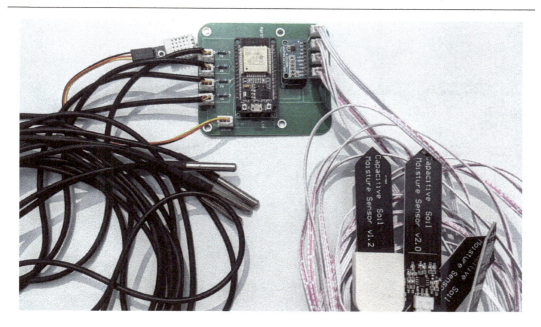

Figure 9.8: Smart agriculture system with all sensors and modules

The preceding figure shows all the components stacked on the PCB. We can see that soil moisture sensors are extended with custom cabling with the help of connectors, while the DS18B20 naked terminal is connected to female connectors, and the same for the DHT22 module. After hardware assembly, we need to calibrate the soil moisture and DS18B20 temperature before deploying the node into the field.

Perfecting sensor calibration

Sensor calibration is a very important aspect of product development, especially when you have a plan to deploy your product in a real-time environment. So, before moving on, first we need to calibrate the capacitive soil moisture and DS18B20 sensors. The soil moisture sensor operation varies from area to area due to air humidity and water levels.

So firstly, we will calibrate the soil moisture sensor by taking the values of sensors in the air and then putting sensors in the water. These values will be used to bind the final readings and, finally, we will convert the soil moisture sensor value from 0 to 100% via the map method. The soil moisture sensor is an analog sensor, so there is no requirement for an extra helping library, except the **ADS module library**, which is shown in the following figure with the name **Adafruit ADS1X15**.

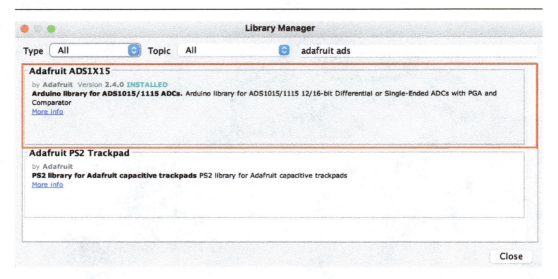

Figure 9.9 – ADS1115 library

Here, we need to install a library for ADS1115/ADS1015 in the Arduino IDE so we can use the ADS module. Navigate to **Sketch | Include Library | Manage Libraries…**, type `Adafruit ADS1X15`, and install the latest version, which is shown in the preceding figure. After installation of the library, download the code from the official GitHub book repository and open the code from the `Soil-Moisture-Calibration` folder:

```
int AirValue[]={0,0,0,0};
int WaterValue[]={0,0,0,0};
```

The preceding code snippet contains two arrays: one for air values and one for sensor values when they are dipped into the water. For soil sensor calibration, we need to get `AirValue` and then `WaterValue` values only by one time. Upload the code to the development board and make sure your soil moisture sensors are dry. Open the serial monitor and note down the `AirValue` value for each sensor. After that, dip the sensors into a pot of water and note down the `WaterValue` value of the sensors.

Let's look at the `AirValues` of AIN0, AIN1, AIN2, and AIN3, as shown in *Figure 9.10*. **AIN** is short for **Analog Input** and the proceeding 0, 1, 2, and 3 are the pin numbers of the ADC1115 module where soil moisture sensors are connected:

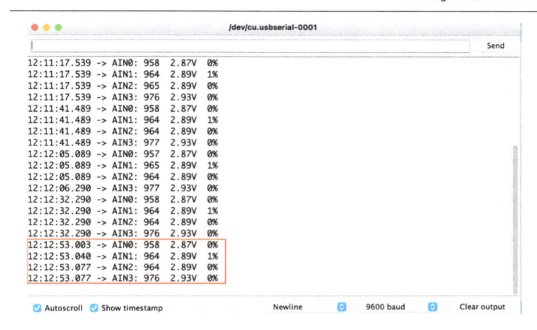

Figure 9.10: Air values of soil moisture sensors

Now let's look at the `WaterValues` after putting the soil moisture sensors in the water:

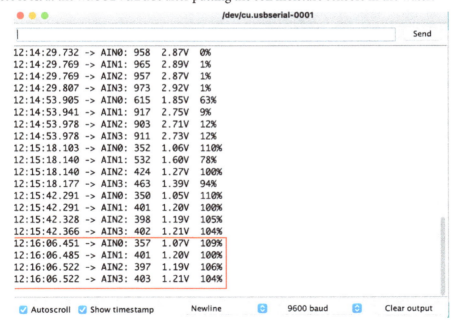

Figure 9.11: Water values of soil moisture sensors

Wait for some time and note down the values when they become stable. After fetching the `Air` and `Water` values, put these values into the preceding arrays and upload the code again to the development board. Verify the values of the soil moisture percentage levels by putting the sensors into the water and then cleaning them. Here, you will get 100% when sensors are deeply in water and 0% when they are dry.

After the soil moisture levels, it's time to verify the DS18B20 temperature probe sensor readings. Firstly, we need to install a library for the DS18B20 temperature sensor. Navigate to **Sketch | Include Library | Manage Libraries…**, type `Dallas Temperature by Miles Burton`, and install the latest version. After installation of the library, download the code from the official GitHub book repository and open the code from the `DS18B20-Calibration` folder:

```
OneWire ds18x20[] = {32,33,25,26};
```

In the preceding code, we have mentioned digital pin numbers, which are reserved on the PCB to connect DS18B20 sensors. If you are using different pins on the breadboard, then update the pin number according to your selection. Upload the code on the development board, then after uploading, open up the serial monitor and see whether you are getting the values from the sensors or not. The following figure shows the DS18B20 temperature probe readings on the serial monitor for calibration purposes.

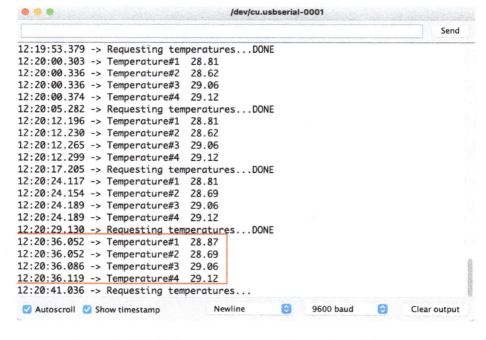

Figure 9.12: DS18B20 temperature sensor values on the Serial Monitor

The preceding figure shows that the DS18B20 temperature sensors are working fine and the values are stabilized. Now, we can move forward with lab calibration.

> **Important note**
>
> A 4.7k **pull resistor** is mandatory for DS18B20. Without pull-up resistor, you will not get the values.

After the soil moisture sensors have tested with the `Air` and `Water` values, it's time to calibrate both sensors in the lab. For moisture testing, we used the hot air oven method to verify the accuracy of the soil moisture sensor. We added water to soil, sand, and salt at different levels and measured it with sensors. After that, we inserted these samples into a hot air oven and compared the sensor readings between the two methods; the results were incredible: only a ±0.5 difference. For DS18B20, we used a calibrated analog thermometer and observed only a ±0.5 difference. The following figure shows a photo of the lab where we calibrated the soil moisture and DS18B20 sensors to industry standards.

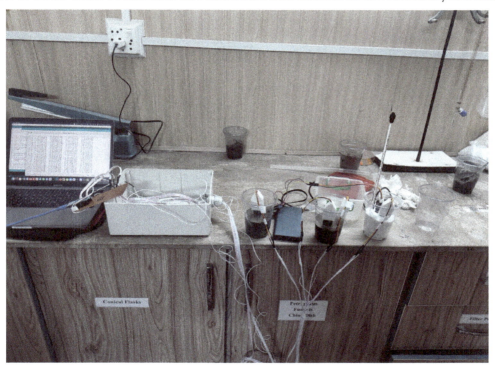

Figure 9.13: Moisture sensor and temperature sensor calibration in the lab

The preceding figure shows the calibration of sensors in the lab. Here, we have tested the sensors with soil, sand, and salt.

In this section, we discussed sensors and their connection to ES32-DevKit V1 using a schematic diagram, as well as PCB design and its implementation. After that, we discussed soil moisture and DS18B20 sensor calibration. In the upcoming section, we will set up things, network credentials, and cloud variables and look into the code.

Setting up things, networks, and cloud variables

After setting up the hardware, it's time to set up a thing in the Arduino IoT Cloud. For this project, we need 10 cloud variables to fetch monitoring parameters from the device; the network settings will be different due to the ESP series board. The following figure gives a complete overview of the **AgriStack** Thing we will set up.

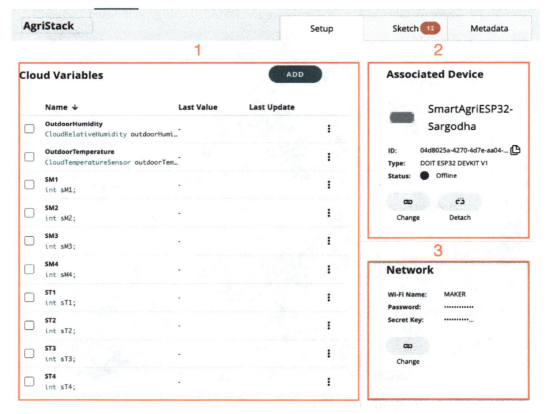

Figure 9.14: Smart agriculture system thing setup

Set up a new thing with the name `AgriStack`. Follow these steps to create variables, an associated device, network configuration, and, finally, the code. We have marked the preceding figure with different red boxes and assigned numbers. These numbers correspond to the following steps, which will help you to set up the Thing:

1. Firstly, we need to set up 10 cloud variables, as shown in *Figure 9.14*. There are two cloud variables for outdoor temperature and humidity; these values will be taken from DHT22. There are four cloud variables for soil moisture and four variables for soil temperature. The previous four will use soil moisture sensor and the latter four will use the DS18B20 temperature probe. More details about cloud variables are available in the next subsection.

2. After that, we need to associate the device with the Thing. In the current project, we are going to use ESP32-DevKit V1, so the wizard will be different compared to Arduino boards. Complete details are available in the *Associating a device* section.

3. Finally, we need to set up the network configuration for the device, but this time, we need to provide a security key for ESP series boards to make the connection secure, whereas Arduino-compatible boards are configured by the Arduino IoT Cloud automatically during the device setup wizard.

Here, we have discussed the different steps that help us to set up our thing. In the proceeding section, we will start looking into cloud variables.

Cloud variables

The following table explains all the properties of variables that we need to use during cloud variable creation. An integer (`int`) is a very famous data type, but here you will observe two new variable types regarding humidity and temperature, which take values in percentage and Celsius, respectively. Also, ensure you have the same variable declaration as per the table; otherwise, you will need to modify the example code according to your naming.

We have set the permission of all cloud variables to **Read Only**, but we also have the **Read/Write** option. In this project, we only want to receive data from the device instead of sending data from dashboard, which is why **Read Only** mode is used, to avoid issues with data consistency. **Update Policy** is set to **On change**, as the device will send the data after five minutes, so this option is more appropriate compared to **Periodically update**:

Serial no.	Variable Name	Variable Type	Declaration	Permission	Update Policy
1	Humidity	CloudRelativeHumidity	humidity	Read Only	On change
2	Temperature	CloudTemperatureSensor	temperature	Read Only	On change
3	SM1	int	sM1	Read Only	On change
4	SM2	int	sM2	Read Only	On change
5	SM3	int	sM3	Read Only	On change
6	SM4	int	sM4	Read Only	On change
7	ST1	int	sT1	Read Only	On change
8	ST2	int	sT2	Read Only	On change
9	ST3	int	sT3	Read Only	On change
10	ST4	int	sT4	Read Only	On change

Table 9.7: Cloud variables list with complete parameters

After the successful creation of cloud variables, we will proceed further with the device association step, where we will add and associate the ESP32-DevKit V1 with our thing.

Associating a device

After variable creation, it's time to add a device and associate it with the Thing. Before adding the device, connect the development board to the computer, and open the **Arduino Create Agent** application. We discussed the Arduino Create Agent in *Chapter 2*, in the *What is the Arduino Create Agent?* section.

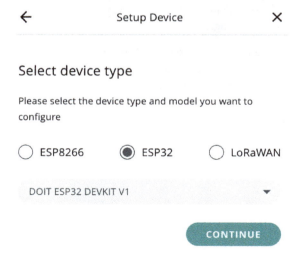

Figure 9.15: Device selection wizard

Click on the **Select Device** button under the **Associated Device** section on the Thing page. A popup will appear where you can see all the devices that are already available. If you have already added your WeMos D1 mini, select it. Otherwise, click on **SET UP NEW DEVICE**. Next, click on the **Set up a 3rd party device** option. Select **ESP32** and **DOIT ESP32 DEVKIT V1** from the dropdown and click on the **CONTINUE** button. Provide the device name and click on the **Next** button. In the final wizard, the **Device ID** and **Secret Key** details will be displayed. Copy the secret key to a safe place as it will be used during the network configuration.

Network configuration

After associating the device with the Thing, it is time to configure the Wi-Fi settings for device communication, as shown in *Figure 9.14*, in the area marked *3*. Under **Network**, you will find the option to fill in the form with the Wi-Fi name and password. In the last field, you will find a new field for the secret key. Paste the secret key that we received from the system during device creation.

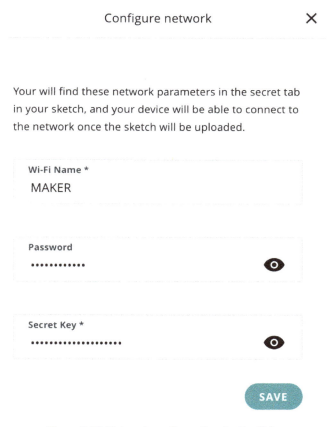

Figure 9.16: Network configuration for the Thing

After network configuration, we are done with our main task; now, the coding task remains, and in the next section, we will go through it.

Coding

The project code is available in the book's official GitHub repository in a ZIP file named AgriStack_ mar05a. Download it and import it to your Arduino Web Editor.

You can download the code and put it into your thing by navigating to the **Sketch** tab. I am not going to discuss that code as you will get the idea after reading it. But here, I will explain the main workflow: we initialize all the things in the setup method and use the timer library to delay calling; remember, never try to use the delay method as it will block the ArduinoCloud.update() method. Then, a method called SmartAgri() is called every five minutes. The following is the complete SmartAgri() method. After this, we will explore what operations are carried out by this method:

```
bool SmartAgri(void *){

  //Fetch Soil Moisture
  FetchSoilMoisture();

  //Fetch Soil Temperature
  FetchTemperature();

  //Fetch DHT Temp & Humiditiy
  FetchDHTTempHum();

  //Send Data To Arduino IoT Cloud
  SendToArduinoIoTCloud();


  //Print The Readings on Serial Port
  PrintTheReadingsSerialPort();

  return true;
}
```

In this project, we have divided all the operations into different methods for easiness. So, firstly, we are calling FetchSoilMoisture(), which is responsible for fetching soil moisture readings from sensors and storing them in an array. Before storing the data in an array, it maps the value for the percentage. Next, we have the FetchTemperature() method, which is responsible for fetching the temperatures from all DS18B20 sensors and saving them into the soil temperature array for further usage. Finally, we call FetchDHTTempHum() to fetch the outdoor temperature and humidity values from the DHT22 module, which will be stored in two variables. Now, we will explore how we get the values from the soil moisture sensors in the following method:

```
float getSoilMoisture(int Pin){

  float SoilMoisture=0;

    //loop 10 times for averaging
  for(int j = 0; j < 5; j++){
    delay(1000);
    SoilMoisture+= ads.readADC_SingleEnded(Pin);
  }

  //divide by 5 to get the average
  SoilMoisture /= 5;

  return SoilMoisture;
  }
```

The preceding technique is used in the FetchSoilMoisture() method to fetch the readings for soil moisture. Here, you will see that the method takes values from the sensor five times with a delay of one second and adds them to the variable; then later, it divides the sensor readings by 5 to get the average. The benefit of this technique is that you will get the best possible value from the soil sensor.

The previous three methods have been used to fetch values from different sensors and store them in global variables and arrays. Now it's time to send these values to the Arduino IoT Cloud; for that reason, we have the SendToArduinoIoTCloud() method, which assigns all the values of sensors to cloud variables, and these values will be updated on the cloud with the help of the ArduinoCloud. update() method. At the end, we have the PrintTheReadingsSerialPort() method, which is optional for use at runtime and is used to display all the sensor values on the serial monitor.

Upload the code to the device and verify the connectivity and readings. If you want to change the reading time, then just modify the `timer.every(600000, SmartAgri);` value. Make sure you are providing the time in milliseconds, where 1 second equals 1,000 milliseconds.

> **Important note**
>
> If you used a different naming scheme in the variable declaration, then update the code according to your naming scheme. But first, you should follow all the steps according to the book and then you can later change the cloud variable names and modify your code, respectively.
>
> Never try to use the `delay` method, as it will block the `ArduinoCloud.update()` method. Always use milliseconds to calculate the waiting time. Review the `loop()` method to call the other methods after five minutes.
>
> The Arduino IoT Cloud only updates the value on the dashboard whenever the variable value is changed. For example, if the temperature is 30°C and it's the same after five minutes, then the Arduino IoT Cloud will not record the value, so don't get confused if values are not changing on the graph. Another benefit of this feature is you will not get duplicated data when you are exporting the content.

After successfully discussing the different methods in the code and uploading the code to ESP32-DevKit V1, it's time to explore how to visualize all the data using awesome Arduino IoT Cloud dashboard widgets.

Creating web and mobile dashboards

After uploading the code to the device, it's time to set up a dashboard for web and mobile to visualize the data with different widgets. The following figure shows the visualization of readings with different widgets:

Figure 9.17: Thing dashboard

We have 10 different readings: **Outdoor Temperature**, **Outdoor Humidity**, four **Soil Moisture** readings, and four **Soil Temperature** readings. For every reading, we are using the gauge widget control, and advanced charts have been used to compare **Soil Moisture** and **Soil Temperature** to visualize the proper correlation between these two attributes. But we also want to monitor historical data; graphs are the best widgets to display live as well as older data. Here, as seen in the lower part of the preceding figure, we have used four graphs, and each graph is connected to a specific cloud variable.

In this section, we have successfully created a dashboard for a smart agriculture thing that shows all the sensor readings in text format, as well as used graphs for comparison purposes.

What next?

We still have a lot of options available to explore, but now it's your turn to use different sensors and development boards to do some more experiments and learn from them. In this chapter, we used 10 sensors but only 3 different types, that is, moisture, temperature, and outdoor temperature and humidity. However, on the market, there are a lot of sensors that provide a wide variety of functionalities for soil, such as **NPK** (which stands for **nitrogen, phosphorus, and potassium**), **EC** (which stands for **electrical conductivity**), and pH sensors and different gas sensors for outdoor measurement.

Try the following sensors to enhance your practical knowledge and compare them with other sensors in terms of features, ranges, and cost:

- NPK sensor
- Soil EC sensor
- Soil pH sensor
- MQ series sensors, which are designed to sense specific gases, including MQ-2, MQ-3, MQ-4, MQ-5, MQ-7, MQ-8, and MQ-9, to find the correlation of gases and their effects on soil and crops
- Seeed Studio SCD30 (temperature, humidity, and CO_2) for outdoor monitoring

Summary

In this chapter, we explored how to develop a smart agriculture monitoring system using DHT22, capacitive soil moisture sensors, a DS18B20 probe for soil temperature, and an ESP32 development board along with the ADS1115 ADC module. We calibrated soil moisture and temperature sensors in the lab before using them in the field. We also set up a thing, which included creating cloud variables, device association, network configuration, and coding of the development board. Then, we created a dashboard to visualize the Thing's sensor readings with different types of widgets to display current readings as well as historical data with the help of graphs.

This project will help you and give you the confidence to collaborate with agriculture researchers and soil scientists to work on a more advanced level. It will help you to add IoT systems to real fields and tunnel farms, as well as help you in home gardening.

In the next chapter, we will work on a smart home project where we will develop a smart RGB LED light that will be connected to the Amazon Alexa Voice assistant and help you to understand and develop smart home solutions.

10

Project #6 – Making Your Home Smarter with a Voice Assistant

This chapter is dedicated to smart homes. **Smart homes** is a wide field that aims to automate everything in your home to make your life experience better and more comfortable, for example, smart light systems, smart air conditioning, smart TVs, and so on. But in this chapter, we will explore how we can build a multi-color smart bulb that is controlled by the **Arduino IoT Cloud** web and mobile dashboard. We'll also add the Amazon Alexa voice assistant to control the smart bulb using voice commands.

Here, we will practically explore smart homes, picking up the **WS2812 RGB LED** ring and Seeed Studio's newest, and very small, development board in the XIAO series, which is based on ESP32 with a lot of features. With the help of the light module, development board, and the Arduino IoT Cloud, we will build a smart light system.

By the end of this chapter, you will have the confidence to build smart home solutions with the help of any open source ESP32/ESP8266 or Arduino series development board using the Arduino IoT Cloud. In particular, you will learn how easy it is to integrate Amazon Alexa Voice assistant into your smart home projects to make them more convenient for end users.

In this chapter, we're going to cover the following main topics:

- Creating smarter homes with IoT
- Essential components – sensors and development boards
- Blueprint for your smart home IoT project
- Initial setup – Thing, network credentials, cloud variables, and code
- User-friendly controls – building web and mobile dashboards
- Enhancing controls – integrating the Arduino IoT Cloud with Amazon Alexa

Technical requirements

The following hardware components are required to complete this chapter's exercise:

- Seeed Studio XIAO ESP32C3

- USB type-C cable for XIAO ESP32C3

- WS2812 RGB LED ring

- Male headers, female headers, and a veroboard

- Jumper cables

- Soldering iron

- Amazon Echo Dot and the Amazon Alexa mobile app

For coding, we will use the **Arduino Web Editor**, which includes a large collection of development boards and sensor libraries, and the Arduino IoT Cloud for the Thing and dashboard setup. To develop hardware and sensor designs, we need the **Fritzing** desktop software and the **Arduino IDE** for testing the WS2812 ring.

Here, we will use the **Amazon Echo Dot** as a voice assistant for voice commands to control the smart bulb. If you don't have an Echo Dot, then you can use the **Amazon Alexa** app for Android/iOS. The chapter's code is available in the official GitHub repository for the book by following this link: https://github.com/PacktPublishing/Arduino-IoT-Cloud-for-Developers.

Creating smarter homes with IoT

Internet of Things (**IoT**) technology plays a crucial role in the development of smart homes. It enables various devices and appliances within a home to connect, communicate, and automate tasks for the convenience, comfort, and efficiency of homeowners. Here are some key aspects of IoT for smart homes:

- **Connectivity**: IoT devices in a smart home are connected to the internet, allowing them to communicate with each other, as well as with the homeowner, remotely. This connectivity facilitates the control, monitoring, and automation of devices from anywhere, using smartphones, tablets, or computers.

- **Home automation**: IoT enables the automation of various tasks within a smart home. For example, lights can automatically turn on or off based on occupancy or the time of day. Thermostats can adjust temperature settings based on the homeowner's preferences or presence in the house. IoT-powered automation helps optimize energy usage, enhance security, and simplify routine activities.

- **Security and surveillance**: IoT devices can enhance the security of a smart home. Smart locks provide keyless entry and allow remote access control. Video doorbells enable homeowners to see and communicate with visitors remotely. Surveillance cameras can be accessed and monitored from anywhere, providing an additional layer of security.

- **Energy management**: IoT devices help optimize energy consumption within a smart home. Smart thermostats learn user preferences and adjust temperature settings accordingly, conserving energy when rooms are unoccupied. Smart plugs and power strips can monitor and control the energy usage of appliances and electronics, helping identify energy-hungry devices and promoting efficient usage.

- **Voice control**: Voice assistants, such as Amazon Alexa or **Google Assistant**, integrated with IoT devices enable hands-free control of various functions in a smart home. Homeowners can use voice commands to control lights, adjust thermostats, play music, check the weather, and perform other tasks, enhancing convenience and accessibility.

- **Health and wellness**: IoT devices can contribute to health and wellness within a smart home. Wearable devices, such as fitness trackers or smartwatches, can integrate with other home devices, such as smart scales or health monitors, to provide comprehensive health data and insights. This data can be shared with healthcare professionals or used to automate certain health-related tasks.

- **Appliance control**: IoT enables the remote control and monitoring of various appliances in a smart home. Refrigerators, ovens, washing machines, and other appliances can be connected to the internet, allowing homeowners to check their status, receive alerts, or control their operation remotely. This connectivity adds convenience and flexibility to household chores and management.

- **Integration and interoperability**: A crucial aspect of IoT for smart homes is the integration and interoperability of devices from different manufacturers. Standards and protocols, such as **Zigbee** or **Z-Wave**, facilitate the seamless connection and communication between devices, ensuring that different IoT products can work together in a unified ecosystem.

It's important to note that while IoT technology brings numerous benefits to smart homes, it also introduces potential security and privacy risks. Homeowners should take measures to secure their IoT devices, such as using strong passwords, keeping firmware up to date, and ensuring proper network security configurations.

Here, we have discussed in detail how IoT is reshaping the lives of human beings in homes and offices. Next, we are going to talk about the hardware and components that we require to carry on with this chapter's project.

Essential components – sensors and development boards

In the ESP32 series, we have a wide collection of development boards, which vary in size and pins. In this chapter, we are using Seeed Studio's latest development board, the **XIAO ESP32C3**, as it's very compact and smaller in size than other boards, and of course, cheaper and is suitable for 5V as well as 3.3V. The following figure is the pin layout diagram of XIAO ESP32C3.

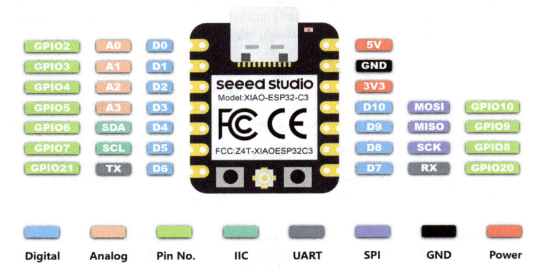

Figure 10.1 – XIAO ESP32C pinout diagram

XIAO ESP32C provides multiple pins for digital input/output. In the previous ESP series board, we found only one analog pin, but on this development board, we have four analog pins, which removes the biggest hurdle while developing a solution that uses multiple analog pins. With previous ESP series boards, we used ADS1115/ADS1015 for extra analog pins, so this development board will save us some bucks as we will get four analog pins by default on the development board.

Besides all those features, XIAO provides a built-in battery charge module and the board is optimized for power consumption, which helps to use this board as a wearable device. For connectivity, there are both Wi-Fi and Bluetooth options available. It also supports **Bluetooth Low Energy** (**BLE 5**), which is more specific to IoT use cases. For further details, please visit `https://wiki.seeedstudio.com/XIAO_ESP32C3_Getting_Started/`.

In the current project, we need one digital pin for the WS2812 RGB LED ring. One of the good features of the development board is that we have a 5V power pin, which is not available on most of the ESP32 series development boards.

We are using the WS2812 16-pixel RGB ring but it comes in different pixels and shapes, such as a stick, matrix, and strip. For the lamp, we prefer the ring shape, but you guys can choose according to your preferences. WS2812 also comes in long strip cables for room decoration and computer tables – especially for gamers, hotels, and so on. There are different vendors who provide the WS2812 module, but we are using a WS2812 that we purchased from AliExpress and it's working perfectly. You can buy it from Amazon, AdaFruit, SparkFun, or from AliExpress.

WS2812 comes with RGB color, and it also allows you to control the brightness of the module, which varies from 1–100%. It also allows you to control every single pixel of the LED – either on/off, or any color, which provides a broad range of use cases to develop interesting solutions and prototypes. The WS2812 RGB LED comes in different sizes and shapes. The following figure shows the RGB LED ring with both the front and back sides.

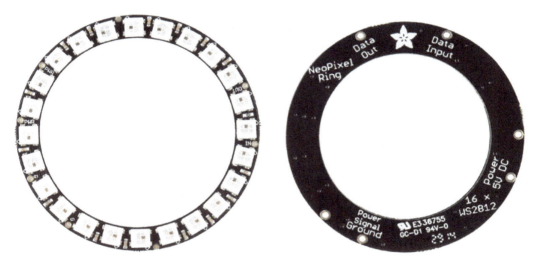

Figure 10.2 – WS2812 RGB LED ring and pinout diagram

The preceding diagram depicts the pinout layout of the WS2812 RGB ring. The complete configuration of the pin connections of WS2812 with XIAO ESP32C3 is shown in *Table 10.1*. *Pin #1* is a GND pin that connects with the onboard GND pin of XIAO ESP32C3. *Pin #2* is a Power 5V DC pin that works with both 3.3V and 5V. *Pin #3* is **Data Input**, which connects with any digital pin. *Pin #4* is **Data Out**, which is only used if you want to extend the WS2812 ring with another ring or stick – this pin will connect to the other ring's data input pin as an extension. Here, I am connecting **Data Input** with *Pin #D3* of the board. You can solder the male headers with WS2812 or directly solder the cables without any header pins.

> **Important note**
> The WS2812 module works perfectly, but still it's necessary to verify that all pixels of the ring/strip are working perfectly. In my case, my last pixel is not working.

In the current section, we have discussed the XIAO ESP32C3 and WS2812 RGH LED ring, as well as its pins. Next, we are going to discuss the project architecture in detail, which includes the project schematics and assembly.

Blueprint for your smart home IoT project

In the preceding sections, we discussed the sensors and development board in detail. Now, it's time to cook the recipe. In hardware development, before starting to work with sensors and development boards, we need to develop the design concepts to get a better understanding of how things will be connected. There is a lot of software available to design and develop design concepts regarding electronics projects, but we are going to use Fritzing.

In the following two subsections, first, we will talk about the schematics and design of a project and explain how to connect the pins of the development board with soldering. Next, we will do some testing of the WS2812 to check all the colors and pixels are working.

Schematic design and assembly

The purpose of the design is to clearly understand how sensors will connect with the development board. It helps engineers to develop a prototype on a breadboard or on a veroboard by using these design files. Another major benefit of designing is that Fritzing builds hardware schematics and a **Printed Circuit Board** (**PCB**) design in the background according to your design, which could be adjusted by designers according to system requirements. The complete connection diagram of the XIAO ESP32C3 and WS2812 RGB LED ring is shown in the following figure.

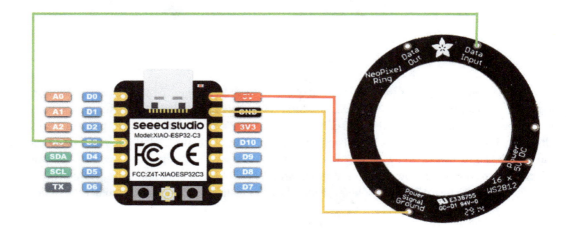

Figure 10.3 – XIAO ESP32C and WS2812 system design

Figure 10.3 illustrates the pin diagram of the whole setup, but for easy guidance, we also created *Table 10.1*, which explains, in a simple way, how to connect the pins of WS2812 to XIAO ESP32C.

XIAO ESP32C	WS2812 Ring
A3	Data Input
5V	Power 5V DC
GND	Power Signal Ground

Table 10.1 – XIAO ESP32C and WS2812 connection

The preceding design and table provide a full overview of how you can connect the sensors to the development board. According to the design, we have common 5V and GND pins from the XIAO ESP32C3 board to the WS2812 module. WS2812 is a digital module so we connected its **Data Input** pin to the D3 pin of the development board. The following figure shows the final prototype of the smart bulb on the veroboard.

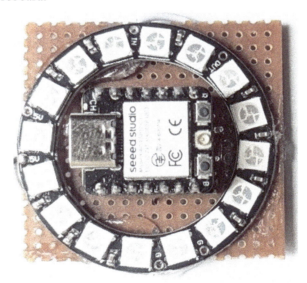

Figure 10.4 – Final prototype

After soldering cables to the module and the male header to the XIAO ESP32C3, connect the pins according to the schematic diagram. There is only one module, so there is no requirement for a veroboard. But I am developing a proper prototype this time – that's why I used a Veroboard. Now it's time to verify the colors and pixels of the WS2812 using ESP32C3.

Testing the WS2812 with the Arduino IDE

To install the ESP32 series development board in the Arduino IDE, first, add the board's definition file in the preferences. To proceed further, follow these steps:

1. Navigate to **File** > **Preferences** and fill **Additional Boards Manager URLs** with the URL `https://raw.githubusercontent.com/espressif/arduino-esp32/gh-pages/package_esp32_dev_index.json`, as shown in the following figure.

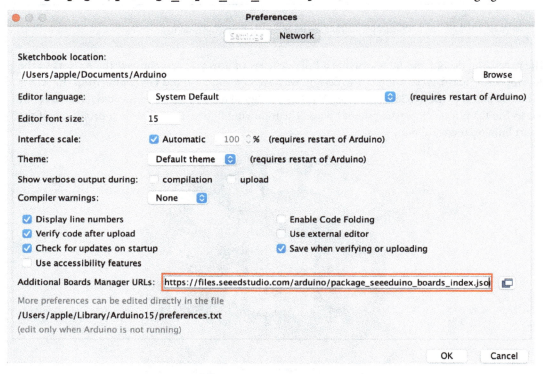

Figure 10.5 – ESP32 board information in the Arduino IDE

2. Later on, navigate to **Tools** > **Board** > **Boards Manager...**, type the keyword `esp32` in the search box, select the latest version of **esp32**, and install it, as shown in the following figure.

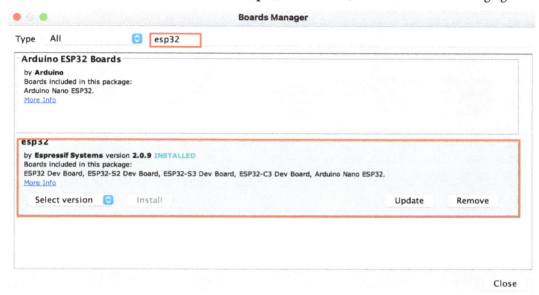

Figure 10.6 – ESP32 series board installation in the Arduino IDE

3. Finally, select the board, navigate to **Tools** > **Board** > **ESP32 Arduino**, and select **XIAO_ESP32C3**. The list of boards is a little long and you need to scroll to the bottom, as shown in the following figure.

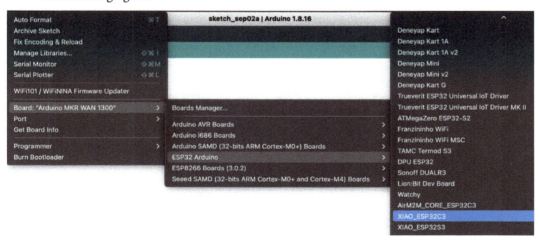

Figure 10.7 – XIAO ESP32C3 board selection in the Arduino IDE

It's time to install the WS2812 library. Navigate to **Sketch** > **Include Library** > **Manage Libraries**. Type Adafruit neopixel in the search bar. Here, you will get different libraries, but you need to install the specific library that matches the search query.

Now we are ready to proceed with the testing steps. Download the code from the official GitHub repository for the book, navigate to the WS2812_Testing folder, and open up the code:

```
#include <Adafruit_NeoPixel.h>

#define LED_PIN      D3
// How many NeoPixels are attached to the Arduino?
#define LED_COUNT 16
// Declare our NeoPixel strip object:
Adafruit_NeoPixel strip(LED_COUNT, LED_PIN, NEO_GRB + NEO_KHZ800);

void setup() {
  strip.begin();            // INITIALIZE NeoPixel strip object
(REQUIRED)
  strip.show();             // Turn OFF all pixels ASAP
  strip.setBrightness(50); // Set BRIGHTNESS to about 1/5 (max = 255)
}
```

Change the LED_PIN constant to D3 or D5. Next, assign the number of pixels to the LED_COUNT constant. Right now, I have 16 pixels in the WS2812 – that's why I am inserting 16. After making modifications, upload the code to the board. Later, you will see the color white on the LED and a moving animation in a circular form. In the setup() method, we initialized NeoPixel strip and set the brightness to 50%:

```
// loop() function -- runs repeatedly as long as board is on --------
-------
void loop() {

  for(int i=0; i<LED_COUNT+1; i++){
    strip.setBrightness(50);
    strip.setPixelColor(i, strip.Color(127+i, 127, 127)); // Set
pixel's color (in RAM)
    strip.show();
    delay(200);
  }

    for(int i=0; i<LED_COUNT+1; i++){
    strip.setBrightness(0);
    strip.setPixelColor(i, strip.Color(0, 0, 0)); // Set pixel's
color (in RAM)
```

```
        strip.show();
    }

}
```

Later, in the `loop()` method, there are two loops. The first loop is used to assign the white color to each pixel and turn on the pixel according to the loop value, with a delay of 200 milliseconds, while in the second loop, we turn off all the pixels one by one by changing the brightness to 0 and RGB colors to 0.

In this section, we have assembled the hardware component on the veroboard and used the code to verify that the WS2812 RGB LED is working. Next, we will set up the Thing and cloud variables in the Arduino IoT Cloud to make our prototype live.

Initial setup – Thing, network credentials, cloud variables, and code

After setting up the hardware, it's time to set up Thing in the Arduino IoT Cloud. For this project, we need one cloud variable to control the LED brightness and color, and turn on/off the WS2812 ring, but I am using three different cloud variables so you will get an idea of when and why we need to use these cloud variables, and every variable connects with a specific widget. The network settings will be different from Arduino development boards due to using ESP series board.

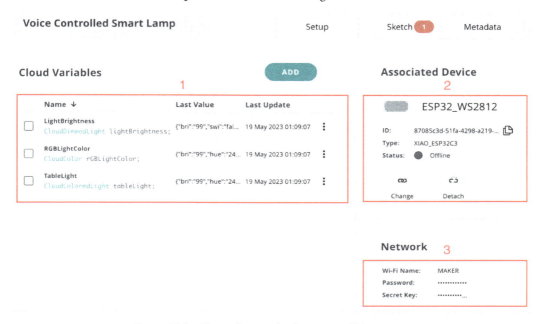

Figure 10.8 – Air quality monitoring system Thing setup

Set up a new **Thing** with the name `Voice Controlled Smart Lamp` and follow these steps to create variables, associate a device and network configuration, and finally, write the code:

1. Firstly, we need to set up three cloud variables for the WS2812. Complete details regarding cloud variables are available in the following section.

2. After that, we need to associate the device with the Thing. In the current project, we are using the XIAO ESP32C3, so the wizard will be different than for Arduino boards. The complete details are available in the *Associating a device* section.

3. Finally, we need to set up the network configuration for the device, but this time we need to provide a security key for ESP series boards to make the connection secure. Arduino-compatible boards are configured by the Arduino IoT Cloud automatically during the device setup wizard.

Cloud variables

The following table provides all the properties of the variables that we need to use during cloud variable creation. For the WS2812, we can use the integer and bool data types, which creates a lot of mess, but thanks to the Arduino IoT Cloud's extended group of variables, we have the **Dimmed light**, **Color**, and **Colored Light** type variables. Next, make sure the same variables are declared as shown in *Table 10.2*, otherwise, you'll need to modify the example code according to your naming.

Here, I made the permission read and write, as this time we will send commands from the cloud dashboard or voice assistant, so it's mandatory to give cloud variables permission to read and write.

S#	Variable Name	Variable Type	Declaration	Permission	Update Policy
1	`LightBrightness`	Dimmed light	`lightBrightness`	Read and write	On change
2	`RGBLightColor`	Color	`rGBLightColor`	Read and write	On change
3	`TableLight`	Colored Light	`tableLight`	Read and write	On change

Table 10.2 – Cloud variables properties table

Previously, I mentioned that we only need one cloud variable, but I am using three different cloud variables and will explain their usage. If I start from the **Dimmed light** type cloud variable, then it has only two options to control the WS2812 – one is brightness and the second is the on/off switch. The **Color** type cloud variable, which is `RGBLightColor`, has only one option regarding the color change. But if we come to the **Colored Light** type cloud variable, then it provides all three options: brightness, color, and an on/off switch. This cloud variable is also compatible with Amazon Alexa and that type cloud variable will be represented as a device in the Amazon Alexa Smart Home skills portal, which is discussed in the *Enhancing control – Integrating Arduino IoT Cloud with Amazon Alexa* section.

Associating a device

After variable creation, it's time to add a device associated with the Thing. Before adding the device, connect the development board to the computer and open the **Arduino Create Agent** application. The following figure shows how to select the ESP32 and then the XIAO_ESP32C3 development board in the popup.

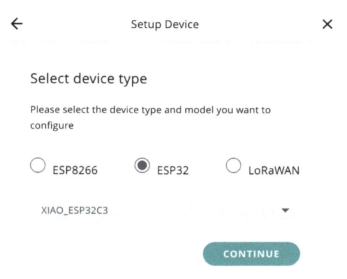

Figure 10.9 – Device selection wizard

Follow these steps to associate the XIAO ESP32C3 to the Thing:

1. Click on the **Select Device** button under the **Associated Device** section on the Thing page shown in *Figure 10.8*.

2. A popup will appear where you can see all the devices that are already available. If you have already added your XIAO ESP32C3, select it. Otherwise, click on **SET UP NEW DEVICE**.

3. Next, click on the **Third party device** option.

4. Select **ESP32** and **XIAO_ESP32C3** from the dropdown and click on the **CONTINUE** button shown in *Figure 10.9*.

5. Fill in **Device Name** and click on the **Next** button.

6. In the final wizard, **Device ID** and **Secret Key** will be displayed. Copy the secret key to a safe place as it will be used during the network configuration.

Now, let's move to the network configuration.

Network

After associating the device with the Thing, it is time to configure the Wi-Fi settings for device communication. The following figure shows the network configuration popup with the **Wi-Fi Name** and **Password** fields.

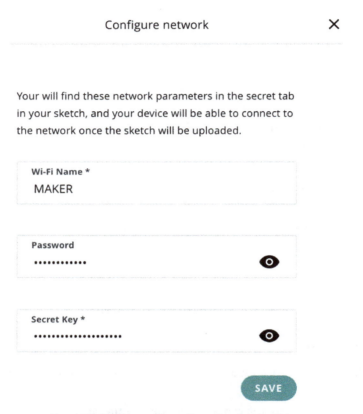

Figure 10.10 – Network configuration for the Thing

You will find a new field – **Secret Key**. Paste the secret key that we received from the system during device creation.

Coding

The chapter's code is available at the official GitHub repository for the book. Download the Voice_ Controlled_Smart_Lamp_may13a code from the repository and import it to the Arduino Web Editor.

You can download the code and put it into your Thing by navigating to the **Sketch** tab. I am not going to discuss that code as you will get the idea after reading it. But here, I will explain the main workflow that initializes all the things in the setup. Remember, never try to use the delay() method – it will block the ArduinoCloud.update() method. But before moving forward, at the start of the code, we need to change the **Pin#** of the LED_PIN constant to 5 and assign a value to LED_COUNT according to the number of pixels in the ring/strip. Here, I am assigning the value 16 as I am using a 16-pixel ring:

```
#define LED_PIN    5
// How many NeoPixels are attached to the Arduino?
#define LED_COUNT 16
// Declare our NeoPixel strip object:
Adafruit_NeoPixel strip(LED_COUNT, LED_PIN, NEO_GRB + NEO_KHZ800);
//Sync Variables
bool swi;
float bright;
float sat;
float hue;
```

If we review the preceding code for the constant, then we will see there is one NeoPixel strip object and four global variables for the switch (swi), brightness (bright), saturation (sat), and hue that will be used later to sync the values from one widget control to another widget control to enable the synchronization between widgets.

After filling the preceding constants with appropriate values, it's time to explore some other methods. If we talk about the setup, then there are only a few lines that initiate the NeoPixel strip object as well as the Arduino IoT Cloud and some other operations. In this project, our loop() method will include one line regarding an Arduino Cloud update and nothing else. Actually, in this project, code will be executed where any change happens on the widget side.

In the project, we have four more methods. Three are event-oriented and one is a common helper method that will be used by three **event-oriented methods** to perform operations on WS2812. Here, the onLightBrightnessChange(), onRGBLightColorChange(), and onTableLightChange() methods are event-oriented and the ControlTheWS2812() method is a **common helper method**. Next, we are going to explore all the methods step by step:

```
void onLightBrightnessChange()  {
  // Add your code here to act upon LightBrightness change
  swi=lightBrightness.getSwitch();
  bright=lightBrightness.getBrightness();

  //Sync the values to tableLight Cloud Variable
  tableLight.setSwitch(swi);
  tableLight.setBrightness(bright);
```

```
//Call the method for operations on WS2812
ControlTheWS2812();
}
```

In the `onLightBrightnessChange()` method, we take brightness and switch values from the `lightBrightness` cloud variable and later assign the values with global variables. The last calling method, `ControlTheWS2812()`, performs the operation on the WS2812 ring according to global variable values:

```
void onRGBLightColorChange()  {
  // Add your code here to act upon RGBLightColor change
  hue=rGBLightColor.getValue().hue;
  sat=rGBLightColor.getValue().sat;
  bright=rGBLightColor.getValue().bri;

  //Sync the values with LightBrightness & tableLight widget
  tableLight.setBrightness(bright);
  tableLight.setHue(hue);
  tableLight.setSaturation(sat);
  lightBrightness.setBrightness(bright);

  //Call the method for operations on WS2812
  ControlTheWS2812();
}
```

The `onRGBLightColorChange()` method is the second method that will be called when there is any change in the color widget control. This method fetches hue, saturation, and brightness values from the `Color` type cloud variable and later assigns these values to other cloud variables as well as global variables. The last calling method, `ControlTheWS2812()`, performs the operation on the WS2812 ring according to global variable values:

```
void onTableLightChange()  {
  // Add your code here to act upon TableLight change
  swi=tableLight.getSwitch();
  bright=tableLight.getBrightness();
  hue=tableLight.getHue();
  sat=tableLight.getSaturation();

  //Sync the values with LightBrightness & RGBLightColor widget
  lightBrightness.setSwitch(swi);
  lightBrightness.setBrightness(bright);
  rGBLightColor= Color(hue,sat,bright);
```

```
   //Call the method for operations on WS2812
   ControlTheWS2812();
}
```

The onTableLightChange() method is associated with the **Colored Light** control widget and it will be called when there is any change to the switch, brightness, or color. This method will fetch four values from the tablelight cloud variable and assign these values to global variables as well to two other cloud variables for synchronization. The last calling method, ControlTheWS2812(), will perform the operation on the WS2812 ring according to global variable values:

```
void ControlTheWS2812(){
   // declare a variable of the Color data type and define it using the
HSB values of the color variable
   Color currentColor=Color(hue,sat, bright);
   byte RValue;
   byte GValue;
   byte BValue;
   currentColor.getRGB(RValue, GValue, BValue);  // the variables will
contain the RGB values after the function returns

   if(swi==true){
      strip.setBrightness(bright);
      for(int i=0; i<LED_COUNT+1; i++){
      strip.setPixelColor(i, strip.Color(RValue, GValue, BValue));
//   Set pixel's color (in RAM)
      strip.show();
   }
   }else{
      for(int i=0; i<LED_COUNT+1; i++){
      strip.setBrightness(0);
      strip.setPixelColor(i, strip.Color(0, 0, 0)); //  Set pixel's
color (in RAM)
      strip.show();
      }
   }
}
```

Finally, we have our last, common helper method, ControlTheWS2812(). This method will first generate RGB color from hue, saturation, and brightness. Then it will check the switch value – if it is true, then the condition will assign the brightness and color to the WS2812 ring and turn on every pixel of the ring with the help of the for loop. Otherwise, it will set the brightness to 0 and turn off all the pixels of the WS2812.

Important note

If you used different *naming* in the variable declaration, then update the code according to your naming scheme. But it's better if you first follow all the steps according to the book and later change the cloud variable names and modify your code respectively.

The Arduino IoT Cloud only updates the values on the dashboard whenever a variable value is changed. For example, if the temperature is 30 and after 5 minutes it's the same, then the Arduino IoT Cloud will not record the value. So, don't get confused if values are not changed on the widget controls. Another benefit of this feature is you will not get duplicated data when you are exporting the content.

In this section, we set up the Thing, associated the XIAO ESP32C3 with the Thing, and set up cloud variables of different types to control LED operations. We also discussed the code for the device in detail, step by step, according to different methods. Now, in the next section, we will set up the dashboard.

User-friendly controls – building web and mobile dashboards

After uploading the code to the device, it's time to set up a dashboard for web and mobile to visualize the data with different widgets. The following screenshot shows a visualization of light controls with different widgets.

Voice Controlled Smart Lamp

Figure 10.11 – Thing dashboard

We have three core functionalities of WS2812, which include RGB color, brightness, and the on/off switch. In the previous section, we created three different cloud variables, which provide different functionalities. That's why here we have three different widget controls, which only work with these cloud variables. The first widget is **Colored Light**, which is linked to the `tableLight` cloud variable and capable of performing all of the operations on the WS2812, such as color change, brightness control, and switching it on and off.

Next, we have two more controls with limited functionalities. The second widget is **Dimmed light**, which is linked with the `lightBrightness` cloud variable and only provides an on/off switch and brightness control, while our third widget control is **Color**, which is linked with the `rGBLightColor` cloud variable and only provides the option to choose the color. If we compare all three widgets, then the **Colored Light** widget is equal to both **Dimmed light** and the **Color** widget, as the **Colored Light** widget has three functionalities, which include turning it on and off, color selection, and brightness control, while the **Dimmed light** widget control has only two options, brightness control and turning on and off functionality, and the **Color** widget control only has the option to choose the color.

So, the final conclusion is if you have a multi-color strip with a brightness control feature, then the **Colored Light** widget and cloud variable are good to go; otherwise, for a single-color light with brightness control, the **Dimmed light** widget and cloud variable are perfect. And if you have only a strip with the multi-color option without a brightness control, then a simple **Color** widget and cloud variable type are enough but remember the **Color** type cloud variable is not compatible with Amazon Alexa.

In this section, we have set up the dashboard with different types of widget controls, which help you to control WS2812 in different ways, such as controlling the brightness, color, and turning on and off the LED ring. Next, we are going to set up the Amazon Alexa Skill with the Arduino IoT Cloud to control our table lamp with voice commands using Amazon Alexa.

Enhancing controls – integrating the Arduino IoT Cloud with Amazon Alexa

After testing everything on the device using the Arduino IoT Cloud dashboard, it's time to link Amazon Alexa with our thing for the voice control system. We have a physical hardware device for Alexa as well mobile apps for Android/iOS. Please visit `https://alexa.amazon.com/` to set up this project. I am using Amazon Echo Dot second generation, but if you don't have access to an Alexa hardware device, then you can simply use the mobile app.

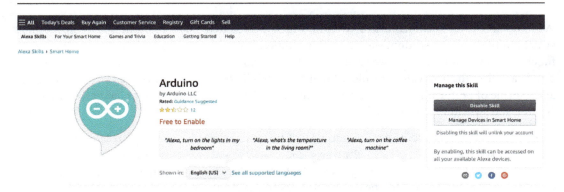

Figure 10.12 – Arduino Skill for Amazon Alexa

The Arduino IoT Cloud natively developed a skill for Amazon Alexa, which can be found at `https://www.amazon.com/Arduino-LLC/dp/B07ZT2PK2H`. Set up your Amazon Alexa and navigate to the preceding URL to enable a skill, which is shown in the preceding figure. When you link the account, it will automatically link the Arduino IoT cloud account that is already logged in with this Skill. So, make sure you are already logged in to the Arduino IoT Cloud. The preceding figure shows the Arduino Skill for Amazon Alexa.

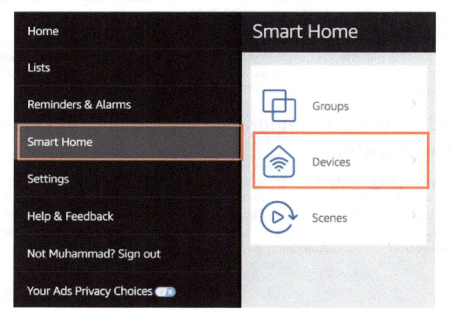

Figure 10.13 – Amazon Alexa Smart Home and devices

After enabling the Arduino skill in Amazon Alexa, navigate to `https://alexa.amazon.com/spa/index.html` and click on the **Smart Home** link, which is located in the left sidebar, then click on **Devices**, shown in the preceding figure. Here, you will see cloud variables will become devices, as shown in the following figure. If you don't see your desired Arduino IoT Cloud variables as a device, then at the bottom, click on the **Discover** button on the **Devices** page, which will take around 20 seconds to load all the stuff.

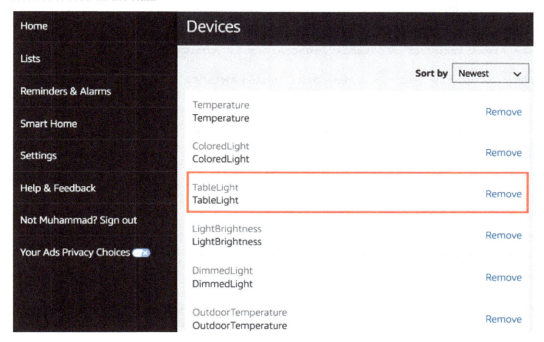

Figure 10.14 – Arduino Cloud variables as devices at Amazon Alexa

Finally, turn on your Amazon Echo Dot and WS2812-based smart lamp and try the following voice commands on Amazon Alexa. Firstly, try these commands, which will help you turn on/off **TableLight**. As shown in the preceding figure, **TableLight** is now acting as a device in the Amazon Alexa smart home:

```
Hey Alexa Turn on the TableLight
Hey Alexa Turn off the TableLight
```

Now it's time to change the brightness and colors of the WS2812 using voice commands. Try the following commands, which will help you to update the brightness and colors. Right now, I have just written four different colors, but you can choose any color name that you want:

```
Hey Alexa set the brightness of TableLight to 99
Hey Alexa set the brightness of TableLight to 50
Hey Alexa change the color of TableLight to red
```

```
Hey Alexa change the color of TableLight to blue
Hey Alexa change the color of TableLight to green
Hey Alexa change the color of TableLight to purple
```

Finally, I am using the Alexa timer functionality to schedule turning on/off the table light after a specific time interval. But you can also use this function just like an alarm and turn on/off the WS2812 for long intervals, such as to turn on the light early in the morning, turning off the lamp at 10:00 P.M., and so on:

```
Hey Alexa turn on the table light after 30 minutes
Hey Alexa turn off the table light after 10 minutes
```

We have discussed different voice commands for Amazon Alexa, but you can search on the internet for more commands regarding light controls and colors.

Now it's time to talk about which Arduino Cloud variables are compatible with Amazon Alexa. You can get up-to-date information at `https://www.amazon.com/Arduino-LLC/dp/B07ZT2PK2H`. At the moment, we have the following list of cloud variables that work perfectly with Amazon Alexa:

- Temperature
- Motion detection
- Light, smart plug, and smart switch
- Dimmed light
- Colored light

According to the preceding list, you can create a thermostat for a room, which will help you to change the room or kitchen temperature according to outdoor and indoor thermostat temperature, you can control your heating and cooling system. To turn on/off any device, we have four different types of cloud variables, which have the same data type Boolean but different names, including light, smart plug, smart switch, and motion detection. These four variables could be used to control any relay/magnetic contactors to turn home appliances on/off, such as cooling/heating systems. We have already discussed **Dimmed light** and **Colored Light** in previous sections.

In this section, we have set up the Amazon Alexa with Arduino Cloud skill and tried different voice commands related to turning lights on and off, as well as how to change the color and brightness of the WS2812 RGB LED ring.

What next?

We still have lots of options available to explore, but now your assignment is to use different relays, sensors, and development boards to do some more experiments and learn from them. In the current chapter, we have only used one WS2812 module for light control, but you can use temperature sensors, relays, and motion sensors to automate your devices in your home, such as automating room switches to control fans, exhaust fans, lights, and air conditioning systems according to room temperature.

> **Important note**
> Be careful when playing with high-voltage power cables when patching the cables to relays.

Summary

In this chapter, we have explored how to develop a low-cost, multi-color smart table lamp for our room using the XIAO ESP32C3 and WS2812. We have set up the Thing, which included cloud variable creation, device association, network configuration, and coding of the development board. Later, we created a dashboard using different widgets to control the WS2812 RGB ring. Finally, we used the Amazon Alexa voice assistant to turn our table lamp on/off and control its color and brightness with voice commands.

This chapter will give you the confidence to build more interesting stuff to make your home and office smarter. In the next chapter, we will talk about Cloud Scheduler and over-the-air update' features. Both features are interesting and specially designed to carry out operations on IoT nodes.

Part 4: Learning Advanced Features of the Arduino IoT Cloud and Looking Ahead

In *Part 4*, the reader is guided through the advanced features of the Arduino IoT Cloud platform, how to use them to develop professional applications, and the tools for maintaining solutions during their life cycle. The book ends with some suggestions for further learning, experimenting, and sourcing information.

This part has the following chapters:

- *Chapter 11, Implementing the Arduino IoT Cloud Scheduler and Over-the-Air Features*
- *Chapter 12, Project #6 – Tracking and Notifying about Your Heart Rate*
- *Chapter 13, Scripting the Arduino IoT Cloud with Cloud CLI*
- *Chapter 14, Moving Ahead in the Arduino IoT Cloud*

11

Implementing the Arduino IoT Cloud Scheduler and Over-the-Air Features

The world is full of different and interesting use cases that vary according to different circumstances. In the world of full automation, many use cases require applications to perform a specific operation at a certain time or frequency, defined by an end user. To handle this situation, the **Arduino IoT Cloud** has a **Scheduler** feature to let end users configure the execution time and frequency through a dashboard, without any modification to code on end devices. Initially, in this chapter, you will learn about the Arduino IoT Cloud Scheduler feature and its implementation.

Then, this chapter will cover the **Over-the-Air** (**OTA**) feature, which is becoming increasingly popular in remote devices such as mobile nodes, especially remote IoT nodes. The OTA feature allows you to broadcast the firmware update to IoT nodes, which will update wirelessly without any physical connection. This procedure enables the remote maintenance of commercial Arduino-based/ESP-series IoT nodes during their life cycle, reducing the related service costs when new features and security fixes become available.

The Arduino IoT Cloud Scheduler provides the ability to schedule operations via a dashboard widget, which helps to execute the operations on devices without modifying the code, and a user can simply adjust the time for routine operations. OTA helps you to send the latest code and updates to devices over the air without any physical connection to a device, which will save operational costs and time.

In this chapter, we will cover the following topics:

- The importance of the Scheduler in IoT
- Using the Arduino IoT Cloud Scheduler – an MKR Wi-Fi 1010 illustration
- Initial configuration – Things, network credentials, cloud variables, and code
- Dashboard creation and a deep dive into the Scheduler widget

- The task at hand – an assignment
- Exploring OTA updates in IoT
- Leveraging the Arduino IoT Cloud for OTA updates

Technical requirements

Before we go any further, first of all, you need to have an Arduino IoT Cloud-compatible board. I recommend Arduino **MKR Wi-Fi 1010** with a bunch of 5 mm LEDs, but here is the complete list of compatible boards: `https://store-usa.arduino.cc/pages/cloud-compatible-boards`. You can choose one according to your requirements.

Second, you need to have an Arduino IoT Cloud account. If you don't already have one, you can sign up at `https://cloud.arduino.cc/` and select a plan according to your requirements.

Third, we need to download and install the **Arduino Create Agent**. Arduino has created a very beautiful web-based guide for installation at `https://create.arduino.cc/getting-started/plugin/welcome`. The code for this chapter is available in the book's official GitHub repository at `https://github.com/PacktPublishing/Arduino-IoT-Cloud-for-Developers`.

> **Important note**
>
> All the Arduino IoT Cloud plans were discussed in detail in *Chapter 1*. You can also visit the following link for updated plan pricing and features: `https://cloud.arduino.cc/plans/`. If you are from an educational institute, then there are plenty of good plans for students and faculties. Arduino also offers customized plans to business organizations according to their requirements.

The importance of the Scheduler in IoT

Within the realm of IoT and cloud computing, a scheduler refers to a component or system that is responsible for managing and controlling the timing and execution of tasks, processes, or events. Its primary function is to ensure the smooth and efficient operation of various activities within an IoT cloud setup. Here are some advantages of employing a scheduler in an IoT cloud environment:

- **Task coordination**: The scheduler facilitates the orchestration of multiple tasks and processes in an IoT cloud by allowing users to define dependencies and priorities. This ensures that tasks are executed in the desired sequence, which is particularly crucial in complex IoT systems involving interconnected devices and services.

- **Resource optimization**: With the limited computational resources typically found in an IoT cloud, a scheduler optimizes its utilization by intelligently assigning tasks based on requirements, available resources, and priorities. This prevents resource overloading or underutilization, leading to enhanced efficiency and cost-effectiveness.

- **Time synchronization**: Achieving synchronized timing for specific operations or events is critical in IoT systems. The scheduler aids in time synchronization by coordinating task execution according to precise timing requirements. This synchronization guarantees that devices, sensors, and services are triggered or activated at the intended moments, enabling accurate data collection, analysis, and decision-making.

- **Energy efficiency**: Many IoT devices operate on constrained battery power, making energy efficiency a vital concern. The scheduler optimizes task scheduling to minimize devices' active time and maximize sleep or low-power mode, thereby conserving energy. This prolongs the battery life of IoT devices, reduces maintenance needs, and enhances overall system reliability.

- **Fault tolerance**: IoT systems are susceptible to failures and disruptions caused by network issues, device malfunctions, or service unavailability. By monitoring task statuses and detecting failures, the scheduler incorporates fault tolerance mechanisms. It automatically reschedules failed or interrupted tasks, ensuring operational continuity and reliability within the IoT cloud.

Overall, a scheduler in an IoT cloud environment brings organization, efficiency, and reliability by coordinating tasks, optimizing resources, synchronizing time, conserving energy, ensuring fault tolerance, and supporting scalability. Its presence is instrumental in managing the complexities of IoT systems and maximizing their performance.

In this section, we have discussed in detail what a scheduler is and how we can benefit from it in product development. In the following section, we will take a look at how the Arduino IoT Cloud Scheduler benefits us in terms of real-world scenarios, and we will also learn how to implement the Arduino IoT Cloud Scheduler using MKR Wi-Fi 101.

Using the Arduino IoT Cloud Scheduler – an MKR Wi-Fi 1010 illustration

In this section, we will take a look at how the Arduino IoT Cloud Scheduler provides different benefits and when and where we require scheduler functionality. Later, we will implement a practical example of a Scheduler using MKR Wi-Fi 1010.

The Arduino IoT Cloud Scheduler

The **Arduino IoT Cloud Scheduler** is a feature integrated into the Arduino IoT Cloud platform that empowers users to schedule and automate actions and events for their connected Arduino devices. It provides a convenient way to define and manage the timing of various tasks and functions within IoT projects. Here are some key aspects and benefits of the Arduino IoT Cloud Scheduler:

- **Task scheduling**: The Arduino IoT Cloud Scheduler allows users to schedule tasks and events on their Arduino devices. It enables the definition of specific timings, intervals, or triggers for actions such as data collection, device control, and sensor readings.

- **Remote control**: By leveraging the Scheduler, users can remotely trigger actions on their Arduino devices. This capability enables the control and automation of functions from any location, without the need for direct physical access to the devices. It enhances flexibility and enables the efficient remote management of IoT projects.

- **Event-based triggers**: The Scheduler supports event-based triggers, empowering users to automate actions based on specific events or conditions. For instance, tasks can be scheduled to execute when a particular sensor value surpasses a defined threshold or when an external event is detected.

- **Time zone management**: The Arduino IoT Cloud Scheduler handles time zone management, ensuring that tasks are executed according to the desired time zone. This functionality is particularly useful when operating across different time zones or serving users in diverse regions.

- **Integration with IoT cloud services**: The Scheduler seamlessly integrates with other features and services offered by the Arduino IoT Cloud platform. This includes data storage, visualization, and notification services. Users can combine scheduling with data logging, charting, and alerting to create comprehensive and cohesive IoT applications.

- **Flexibility and customization**: The Arduino IoT Cloud Scheduler provides a high degree of customization, enabling users to define complex schedules and conditions for their tasks. Users can specify the task frequency, duration, and intervals, and configure advanced parameters to align with their specific requirements.

By harnessing the power of the Arduino IoT Cloud Scheduler, users can automate tasks, remotely control devices, and establish time-based or event-driven workflows for their Arduino-based IoT projects. This feature simplifies the management and coordination of actions across devices, elevating the functionality and efficiency of IoT applications.

In this section, we discussed how the Arduino IoT Cloud Scheduler provides a benefit to schedule our tasks. In the next section, we will implement a Scheduler using MKR Wi-Fi 1010.

An MKR Wi-Fi 1010 example

In this chapter, I will not do a complex project to demonstrate how we can use the Scheduler. Instead, we will use a simple MKR Wi-Fi 1010 with three 5 mm LEDs, and we will set up the system so that it will turn LEDs on or off after a specific time interval. This example will simplify the hardware complexity and help you understand how the Arduino IoT Cloud Scheduler works. *Figure 11.1* shows how LEDs connect with the MKR Wi-Fi 1010 for this Scheduler example.

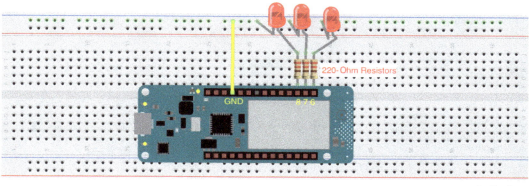

Figure 11.1 – The MKR Wi-Fi 1010 with LEDs

Here, we will just use three LEDs for three different schedulers/timers. We used *Pins 8*, *7*, and *6* to attach the LEDs with the MKR Wi-Fi 1010, using a 220-Ohm resistance, which will control the power from these pins, and one common **ground** (**GND**) goes to all the LEDs via the breadboard.

In this section, we discussed the schematic diagram of our project, where we explained which pins are used to connect the LEDs with the MKR Wi-Fi 1010. In the upcoming section, we will set up a Thing and device association with the Thing, and cloud variable creation and network configuration will be discussed step by step, along with code.

Initial configuration – Things, network credentials, cloud variables, and code

After setting up the hardware, it's time to set up a Thing in the Arduino IoT Cloud. For this project, we need three cloud variables for the Scheduler, which will be linked with dashboard widgets and receive the values from users. Later, the device will perform an operation (in our example, it will turn the LEDs on and off according to a scheduler time) when the Scheduler is active. *Figure 11.2* gives a complete overview of the **Cloud Scheduler** Thing.

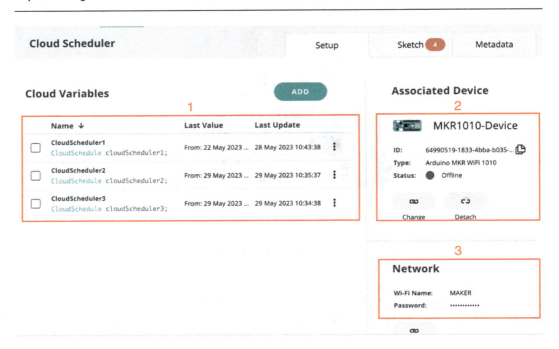

Figure 11.2 – The Cloud Scheduler Thing setup

Set up a new Thing with the name `CloudScheduler`. Take the following steps to create cloud variables, associate a device, set up network configuration, and finally, write the code. In *Figure 11.2*, all the steps are marked with a number above red boxes, which relate to the following steps:

1. Firstly, we need to set up three cloud variables for `CloudScheduler`. The complete details regarding cloud variables are available in the next section.

2. After that, we need to associate the device with the Thing. In the current project, we are using Arduino's MKR Wi-Fi 1010, so the wizard will be the same for Arduino boards. The complete details are available in the *Associating a device* section.

3. Finally, we need to set up the network configuration for the device. Arduino-compatible boards are configured by the Arduino IoT Cloud automatically during the device setup wizard, so you just need to provide the Wi-Fi **service set identifier** (**SSID**) and password.

Cloud variables

The following table explains all the properties of the variables that we need to use during cloud variable creation. For the Scheduler, we will use a custom data type, `Schedule`, which we have thanks to Arduino IoT Cloud's extended group of variables. Then, make sure you have the same `declaration` variable as per the table; otherwise, you will need to modify the example code according to your naming.

S#	Variable Name	Variable Type	Declaration	Permission	Update Policy
1	CloudScheduler1	Schedule	cloudScheduler1	Read and write	On change
2	CloudScheduler2	Schedule	cloudScheduler2	Read and write	On change
3	CloudScheduler3	Schedule	cloudScheduler3	Read and write	On change

Table 11.1 – The cloud variables declaration list

Here, I set the permission as *read* and *write* because we will input the date, time, and interval from the Arduino dashboard, which will be controlled by the end user, and the device will only perform the LED on/off operation when the Scheduler is in a state of `true`. **Update Policy** is set to **On change**, as the dashboard will send data to the device when there is any change in Scheduler values by the user.

Associating a device

After creating the variable, it's time to add a device and associate it with the Thing:

1. Before adding the device, connect the development board to the computer and open the **Arduino Create Agent** application.

2. After assigning a name to the Thing, we need to attach the device to it. When you click on the **Select Device** button, you will see a popup that shows you the available devices and an option to add a new device. In our case, we don't have a device in the portal, so we can just click on **SET UP NEW DEVICE** to configure a new device in the account.

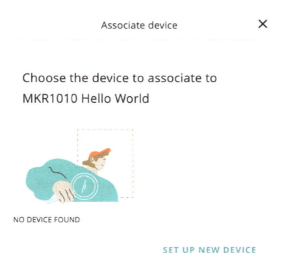

Associate device   ✕

Choose the device to associate to
MKR1010 Hello World

NO DEVICE FOUND

SET UP NEW DEVICE

Figure 11.3 – The associated device

3. Then, you will see two options in the popup. The first option is **Set up an Arduino device**, and the second option is **Set up a 3rd Party device**. Here, you will see a note under both options that says **Compatible devices**. This means you cannot use all types of Arduino devices and third-party devices with the Arduino IoT Cloud.

Figure 11.4 – Choosing the device

Select one option from the popup according to the available device. For this example, we will click on **Set up an Arduino device**, as in this chapter, we are using an MKR Wi-Fi 1010 board. Before adding the device, make sure the **Arduino Create Agent** is running on your machine.

> **Important note**
>
> Here is the link where you can find the Arduino IoT Cloud-compatible boards: `https://store-usa.arduino.cc/pages/cloud-compatible-boards`. For third-party devices, we have three options, which are ESP8266, ESP32, and **LoRaWAN** devices. For other devices, we have API access, which was discussed in the second part of *Chapter 2*.

4. Now, you will see the **Setup Device** popup, which will start searching for your device. Make sure the device is properly connected to the machine.

←   Setup Device   ✕

Arduino MKR WiFi 1010 found

An Arduino MKR WiFi 1010 has been detected on port /dev/cu.usbmodem14101 and ready to be configured.

CONFIGURE

If the detected type of the device you want to configure is not correct, try to reset your board and then refresh

Figure 11.5 – Setup Device

The wizard will find and list all the connected boards with their name and port details. Click on the **CONFIGURE** button to move forward. If the wizard didn't show the device after searching, try to plug it into a different port, and click on the **refresh** link located at the bottom.

5. In the next configuration wizard, provide the device name. Spaces and special characters are not allowed in the device name. Then, click on the **NEXT** button.

Figure 11.6 – The device configuration name

After that, the wizard will start the device configuration process. This will take up to five minutes, but in most cases, it only takes one minute to configure the device.

6.   You will then see the **Congratulations! You are all set** message in the next popup. Click on the **Done** button, and the device will be attached to your Thing.

In this section, we associated the MKR Wi-Fi 1010 development board with our Thing. In the next section, we will configure the Wi-Fi network configuration for the MKR Wi-Fi 1010.

Network configuration

After the attachment of the device with the Thing, we can see that the device is offline. To get it online, we need to provide the Wi-Fi details.

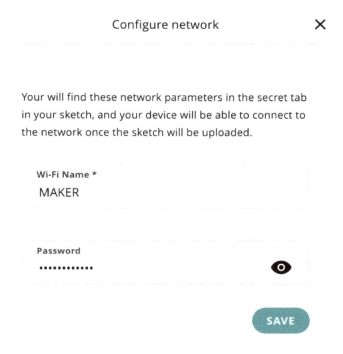

Figure 11.7 – Network configuration

On the Thing page under the **Network** tab, click on the **CONFIGURE** button. You will see the **Configure network** pop-up box with two fields – **Wi-Fi Name** and **Password**. Type in the Wi-Fi SSID and password, and click on the **SAVE** button.

We are done with the device and network configuration; only the coding part is left. In the next section, we will look at the code for the device.

Coding

The code for this chapter is available in the book's official GitHub repository. Download the `Cloud_ Scheduler_may22a` code from the repository, and import it to your **Arduino Web Editor**.

You can download the code and put it into your Thing by navigating to the **Sketch** tab. The whole project code is very small and simple; that's why I will go through all the code here and discuss it in detail. Remember, never try to use the `delay()` method, as it will block the `ArduinoCloud. update()` method:

```
#define LED1 8
#define LED2 7
#define LED3 6
```

Here, we have very simple code. Firstly, we will define the pins' LED1, LED2, and LED3 constants, which will be initialized in the setup() method as output, using the pinMode() method:

```
void setup() {
  pinMode(LED1,OUTPUT);
  pinMode(LED2,OUTPUT);
  pinMode(LED3,OUTPUT);
  // Initialize serial and wait for port to open:
  Serial.begin(9600);
  // This delay gives the chance to wait for a Serial Monitor without
blocking if none is found
  delay(1500);

  // Defined in thingProperties.h
  initProperties();

  // Connect to Arduino IoT Cloud
  ArduinoCloud.begin(ArduinoIoTPreferredConnection);

  setDebugMessageLevel(2);
  ArduinoCloud.printDebugInfo();
}
```

Then, we have all the code regarding Schedulers in the loop() method, which will perform an operation when a scheduler/timer is in an active state. In the following code, we have a separate if-else statement for each cloudScheduler cloud variable; here, we check whether cloudScheduler is active and then turn on the LED; otherwise, we turn off the LED. We have cloudScheduler1, cloudScheduler2, and cloudScheduler3, plus three if-else statements to check their values:

```
void loop() {
  ArduinoCloud.update();
  // Your code here

  //Cloud Scheduler 1 Code
  if(cloudScheduler1.isActive()){
    digitalWrite(LED1,HIGH);
  }else{
    digitalWrite(LED1,LOW);
  }

    //Cloud Scheduler 2 Code
  if(cloudScheduler2.isActive()){
```

```
    digitalWrite(LED2,HIGH);
  }else{
    digitalWrite(LED2,LOW);
  }

    //Cloud Scheduler 3 Code
  if(cloudScheduler3.isActive()){
    digitalWrite(LED3,HIGH);
  }else{
    digitalWrite(LED3,LOW);
  }

}
```

The Scheduler widget is very complex in configuration with lots of options, but its code is very simple and straightforward. You just need to verify whether the Scheduler state is `true` or `false`, and if it's `true`, then proceed with the task; otherwise, stop the task. So, in the `loop()` method, we have three `if-else` statements, which check different cloud Schedulers'/timers' states. If a specific Scheduler is active, then a specific LED will be turned on; otherwise, it will be turned off.

I attached the LED in *Pin #8* to `cloudScheduler1`, the LED in *Pin #7* to `cloudScheduler2`, and the LED in *Pin #6* to `cloudScheduler3`. Now, set the first widget's time to 5 seconds for every minute, the second widget to 10 seconds for every minute, and 15 seconds for every minute for the third widget. All the LEDs will turn on at the same time, but the first LED will be on for 5 seconds, the second LED will be on for 10 seconds, and the third will turn off after 15 seconds. In this example project, we have used three different Schedulers to demonstrate how we can use multiple Schedulers/timers to automate our tasks on a single development board.

> **Important note**
>
> If you used different *naming* in the variable declaration, then update the code according to your naming scheme. However, it's better at first if you follow all the steps according to the book and later change the cloud variable names and modify your code, respectively.
>
> Also, don't put the code at the end of the `loop()` method, as it will create a delay with pulse sensor readings.

In this section, we discussed code and how it works with the Arduino IoT Cloud Scheduler to turn the LEDs on and off. In the following section, we will set up a dashboard, where we will place the Scheduler widget and attach it to our cloud variables.

Dashboard creation and a deep dive into the Scheduler widget

After uploading the code to the device, it's time to set up a dashboard for web and mobile to insert the multiple Scheduler widgets that will be linked to the Scheduler variables, for further controls and operations. The following figure shows the visualization Scheduler with different timer options:

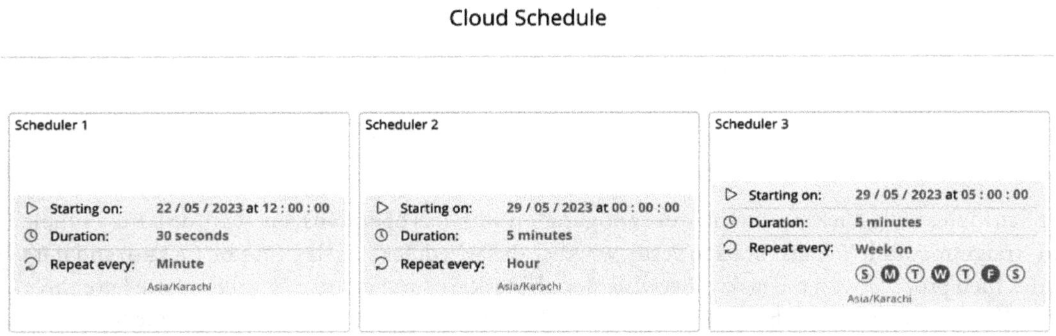

Cloud Schedule

Scheduler 1		Scheduler 2		Scheduler 3	
▷ Starting on:	22 / 05 / 2023 at 12 : 00 : 00	▷ Starting on:	29 / 05 / 2023 at 00 : 00 : 00	▷ Starting on:	29 / 05 / 2023 at 05 : 00 : 00
⏱ Duration:	30 seconds	⏱ Duration:	5 minutes	⏱ Duration:	5 minutes
⟳ Repeat every:	Minute	⟳ Repeat every:	Hour	⟳ Repeat every:	Week on
	Asia/Karachi		Asia/Karachi		Ⓢ Ⓜ Ⓣ Ⓦ Ⓣ Ⓕ Ⓢ
					Asia/Karachi

Figure 11.8 – The Thing dashboard

We have three Scheduler variables. To visualize all of them, three Scheduler widgets will be linked to each cloud variable, respectively. The purpose of the three widgets and variables is to demonstrate how we can set different types of timers. The first widget demonstrates how to use a timer that will be executed every minute for 30 seconds, the second widget demonstrates how to use a timer that will be activated every hour for five minutes, and the third widget demonstrates that we can set the timer for a long period, such as specific days at a specific time. Here, I have set it to be activated on Monday, Wednesday, and Friday for five minutes.

We just set the different widgets with different timer settings. One of the example settings of the Scheduler widget is shown in *Figure 11.9*, and we will explore in depth how to set these settings. This control widget has multiple options for configuration, so I think it's necessary to discuss it in detail for proper guidance.

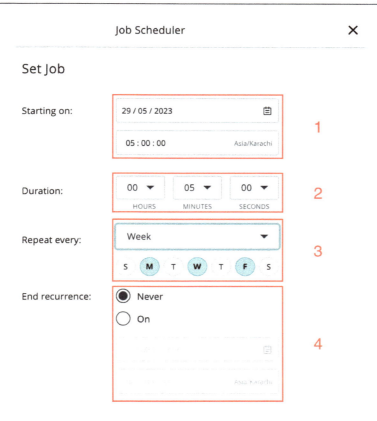

Figure 11.9 – The Scheduler widget options

When you click on the Scheduler widget, a popup will appear with options, just like in the preceding figure. Here, I have divided the screenshot into four different numbered sections. From this popup, you can adjust your time settings from seconds to years and set the start and end date, or choose to execute without any date limitation. Let's look at each section:

1. Here, we have two input controls – one is for the starting date and the other is for the starting time, as indicated by the control headings.

2. Next, we have the **Duration** setting, in which we have three drop-down boxes – **HOURS**, **MINUTES**, and **SECONDS**. This will define how long the timer will be executed on the machine. For example, if you want to perform an operation for 30 seconds, then just select **30** seconds and leave the other fields, or if you want to perform an operation for 5 minutes, then select **5** minutes and leave the other fields, and so on.

3. Then, we have the **Repeat every** setting, which is only applicable for **Week**, **Month**, and **Year**; there is no predefined setting for minutes and hours. I have selected **Week**. Under that, the days are shown (by their first letter), and there, you can select on which day/days you can perform an operation. There are different options for **Month** and **Year**, which will be discussed in a moment.

4.   Finally, we have the **End recurrence** setting. Here, we have two options – **Never** and **On**. When you click on **On**, you will need to enter the date and time when your operation will be stopped. If you want to execute it indefinitely, then just select the **Never** option.

For **Year** and **Month** in the **Repeat every** section, we have different options in the Scheduler. The following figures show all the details regarding both options. First, let's look at **Month**:

Figure 11.10 – The Month option in the Scheduler

Here is the **Year** option:

Figure 11.11 – The Year option in the Scheduler

For **Month**, we have a dropdown that allows us to select the day (such as **1st**), while in the case of **Year**, we have two dropdowns – one for the day and one for the month (such as **1st January**).

In this section, we set up the dashboard with three different Scheduler widgets and assigned them Boolean-type cloud variables, which will be used in our code to check the Scheduler state and whether the Scheduler is active or not. In the following section, you have an assignment to use the Scheduler according to the specified requirements, giving you a proper idea of how you can use the scheduler functionality in your projects to enhance your product development.

The task at hand – an assignment

Continuing from the previous project where you connected three LEDs to the MKR Wi-Fi 1010 and set up the Arduino IoT Cloud Scheduler, complete the following assignment tasks:

- Attach three relays to control any electrical/electronic appliance, such as a fan, light, or heater, using the Scheduler.

- Implement the Scheduler to turn your home's outside/indoor lights on/off.

- Attach a buzzer instead of LEDs, and create an alarm device for your room/classroom.

- Turn on surprise lighting with the Scheduler for a birthday or anniversary. Use the same light strip with multiple Schedulers to turn the light strips on/off for different occasions.

- Control the water solenoid valve for your garden/tunnel farm using the Scheduler (this is optional, and if you have a smart agriculture facility).

In this section, we outlined an assignment that will test your skills with different scenarios and help you explore the usage of the Scheduler feature in different environments. In the following section, we will start to explore the benefits of OTA, the Arduino IoT Cloud's OTA features, supported development boards for OTA, and how to use OTA features in the Arduino IoT Cloud. And, of, course you will also learn about the pros and cons of the Arduino IoT Cloud OTA.

Exploring OTA updates in IoT

OTA is a term that refers to the wireless distribution of software or firmware updates, or other updates to devices. This technology allows updates to be delivered and installed on devices without the need for physical connections or manual intervention. OTA is widely utilized across various industries, including telecommunications, automotive, consumer electronics, and IoT. Here are a few examples of OTA usage:

- **Mobile devices**: OTA updates are commonly employed to distribute operating system updates, security patches, and feature enhancements to smartphones and tablets. Users receive notifications, prompting them to download and install the updates wirelessly.

- **Automotive industry**: Many modern vehicles are equipped with OTA capabilities, enabling manufacturers to remotely update the vehicle software, infotainment systems, navigation maps, and other features. OTA updates can improve vehicle performance, introduce new functionalities, and address security vulnerabilities.

- **IoT devices**: IoT devices, such as smart home devices, wearables, and industrial sensors, often rely on OTA updates to deliver firmware updates, bug fixes, and new features. This enables manufacturers to enhance device performance, address vulnerabilities, and introduce new functionalities without the need for physical access to the devices.

- **Set-top boxes and smart TVs**: OTA updates are utilized to deliver firmware updates and software patches to set-top boxes and smart TVs. This ensures that these devices remain up to date with the latest features, security enhancements, and bug fixes.

OTA updates offer numerous benefits, including convenience, cost-effectiveness, and the ability to quickly address security vulnerabilities or software issues. However, ensuring the integrity and security of OTA updates is crucial to prevent unauthorized access or malicious activities that could compromise the devices or data.

In this section, we explored what OTA is and how it offers benefits in today's world. In the following section, we will discuss in detail the Arduino IoT Cloud OTA feature, which includes compatible devices that are supported by the Arduino IoT Cloud for OTA, and how to use the OTA feature in the Arduino IoT Cloud to send firmware updates to devices.

Leveraging the Arduino IoT Cloud for OTA updates

Arduino IoT Cloud OTA is a feature available in the Arduino IoT Cloud platform, designed to facilitate the remote monitoring and control of Arduino-based IoT devices. This functionality allows users to wirelessly update the firmware of their deployed Arduino IoT devices.

The Arduino IoT Cloud pros

The Arduino IoT Cloud OTA feature offers the following capabilities:

- **Firmware updates**: Users can remotely update the firmware of their Arduino IoT devices as well as ESP-series devices using Arduino IoT Cloud OTA. This enables the deployment of bug fixes, security patches, feature enhancements, and new versions of code without the need for physical access to the devices.

- **Code synchronization**: The OTA feature ensures that the code running on Arduino/ESP-series IoT devices remains synchronized with the latest version stored on the cloud. It eliminates the necessity of manually updating each device individually, thereby maintaining consistency across the entire fleet of IoT devices.

- **OTA configuration**: In addition to firmware updates and code synchronization, Arduino IoT Cloud OTA enables users to remotely configure the parameters or settings of their Arduino/ESP-series IoT devices. This means device behavior can be modified, thresholds can be adjusted, and variables can be changed without the need for physical intervention.

- **Security and integrity**: Arduino IoT Cloud OTA ensures the security and integrity of firmware updates through authentication and encryption mechanisms. This safeguards against unauthorized access or tampering during the transmission process, enhancing the security of IoT devices and preventing potential vulnerabilities.

By providing a convenient and secure method to remotely update firmware and configure devices, the Arduino IoT Cloud OTA simplifies the management and maintenance of Arduino-based IoT deployments. It enhances efficiency, reduces costs, and enables users to keep their IoT devices up to date with the latest features, bug fixes, and security enhancements. In the following subsection, we will discuss the cons of the Arduino IoT Cloud OTA feature.

Arduino IoT Cloud OTA cons

The Arduino IoT Cloud OTA feature is a convenient tool to remotely update the firmware of your Arduino devices connected to the Arduino IoT Cloud platform. However, as with any technology, it has its drawbacks and limitations. Here are some cons of the Arduino IoT Cloud OTA feature:

- **Limited bandwidth**: OTA updates require data transfer over the internet, which can be costly or problematic in areas with limited or expensive data bandwidth. Large firmware updates may consume a significant amount of data.

- **Network stability**: Reliable internet connectivity is essential for OTA updates. If a device loses connection during an update, it can result in failed or corrupt firmware, potentially rendering the device unusable.

- **Version control**: Managing different versions of firmware across multiple devices can become challenging. Keeping track of which devices are running which firmware versions and ensuring compatibility can be time-consuming.

- **Compatibility issues**: OTA updates may not work seamlessly with all types of devices and configurations. Ensuring that your hardware supports OTA updates and that you have the necessary libraries and code in place can be a complex task.

- **Latency**: Depending on the size of the firmware update and the speed of the internet connection, OTA updates can introduce latency, causing devices to be temporarily unavailable during the update process.

- **Dependency on the Arduino IoT Cloud**: To use the Arduino IoT Cloud OTA feature, you must rely on the Arduino IoT Cloud platform. If the platform experiences downtime or changes in its services, it can impact your ability to perform OTA updates.

- **Limited rollback options**: In some cases, if an OTA update fails or causes issues, rolling back to a previous firmware version can be challenging, especially if you didn't plan for rollback mechanisms in advance.

Despite these cons, OTA updates remain a valuable feature for many IoT projects. However, it's essential to carefully assess your project's specific requirements and constraints before implementing OTA updates and to address these challenges through proper planning and security measures.

In this section, we discussed the different benefits of the Arduino IoT Cloud OTA feature as well as its cons. In the following section, we will take a deeper look into which hardware development boards are compatible with the Arduino IoT Cloud OTA feature, as it is currently not supported by all hardware development boards. Therefore, it's necessary for you to keep this point in mind during the product development stage if you need an OTA feature for your product.

A list of compatible development hardware for Arduino OTA

Not all of the official Arduino (or other) development boards are ready for the OTA feature, but here are the ones that are compatible and ready. Go to this link to check out all the information regarding OTA-compatible development boards: `https://docs.arduino.cc/arduino-cloud/features/ota-getting-started`.

These are the official Arduino development boards that are ready for OTA:

- Arduino MKR Wi-Fi 1010
- Arduino Nano 33 IoT
- Arduino Nano RP2040 Connect
- Portenta H7
- Portenta Machine Control
- Nicla Vision
- Arduino Opta (PLC)

These are the ESP32-series development boards that are ready for OTA:

- ESP32-S2-DevKitC
- NodeMCU-32-S2
- WeMos LOLIN D32
- ESP32-S3-DevKitC
- ESP32-CAM
- NodeMCU-32S
- Freenove ESP32 WROVER
- ESP32-DevKitC-32E
- DOIT ESP32 DevKit v1

The good thing is that Arduino provides the latest features to ESP32-series development boards. These boards are very popular among students/researchers and professional developers, due to their cost and availability all around the world. I used the **XIAO ESP32-C3 series** development board for various projects and tested the OTA service for that board. From my personal experience, the OTA service works faster on official Arduino development boards as compared to the ESP32 series, but I hope in the future that the Arduino Cloud team will optimize the OTA feature for the ESP32 series board for a faster and better experience.

> **Important note**
>
> The Arduino IoT Cloud offers the OTA feature to Wi-Fi-enabled devices. This means that LoRaWAN is currently not compatible with the OTA feature.

In this section, we discussed the broad range of compatible boards that support the Arduino IoT Cloud OTA feature. In the following section, we will take a look at how we can use the OTA feature in the Arduino IoT Cloud to send firmware updates via the internet, without any device connection to the host computer.

Implementing the OTA update on the MKR Wi-Fi 1010

Firstly, we will explore how we can use OTA, and then we will dive deep into how OTA works behind the scenes. We need to navigate to a Thing that uses an OTA-supported development board; we will choose a Thing that is already attached to the MKR Wi-Fi 1010 device. Navigate to the **Sketch** tab in the Thing. The following figure shows the OTA feature and port:

Figure 11.12 – The physical port connection with the OTA update feature

My device is connected to my MacBook as well as to the Arduino IoT Cloud via Wi-Fi. That's why you can see two options in the preceding figure for sketch uploading. The first one is the **Port** option, which is only available when your development board is directly connected to your laptop/computer, while the second option is **Over-the-Air**, which is available when your code is configured on your development board with network settings and successfully connected to the Arduino IoT Cloud over the internet.

Select the **Over-the-Air** option, and click on the **Sketch Uploading** (the green arrow icon) button; this will start uploading your updated code to the board via the internet without the intervention of a physical connection. However, how can you confirm that this works via the internet? Just unplug the development board from your computer and power it with any adapter, but make sure your device has access to a Wi-Fi router.

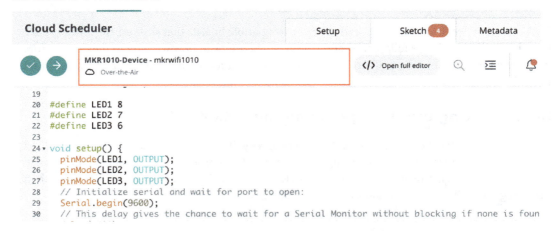

Figure 11.13 – The standalone Over-the-Air update option

After disconnecting from the computer and turning on the device via the power adapter, you will see only the **Over-the-Air** update option in your **Sketch** tab. Just modify your code or add some extra login details, and click on **Sketch Uploading** (the green arrow icon), and within a short time, your code will be on the development board without any hassle.

Based on my experience, I've often thought we should have an option by which we can modify/update the code of remote devices, such as devices for smart agriculture, warehouse monitoring, and industrial monitoring, because it's very difficult to travel to remote places to update/modify the code. However, the Arduino IoT Cloud OTA feature makes our lives easier overall. With the OTA feature, we can save time and cost and provide the correct updates on time to our devices without any delay.

How OTA works

Let's talk about how OTA works behind the scenes. The Arduino IoT Cloud first compiles the code in a cloud environment, according to the selected device, and then stores these compiled files in **AWS S3** storage. There, we will get the URL of the compiled files' location, which is transmitted from the Arduino IoT Cloud to the device directly for further operations. When the device receives the OTA file URL and the OTA_REQ flag is `true`, it will start downloading the compiled files from the specified URL. After download completion, the development board verifies the downloaded files with a length/CRC check. After download verification, the board will start flashing with the latest firmware. The following figure illustrates the whole procedure that happens behind the scenes:

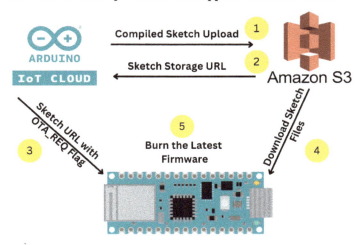

Figure 11.14 – The Arduino IoT Cloud OTA behind the scenes

The Arduino IoT Cloud team has simplified the complexity of this process and provides only a single-click option for developers for OTA. The purpose of this diagram is to give you an overview of how things work, which will hopefully provide you with new ideas for your future developments.

In this section, we learned how to implement the Arduino IoT Cloud OTA feature to send firmware OTA. We also discussed how the Arduino IoT Cloud sends firmware updates to devices using the Amazon S3 service.

Summary

In this chapter, we explored the Scheduler and how we can use the Arduino IoT Cloud to automate tasks that have different patterns or random patterns of operation. We used simple LEDs with the MKR Wi-Fi 1010 to demonstrate multiple Scheduler/timer operations, which helped you to understand how to use this function in real-world projects, such as in smart agriculture and smart industry.

In the second part of the chapter, we explored OTA. Firstly, we discussed the pros and cons of OTA and how we can save time and costs with it. Then, we used OTA-enabled development boards to demonstrate the use of the OTA feature, and finally, we explored how OTA works behind the scenes.

In the following chapter, we will implement a healthcare project. You will learn how to use a heartbeat sensor as well as the Arduino IoT Cloud webhooks feature, which will send data to a third-party service (**Zapier**). We will use Zapier to set up a *Zap*, which will receive the heartbeat readings and send an email notification to a designated person if the reading is over or under the threshold.

12

Project #6 – Tracking and Notifying about Your Heart Rate

This chapter is dedicated to smart healthcare and wearables. It shows how healthcare devices can be integrated with the **Arduino IoT Cloud platform** and offers an example of an interface between the Arduino IoT Cloud and a third-party service. The notification service sends notifications to recipients when the measured heart rate exceeds the defined heart rate threshold.

In this chapter, we will embark on a practical exploration of smart health and wearables by working with a **heart rate sensor** and Seeed Studio's newest and very small development board in the **XIAO series**, based on **ESP32** with a lot of features. With the help of a sensor, a development board, and the Arduino IoT Cloud, we will build an IoT-enabled wearable healthcare solution. You will also learn how to set up webhooks for sending the latest heart rate values to Zapier. Finally, you will see how to set up Zaps in Zapier for email/mobile notifications on heart rate data.

In this chapter, we're going to cover the following main topics:

- Exploring IoT for smart health solutions
- Knowing the hardware components – sensors and development boards
- Understanding the project architecture
- Setting up Things, network credentials, cloud variables, and code
- Setting up a dashboard for web and mobile
- Setting up the notification service

Technical requirements

The following hardware components are required to complete this chapter's exercise:

- Seeed Studio XIAO ESP32C3

- USB Type-C cable for the XIAO ESP32C3

- Pulse sensor (find the complete details and store links in the *Knowing the hardware components – sensors and development boards* section)

- Male headers for the development board

- Jumper cables

For coding, we will use the **Arduino Web Editor**, which includes a large collection of development boards and sensor libraries, along with Arduino IoT Cloud for Thing and dashboard setup. To develop hardware and sensor designs, we need the **Fritzing** desktop software and the **Arduino IDE** desktop software for pulse-sensor calibration using the **Serial Plotter**, which is not available in the Arduino Web Editor.

We will also use **Zapier** to send alerts by email when our sensor detects a heart rate above our specified **beats-per-minute** (**BPM**) threshold. You can use a Free/trial account or buy a Zapier Professional plan according to the requirements of your project as Zapier Professional provides more features and functions compared to a Free account. The code used in this chapter is available from the book's official GitHub repository at `https://github.com/PacktPublishing/Arduino-IoT-Cloud-for-Developers`.

Exploring IoT for smart health solutions

The **Internet of Things** (**IoT**) is playing a significant role in providing smart healthcare solutions that can improve patient outcomes and reduce healthcare costs. IoT devices can collect real-time data, communicate with other devices, and generate insights that can help healthcare providers make better decisions.

Here are some examples of how IoT can be used in smart health solutions:

- **Remote patient monitoring**: IoT devices can be used to monitor patients' health in real time, even when they are not in the hospital. Wearable devices, sensors, and medical-grade IoT devices can collect data on vital signs, BPM rates, blood-glucose levels, and medication adherence. Healthcare providers can use this data to provide personalized care and prevent complications.

- **Telemedicine**: IoT devices can enable virtual consultations and remote medical services. Patients can communicate with their healthcare providers using video conferencing, and healthcare providers can remotely monitor patients' health through IoT devices. This can improve access to healthcare services, reduce healthcare costs, and improve patient outcomes.

- **Smart medication management**: IoT devices can help patients manage their medications more effectively. IoT-enabled pill dispensers can remind patients when it's time to take their medication and can track medication usage. Healthcare providers can use this data to provide personalized care and prevent medication errors.

- **Predictive maintenance**: IoT devices can be used to monitor medical equipment and predict when maintenance is required. This can help prevent equipment failures, reduce downtime, and improve patient outcomes.

- **Smart hospital management**: IoT devices can be used to manage hospital resources more efficiently. For example, IoT-enabled asset tracking systems can help healthcare providers locate medical equipment quickly, reducing waiting times for patients.

In conclusion, IoT can enable smart health solutions that improve patient outcomes and reduce healthcare costs. Healthcare providers can use IoT data to provide personalized care and make more informed decisions. As IoT technology continues to evolve, we can expect to see even more innovative healthcare solutions in the future.

In this section, we have discussed IoT and smart healthcare and how IoT is beneficial to us in the development of smart healthcare products. Next, we will take a look at what types of hardware and sensors are required to carry out the exercise in this chapter.

Knowing the hardware components – sensors and development boards

The ESP32 series offers a wide array of development boards that vary in the sizes and pins offered. In this chapter, we are using Seeed Studio's latest development board, the **XIAO ESP32C3**, as it's very compact and smaller in size than other boards, cheaper in cost, and provides 5V along with 3.3V. *Figure 12.1* shows a pin diagram of the XIAO ESP32C3 we will use:

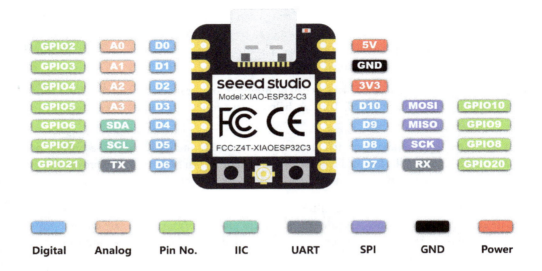

Figure 12.1 – XIAO ESP32C3 pinout diagram

The XIAO ESP32C3 provides multiple pins for digital input/output. In previous ESP-series boards such as the ESP8266, we only had one analog pin, but we have four on this development board, which removes the biggest hurdle encountered when developing solutions using multiple analog pins. To get around this on previous ESP-series boards, we had to use **ADS1115/ADS1015** for extra analog pins, so this development board will save you some bucks with its four analog pins by default.

Besides these features, XIAO provides a built-in battery charge module and the board is optimized for power consumption, which make this board appropriate for developing wearable devices. For connectivity, both Wi-Fi and Bluetooth are available, including **Bluetooth Low Energy** (**BLE**) **5 support**, which is more specific to IoT use cases. For further details, please visit `https://wiki.` `seeedstudio.com/XIAO_ESP32C3_Getting_Started/`.

For our current project, we need one analog pin for the **pulse sensor**, and a5V pin for power. One of the good features of our chosen development board is that we have a 5V power pin, which is not available in most of the ESP32 series development boards.

We use the pulse sensor to measure the BPM but there is a variety of other pulse oximeters on the market for BPM and pulse measurement. The following pulse sensor (*Figure 12.2*) is open source, cheaper, and easier to use than other sensors. You can also use Chinese-made pulse sensors but you will require controlled conditions while using these sensors.

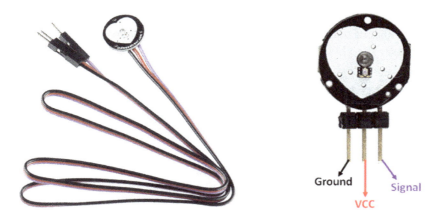

Figure 12.2 – Pulse sensor and its pinout diagram

The following is a list of official stores where you can buy the original pulse sensor:

- **SparkFun**: https://www.sparkfun.com/products/11574

- **Adafruit**: https://www.adafruit.com/product/1093

- **Amazon UK**: https://www.amazon.co.uk/dp/B01CPP4QM0

- **Amazon USA**: https://www.amazon.com/PulseSensor-com-Original-Pulse-Sensor-project/dp/B01CPP4QM0

The preceding figure shows the pinout layout of the pulse sensor. *Pin #1* is the GND pin, which connects to the onboard GND pin. *Pin #2*, VCC, works with both 3.3V and 5V. *Pin #3* connects to any analog pin on the board. I connect it to *Pin #A1* on the board. You can solder the male headers to the pulse sensor or directly solder the cables without any header pins.

Measuring a pulse is a very critical and difficult task, but we can benefit from pulsesensor.com, started by **World Famous Electronics LLC** as a crowd-funding project. On this site, you can find all the official details including specifications, how the sensor works, and development board code samples.

> **Important note**
> Chinese-made pulse sensors are good for DIY projects, but even sensors from official stores can't be deployed in real-world use cases without professional calibration using a real-time **electrocardiogram (ECG)**, BPM equipment, and a doctor's verification.

In this section, we discussed the pulse sensor and where you can buy it, as well as examining its pinout diagram for better understanding. Next, we will examine the project architecture, covering how to connect the sensors to the XIAO ESP32C3.

Understanding the project architecture

In the preceding sections, we discussed the sensors and development board in detail. Now it's time to get started on the recipe. In hardware development, before we start working with sensors and development boards, we need to develop the design concepts to get a better understanding of how things will be connected. There are many pieces of software available to design and develop design concepts for electronics projects, but we are going to use Fritzing.

In the following two subsections, we will cover schematics and project design, explaining how to connect the pins to the development board and soldering. Next, we will do some calibration of the *pulse sensor fetch-reading threshold*, as this is different for different development boards. This is very important to do before we send the data to the cloud.

Schematics design and assembly

The purpose of design is to get a clear understanding of how the sensors will be connected to the development board. A clear design helps engineers to develop a prototype on a **breadboard** or **veroboard**. Another major benefit of effective design is that Fritzing builds hardware schematics and PCB designs in the background according to your design, which can then be adjusted by designers according to the system requirements. *Figure 12.3* shows the project schematic diagram demonstrating how to connect the pulse sensor to the XIAO ESP32C3:

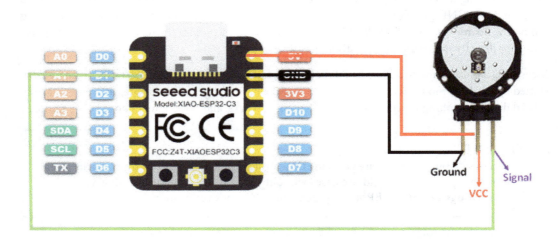

Figure 12.3 – XIAO ESP32C and pulse sensor system design

The design in the preceding figure provides an overview of how to connect the sensors to the development board. According to our design, we have 5V and GND from the development board to the pulse sensor. The pulse sensor is an analog sensor, so we connected its *Signal* pin to the *A1* pin of the development board.

Figure 12.4 – Final prototype

After soldering the male headers to the pulse sensor and the XIAO ESP32C3, connect the pins according to the schematic. There is only one sensor, so no veroboard is required. *Figure 12.4* shows the pulse sensor connected to the XIAO ESP32C3 without any breadboard or Veroboard, but rather, directly connected with jumper wires. Now, it's time to calibrate the pulse sensor and get an appropriate threshold value by putting your fingertip on the sensor.

Sensor calibration

For sensor calibration, we need the Serial Plotter to identify the pulse value threshold. Currently, the Arduino Web Editor does not support the Serial Plotter, so we are going to use the Arduino IDE. To work with the Arduino IDE, we need to install the **Seeed Studio XIAO ESP32C3 series** development board and the pulsesensor.com library.

To install the ESP32 series development board in the Arduino IDE, firstly, add the board's definition file in the preferences:

1. Navigate to **File** > **Preferences**, and fill the **Additional Boards Manager URLs** field with the following URL: https://raw.githubusercontent.com/espressif/arduino-esp32/gh-pages/package_esp32_dev_index.json.

2. Then, navigate to **Tools** > **Board** > **Boards Manager...**, type esp32 in the search box, select the latest version of ****esp32****, and install it.

3. Finally, select the board by navigating to **Tools** > **Board** > **ESP32 Arduino** and selecting **XIAO_ESP32C3**. The list of boards is a little long and you will need to scroll to the bottom to find it.

It's time to install the pulse sensor library. Navigate to **Sketch** > **Include Library** > **Manage Libraries**. Type `pulsesensor playground` into the search bar. Only one library will be returned here – install it.

Now we are ready to proceed to the calibration step. Navigate to **File** > **Examples** > **PulseSensor Playground** > **Getting Started Project**. Here, you will get the template code for calibration, to which we will make the following changes:

```
// Variables
int PulseSensorPurplePin = A1;           // Pulse Sensor PURPLE WIRE
connected to ANALOG PIN 0
int LED = 10;     //  The on-board Arduino LED
```

Set the `PulseSensorPurplePin` variable to `A1`. Remember to never use a simple `1` as it will give you different values. Next, assign `10` to the `LED` variable. After these modifications, upload the code to the board. To monitor the recorded values in graph format, navigate to **Tools** > **Serial Plotter**. *Figure 12.5* shows the Serial Plotter presenting all the values in the form of a graph. The threshold values are marked by the red box.

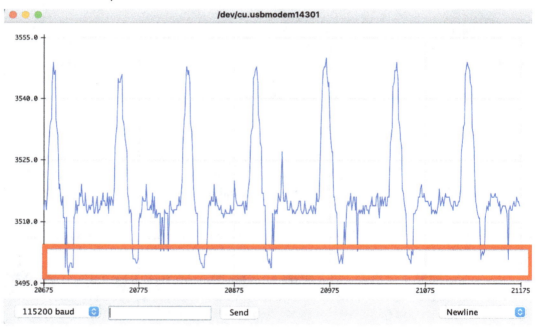

Figure 12.5 – Pulse sensor raw-readings graph using the Serial Plotter

Put a finger on the front side of the pulse sensor, which is marked with a white heart shape. Wait for some time for the readings to stabilize on the Serial Plotter. After a few seconds, you should see stable readings as shown in the preceding figure. Mark the lowest level as the threshold. In my case, I take **3500** as the threshold value to avoid noise.

After that, download the `PulseSensor_BPM_Alternative` code from the GitHub repository under `Chapter 12`. This is some code modified by us that we'll use to display the BPM. But before uploading the code to the board, modify the values as follows:

```
const int PULSE_INPUT = A1;
const int PULSE_BLINK = 10;
const int PULSE_FADE = 5;
const int THRESHOLD = 3450;    // Adjust this number to avoid noise
when idle
```

Assign A1 to the `PULSE_INPUT` variable, 10 to `PULSE_BLINK`, and set the `THRESHOLD` value according to your stabilized reading taken from the Serial Plotter. As stated, I am using 3500 from my graph. Upload the code to the board and observe the BPM readings in the Serial Monitor. Place a finger on the top of the sensor and you will get different BPM readings. *Figure 12.6* demonstrates what this should look like:

Figure 12.6 – BPM values in the Serial Monitor

The preceding figure shows random BPM values, and when we put a finger on the sensor, it detects **96** and **100** BPM. You can play with the sensor and verify the readings with any professional smartwatch. Next, we need to set up a Thing, some code, and a dashboard in the Arduino IoT Cloud to prepare our IoT project.

Setting up a Thing, network credentials, cloud variables, and code

After setting up the hardware, it's time to set up a Thing in the Arduino IoT Cloud. For this project, we need one cloud variable to fetch BPM reading from the device. The network settings will be different from those of Arduino IoT development boards as we are using an ESP series board. *Figure 12.7* shows the complete Thing details including cloud variables, device info, and network configurations:

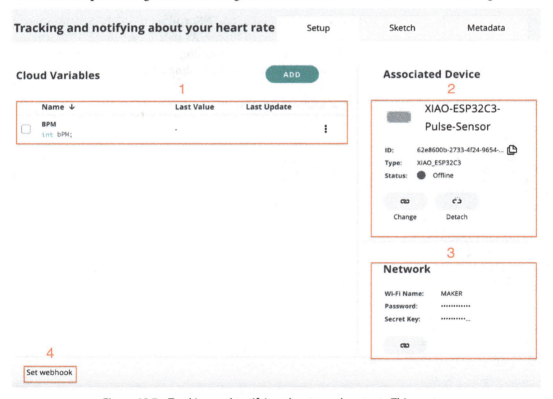

Figure 12.7 – Tracking and notifying about your heart rate Thing setup

Set up a new **Thing** with the name `Tracking and notifying about your heart rate`. Then, proceed to the following sections of this chapter, which will take us through the following steps to create the variables, associate the device, set up the network configuration, and finally, apply the code:

1. Firstly, we need to set up one cloud variable for **BPM**. The complete details regarding cloud variables are available in the following *Cloud variables* section.

2. After that, we need to associate the device with the Thing. In our current project, we are using the XIAO ESP32C3, so the wizard will be different from that for Arduino boards. The complete details are available in the *Device association* section.

3. Next, we need to set up the network configuration for the device, but this time, we need to provide a security key for ESP-series boards to make the connection secure (whereas Arduino-compatible boards are configured by the Arduino IoT Cloud automatically during the device setup wizard).

4. Lastly, we will set up the webhook toward the end of the chapter, along with the notification service using Zapier.

Cloud variables

The following table outlines the properties that we need to use during cloud variable creation. For BPM, we could just use the `integer` data type, but thanks to the Arduino IoT Cloud extended group of variables, we can choose the specific `Heart rate` variable type. Next, make sure you use the same variable declaration as in the table; otherwise, you will need to modify the example code according to your own naming.

For **Permission**, while we do have a **Read/Write** option, I chose **Read Only** as we only want to receive data from the device, as opposed to dashboard modification, so **Read Only** mode will avoid issues in data consistency. **Update Policy** is set to **On change** as the device will send the data whenever there is any change detected in the BPM value:

S#	Variable Name	Variable Type	Declaration	Permission	Update Policy
1	BPM	Heart rate	bPM	Read Only	On change

Table 12.1 – Cloud variable for our Thing

In this section, we have created the cloud variable that receives the heart rate value in BPM from the sensor device. In the next section, we will associate the device with the Thing.

Device association

After variable creation, it's time to add the device and associate it with the Thing. Before adding the device, connect the development board to the computer and open the **Arduino Create Agent** application. *Figure 12.8* shows the device setup wizard where we have selected **ESP32** and then **XIAO_ESP32C3** from the dropdown:

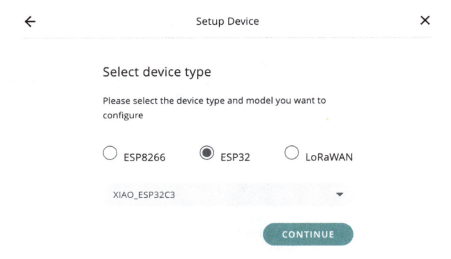

Figure 12.8 – Device selection wizard

1. Click on the **Select Device** button under the **Associated Devices** section on the Thing page. A popup will appear showing all the devices that are already available. If you have already added your XIAO ESP32C3, select it. Otherwise, click on **SET UP NEW DEVICE**.

2. Next, click on the **Third Party device** option. Select **ESP32** and **XIAO_ESP32C3** from the dropdown and click on the **CONTINUE** button.

3. Fill in the **Device Name** field and click on the **Next** button.

4. On the final wizard screen, the **Device ID** and **Secret Key** values will be displayed. Copy the **Secret Key** value to a safe place as it will be needed later during the network configuration.

In this section, we associated the XIAO ESP32C3 device with the Thing. The device association process is somewhat different to adding the Arduino MKR1010 to a Thing. Next, let's complete the network settings.

Network

After associating the device with the Thing, it is time to configure the Wi-Fi settings for device communication. Fill in the form shown in *Figure 12.9* with your **Wi-Fi Name** and **Password** values. The last field here is the **Secret Key** field. Paste the secret key value in here that we received from the system during device creation.

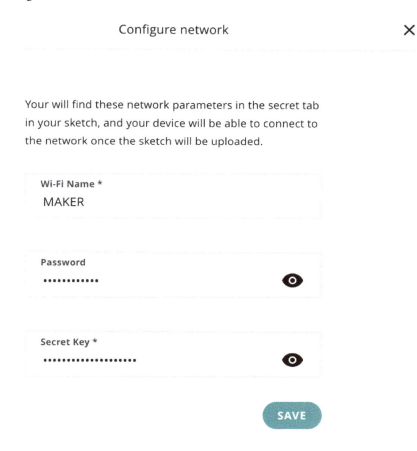

Figure 12.9 – Network configuration for the Thing

Figure 12.9 shows how it should look once you've entered all the relevant values. In the next subsection, we will cover the coding for the device.

Coding

The code for this chapter is available in the book's official GitHub repository. Download the `Tracking_and_notifying_Your_Heart_Rate_mar31a` code from the repository and import it to the Arduino Web Editor.

You can download the code and add it to your Thing by navigating to the **Sketch** tab. We will not discuss the code at length as you will get the gist after reading the code yourself, but I will explain the main workflow with which we initialize all the variables and constants in the setup.

Remember to never use the `delay` method as it will create blocking in the `ArduinoCloud.update()` method. But before moving on to the code, we need to set the `PULSE_INPUT` variable to pin A1, `PULSE_BLINK` to digital pin 10 for the LED, and set `THRESHOLD` with your calibration value:

```
const int PULSE_INPUT = A1;
const int PULSE_BLINK = 10;
const int PULSE_FADE = 5;
const int THRESHOLD = 3450; // Adjust this number to avoid noise when
you will start getting values from sensor
```

After configuring the preceding variables with the appropriate values, it's time to explore the loop method:

```
if (pulseSensor.sawNewSample()) {
  if (--samplesUntilReport == (byte) 0) {
    samplesUntilReport = SAMPLES_PER_SERIAL_SAMPLE;

    //pulseSensor.outputSample();

    if (pulseSensor.sawStartOfBeat()) {
        bPM=pulseSensor.getBeatsPerMinute();
        Serial.print(bPM);
        Serial.println(" bpm");
    }
  }
  /*******
    Here is a good place to add code that could take up
    to a millisecond or so to run.
  *******/
}
/******
    Don't add code here, because it could slow the sampling
    from the PulseSensor.
******/
```

In the loop method, the development board calls `pulseSensor.sawNewSample()` to fetch new samples if they exist. Other than that, it will not call any activity, which is why you will see a delay in readings returned if there is no change found by the system in the BPM data. If any change occurred in the sensor readings, then BPM readings will verify using the `pulseSensor.sawStartOfBeat()` method.

In the previous section where we created the cloud variable, recall the cloud variable declaration – our `pulseSensor.getBeatsPerMinute();` method assigns the sensor reading to that **bPM** variable. This cloud variable declaration is available in the `thingProperties.h` file. So, when you assign the values to these constants, the `ArduinoCloud.update()` method in the loop will automatically send the data to the cloud. Finally, upload the code to the device and verify the readings returned using the Serial Monitor.

Important note

If you used different *naming* in the variable declaration, then update the code according to your naming scheme. It would be better, however, if you followed the steps according to the book first and then change the cloud variable names later and modify your code respectively.

Never use the `delay` method, which will create a block for the `ArduinoCloud.update()` method, and don't put code at the end of the loop method, as it will cause a delay in the pulse sensor readings.

The Arduino IoT Cloud only updates the value on the dashboard whenever the variable value is changed. For example, if the heart beat is 80 and after 5 minutes it's still the same, then the Arduino IoT Cloud will not record the value, so don't get confused if values do not appear to change on the graph. Another benefit of this feature is you will not get duplicated data when you export the content.

In this section, we discussed the code in depth and guided you through the code operation and how to set the threshold values. In the next section, we are going to set up the dashboard to visualize the BPM value in different formats for better understanding.

Setting up a dashboard for web and mobile

After uploading the code to the device, it's now time to set up the dashboard for web and mobile to visualize the data with different widgets. The following figure demonstrates how this visualization might look:

Figure 12.10 – Thing dashboard

In the preceding figure, we have a BPM reading, and to visualize it, we have used two widgets, **Value** and **Advanced Chart**. The **Value** widget on the left of the screen shows the real-time **BPM** values, while the **Advanced Chart** widget illustrates the real-time readings as well as historical readings for proper analysis, just like an ECG machine display. Both widgets are attached to the BPM cloud variable.

The **Advanced Chart** widget is a new addition to the widgets on offer, and comes with a variety of features including different chart formats such as line, spline, spline/line area, and bar charts, with the option to customize the color of the plot. Another big feature is the ability to visualize multiple cloud variables on the same chart, which is not available in simpler chart widgets. We will use that feature in upcoming projects for a proper demonstration.

In this section, we briefly discussed some widgets and why these widgets are used in our dashboard. Next, we will set up the notification service using Zapier, which will send an email/SMS when the pulse is detected as going above or below our thresholds.

Setting up the notification service

Multiple platforms provide **Software-as-a-Service** (**SaaS**) infrastructure and operate as a bridge between a variety of applications to make interoperability easy. Platforms for this purpose include **Zapier**, **IFTTT**, and **Integromat**, and provide an interface to integrate other platforms into the Arduino IoT Cloud platform to fulfill the requirements instead of developing the required features from scratch.

So firstly, we need to understand why we need the Zapier automation platform. In our current project, we want to send notifications by email/SMS when a specific threshold is met, but the Arduino IoT Cloud only provides the data visualization, webhooks, and API functionalities. We have two options to solve this problem. Either we need to develop a custom solution to send notifications by email/SMS using Arduino webhooks and APIs, or we can use an automation platform such as Zapier or IFTTT, which will save time and reduce costs compared to the first option.

For this exercise, we will use Zapier, which will receive the data via **Arduino webhooks**. We will apply Zapier filters in Zaps to manage the threshold, and when the threshold is crossed, Zapier will send an email notification about BPM levels. A *Zap* is a term used in Zapier to describe an automated workflow that allows you to connect apps and services together, and each Zap can consist of multiple actions.

Before moving onto the main steps, first sign up to `zapier.com` and use the trial version, as the Zapier webhooks we are going to use are only available under the *Professional plan*. The following screenshot demonstrates the trigger and two actions required to set up our notification functionality:

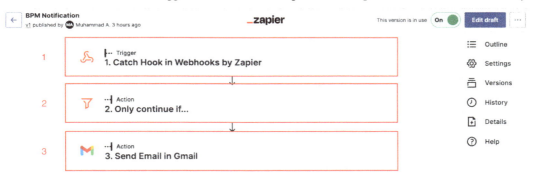

Figure 12.11 – Zapier complete notification Zap

The steps to create this, which we will work through for the remainder of this section, are as follows:

1. Firstly, we need to set up the **webhook trigger**, which will provide a URL. This URL should be inserted into the **Thing** by clicking on **Set Webhook** on the Arduino IoT Cloud Thing page. This trigger will be responsible for receiving the data from the Arduino IoT Cloud.

2. In the second step, we apply the filter on the BPM value, which specifies that if the BPM is greater than 100 or less than 60, then proceed to the next action; otherwise, the BPM is normal and there is no need to send a notification.

Finally, we will use the **Email by Zapier** or **Gmail** option to send the notification. We add multiple actions to the Zap. To keep things easy and manageable, we chose to use a simple email notification. Alternatively, you could also use **Twillo** to send SMS notifications to recipients.

Previously, we have discussed the different triggers and actions step by step that are required for notifications to be triggered and sent. The following points will guide you through these steps in Zapier:

1. The preceding screenshot gives a rough idea of how our setup looks in Zapier. To create a new Zap in Zapier, click the **Create** button and select **New Zap**, which will open a new page where you select the required triggers and actions.

2. Type `Webhook` in the search bar and select the **Webhooks By Zapier** option, which is available under the Professional plan. Click on **Event** and select **Catch Hook**, then click **Continue**. In the **Trigger** tab, just leave the empty **Pick off a Child Key** textbox as is and proceed to the next step by clicking on the **Continue** button.

3. In the **Test** tab, you will get the **webhook URL** – copy that and navigate to **Thing** in the Arduino IoT Cloud, then click on **Set Webhook**. Insert the URL into the window that pops up, then hit the **Save** button.

Come back to Zapier and click the **Test Trigger** button to verify whether data is arriving or not. Before you can verify this, the device must be powered on and connected to the internet to send the values. This might not work on your first try; if not, try again and you should see the data arriving, which means you are receiving the data successfully from the Arduino Thing. *Figure 12.12* shows a trigger test, demonstrating the values received from the Arduino IoT Cloud pulse monitoring Thing:

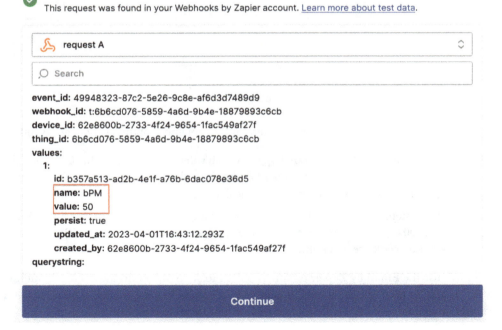

Figure 12.12 – Trigger test

The preceding screenshot shows Zapier successfully receiving the data from the Arduino IoT Cloud Thing. In the red box, we can see **bPM** and **value**. The **value** parameter will be used in the next action. Click the **Continue** button and a new **Action** popup will appear. Here, we need to configure the filter action where we will set the threshold for our BPM notification, as shown in *Figure 12.13*:

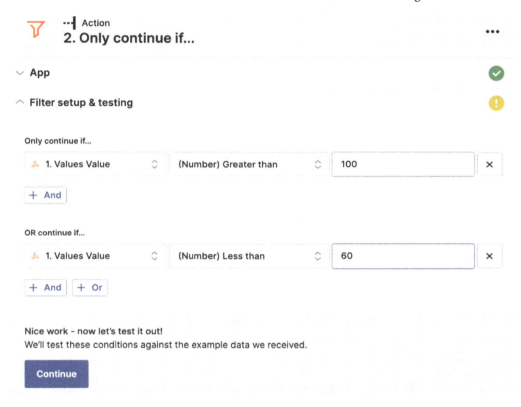

Figure 12.13 – Filter action

Type `Filter` in the search box and select **Filter by Zapier**. Click on **Choose Field…** and select **Values Value** from the dropdown. Then, click **Choose Condition**, select **Number (Greater than)**, and put `100` in the next input field. This sets the upper threshold value to 100 BPM. Next, click **OR**, and leave the value field as it is, but in **Choose Condition**, select **Number (Less than)** and insert `60` in the next field. Lastly, click on **Continue**.

Our filter is ready; now, our email notification action is required to finish the setup. We have two options to send email notifications: either **Email by Zapier** or **Gmail**. I opted to use **Email by Zapier**. Next, the **Action** popup window will appear; type `Email` in the search box and click on **Email by Zapier**. Click on **Event** and select **Send Outbound Email**. In the next window, set all the parameters for the email receiver, subject, and body, as shown in the following screenshot:

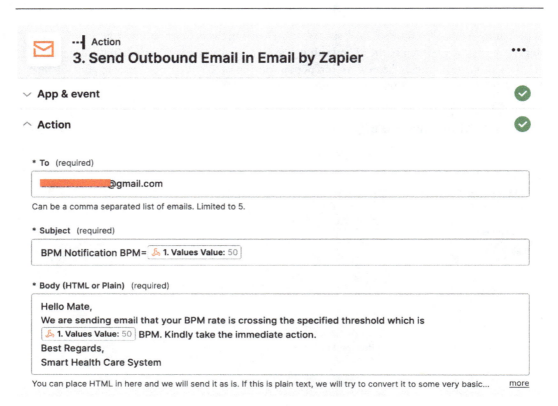

Figure 12.14 – Email notification settings

Only three fields are mandatory here – insert the recipient email in the **To** field, write a relevant entry for the **Subject** field, and insert a message in the **Body** area. It's up to you whether you fill the other fields or leave them blank. If you observe the preceding screenshot, you may notice I added **Values Value** to both the **Subject** and **Body** fields, which will display the values that triggered the notification in the email. Click the **Continue** button at the bottom of the page and test the action – if you receive the email with the BPM values, then publish the Zap and you are good to go.

In this section, we set up the notification services for our pulse monitor using Zapier. We created a Zap that consists of three steps. Firstly, we set up the webhook responsible for receiving the data. The second step deals with the threshold, and the third and final step handles sending the email notification.

What next?

There are many more options available to explore, but these are left to you to work on, using different health sensors and development boards to do some more experiments and learn from them. In the current chapter, we only used one sensor that provided only one parameter, but there are many sensors on the market that provide a wide variety of functionalities including the monitoring of blood sugar, blood oxygen, blood pressure, body temperature, and more.

Try the following sensors to enhance your practical knowledge and compare this selection with other sensors in terms of features, ranges, and cost:

- LilyPad temperature sensor (`https://www.sparkfun.com/products/8777`)
- High-sensitivity pulse oximeter and heart-rate sensor for wearables (`https://www.seeedstudio.com/MAXREFDES117-HEART-RATE-AND-PULSE-OXIMETRY-MONITOR-p-2762.html?queryID=51de6141574a711bbe455cb4894ce3fb&objectID=411&indexName=bazaar_retailer_products`)
- Fall detection module (`https://www.seeedstudio.com/24GHz-mmWave-Radar-Sensor-Fall-Detection-Module-p-5268.html`)
- Open source Arduino blood glucose meter shield
- MIKROE series health sensors

Summary

In this chapter, we explored how to develop a low-cost wearable smart heart-rate monitoring system using the XIAO ESP32C3 and a pulse sensor. One important thing to note was the necessity of calibrating medical sensors before using them in the field. We set up a Thing, which included cloud variable creation, device association, network configuration, and coding for our development board. Later, we created a dashboard to visualize our sensor readings with different widgets to display both current readings and historical data with the help of graphs. Finally, we used Zapier to set up an email notification service based on thresholds using webhooks and saw how to employ webhooks to integrate third-party services with the Arduino IoT Cloud.

In the next chapter, we will learn about scripting in the Arduino IoT Cloud with the **Arduino Cloud CLI (CCLI)**. This is a command-line tool that provides access to Arduino IoT Cloud services via terminal commands. We will use the Arduino IoT Cloud CLI to automate bulk operations, including bulk device creation, which will help us to minimize the time required for operations and maintenance.

13

Scripting the Arduino IoT Cloud with Cloud CLI

The Arduino Cloud **Command-Line Interface** (**CLI**) is an automation tool that is useful for scripting and creating devices, Things, and dashboards. It also provides the option to perform mass uploads (**OTA**), enabling the fleet management of deployed IoT nodes. This chapter will explore the advanced functionalities of the tool and propose some scenarios for its usage.

The Arduino Cloud CLI is a cross-platform tool that lets you perform bulk management and operations via the command line, which helps you to increase your productivity, and provides the option to automate Things via command-line scripts. In this chapter, we will explore all the commands and observe their context.

By the end of this chapter, you will understand how to interact with the Arduino IoT Cloud platform via a CLI to create, delete, or extract templates from devices, Things, and dashboards and send OTA updates to devices via the command line. This chapter will show you how to perform all the operations via the command line to boost your productivity. The commands you will learn will help you write custom scripts for use in mass deployments and bulk management operations.

In this chapter, we will cover the following main topics:

- What is the Arduino Cloud CLI?
- Securing access – unveiling API keys and authentication
- Installing the Arduino Cloud CLI
- Interacting with devices
- Engaging with Things
- Crafting dashboards – unleashing potential via the command line
- OTA management
- What's next?

Technical requirements

There are no specific hardware requirements for this chapter as we will focus on the Arduino Cloud CLI and work through different command exercises to perform operations on the Arduino IoT Cloud platform using a CLI. However, before we proceed, we will need the following software to complete the different exercises in this chapter:

- The Arduino Cloud CLI
- The Arduino IDE
- An Arduino IoT Cloud account

For the commands, we need the Arduino Cloud CLI and an active Arduino IoT Cloud account. This chapter only contains commands, so there is no folder for it on GitHub.

What is the Arduino Cloud CLI?

The Arduino Cloud CLI is a powerful tool to manage and interact with your Arduino projects on the cloud. It allows you to perform various operations, such as deploying and managing devices and generating a dashboard and Things template for bulk creations, all from the comfort of your command line.

The benefits of using the Arduino Cloud CLI are numerous. Firstly, it provides a convenient and efficient way to manage your projects without the need for a graphical user interface. This can be particularly useful if you prefer working with command-line tools, or if you integrate Arduino into an automated workflow.

The Arduino Cloud CLI serves as a command-line utility, enabling you to interact with the key functionalities of the Arduino IoT Cloud through a terminal. It provides the capability to accomplish the following tasks:

- Duplicate existing Things and dashboards by extracting their templates
- Execute mass OTA uploads
- Generate devices, Things, and dashboards directly through the CLI

Here are some of the benefits of using the Arduino Cloud CLI:

- **Automation**: The Arduino Cloud CLI can be used to automate tasks that you would otherwise have to do manually. For example, you could use it to create a script that clones a Thing and then performs a mass OTA upload to all of the devices that are associated with that Thing.

- **Efficient device management**: The Arduino Cloud CLI can help you manage a large number of devices more efficiently. For example, you could use it to list all of the devices that are associated with a particular tag or to get the status of a particular device.

- **Access to advanced features**: The Arduino Cloud CLI can be used to access features of the Arduino IoT Cloud that are not available in a web interface. For example, you could use it to create a script that checks the status of a device every minute and then sends an email alert if the status changes.

- **Customization**: Being open source, users have the flexibility to customize the Arduino Cloud CLI to suit their specific needs and integrate it into their workflows.

- **Active development and community support**: The tool is actively developed, meaning it continually receives updates, new features, and bug fixes. Additionally, the presence of a large community can provide assistance and support for users.

- **Time and effort savings**: The Arduino Cloud CLI can save time and effort in managing IoT projects, making it a valuable resource for developers working with Arduino devices.

Overall, the Arduino Cloud CLI is a powerful tool that can be used to automate tasks, manage a large number of devices, and access features of the Arduino IoT Cloud that are not available in a web interface.

In this section, we have discussed what the Arduino Cloud CLI is and what the benefits of the Arduino Cloud CLI are. In the next section, we will explore how to set up API keys and how to use API keys to authenticate the Arduino Cloud CLI with the Arduino IoT Cloud.

Securing access – unveiling API keys and authentication

Before getting into the meat of the chapter, we first need to talk about the authentication mechanism of the platform. The Arduino IoT Cloud uses a **token authentication mechanism** to validate Arduino Cloud CLI requests.

Before we start to install and test the Arduino Cloud CLI, we need to set up the API keys in Arduino Cloud that will provide us with the client ID and secret. In older versions of the interface, the API options were under the **Integrations** tab, but they have now moved to Arduino Cloud, which is available at `https://cloud.arduino.cc/home/`.

After visiting the **Integration** page, click on **API Keys**, and then you will be taken to the API page. Click on **CREATE API KEY**. A popup will appear; provide a name for the API, and click on the **CONTINUE** button. The wizard that appears will take a few seconds to generate the keys, and then a new popup will appear displaying the keys, as shown in *Figure 13.1*.

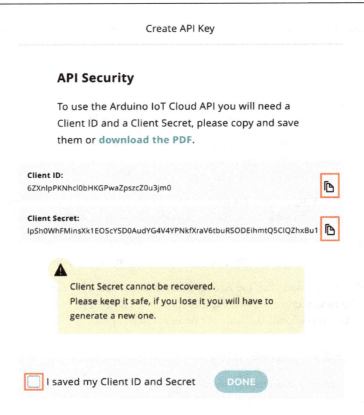

Create API Key

API Security

To use the Arduino IoT Cloud API you will need a
Client ID and a Client Secret, please copy and save
them or download the PDF.

Client ID:
6ZXnIpPKNhcl0bHKGPwaZpszcZ0u3jm0

Client Secret:
IpSh0WhFMinsXk1EOScYSD0AudYG4V4YPNkfXraV6tbuRSODEihmtQ5ClQZhxBu1

⚠ Client Secret cannot be recovered.
Please keep it safe, if you lose it you will have to
generate a new one.

☐ I saved my Client ID and Secret   DONE

Figure 13.1 – The API keys

Copy the **Client ID** and **Client Secret** values by clicking on the copy icons – never try to copy by manual selection, as the client secret is very long, so clicking on the copy icon is the best option. Save both the **Client ID** and **Client Secret** values in a secure location, and then click the checkbox, confirming that you have saved your keys. Lastly, click on **DONE**, and you will see your API key in the panel – it's now ready for use.

> **Important note**
>
> A single API key is used to give access to all the Things and their variables. Having access to all the infrastructure with just one API key is handy, instead of having to create separate API keys for each Thing, but you must take care of your key! This is a big security risk as, if you were to lose the key, a hacker could gain access to your whole account.

In this section, we created API authentication keys, which consist of a client ID and a client secret. This section is most important, as without these keys, we can't execute any command via the Arduino Cloud CLI. In the following section, we will install the Arduino Cloud CLI.

Installing the Arduino Cloud CLI

In this section, we will install the Arduino Cloud CLI tool. The Arduino team developed the CLI tool for all three major operating systems: macOS, Windows, and Linux. You can download the Arduino Cloud CLI tool for your operating system from `https://github.com/arduino/arduino-cloud-cli/releases`. The official Arduino Cloud CLI page can be found at `https://docs.arduino.cc/arduino-cloud/getting-started/arduino-cloud-cli`; here, you can get updated information regarding commands and their usage.

Always try to download the latest and most stable release of the Arduino Cloud CLI. After downloading the ZIP file according to your operating system, extract the files from it. You will find one executable file named `arduino-cloud-cli` and another called `LICENSE.txt`, and can set up Environmental variables for an `arduino-cloud-cli` executable file in your operating system, which will help you to execute `arduino-cloud-cli` in the terminal without specifying the location of the `arduino-cloud-cli` folder.

Just open up the terminal and enter the following command:

```
arduino-cloud-cli
```

Then, you will see the following output on your terminal (*Figure 13.2*).

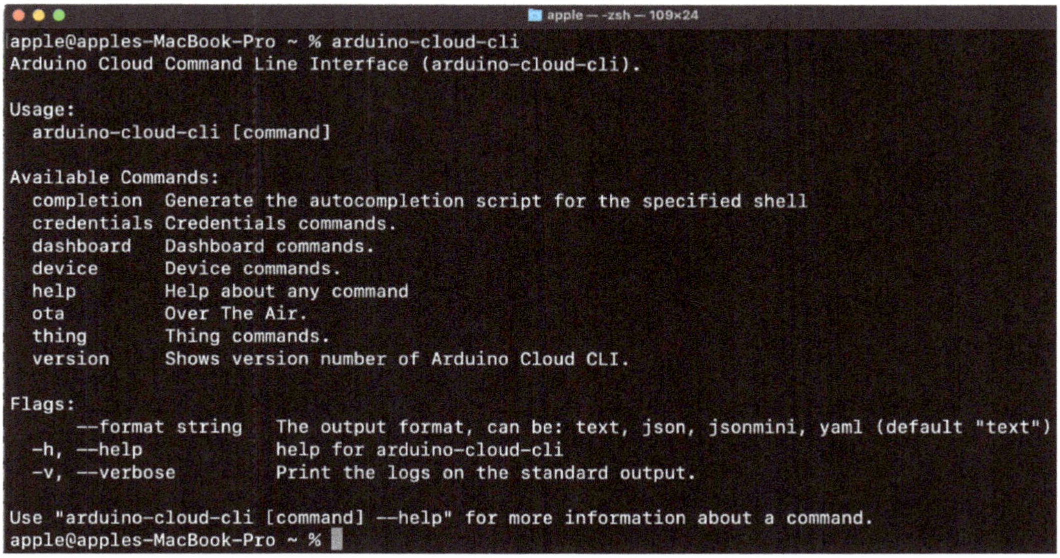

```
apple@apples-MacBook-Pro ~ % arduino-cloud-cli
Arduino Cloud Command Line Interface (arduino-cloud-cli).

Usage:
  arduino-cloud-cli [command]

Available Commands:
  completion  Generate the autocompletion script for the specified shell
  credentials Credentials commands.
  dashboard   Dashboard commands.
  device      Device commands.
  help        Help about any command
  ota         Over The Air.
  thing       Thing commands.
  version     Shows version number of Arduino Cloud CLI.

Flags:
      --format string   The output format, can be: text, json, jsonmini, yaml (default "text")
  -h, --help            help for arduino-cloud-cli
  -v, --verbose         Print the logs on the standard output.

Use "arduino-cloud-cli [command] --help" for more information about a command.
apple@apples-MacBook-Pro ~ %
```

Figure 13.2 – The Arduino Cloud CLI terminal

This simply shows you how to use the Arduino Cloud CLI with different parameters, as we didn't specify any parameters during the command execution.

Now, it's time to initiate the Arduino Cloud CLI authentication with Arduino Cloud, using the API keys that we generated in the previous section. Type the following command into the terminal:

```
arduino-cloud-cli credentials init
```

After executing the preceding command, you will be asked for your client ID and client secret, respectively. Finally, you will be asked for your organization ID, which is not mandatory, and you can leave this empty, as shown in *Figure 13.3*.

Figure 13.3 – The Arduino Cloud CLI authentication process with Arduino Cloud

After successful authentication, you will see a success message on the terminal, as shown in *Figure 13.3*. Congratulations! You are now ready to execute the commands on the terminal and able to perform operations on the Arduino IoT Cloud via commands.

In this section, we downloaded the `arduino-cloud-cli` file and installed it on our operating system, and we also initialized the authentication process for the `arduino-cloud-cli` tool with the Arduino IoT Cloud. In the next section, we will start playing with devices using the command line.

Interacting with devices

In this section, we will get hands-on and practical with devices. We will perform create, list, delete, tag, and untag operations on a device, as well as list all the devices and show all the parameters of specific devices. Open up the command terminal, and then we'll execute the commands in the following sections.

Creating a device

Firstly, we will start by creating a device. The documentation on device creation can be found at `https://docs.arduino.cc/arduino-cloud/getting-started/arduino-cloud-cli#device`. Before you execute the command, connect your development board to your computer and find out the port number and FQBN for your device from the documentation page. The following is the syntax of the `device create` command:

```
arduino-cloud-cli device create --name <deviceName> --port <port>
--fqbn <deviceFqbn>
```

I attached the MKR Wi-Fi 1010 to my computer, which is available on port `/dev/cu.usbmodem101`, and its FQBN is `arduino:samd:mkrwifi1010`. Therefore, the following will be my command:

```
arduino-cloud-cli device create -n ArduinoDevBoardByCLI  -p /dev/
cu.usbmodem101 -b arduino:samd:mkrwifi1010
```

After executing the preceding command, you will get the following output, which shows the device has been successfully created (*Figure 13.4*).

```
apple@apples-MacBook-Pro ~ % arduino-cloud-cli device create -n ArduinoDevBoardByCLI
 -p /dev/cu.usbmodem101 -b arduino:samd:mkrwifi1010
name: ArduinoDevBoardByCLI
id: cda148e4-b011-459a-95fd-a7510c9601c2
board: mkrwifi1010
serial_number: 1B2739FE5154305146202020FF022F2C
fqbn: arduino:samd:mkrwifi1010
apple@apples-MacBook-Pro ~ %
```

Figure 13.4 – Device creation using arduino-cloud-cli

After creating the device, the terminal will show the device name, ID, board, serial number, and FQBN. Just imagine how easy it would be to attach dozens of development boards to the Arduino IoT Cloud using the command line, compared to a graphical user interface. The Arduino Cloud CLI is also able to create **LoRaWAN** devices as well as ESP32/ESP8266 devices via the CLI.

In this subsection, we created a device in the Arduino IoT Cloud using the command line. In the following subsection, we will explore how to list the device.

Listing devices

In this section, we will list all the devices. *Listing* devices means displaying all the devices with their properties. The documentation on listing devices is available at `https://docs.arduino.cc/arduino-cloud/getting-started/arduino-cloud-cli#list-devices`. The following is a very simple command to list all the devices:

```
arduino-cloud-cli device list
```

After executing the preceding command, we will see a complete list of devices, as shown in the following figure.

Figure 13.5 – The device list command

In the output, we can see the device name, ID, board, FQBN, serial number, and tags. Here, the ID is very important, as it will be used in the following commands for device deletion, as well as for tag creation and deletion. In this subsection, we have seen how to list the devices, and in the next subsection, we will explore how to delete a device using its ID.

Deleting a device

In this section, we will explore how we can delete a device using the device ID. The documentation for deleting devices is available at `https://docs.arduino.cc/arduino-cloud/getting-started/arduino-cloud-cli#delete-a-device`. The following is the command syntax for device deletion:

```
arduino-cloud-cli device delete --id <deviceID>
```

According to the preceding command syntax, we need a device ID for deletion. You can retrieve the device ID by using the `device list` command:

```
arduino-cloud-cli device delete -i ca711f68-6de9-497a-ac45-
780219ad2bb8
```

After successfully deleting the device, you will not see any error message; otherwise, you will see a `401 error` on the screen.

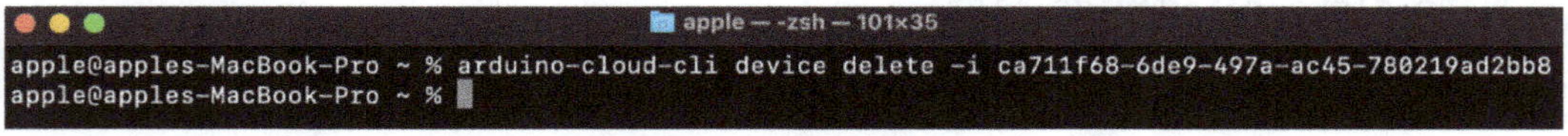

Figure 13.6 – The device delete command

Figure 13.6 shows the completed command for device deletion, and there is no error on the screen, which means the device has been deleted successfully. In this subsection, we discussed the `delete` command. In the upcoming subsection, we will tag and untag a device.

Tagging and untagging a device

In this section, we will explore how we can tag and untag a device using the device ID. The documentation for tagging a device is available at `https://docs.arduino.cc/arduino-cloud/getting-started/arduino-cloud-cli#tag-device`, and the documentation for untagging a device is available at `https://docs.arduino.cc/arduino-cloud/getting-started/arduino-cloud-cli#untag-device`. The following is the command syntax to tag a device:

```
arduino-cloud-cli device create-tags --id <deviceID> --tags
<key0>=<value0>,<key1>=<value1>
```

The following is the command syntax to untag a device:

```
arduino-cloud-cli device delete-tags --id <deviceID> --keys
<key0>,<key1>
```

You might ask the question, why do we need a tag for a device? Let's say you have a generic product for warehouse monitoring, and you have deployed this product in different organizations and different rooms. Now, the issue is that it's very difficult to assign the organization name and location in the **Device Name** field. So, an optimal solution is tagging. You can use tags as many times as you want. A tag has two options – one is a key and the other is a value.

In the following example, we will attach two tags – one for the organization name and another for the location. Pick a device ID by using the `device list` command to attach the tags. The following is the command to attach tags to a device:

```
arduino-cloud-cli device create-tags -i cda148e4-b011-459a-95fd-
a7510c9601c2  --tags Org=ASNAGroup,Location=Warehouse1
```

According to the following command syntax, we need a device ID to remove the tag from the device. You can fetch the device ID by using the `device list` command. The following command is used to remove the tag from the device:

```
arduino-cloud-cli device delete-tags -i cda148e4-b011-459a-95fd-
a7510c9601c2 -k Location
```

Here, the command is a little different, as we have used `delete-tags` and `-k` to specify the tag key. If you want to remove multiple tags, then use a comma to separate the keys.

In this and the preceding subsections, we performed various operations on devices using commands, including ones for device creation, listing devices, device deletion, tagging, and untagging. In the next section, we will explore how to practically perform operations on Things.

Engaging with Things

A Thing is one of the most important elements in the Arduino IoT Cloud, which acts as a separate container holding all of its ingredients, such as cloud variables, the device, a sketch for the device, and the device's network configuration. In this section, we will try a range of different operations via commands, such as extracting a template from a Thing, creating a Thing from a template, making a clone of a Thing, and deleting a Thing.

Extracting a template from a Thing

In the Arduino Cloud CLI, we deal with commands and provide different parameters to perform different types of operations. Therefore, it is difficult to create a new Thing via the command line, as it will make it more complex to pass different parameters, such as cloud variables and network configurations.

To solve this issue, the Arduino team introduced the concept of template extraction from a Thing. For example, say you want to deploy hundreds of environmental monitoring nodes. It's difficult to create hundreds of Things via the Arduino graphical user interface and to create a long command for Thing creation that includes all the information regarding the Thing. Therefore, Arduino introduced the template extraction technique. Firstly, we will create a Thing via the Arduino graphical user interface, and then we will extract its template via the command line. Then, using the template, we will create the Thing in the Arduino IoT Cloud via the command line, as the Arduino Cloud CLI does not allow you to create a Thing from scratch. You can find out more about Thing template extraction in the official documentation at `https://docs.arduino.cc/arduino-cloud/getting-started/arduino-cloud-cli#extract-thing-template`.

The following is the command syntax for template extraction. With this command, we need to provide a Thing ID, with which the command will fetch the template of the Thing. Then, we need to provide the format for the template file – either JSON or YAML:

```
arduino-cloud-cli thing extract --id <thingID> --format <json|yaml>
```

For the Thing ID, either visit the Arduino IoT Cloud to find it or refer to the upcoming subsections, in which we will show you how to list Things, which provides the Thing name, ID, and so on, so you can also retrieve the Thing ID from the output. Now, we will assign the format; we want the template output in JSON format, so I used JSON here:

```
arduino-cloud-cli thing  extract -i 91c90962-56b6-4094-abe0-
1b5ad4828721 --format json
```

After executing the command, we will get the template output on the screen in JSON format, as shown in *Figure 13.7*.

```
● ● ●                          apple — -zsh — 127x35
apple@apples-MacBook-Pro ~ % arduino-cloud-cli thing  extract -i 91c90962-56b6-4094-abe0-1b5ad4828721 --format json
{
    "name": "Sense the Environment",
    "variables": [
        {
            "name": "Temperature",
            "permission": "READ_ONLY",
            "type": "HOME_TEMPERATURE_C",
            "update_parameter": 0,
            "update_strategy": "ON_CHANGE",
            "variable_name": "temperature"
        },
        {
            "name": "AirQuality",
            "permission": "READ_ONLY",
            "type": "INT",
            "update_parameter": 0,
            "update_strategy": "ON_CHANGE",
            "variable_name": "airQuality"
        },
        {
            "name": "Humidity",
            "permission": "READ_ONLY",
            "type": "PERCENTAGE_RELATIVE_HUMIDITY",
            "update_parameter": 0,
            "update_strategy": "ON_CHANGE",
            "variable_name": "humidity"
        }
    ]
}
apple@apples-MacBook-Pro ~ %
```

Figure 13.7 – Extracting the Thing template

Our Thing template shows all the information regarding cloud variables. Copy the text and save it in a file, which will be used in the following section for Thing creation.

Creating a Thing

After extracting the Thing template, we will now start to create the Thing. The documentation on Thing creation can be found at https://docs.arduino.cc/arduino-cloud/getting-started/arduino-cloud-cli#create-things. The following is the syntax of the Thing creation command, which takes two parameters. Firstly, it will take the name, and secondly, it will take the template filename for the Thing creation, which contains the Thing template in JSON format that we saved in the previous section:

```
arduino-cloud-cli thing create --name <thingName> --template
<template.(json|yaml)>
```

Here, I have provided a Thing name, EnvSense101, and in the previous section, I saved the JSON template in the file named EnvSenseTemplate.json. Then, we provide the name with the -n parameter and the template file with the -t parameter:

```
arduino-cloud-cli thing create -n EnvSense101 -t EnvSenseTemplate.json
```

After executing the preceding command, you will get the following output for successful Thing creation (*Figure 13.8*).

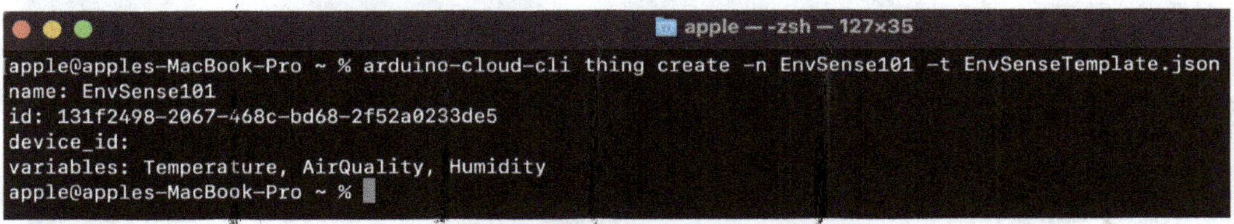

```
apple@apples-MacBook-Pro ~ % arduino-cloud-cli thing create -n EnvSense101 -t EnvSenseTemplate.json
name: EnvSense101
id: 131f2498-2067-468c-bd68-2f52a0233de5
device_id:
variables: Temperature, AirQuality, Humidity
apple@apples-MacBook-Pro ~ %
```

Figure 13.8 – Thing creation using arduino-cloud-cli

After creating the Thing, the terminal will show the Thing name, ID, device ID (which is empty right now, but in the upcoming sections, we will associate the device with this Thing), and variable name.

In this subsection, we created a Thing in the Arduino IoT Cloud using the command line. In the following section, we will explore how to clone the Thing for bulk creations.

Cloning a Thing

After creating a Thing from a template, we will now explore how we can use the clone operation for large-scale deployments. The documentation on the Thing clone can be found at https://docs. arduino.cc/arduino-cloud/getting-started/arduino-cloud-cli#clone-things. The following is the syntax of the thing clone command, which will take two parameters. Firstly, it will take a name, and secondly, it will take a Thing ID:

```
arduino-cloud-cli thing clone --name <thingName> --clone-id
<thingToCloneID>
```

Here, I have provided a Thing name, EnvSense102, and in the previous section, we created the Thing, so I can get its ID from the terminal, as shown in *Figure 13.8* (use your own Thing ID in the command line). Then, provide the name with an -n parameter and the Thing ID with a -c parameter:

```
arduino-cloud-cli thing clone -n EnvSense102 -c 131f2498-2067-468c-
bd68-2f52a0233de5
```

After executing the preceding command, you will get the following output for a successful Thing clone (*Figure 13.9*).

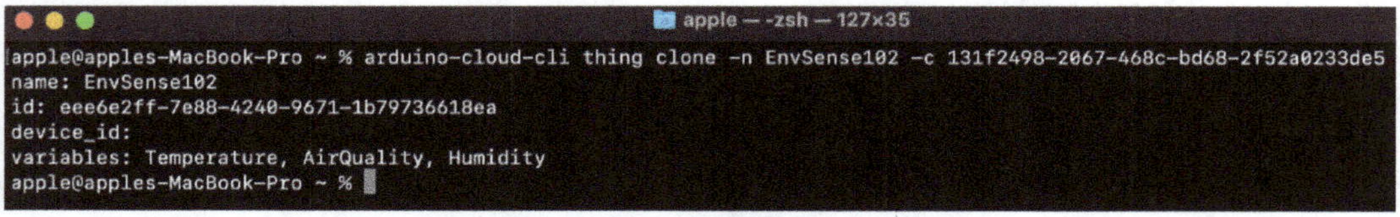

```
apple@apples-MacBook-Pro ~ % arduino-cloud-cli thing clone -n EnvSense102 -c 131f2498-2067-468c-bd68-2f52a0233de5
name: EnvSense102
id: eee6e2ff-7e88-4240-9671-1b79736618ea
device_id:
variables: Temperature, AirQuality, Humidity
apple@apples-MacBook-Pro ~ %
```

Figure 13.9 – A Thing clone using arduino-cloud-cli

This is the output of a successful Thing clone by the Arduino Cloud CLI. After cloning the Thing, the terminal will show the Thing name, ID, device ID (which is empty right now, but in the upcoming section, we will associate the device with this Thing), and variable name. You can see how easy it is to create hundreds of Things with just the `clone` command. Here, you can just create a batch script, which will only change the name of the Thing by using the `for` loop and create hundreds of Things in just a few minutes.

In this subsection, we learned how to clone a Thing in the Arduino IoT Cloud using the command line. In the following section, we will explore how to list Things.

Listing Things

In this section, we will list all the Things. The documentation on listing Things is available at `https://docs.arduino.cc/arduino-cloud/getting-started/arduino-cloud-cli#list-things`. The following is a very simple command to list all the Things:

```
arduino-cloud-cli thing list
```

After executing the preceding command, we will see a complete list of Things, as shown in the following figure.

```
apple@apples-MacBook-Pro ~ % arduino-cloud-cli thing list
Name                                                   ID                                      Device                                  Tags
EnvSense101                                            131f2498-2067-468c-bd68-2f52a0233de5
A remote asset tracking using LoRaWAN                  629d48df-c0c5-4708-9eb0-c77407c5b2b2    648d742f-2126-42ad-8ac4-55f885e2e818
Voice Controlled Smart Lamp                            659e7bf9-42fc-4737-ae25-9be5194334c3    87085c3d-51fa-4298-a219-5fd20703ab9b
Tracking and notifying about your heart rate           6b6cd076-5859-4a6d-9b4e-18879893c6cb    62e8600b-2733-4f24-9654-1fac549af27f
Thing Via API-Name-Update                              6e3d308c-dfb2-49ad-aa61-998227f214ab
Indoor Device MKR Wi-Fi 1010                           79a7776b-9fa9-498c-96b9-50dc355eacac    64990519-1833-4bba-b035-978fcaa33466
Cloud Scheduler                                        82f7112f-8010-4789-86ba-d242e0dcd794
AgriStack                                              85b04a9c-e335-4842-bf4b-c13f726e0522    04d8025a-4270-4d7e-aa04-45db87a594f5
A portable thing tracker using MKR GSM1400              8aee742e-4492-423d-9f19-79fec856b917    5aae7e1f-940b-4426-80ac-1c953839cdb2
Sense the Environment                                  91c90962-56b6-4094-abe0-1b5ad4828721    ef63111f-72bb-4826-84bb-02093d4d85f1
MKR1010 Hello World                                    bf8e11ea-1a78-4f95-b6a0-c6d50b868402
Sense the Env Thing Via API Update                     d99e244d-f245-4e27-9ead-717e52ac5a96    e88b84a7-7ad7-4c2b-b79c-ab426e47dc67
EnvSense102                                            eee6e2ff-7e88-4240-9671-1b79736618ea

apple@apples-MacBook-Pro ~ %
```

Figure 13.10 – The thing list command

In the output, we can see the Thing name, ID, device, and tags. Again, the ID is very important, as it will be used in the following commands for Thing deletion, as well as for tag creation and deletion. In the preceding sections, we also used the ID for Thing template extraction and creation, as well as Thing cloning.

The Arduino Cloud CLI also provides different parameters to get more detailed output on the terminal, such as a variable list along with a list of Things. We can attach the -s parameter to the Thing, and we can also list a Thing by providing a device ID as well as list a series of Things by providing a Thing ID. Here, I want to explore how we can get a variable list along with Things. The following is a simple command to list cloud variables:

```
arduino-cloud-cli thing list -s
```

After executing the preceding command, you will see the output shown in *Figure 13.11*.

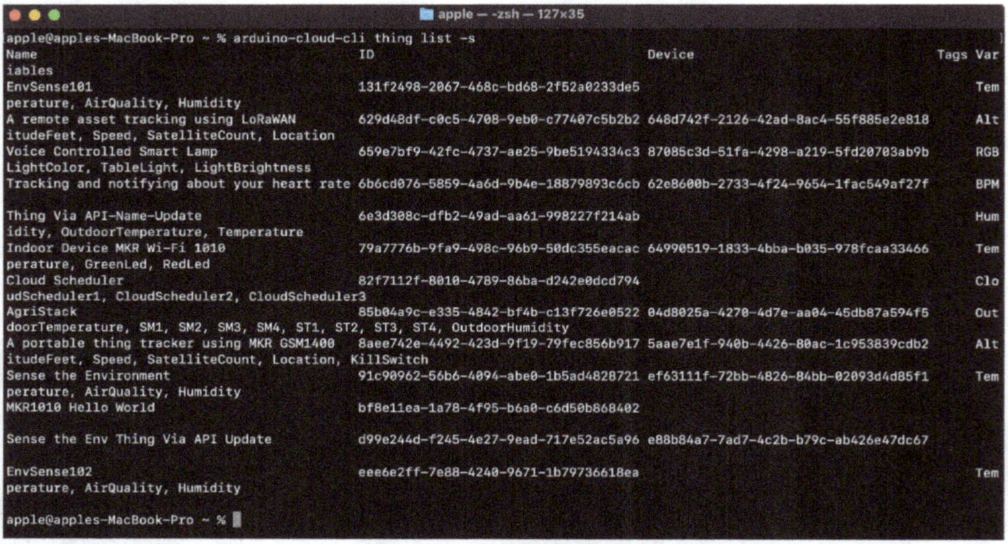

Figure 13.11 – The thing list command with variables

Here, you can see all the cloud variables along with the Thing names, but it looks a little bit complicated. Now, we will try to list a single Thing with cloud variables. The following is the command syntax to list a Thing with cloud variables. It will take two parameters as input – one Thing ID and an -s parameter:

```
arduino-cloud-cli thing list -i eee6e2ff-7e88-4240-9671-1b79736618ea
-s
```

Execute the preceding command, and you will see the complete and readable output shown in *Figure 13.12*.

Figure 13.12 – Displaying a single Thing with cloud variables

Now, it's time to explore how we can find a Thing by using a device ID. The following is a simple command to retrieve a Thing based on a device ID:

```
arduino-cloud-cli thing list -d ef63111f-72bb-4826-84bb-02093d4d85f1
-s
```

After executing the preceding command, we will get specific Thing data using the device ID, as well as its cloud variables, as we used the -s parameter in the command (as shown in *Figure 13.13*).

Figure 13.13 – Displaying a single Thing based on a device ID, with cloud variables

In this subsection, we explored how to list Things by using different parameters. In the next subsection, we will explore how to delete a Thing.

Deleting a Thing

In this section, we will explore how to delete a Thing using a Thing ID. The documentation for deleting a Thing is available at https://docs.arduino.cc/arduino-cloud/getting-started/arduino-cloud-cli#delete-things. The following is the command syntax for Thing deletion:

```
arduino-cloud-cli device delete --id <deviceID>
```

According to the command syntax, we need a Thing ID for deletion. You can fetch the Thing ID by using the thing list command:

```
arduino-cloud-cli thing delete -i eee6e2ff-7e88-4240-9671-1b79736618ea
```

After the successful deletion of the device, you will not see an error message; otherwise, you will get a 401 error message on the screen.

Figure 13.14 – The Thing delete command

Figure 13.14 shows the complete command for Thing deletion, and there is no error on the screen, which means the Thing has been deleted successfully. In this subsection, we discussed the delete command, and in the upcoming subsection, we will explore how to associate the device with a Thing.

Associating a device with a Thing

In the previous Thing subsections, we extracted the Thing template, created the Thing from that template, and also performed Thing cloning operations. However, throughout all the processes, we didn't associate a device with a Thing, and without a device, a Thing is just an empty JAR that is not capable of performing any operation.

In this subsection, we will explore how to attach the device with a Thing by using a device ID and a Thing ID. The documentation for associating a device with a Thing is available at `https://docs.arduino.cc/arduino-cloud/getting-started/arduino-cloud-cli#bind-thing-to-device`. The following is the simple command syntax to bind a device with a Thing in the Arduino IoT Cloud:

```
arduino-cloud-cli thing bind --id <thingID> --device-id <deviceID>
```

Here, you can get a specific device ID by using the `arduino-cloud-cli device list` command and a Thing ID with `arduino-cloud-cli thing list`:

```
arduino-cloud-cli thing bind -i 131f2498-2067-468c-bd68-2f52a0233de5
-d cda148e4-b011-459a-95fd-a7510c9601c2
```

In the preceding command, we have assigned a Thing ID by using `-i` and a device ID with the `-d` parameter. Execute the preceding command, and you will see the output shown in *Figure 13.15*.

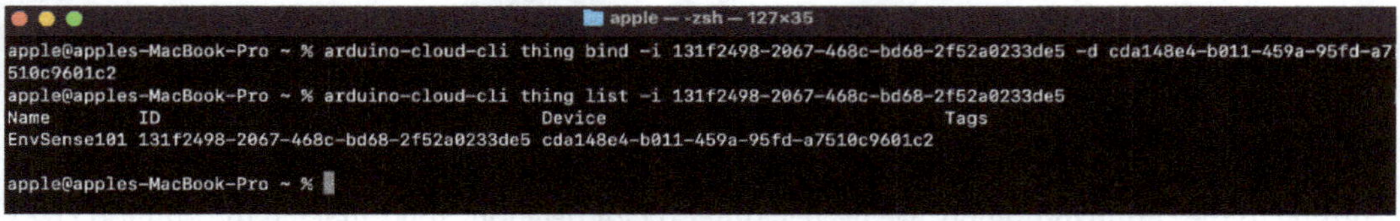

Figure 13.15 – Device binding with Thing

Figure 13.15 shows a device successfully binding with a Thing. To confirm, we used the `thing list` command with the `-i` parameter to verify the device ID. In both the command as well as in the `thing list` output, the device ID is the same.

In this subsection, we explored how to bind/associate a device with a Thing. In the next subsection, we will discuss how to assign and remove tags from a Thing.

Tagging and untagging a Thing

In this section, we will explore how we can tag and untag a Thing using the Thing ID. The documentation for tagging a Thing is available at `https://docs.arduino.cc/arduino-cloud/getting-started/arduino-cloud-cli#tag-a-thing`, and for untagging a Thing, documentation is available at `https://docs.arduino.cc/arduino-cloud/getting-started/arduino-cloud-cli#untag-a-thing`. The following is the command syntax to tag a Thing:

```
arduino-cloud-cli thing create-tags --id <thingID> --tags
<key0>=<value0>,<key1>=<value1>
```

The following is the command syntax to untag a Thing:

```
arduino-cloud-cli thing delete-tags --id <thingID> --keys
<key0>,<key1>
```

You might question the necessity of assigning a tag to a Thing. Consider this scenario. You have a versatile product designed for monitoring warehouses, and you've deployed this product in various organizations and different rooms within those organizations. The challenge arises when attempting to incorporate the organization's name and location directly into the **Device Name** field, which can be quite cumbersome. In this context, a more efficient solution presents itself through the use of tags. Tags can be applied without limitations, much like when we previously established tags for devices. Each tag consists of two components: a key and a corresponding value.

So, in the following example, we will attach two tags – one for the organization name and another for the location. Pick the Thing ID by using the `thing list` command to attach tags. The following is the command to attach tags to a Thing:

```
arduino-cloud-cli thing create-tags -i 131f2498-2067-468c-bd68-
2f52a0233de5 --tags Org=ASNAGroup,Location=MainUnit
```

After executing the preceding command, you can verify the tags by using the `thing list` command, as shown in *Figure 13.16*.

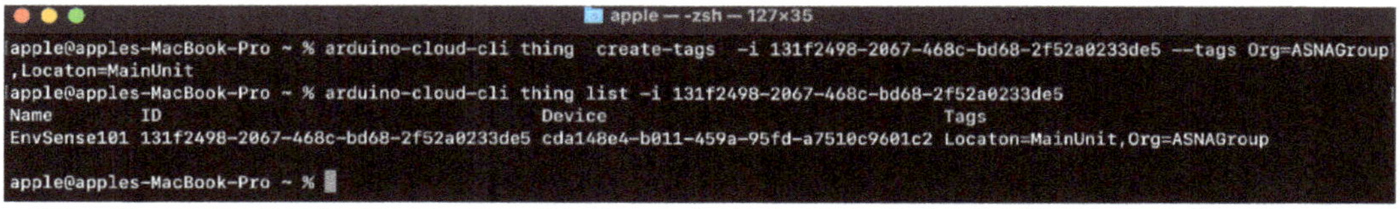

Figure 13.16 – Assigning tags to a Thing

Figure 13.16 shows the full command that is used to assign tags to a Thing, and it also clearly shows the `thing list` command we used to verify the tags.

Now, it's time to explore how we can remove a tag from a Thing. Previously, we saw the syntax to untag a tag from a Thing. The following is the complete command that will remove the location tag from a specific Thing:

```
arduino-cloud-cli thing delete-tags -i 131f2498-2067-468c-bd68-
2f52a0233de5 -k Location
```

After executing the preceding command, you can verify the tags by using the `thing list` command, as shown in *Figure 13.17*.

Figure 13.17 – Deleting a tag from a Thing

Figure 13.17 shows the full command that is used to delete a tag from a Thing, and it also clearly shows the `thing list` command we used to verify the tags.

Here, the command is a little different, as we have used `delete-tags` and `-k` to specify the tag key. If you want to remove multiple tags, then use a comma to separate the keys. In the following section, we will explore how to work with dashboards using the Arduino Cloud CLI.

Crafting dashboards – unleashing potential via the command line

Dashboards are the most important ingredient in the Arduino IoT Cloud pertaining to **data visualization**. In the Arduino Cloud CLI, we have dashboard-specific commands to perform operations on dashboards, such as extracting a template from an existing dashboard, viewing a list of dashboards, deleting the dashboard, and creating a dashboard from an extracted template. Firstly, we will start with dashboard template extraction.

Extracting a template from a dashboard

In the Arduino Cloud CLI, we deal with commands and provide different parameters to perform various operations. Therefore, it is difficult to create a new dashboard via the command line, as it will make it more complex to guide the Arduino IoT Cloud about widgets and attach these widgets with cloud variables via commands.

To solve this issue, the Arduino team introduced the concept of template extraction from a dashboard. For example, if you want to deploy hundreds of environmental monitoring nodes, it's difficult to create hundreds of dashboards via the Arduino graphical user interface. It's also difficult to create long commands for dashboard creation, which includes all the information regarding the dashboard. So, Arduino introduced the template extraction technique. Firstly, we will create the dashboard via the Arduino graphical user interface, and then we will extract its template via the command line. Then, using a template, we will create dashboards in the Arduino IoT Cloud via the command line, as the Arduino Cloud CLI does not allow you to create a dashboard from scratch. The official documentation for dashboard template extraction is available at `https://docs.arduino.cc/arduino-cloud/getting-started/arduino-cloud-cli#extract-dashboard-template`.

The following shows the command syntax for template extraction. With this command, we need to provide a dashboard ID with which the command will fetch the template of the dashboard. Then, we need to provide the format for the template file – either JSON or YAML:

```
arduino-cloud-cli dashboard extract --id <dashboardID> --format
<json|yaml>
```

For the dashboard ID, either visit the Arduino IoT Cloud to find it or refer to the upcoming subsections, in which we will show you how to list dashboards, which will provide their name, ID, and so on. Now, we will assign the format; we want the template output in JSON format, so I used JSON here:

```
arduino-cloud-cli dashboard  extract -i f00aaaab-7faa-4ba6-bdd7-
814377f296ba --format json
```

After executing the command, we will get the template output on the screen in JSON format, as shown in *Figure 13.18*.

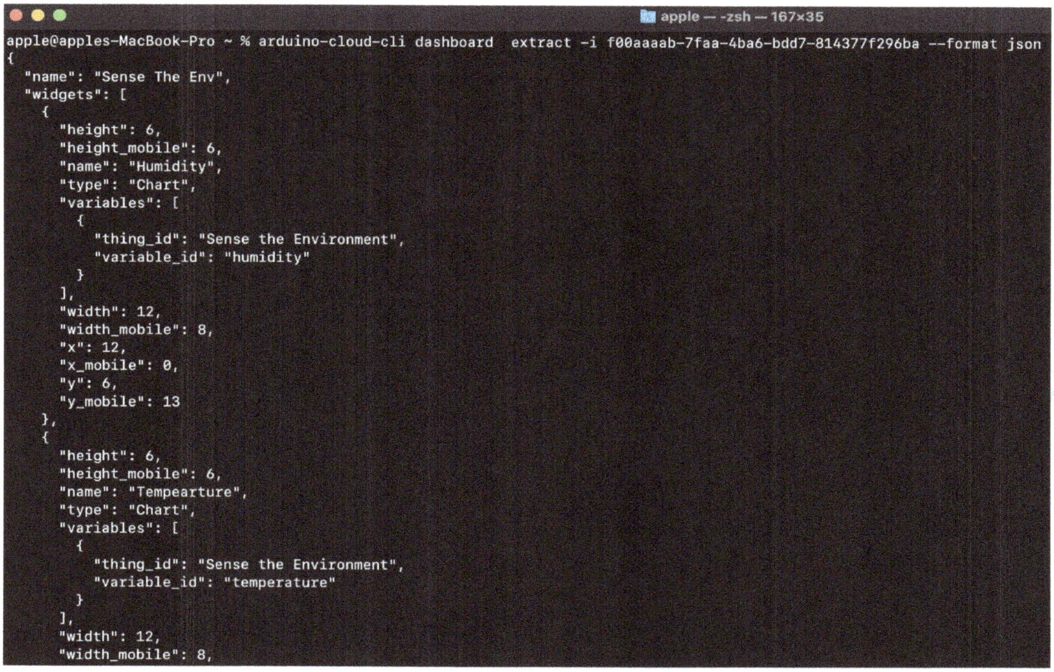

Figure 13.18 – Extracting a dashboard template

Figure 13.18 shows partial output on the screen. We have our dashboard template in JSON format, which shows all the information regarding widgets and their configuration, including `thing_id` and `variable_id`. Copy the JSON format output and save it in a file, which will be used in the following section for dashboard creation.

> **Important note**
>
> There is a bug in the Arduino Cloud CLI for dashboard extraction, as it shows the Thing name instead of the Thing ID in the `thing_id` value. Therefore, you need to replace the text with the Thing ID; otherwise, an error will occur during the execution of the dashboard creation command.

In this subsection, we explored how to extract a template from an existing dashboard. In the following subsection, we will explore how to list dashboards.

Listing dashboards

In this section, we will list all the dashboards. The documentation on listing dashboards is available at `https://docs.arduino.cc/arduino-cloud/getting-started/arduino-cloud-cli#list-dashboards`. The following is a very simple command to list all the dashboards:

```
arduino-cloud-cli dashboard list
```

After executing the preceding command, we will see a complete list of dashboards, as shown in the following figure.

```
apple@apples-MacBook-Pro ~ % arduino-cloud-cli dashboard list
Name                                                        ID                                    UpdatedAt
MKR1010 Hello World Dashboard                               78441d91-250b-4bcd-9cf5-3b295a16ef79  2023-02-19 07:03:24.901079 +0000 UTC
SmartAgri-Sangodha                                          36287c03-5834-4a64-b40a-102740c998c6  2023-05-06 19:36:31.935033 +0000 UTC
Cloud Schedule                                              e17b56e0-2d50-4c38-838b-1b4abfe8c92e  2023-05-30 04:37:54.815238 +0000 UTC
Sense The Env                                               f00aaaab-7faa-4ba6-bdd7-814377f296ba  2023-03-24 19:03:46.605656 +0000 UTC
Tracking and notifying Your Heart Rate Dashboard            28ea7839-7a81-460e-a871-36f8d45d82cee  2023-04-19 16:41:36.604465 +0000 UTC
Voice Controlled Smart Lamp                                 ed4b5e08-7655-483a-9f06-94c5777e2f24  2023-05-20 18:07:40.757867 +0000 UTC
Thing to Thing Dashboard                                    95a2a11b-7bea-43af-89a7-4e4731aefa7e  2023-09-08 05:10:29.827417 +0000 UTC
Untitled                                                    5e658ff8-2519-4d00-b556-41bad8b15571  2023-04-06 16:27:35.17932 +0000 UTC
A portable thing tracker using MKR NB 1500 Dashboard        c6456aca-c41e-4016-bb63-93feabe4d7bb  2023-04-06 16:33:10.633876 +0000 UTC
Multiple Things Dashboard                                   782eda2a-254d-44b9-8dfe-dd06f929ad4b  2023-09-08 05:13:37.325745 +0000 UTC
A portable thing tracker using MKR WAN 1300                 e62fa4ac-efa5-4d43-bc40-b05488cdf144  2023-08-30 14:45:25.660177 +0000 UTC

apple@apples-MacBook-Pro ~ %
```

Figure 13.19 – The dashboard list command

In the output shown in *Figure 13.19*, we can see the dashboard **Name**, **ID**, and **UpdatedAt** details. Here, **ID** is very important, as it will be used in the following commands for dashboard deletion. It also helps you in dashboard template extraction, as we used the dashboard ID in the preceding subsection to extract the template.

In this subsection, we explored how to list dashboards by using a very simple command. In the next subsection, we will explore how to delete a dashboard using the dashboard ID.

Deleting a dashboard

In this subsection, we will explore how to delete a dashboard using the dashboard ID. The documentation for deleting dashboards is available at `https://docs.arduino.cc/arduino-cloud/getting-started/arduino-cloud-cli#delete-dashboards`. The following is the command syntax for dashboard deletion:

```
arduino-cloud-cli dashboard delete --id <dashboardID>
```

According to the preceding command syntax, we need to provide a dashboard ID for deletion. You can fetch the dashboard ID by using the `dashboard list` command:

```
arduino-cloud-cli dashboard delete -i 5e658ff8-2519-4d00-b556-
41bad8b15571
```

After the successful deletion of the device, you will not see an error message; otherwise, you will get a `401 error` message on the screen.

```
apple@apples-MacBook-Pro ~ % arduino-cloud-cli dashboard delete -i 5e658ff8-2519-4d00-b556-41bad8b15571
apple@apples-MacBook-Pro ~ %
```

Figure 13.20 – The dashboard delete command

Figure 13.20 shows the complete command for dashboard deletion, and there is no error on the screen, which means the dashboard has been deleted successfully. In this subsection, we discussed the `delete` command. In the upcoming subsection, we will explore how to create a dashboard using a template, which we extracted in the first subsection of this section.

Creating a dashboard

After extracting a dashboard template, we can start to create a dashboard. The documentation on dashboard creation can be found at `https://docs.arduino.cc/arduino-cloud/getting-started/arduino-cloud-cli#create-dashboard`. The following is the syntax of the dashboard creation command, which takes two parameters. Firstly, it takes the name of the dashboard, and secondly, it takes the template filename for dashboard creation, which contains the dashboard template in JSON format that we saved in the previous section:

```
arduino-cloud-cli dashboard create --name <dashboardName> --template
<template.(json|yaml)> --override <thing-0>=<actualThingID>,<thing-
1>=<otherActualThingID>
```

Here, I have provided the Thing name, `EnvSense101`, and in the previous section, I saved the JSON template in a file named `EnvSenseTemplate.json`. Then, we provide the name with the `-n` parameter and the template file with the `-t` parameter:

```
arduino-cloud-cli dashboard create -n EnvSensedashboard101 -t
EnvSensedashboard.json
```

After executing the preceding command, you will get the following output for successful dashboard creation (*Figure 13.21*):

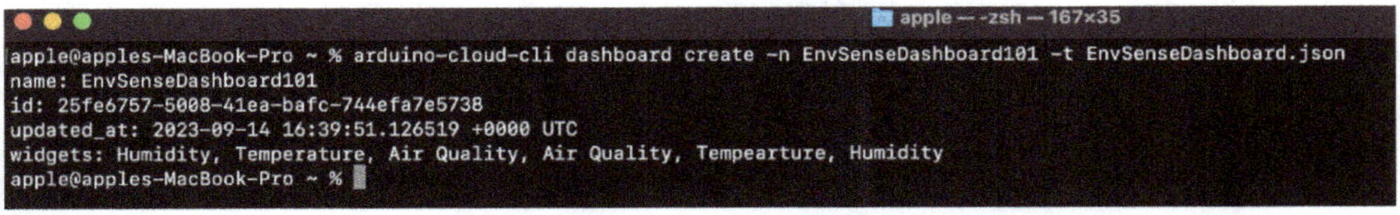

Figure 13.21 – Dashboard creation using arduino-cloud-cli

Figure 13.21 shows the command and the output of successful dashboard creation by the Arduino Cloud CLI. After creating the dashboard, the terminal shows the dashboard **name**, **id**, **updated_at**, and **widgets** details.

> **Important note**
>
> There is a bug in the Arduino Cloud CLI for dashboard extraction, as it shows the Thing name instead of the Thing ID in the `thing_id` value. Therefore, you need to replace the text with the Thing ID; otherwise, an error will occur during the execution of the dashboard creation command.

In this subsection, we created a dashboard in the Arduino IoT Cloud using the command line. In the following section, we will explore how OTA updates work via a CLI.

OTA management

In *Chapter 11*, we explored what OTA is and how we can easily use this feature to send updates to remote devices. In that chapter, we used a graphical user interface, which is a good option for a single device. However, when we have bulk Things to send OTA, then the situation becomes complex, as we need to go through different things one at a time to send OTA updates, which is very time consuming and a difficult operation at the enterprise level.

That's why the Arduino team created commands for the Arduino Cloud CLI to send OTA updates to single or multiple devices automatically, to minimize the complexity and operation time. So, firstly, we will explore how to export the compiled binary by using the Arduino IDE, and then we will send an OTA update to a device using its ID. For official documentation and updates, visit `https://docs.arduino.cc/arduino-cloud/getting-started/arduino-cloud-cli#ota-over-the-air`.

Exporting a binary using the Arduino IDE

In this section, we will use the Arduino IDE to generate the complied binaries of our program for a device OTA. Firstly, download your Thing code from the Arduino IoT Cloud. Then, extract your downloaded code and open it up in the Arduino IDE. Select the development board in the Arduino IDE, and then click on **Sketch | Export Compiled Binary**, as shown in *Figure 13.22*.

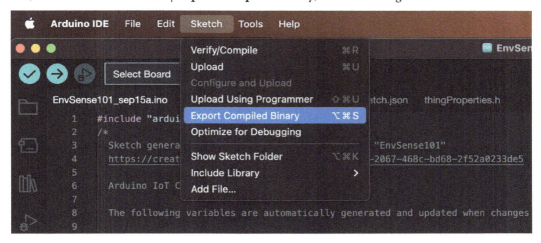

Figure 13.22 – Export Compiled Binary in the Arduino IDE

Clicking on **Export Compiled Binary** will generate the `build` directory under your `sketch` directory, where you will find lots of files generated by the Arduino compiler. You need to select the file that ends with the `ino.bin` extension, as shown in *Figure 13.23*.

Figure 13.23 – The sketch build files

In this section, we explored how to generate the build files of a sketch using the Arduino IDE. In the next subsection, we will send this build file to a device OTA via the command line.

Uploading a sketch to a device

The Arduino Cloud CLI provides a single upload option as well as a mass deployment option. This is the official documentation link: `https://docs.arduino.cc/arduino-cloud/getting-started/arduino-cloud-cli#upload`. You can visit the page for the latest updates and news. Firstly, we will explore how to send an update to a single device. The following is a simple command syntax for a single-device OTA operation:

```
arduino-cloud-cli ota upload --device-id <deviceID> --file <sketch-
file.ino.bin>
```

Here, we need to specify the device ID and the filename, including its path, which is done with the following command:

```
arduino-cloud-cli ota upload -d cda148e4-b011-459a-95fd-
a7510c9601c2  --file EnvSense101_sep15a.ino.bin
```

After the successful execution of the command, you will see an empty terminal without any errors, as shown in *Figure 13.24*. However, if the device is unavailable or any other issue arises, then the details will be printed on the terminal.

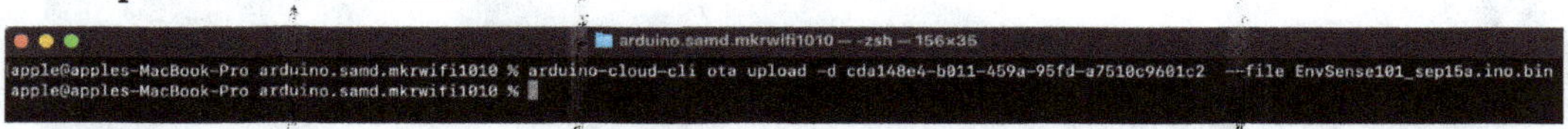

Figure 13.24 – A successful command execution of the OTA upload

Figure 13.24 shows that our upload has been completed successfully without any errors. It will take some time on the terminal to upload the file, depending on your internet speed as well as your sketch size, but you need to wait till the final output. Never interrupt the upload procedure.

Then, we have the mass deployment option in OTA, where you can upload firmware to multiple devices by using FQBN, as well as tags. The following is a simple command for mass deployment that uses FQBN, and you can also assign specific device IDs:

```
arduino-cloud-cli ota mass-upload --fqbn <deviceFQBN> --device-ids
<deviceIDs> --file <sketch-file.ino.bin>
```

However, with this specific command, I will only use `fqbn` to send the update to all the same device types:

```
arduino-cloud-cli ota mass-upload -b arduino:samd:mkrwifi1010 --file
EnvSense101_sep15a.ino.bin
```

You can also explore the OTA mass upload by adding tags, to send an update to specific groups of devices. In this section, we explored how to build binaries of a sketch using the Arduino IDE and how to upload an update using the OTA command.

What next?

After playing around with some commands, it's now time to do some more experiments so that you can apply your learning to new scenarios and learn new stuff. We explored the complete list of commands available on the Arduino Cloud CLI. However, you can check out Arduino's official page for the latest updates and news to keep yourself up to date with the latest features. Now, it's your turn to create batch scripts using the Arduino Cloud CLI to automate your operations, such as bulk device addition in the Arduino IoT Cloud, bulk Thing creation using templates, binding devices with Things, and creating a dashboard for every Thing from dashboard templates.

Summary

In this chapter, we covered all the types of commands that are officially available to us on the Arduino Cloud CLI. Firstly, we explored device-related commands, which include device creation, listing devices, deletion, tagging, and untagging. Then, we explored how to work with Things; in that section, we started with template extraction and then created a Thing using a template. We also explored how to clone a Thing, how to bind a device with a Thing, and so on. In the penultimate section, we played around with dashboard commands, and in the last section, we explored how OTA commands can benefit us by sending updates to devices via the command line in different ways.

This chapter was specially designed for backend developers and administrators who want to use the Arduino Cloud CLI to optimize their daily tasks, by using terminal commands instead of a graphical user interface. This chapter will have helped them interact with the Arduino IoT Cloud using a CLI. It will also have helped them to create custom scripts, automating their daily tasks.

The following chapter is the last chapter of this book, and in this chapter, we will explore different Arduino IoT Cloud plans for educational and enterprise organizations. We will also explore industrial IoT hardware devices and different types of Arduino IoT Cloud services that are especially available to enterprise organizations. This chapter will give you a complete overview of how to scale your product from a smaller scale to an enterprise level.

14

Moving Ahead in the Arduino IoT Cloud

The **Arduino IoT Cloud** offers various plans, with different features for each plan enabled to certain levels. In the chapter, you will be guided through the different options available at the time of writing, including the enterprise plans, and a description of the additional functionalities they provide.

Then, you will be invited to put into practice what was learned in previous chapters by implementing and expanding the examples with further functionalities. The Arduino IoT Cloud is a live product, always evolving, and this chapter will list official Arduino sources of information, allowing you to monitor any updates and future releases.

You will also get an insight into the Arduino PRO hardware and software tools, which are specially designed for industrial IoT solutions. This information will help you to design and build professional solutions for your industry.

In this chapter, we will cover the following main topics:

- Arduino IoT Cloud plans
- Arduino PRO
- Further resources and insights

Arduino IoT Cloud plans

The Arduino IoT Cloud comes with different plans for different types of entities, and every entity comes with different types of pricing plans for its users. In the Arduino IoT Cloud, there are mainly three entities, which include individuals, schools, and organizations, as shown in *Figure 14.1*.

Figure 14.1 – The Arduino IoT Cloud plans' different categories

The Arduino IoT Cloud team divided the pricing plans according to different categories and users, and pricing varies from category to category. There are also different pricing plans available in those categories. For the updated pricing plans and features, visit `https://cloud.arduino.cc/plans/`.

We will discuss all the categories step by step in the following subsections, and the business plan will be discussed in a separate section. Firstly, we will look at plans for individuals in the next subsection.

Plans for individuals

First, we will start with pricing plans for individuals. This category is specially designed for learners, professionals, makers, hobbyists, or anyone who wants to learn or use the Arduino IoT Cloud as an individual entity. For them, the Arduino IoT Cloud has four different plans, which include the free, entry, maker, and maker plus plans. All the plans have different pricing according to their features, except for the free plan, which is freely available to everyone without any cost.

Now, we will discuss how each plan is different from another by comparing their limitations and features, as well as their cost, in *Table 4.1*. We will not compare all the features here, as the complete details are available on the Arduino IoT Cloud plans page. Here, we will only discuss the important features.

Features	Free	Entry	Maker	Maker plus
Number of Things	2	10	25	100
Data retention	1 day	15 days	90 days	1 year
Cloud triggers	Not available	Not available	100 notifications a day	400 notifications a day
Cloud variables	5	10	Unlimited	
API	Not available	1 request a second	10 requests a second	
Shareable dashboard	Not available	Not available	Available	
OTA	Not available	Available		
Price yearly	Free	USD 23.88	USD 71.88	USD 239.98
Price monthly	Free	Not available	USD 6.99	USD 23.99

Table 14.1 – The plan for individuals' features comparison

In *Table 14.1*, we compare different plans with respect to some important features. Firstly, we will explore the *free plan*, which only allows you to create two Things. One-day data retention is available, and you can create up to five cloud variables for your Thing. However, cloud triggers, API access, a shareable dashboard, and (**OTA**) features are not available. The free plan is good from a learning point of view, and you can even host up to two personal IoT devices.

Then, we have the *entry plan*, which is perfect for students and hobbyists if they want to expand their IoT devices on a smaller scale. This plan will cost them USD 23.88 per year and is only available in yearly billing, not monthly. In this plan, you will get 10 Things and 15-day data retention, with up to 10 cloud variables for each Thing. Users will also get the benefit of the API and OTA features, but cloud triggers and shareable dashboard features are still not available.

The *maker plan* is the third plan in this category, which is good for users who design and develop IoT solutions and want to taste all the features of the Arduino IoT Cloud. It costs USD 71.88 per year and can be paid on a monthly basis. With this plan, users are able to create 25 Things, and 90-day data retention is allowed (which is a very good option for data recording). Also, users are allowed to set up cloud triggers for 100 notifications per day, and 10 API requests per second are allowed.

Finally, we have the *maker plus plan*, which is the perfect choice for IoT freelancers or small-scale IoT start-ups. In this plan, users are allowed to host up to 100 Things with one-year data retention, which is a perfectly good combination for professional, small-scale deployments, and they only need to pay USD 239.98 per year or USD 23.99 per month. You can see all the features of the Maker Plus plan, as well as the aforementioned plans, in *Table 4.1* or on the official website.

Machine learning tools are available to all plans equally, so anyone can enjoy the benefit of this feature and integrate machine learning into their IoT solutions, making them more advanced. This offers the benefit of powerful machine learning on the cloud side without any hassle.

Let's explore the maker plus plan with respect to its cost for freelancers and small IoT start-ups. This plan costs USD 239.98 per year and allows you to host up to 100 IoT Things. If we calculate the cost per Thing, then it will be around USD 2.40 per Thing for one year, which is very reasonably priced, and there is also zero cost for infrastructure and security maintenance, as all these requirements are managed by the Arduino IoT Cloud team.

In this subsection, we discussed the different Arduino Cloud plans that are available for individuals in detail. In the upcoming subsection, we will explore the plans for educational institutes.

Plans for schools

Every organization, such as Google, Microsoft, and Amazon AWS, provides a special pricing plan for education institutes to help them grow their students' knowledge and skills, preparing them according to the latest industry trends. The Arduino IoT Cloud also has a special pricing plan for schools, colleges, and universities.

Besides their special pricing plan, the Arduino IoT Cloud also provides a free plan for students, similar to the free plan for individuals. Therefore, we will not discuss this and focus instead on the customized school plan. In the school plan category, the pricing changes according to the number of students, but the features available to them all remain the same. *Table 14.2* provides a detailed pricing plan according to the number of students. For updated pricing for schools, visit `https://cloud.arduino.cc/plans`.

Number of students	Pricing per member/per year
5 to 50 members	USD 20 per member per year
51 to 100 members	USD 18 per member per year
101+ members	USD 15 per member per year

Table 14.2 – The pricing plan for schools according to the number of students

Table 14.2 states the pricing according to student numbers and per member. Let's explore what features they provide to every school member. In the school plan, every member can create up to 5 Things, with unlimited cloud variables and six-month data retention, which is very good, especially for PhD and master's students, as they may want to collect data from IoT devices for further research and experiments, or are building a prototype to solve a real-world problem. Also, the plan provides 10 notifications per day for cloud triggers and 10 requests per second for APIs.

The Arduino IoT Cloud school plan can also natively integrate with Google Classroom users. This makes it easy for faculty members to manage their students, assignments, and lots of other stuff in the Arduino IoT Cloud via Google Classroom. The Arduino IoT Cloud also provides centralized billing and user management that is **General Data Protection Regulation** (GDPR)-compliant.

There is another offer available to students via **GitHub Education** – the **Student Developer Pack**. Students can visit the official GitHub page for further updates and news: `https://education.github.com/pack#offers`. According to the current agreement between Arduino and GitHub, Arduino provides six free months of the Arduino IoT Cloud maker plan, as well as a discount on selected development boards.

In this subsection, we dived deep into educational pricing plans and their features for each student. In the following section, we will explore the Enterprise Base Plan in detail, which helps you to scale your product with enterprise-level features.

The enterprise base plan

In this section, we will first explore the basic features of the enterprise base plan, and then in different subsections, we will explore the specialized features that are only available in the enterprise plan, which allow organizations to perform bulk operations such as fleet and device management.

The enterprise base plan is specially designed for organizations that are interested in using the Arduino IoT Cloud as a main infrastructure for their solution deployment and management. In regard to pricing and devices, the plan starts from USD 42 for 50 devices, increasing in multiples of 50 up to 500. If you have more than 500 devices, then you would need to directly contact the Arduino Support team for a customized pricing plan. Fifty devices cost USD 500 per year, and each device costs USD 10 per year and approximately USD 0.83 per month. This cost per device is very nominal, as you don't need to pay any infrastructure or development charges, security costs, and so on. This plan also provides you with advanced management control, which will make your management and operations easier compared to other plans.

Data retention in the enterprise plan is one year for all devices, and every device is allowed to send 20 notifications via **cloud triggers** and 10 requests per second for **APIs**. Besides all of these features, organizations will receive **technical support** via a ticketing system, which is not available in other plans.

In this subsection, we discussed the basic features of the enterprise base plan. Now, we will explore role-based access control and fleet management in the upcoming subsection.

Role-based access control and fleet management

At the enterprise level, there are several employees in an organization who manage and perform different operations. It's mandatory for an organization to assign different access levels to their employees according to their responsibilities. To aid this, the Arduino IoT Cloud has a role-based access control system for organizations, where they can easily assign their employees access and manage it according to their job description.

Role-based access control ensures the safety and security of your devices and protects them from human mistakes and errors. With the help of role-based access control, you can share access among teams for project collaboration and assign device access to members at different levels, according to their management responsibility.

Another feature of the Arduino IoT Cloud enterprise base plan is fleet management. The Arduino IoT Cloud introduced this feature to manage a large number of devices effectively and easily. Fleet management contains a device filtering and grouping feature, bulk OTA updates, hierarchies, and many other features.

In this subsection, we discussed role-based access control and fleet management for devices. In the following subsection, we will explore machine learning tools and the Portenta X8 Manager.

Machine learning tools and the Portenta X8 Manager

With the rapid growth of AI and machine learning, it's now become vital for IoT solutions to integrate machine learning into their solutions so that customers can benefit from its power to improve their operations, such as predictive maintenance, anomaly detection, and quality control.

The Arduino team collaborated with Edge Impulse to provide machine learning integration in the Arduino IoT Cloud. In Edge Impulse, you can train models using devices' data, by importing them into Edge Impulse or directly connecting the devices, such as Arduino Nano 33 BLE Sense, Arduino Nicla Vision, Arduino Portenta H7, or any Linux-supported device. This feature helps developers and solution providers to train a model using a graphical user interface, with the help of a small amount of code.

Then, you can deploy these models, using TinyML, to Arduino-supported development boards. For further details, please visit `https://cloud.arduino.cc/machine-learning-tools/`. In the enterprise base plan, Arduino charges USD 500 per month for machine learning services, which include 60 minutes per job and a total of 1,000 minutes per month.

The Portenta X8 Manager is a specialized extension integrated with the Arduino IoT Cloud, designed to empower users in safeguarding and managing their Portenta X8 Linux distribution. It facilitates essential functionalities such as **secure maintenance**, **containerized application deployment**, and secure **OTA** differential updates.

The Portenta X8 Manager is designed for businesses and organizations that need to deploy and manage large fleets of Portenta X8 devices securely and reliably. It provides a number of features that make it ideal for enterprise use, including the following:

- **Secure OTA updates**: The Portenta X8 Manager uses a secure OTA update process to ensure that devices are always up to date with the latest firmware and security patches.

- **Containerized applications**: The Portenta X8 Manager allows users to deploy and manage containerized applications on their devices. This makes it easy to deploy and update complex applications without having to reprogram the entire device.

- **Role-based access control (RBAC)**: The Portenta X8 Manager supports RBAC so that organizations can control who has access to their devices and applications.

- **Audit logging**: The Portenta X8 Manager provides audit logging so that organizations can track all activity on their devices and applications.

The Portenta X8 Manager is available as a paid add-on to the Arduino IoT Cloud enterprise base plan, which costs USD 250 per month. For more details, refer to the **Enterprise Base Plan** tab on the Arduino IoT Cloud plans page under the **For business** tab.

In this subsection, we dived deep into machine learning and the Portenta X8 Manager add-on for the Arduino IoT Cloud enterprise base plan. In the following section, we will cover Arduino PRO hardware and software tools in detail.

Arduino PRO

Arduino PRO is a separate line of products that contain professional tools in both the hardware and software categories. These tools are specially designed to carry out industrial operations, such as those found in aviation, industry 4.0, healthcare, robotics, smart cities, and smart homes/offices. We will explore both the hardware and software tools step by step in the following subsections.

Arduino PRO hardware

Arduino PRO is a line of products offered by Arduino LLC, the company behind the popular open source Arduino platform. Arduino PRO boards are designed for users who have a more advanced understanding of microcontrollers and electronics, and who are looking for boards that offer additional features and capabilities compared to the standard Arduino boards. These boards are often used by makers, engineers, and professionals for various applications.

In the following subsections, we will only explore three types of hardware; for a complete list, please visit https://www.arduino.cc/pro/platform-hardware/.

The Portenta family

The Arduino Portenta family is a series of high-performance industry-rated boards. These boards are designed to enable simultaneous execution of high-level code, such as protocol stacks, machine learning, or even interpreted languages such as MicroPython or JavaScript, along with low-level, real-time tasks. The Portenta family adds two 80-pin high-density connectors at the bottom of the board, ensuring scalability for a wide range of applications. *Figure 14.2* shows all the series of development boards from the Portenta family. All the details of these boards will be discussed step by step in the following paragraphs.

Figure 14.2 – The Portenta series development boards

A few of the development boards available in the Arduino Portenta family are shown in *Figure 14.2*, and the following list details some of these boards:

- **Portenta X8**: A powerful, industrial-grade **system-on-module** (**SOM**) with a Linux OS preloaded onboard. It is capable of running device-independent software thanks to its modular container architecture. It also offers onboard Wi-Fi/Bluetooth Low Energy connectivity for secure OS/ application OTA updates.

- **Portenta Max Carrier**: This carrier board transforms Portenta modules into single-board computers or reference designs that enable edge AI for high-performance industrial, building automation, and robotics applications.

- **Portenta H7 Lite Connected**: This is designed to provide the computational power of Portenta H7 for AI applications and low-latency control solutions. It is more cost-effective than the full H7 module by removing the high-resolution video interface feature.

- **Portenta H7 Lite**: A board that allows you to build your next smart project. It is compatible with the Arduino IoT Cloud and enables you to connect devices, visualize data, and control and share your projects from anywhere in the world.

- **Portenta Machine Control**: A fully centralized, low-power industrial control unit that is capable of driving equipment and machinery. It can be programmed using the Arduino framework or other embedded development platforms.

Note that these are just a few examples from the Arduino Portenta family. You can find more information about these boards and other related products at `https://store.arduino.cc/ collections/portenta-family`.

In this subsection, we explored the Portenta Series, which is specially designed for industrial use cases and also supports different programming languages, including MicroPython and JavaScript. It also gives you the option to perform concurrent operations in parallel. In the following subsection, we will explore the Nicla family, which is specially designed for voice and vision.

The Nicla family

The Arduino Nicla family is a series of industrial-oriented boards designed for low-power AI, machine learning, and machine vision applications. These boards are fully equipped with industrial-grade sensors and are designed to work as autonomous, battery-operated systems. *Figure 14.3* shows Nicla Vision, but you can visit the official website to see other variants from the Nicla family.

Figure 14.3 – The Nicla Vision development board

Here are some of the boards available in the Arduino Nicla family:

- **Nicla Voice**: Arduino PRO's smallest form factor board to date. It can be used to upgrade or retrofit existing machines and systems. It is particularly suitable for wearable products, such as helmets and smart bands, due to its long battery-powered autonomy.

- **Nicla Vision**: A square-shaped board, with a 2 Mega Pixel color camera sensor and other built-in devices to collect various environmental data. It is suitable for machine-vision-based applications at the edge.

Note that these are just a few examples from the Arduino Nicla family. You can find more information about these boards and other related products at `https://www.arduino.cc/pro/hardware-nicla-family`.

In this subsection, we discussed Nicla Voice and Nicla Vision, and both these development boards are specially designed for industrial use cases where voice and vision are mandatory requirements to control the machine process, such as logistics and loading and unloading robots. In the following subsection, we will discuss the latest product from Arduino, which is Opta PLC.

Opta PLC

The Arduino Opta is a secure, easy-to-use micro PLC with industrial IoT capabilities, designed in partnership with Finder. It allows professionals to scale up automation projects while leveraging the open and widely known Arduino ecosystem. The Opta board is equipped with a powerful STM32H747XI dual-core Cortex®-M7 + M4 MCU, enabling real-time control, monitoring, and predictive maintenance applications. It supports secure OTA firmware updates and establishes data security from the hardware to the cloud, through its onboard security element and X.509 standard compliance. The Opta board also offers various connectivity options, such as Ethernet, Wi-Fi, and Bluetooth Low Energy. *Figure 14.4* shows Opta PLC; other variants have the same shape but differ in communication features.

Figure 14.4 – Opta PLC

The Arduino Opta family includes the following variants and shown in *Figure 14.4* (all variants look are same in shape but different in connectivity so here I just added one picture):

- **Opta Lite**: This variant features Ethernet onboard and USB-C programming ports

- **Opta RS485**: In addition to Ethernet, this variant also provides an RS485 half-duplex connectivity interface

- **Opta Wi-Fi**: The most versatile variant, this offers Wi-Fi/Bluetooth Low Energy connectivity

To program the Arduino Opta board, you can use the Arduino PLC IDE, which supports the five programming languages defined by the IEC 61131-3 standard – Ladder, Functional Block Diagram, Structured Text, Sequential Function Chart, and Instruction List. This makes PLC programming easy and allows you to quickly code PLC applications, or port existing ones, to Arduino Opta or Portenta Machine Control.

For more information about the Arduino Opta family and its features, visit `https://www.arduino. cc/pro/hardware-arduino-opta`.

In these subsections, we have explored the three main top-of-the-line Arduino PRO hardware products. In the following section, we will explore the Arduino PRO software tools.

Arduino PRO software

Along with its hardware tools, Arduino developed software in its Pro series, which includes the **IoT Cloud, IDE 2, Arduino CLI application**, the **Arduino PLC IDE**, and the **Speech Recognition Engine** library. For complete details about these tools, visit `https://www.arduino.cc/pro/ platform-software/`.

In the following subsections, we will cover the Arduino PLC IDE and the Speech Recognition Engine.

Arduino PLC IDE

The Arduino PLC IDE is an integrated development environment that allows you to program Portenta Machine Control and Arduino Opta, using the five programming languages defined by the IEC 61131-3 standard. These languages are as follows:

- Ladder Diagram
- Functional Block Diagram
- Structured Text
- Sequential Function Chart
- Instruction List

The Arduino PLC IDE interface is shown in *Figure 14.5*. which is totally different from the Arduino IDE. It supports various programming interfaces, as mentioned in the previous bullet points but one of the famous programming interfaces for PLC is the Ladder Diagram, which is specially used by PLC engineers to program the PLC.

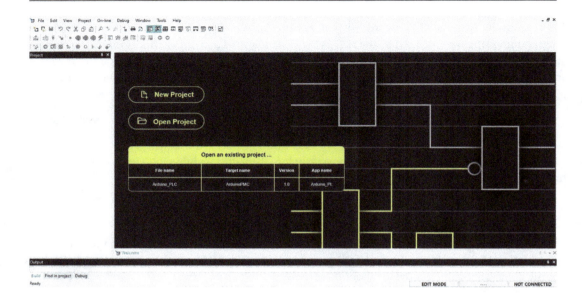

Figure 14.5 – The Arduino PLC IDE

The Arduino PLC IDE offers an intuitive user interface (shown in *Figure 14.5*), complete with a suite of debugging tools, including watch windows, breakpoints with step-by-step execution, triggers, oscilloscope functionality, and live debug mode. It further extends its capabilities with rapid porting solutions and enables the integration of PLC programming alongside Arduino sketches, through an integrated sketch editor. This synergy permits the effortless exchange of variables between these two environments, facilitating the inclusion of deterministic cyclic tasks and multitasking within your software application.

The Arduino PLC IDE supports various industrial fieldbus protocols, including Modbus RTU, Modbus TCP, and CANOpen. It offers a wide set of pre-installed libraries and function blocks, as well as the option to create custom libraries. To program with IEC 61131-3, you will need to unlock the hardware with a lifetime license key, available at the Arduino Official Store.

For more information about the Arduino PLC IDE and its features, please visit the official page at `https://www.arduino.cc/pro/software-plc-ide/`.

In this subsection, we discussed the Arduino PLC IDE, which is specially designed for Arduino Opta PLC to program it. The Arduino PLC supports five different languages to program in. In the following subsection, we will explore the Speech Recognition Engine library.

The Speech Recognition Engine library

The **Arduino Speech Recognition Engine** is a powerful software library that enables you to develop projects based on speech recognition. It allows you to interact with machines using voice commands, without the need for vocal training or an internet connection. The library was developed by Cyberon, a worldwide leader in speech recognition, and is designed to be easy to use and compatible with multiple Arduino boards and the Arduino IDE. It supports voice commands in over 40 languages, regardless of the speaker's voice, tone, or accent. You can configure multiple wake-up words and sequences without retraining for different users.

The Speech Recognition Engine is ideal for various applications, such as smart buildings and home automation, information kiosks, vending machines, smart beds in hospitals, and emergency alert systems. It can listen to anyone speaking to it while ignoring background noise.

To get started with the Arduino Speech Recognition Engine, you can visit the official Arduino website: `https://www.arduino.cc/pro/software-speech-recognition-engine/`. It offers a robust library featuring an integrated AI/ML engine that excels in phoneme-based modeling. This advanced library enables the recognition of multiple wake-up words and sequences of commands without the need for vocal training. The library is compatible with multiple Arduino boards and requires no additional hardware, software, or internet connectivity.

Note that there is also another Arduino board called Nicla Voice, which was discussed in the *Arduino PRO hardware* section. This board implements always-on speech and motion recognition at the edge. It integrates a neural decision processor from Syntiant (NDP120) to run multiple AI algorithms.

In the Arduino PRO section and subsections, we explored the main Arduino PRO top-of-the-line development boards, including the Portenta series, the Nicla series, and the OPTA PLC series. We also explored Arduino PRO software, including the Arduino PLC IDE and the Speech Recognition Engine library. In the following section, we will cover some further resources for your learning.

Further resources and insights

Arduino continuously evolves its products and services according to the latest demands and trends. Hence, it's difficult to cover everything. So far, I have just mentioned some useful resources that will help you to keep yourself updated with the latest news and features.

It's best to keep an eye on the Arduino official blog for the latest news related to its products and updates at `https://blog.arduino.cc/`. Communities always share and help users to learn, so become part of the fastest-growing community by joining the Arduino Community forum, which can be found here: `https://forum.arduino.cc/`. You can also share your projects and learn from others' projects at Arduino Project Hub: `https://projecthub.arduino.cc`. For instant communication with fellow community members, you can join the Discord channel: `https://discord.gg/jQJFwW7`.

Along with the Arduino community, you can also be part of some other globally famous maker communities, such as `https://Hackster.io` and `https://instructables.com/`. On these platforms, you will find the latest projects along with complete descriptions, and they are a good way to keep yourself updated. After learning from these communities, it's your turn to submit your DIY projects to them to educate other community members. The two aforementioned communities also host contests in different categories; try to participate in them.

Here is a list of other Arduino resources that will help you to further your learning:

- *Getting Started with Arduino products*: `https://www.arduino.cc/en/Guide`
- Documentation: `https://docs.arduino.cc/`
- Arduino Cloud documentation: `https://cloud.arduino.cc/resources`
- A reference to the Arduino programming language: `https://www.arduino.cc/reference/en/`
- Built-in examples of Arduino IDE documentation: `https://docs.arduino.cc/built-in-examples/`
- Built-in libraries and their example documentation: `https://docs.arduino.cc/library-examples/`
- Arduino official support and knowledge base: `https://support.arduino.cc/hc/en-us`
- Arduino Education: `https://www.arduino.cc/education`
- Hardware: `https://www.arduino.cc/en/hardware`
- Pro hardware: `https://www.arduino.cc/pro`

In this section, we explored the different online resources that will help you to keep yourself updated with new developments, as well as become part of the online maker communities, keeping yourself engaged for further learning.

Summary

In this chapter, we explored different pricing plans for individuals, educational institutes, and enterprise organizations. All the plans were discussed in depth, and we also compared the plans to explore further differences. The Arduino IoT Cloud provides features with different thresholds for different plans, according to users' needs. Then, we explored the Arduino PRO software and hardware tools in depth, allowing you to make informed decisions when developing industrial solutions. Finally, we explored further resources that can provide you with the latest news and updates about product developments, and we also shared different community resources that a user can benefit from by becoming a member.

So, after reading this chapter, you will be able to identify which pricing plan you need for your usage and also guide your organization or customers, according to their needs, on which Arduino Cloud plan is suitable for them. You also now know the Arduino PRO hardware development boards, including the Portenta, Nicla, and Opta series, as well as Arduino PRO software, including the Arduino PLC IDE and the Speech Recognition Engine. This Pro line will help you to identify and choose specific hardware and software tools for your professional and industrial-grade solutions. Finally, you now know how to keep yourself updated by following the links provided in the *Further resources and insights* section.

As we reach the end of *Arduino IoT Cloud for Developers*, I hope this journey has been as enlightening and rewarding for you as it has been for me. The world of IoT is a realm of limitless possibilities, where the things around us become more intelligent, responsive, and interconnected.

Through these pages, we explored the fundamentals of IoT, delved deep into the capabilities of the Arduino IoT Cloud, and brought our knowledge to life through hands-on projects. We embraced the power of data exchange, advanced scripting, and practical applications that enhance our lives.

Remember that IoT development is a continuous adventure, with countless opportunities waiting for you. As you move forward, keep experimenting, creating, and innovating. The world needs your ideas, your solutions, and your vision for a smarter, more connected future.

Whether you're a novice or an experienced developer, I encourage you to stay curious, keep learning, and never stop exploring. The intersection of IoT and Arduino is a place where innovation thrives, and it's now your playground.

Thank you for embarking on this journey with me. Here's to the endless possibilities that IoT and the Arduino IoT Cloud bring to our lives. The future is yours to create.

Index

Packtpub.com

Subscribe to our online digital library for full access to over 7,000 books and videos, as well as industry leading tools to help you plan your personal development and advance your career. For more information, please visit our website.

Why subscribe?

- Spend less time learning and more time coding with practical eBooks and Videos from over 4,000 industry professionals

- Improve your learning with Skill Plans built especially for you

- Get a free eBook or video every month

- Fully searchable for easy access to vital information

- Copy and paste, print, and bookmark content

Did you know that Packt offers eBook versions of every book published, with PDF and ePub files available? You can upgrade to the eBook version at Packtpub.com and as a print book customer, you are entitled to a discount on the eBook copy. Get in touch with us at customercare@packtpub.com for more details.

At www.packtpub.com, you can also read a collection of free technical articles, sign up for a range of free newsletters, and receive exclusive discounts and offers on Packt books and eBooks.

Other Books You May Enjoy

If you enjoyed this book, you may be interested in these other books by Packt:

Architectural Patterns and Techniques for Developing IoT Solutions

Jasbir Singh Dhaliwal

ISBN: 978-1-80324-549-2

- Get to grips with the essentials of different architectural patterns and anti-patterns
- Discover the underlying commonalities in diverse IoT applications
- Combine patterns from physical and virtual realms to develop innovative applications
- Choose the right set of sensors and actuators for your solution
- Explore analytics-related tools and techniques such as TinyML and sensor fusion
- Overcome the challenges faced in securing IoT systems
- Leverage use cases based on edge computing and emerging technologies such as 3D printing, 5G, generative AI, and LLMs

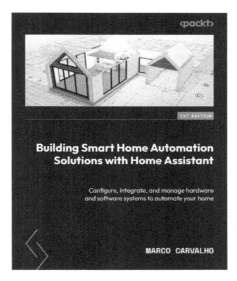

Building Smart Home Automation Solutions with Home Assistant

Marco Carvalho

ISBN: 978-1-80181-529-1

- Understand the fundamental concepts of home automation systems
- Set up a home automation system using Home Assistant and Raspberry Pi
- Create and configure ESP8266-based sensors to work with Home Assistant
- Hack a commercial actuator to work with Home Assistant using Tasmota
- Create automations, customize, and use applications with Home Assistant
- Leverage IoT software tools to take your home automation to the next level
- Work on hands-on projects, including LED strip lights and an ESP32 five-zone temperature logger
- Explore home automation FAQs, emerging technologies, and trends

Packt is searching for authors like you

If you're interested in becoming an author for Packt, please visit `authors.packtpub.com` and apply today. We have worked with thousands of developers and tech professionals, just like you, to help them share their insight with the global tech community. You can make a general application, apply for a specific hot topic that we are recruiting an author for, or submit your own idea.

Share Your Thoughts

Now you've finished *Arduino IoT Cloud for Developers*, we'd love to hear your thoughts! Scan the QR code below to go straight to the Amazon review page for this book and share your feedback or leave a review on the site that you purchased it from.

`https://packt.link/r/1837637172`

Your review is important to us and the tech community and will help us make sure we're delivering excellent quality content.

Download a free PDF copy of this book

Thanks for purchasing this book!

Do you like to read on the go but are unable to carry your print books everywhere?

Is your eBook purchase not compatible with the device of your choice?

Don't worry, now with every Packt book you get a DRM-free PDF version of that book at no cost.

Read anywhere, any place, on any device. Search, copy, and paste code from your favorite technical books directly into your application.

The perks don't stop there, you can get exclusive access to discounts, newsletters, and great free content in your inbox daily

Follow these simple steps to get the benefits:

1. Scan the QR code or visit the link below

https://packt.link/free-ebook/9781837637171

2. Submit your proof of purchase
3. That's it! We'll send your free PDF and other benefits to your email directly

www.ingramcontent.com/pod-product-compliance
Lightning Source LLC
Chambersburg PA
CBHW080607060326
40690CB00021B/4613